CAREER EXPLORATION ON THE INTERNET

A STUDENT'S GUIDE TO MORE THAN 500 WEB SITES

Edited by Laura R. Gabler

Ferguson Publishing Company
Chicago, Illinois

Career Exploration on the Internet: A Student's Guide to More Than 500 Web Sites
By Laura R. Gabler

ISBN 0-89434-305-X

Published and Distributed by
Ferguson Publishing Company
200 West Jackson, Suite 700
Chicago, Illinois 60606
800-306-9941
Web: www.fergpubco.com

Printed in the United States of America

X-2

TABLE OF CONTENTS

INTRODUCTION
NAVIGATING THE INTERNET TO EXPLORE YOUR CAREER OPTIONS V

SECTION I. SELF-EXPLORATION AND DISCOVERY
CHAPTER 1: 3
THINKING ABOUT YOUR INTERESTS, SKILLS, AND GOALS
CHAPTER 2: 13
ASSESSMENT TESTS

SECTION II. CAREER PREPARATION
CHAPTER 3: 29
RESEARCHING CAREER FIELDS AND CHOOSING A MAJOR
CHAPTER 4: 41
INFORMATION INTERVIEWING AND NETWORKING
CHAPTER 5: 47
THE FUTURE WORLD OF WORK

SECTION III. EDUCATION AND TRAINING FOR JOB ENTRY AND CAREER DEVELOPMENT
CHAPTER 6: 55
TWO- AND FOUR-YEAR ACADEMIC PROGRAMS AND GRADUATE STUDIES
CHAPTER 7: 69
OTHER POSTSECONDARY TRAINING OPTIONS
CHAPTER 8: 83
GETTING EXPERIENCE
CHAPTER 9: 111
TUITION AND FINANCIAL AID

SECTION IV. GENERAL CAREER EXPLORATION AND PLANNING
CHAPTER 10: 119
JOB SEARCHING ON THE INTERNET
CHAPTER 11: 133
GENERAL CAREER RESOURCES

SECTION V. NARROWING YOUR FOCUS
CHAPTER 12: 153
RESOURCES TO MEET SPECIFIC NEEDS

SECTION VI. LEARNING MORE ABOUT ASSORTED CAREER FIELDS
CHAPTER 13: 201
RESOURCES FOR SPECIFIC INDUSTRIES

SECTION VII. FINDING A JOB
CHAPTER 14: 307
RESUMES
CHAPTER 15: 313
COVER LETTERS
CHAPTER 16: 317
CAREER PORTFOLIO
CHAPTER 17: 323
INTERVIEWING
CHAPTER 18: 329
ON-CAMPUS SERVICES
CHAPTER 19: 341
COMPANIES
CHAPTER 20: 349
JOB LISTINGS, RESUME DATABASES, AND RECRUITING SERVICES

SECTION VIII. CONSIDERING—AND ACCEPTING—A JOB OFFER
CHAPTER 21: 369
SALARY/WAGES
CHAPTER 22: 375
FRINGE BENEFITS
CHAPTER 23: 381
PERSONNEL MANAGEMENT
CHAPTER 24: 389
EMPLOYMENT LAWS
CHAPTER 25: 393
YOUR RIGHTS AS AN EMPLOYEE
SITE INDEX: 399

NAVIGATING THE INTERNET TO EXPLORE YOUR CAREER OPTIONS

There are many tools and resources available to you as you learn about career management, explore your occupational options, and conduct a job search. One of the newest and fastest growing is the Internet. The Internet features thousands of Web sites related to career exploration. Career counselors, educational institutions, employers, recruiting firms, and government organizations are among those who sponsor these sites.

What can you expect to find online? There are Web sites that can help you

identify and assess your interests, skills, and goals,

explore opportunities in a field,

learn about the future of work and specific occupational outlooks,

discover where to acquire appropriate education and training for an occupation,

determine if licenses or certificates are necessary to enter an occupation,

locate professional associations through which you can keep up-to-date with an industry as well as have the support of members,

create a resume, a targeted cover letter, and a career portfolio, track down job openings and learn more about individual employers,

evaluate and negotiate a job offer,

find out what you can expect on the job once you land one, and much more.

No matter what your career needs are, Career Exploration on the Internet will steer you in the right direction to receive guidance in these and other areas. So let's look more specifically at what's in the book and how you can get the most out of it.

First of all, in Section I you'll learn how to begin managing your career by exploring what it is that makes you tick—that is, what you like to do and what you're good at doing. The reviewed sites will nudge you to take a close look at yourself: your skills and interests (academic, creative, interpersonal, athletic, and so on), as well as your goals in life. In fact, many sites feature various assessment tests to assist you in these regards.

Once you've completed the self-exploration and discovery phase, you'll be ready to zero in on a suitable career field. The career guides in Section II provide information on the numerous career options available to you. You'll find occupational information complete with in-depth job descriptions and working condition overviews, as well as articles and essays about specific career fields.

Sites here also cover relevant educational and training requirements for entering a career field. Pay close attention here. If you want to be competitive in the labor market, whether you are just starting a job, seeking to advance, or looking at making a change, you need to know what training is required for jobs that interest you—and then you must find a way to get that training (covered in Section III). In Section II you'll learn how to gather all of this information and more on your own, through information interviewing and networking. By talking directly with people in the field, you get a first-hand glimpse at what you can realistically expect—plus you gain contacts who might be able to help you in future.

Speaking of the future, when considering a career field, you'll want to know something about the job outlook so you can better map out your life plans. Data on occupational trends can be found at certain sites in this section as well.

After identifying a career field and learning what the requirements are for entering that field, it'll be time to decide where to go to get the necessary education, training, or experience. Among the possibilities are course work at educational institutions and work/learning experiences such as apprenticeships, internships, or on-the-job training. Other ways to get training can be through volunteering or service learning. Section III sites suggest where you can go to get experience or how to select a school. Sites here will also guide you in making an informed and appropriate decision matching your criteria. Given that the doors that will be open to you hinge on your decision, this is an important step in your career management. (Though of course it's never too late to go back and try a new direction.) You should realize that just achieving the minimum level of training is not usually sufficient to be competitive in the labor market. It is usually a combination of academic preparation and experience that makes a person most competitive.

At this point you will have completed the preliminary legwork, making it time to kick your Internet career exploration into full gear. Section IV shows you how to conduct online research yourself. You'll learn about search engines, protecting your privacy, and assessing the source of a site (for example, how to discern the useful and "legitimate" sites from the outdated or unauthoritative). You'll already have a taste of what's available online, so you can use search engines to supplement or expand on that. As you continue to work your way through the rest of the book, be sure to apply the site-assessment tools covered in this section.

In addition to this general job search guidance, Section IV introduces you to some of the Web's largest job search sites. These mega-sites basically have it all—plenty of career advice as well as searchable job listings, resume databases, and services that match up your qualifications with jobs or careers. Most of these sites are geared toward folks actively pursuing jobs, but there's a wealth of resources you can use to explore career possibilities. Meet people with similar interests through the discussion groups, read industry projections and salary surveys, research potential employers by studying company profiles, or take more self-assessment tests. Think of these mega-sites as the headquarters of your career search. You can keep going outward, forging ahead to explore new territory, but you'll want to periodically return to headquarters to get grounded.

Moving on to Section V you'll find sites that are narrower in scope. Many of these sites target audiences composed of disabled, minority, or women workers. Others are regional, federal, or international career resources.

Continuing the theme of a narrower focus is Section VI. Here are sites—many of them for professional associations—devoted to specific industries. You'll be able to conduct very specialized career research here when you visit sites developed and maintained by professionals in your chosen field.

When you arrive at Section VII you should feel ready to pound the pavement and get a job. But there are a few details to attend to beforehand, like compiling your resume, composing targeted cover letters, and pulling together a career portfolio—all of which lead to interviewing with employers, at their place of business or perhaps at campus job fairs. Research those potential employers on the Web and check out online job listings and resume databases. Sound like a lot of work? With everything you'll have under your belt at this point, you'll surely be up to the challenge of finding the right job for you. Besides which, Section VII will walk you through each of these steps.

And once you've found that job, it's time to negotiate. Learn what considerations you should keep in mind when you're trying to decide whether to accept or decline a job offer. Assess whether or not the salary offered is in the ballpark for your occupation and also whether the fringe benefits sufficiently supplement the salary offered. Read up on common personnel practices, employment laws, and your rights as an employee. All of this is addressed in Section VII, which brings you to the end of the book—but not to the end of your career management.

Having a career is a process that evolves over a lifetime and that has identifiable stages. Typical stages include (a) exploring what occupation to pursue, (b) entering an occupation and establishing a pattern of working, (c) maintaining a pattern of working, and (d) disengaging from the role of work. One criticism of career development theories has been that people no longer experience working throughout their lives by way of a stage-ordered developmental process. Experts observing today's labor market have noted that there is a growing trend for people to change not just their job positions but their occupations—perhaps several times during their working life. This trend is due both to factors outside of an individual's control, such as losing a position through an employer's downsizing, and to factors within an individual's control, such as deciding to temporarily leave a paid employment situation to engage more actively in other life roles (perhaps parenting or returning to school).

You will find that throughout your life you are faced with career transitions as you move into the workforce, move out of the workforce, and reenter the workforce. You may select an occupation to enter at the beginning of your career but will probably experience career transitions that require you to move not only from job to job but sometimes from occupation to occupation. Therefore, you may want to keep this book handy and refer to it whenever you enter a transitional stage. You might even want to regularly check out the assessment materials in order to stay aware of your interests, skills, and goals. The association pages should be regular visits too so that you can keep on top of industry issues. And be sure to routinely update your resume, not only when you change jobs but as you acquire new skills and take on additional responsibilities.

All of this goes to say that your career management will be an ongoing, ever-changing process throughout your life. Whether you're preparing to enter the workforce or you're in a later transitional, reevaluative point, you're certain to find sites in this book that will motivate, challenge, guide, and assist you in exploring your career dreams and goals.

As you've probably already guessed, even after you narrow your search, it's unlikely that you'll find just one Web site that meets all your needs. Maybe you'll turn up half a dozen sites that you like and will want to visit on a regular basis. And don't forget that the Internet is a dynamic place. New career-related Web sites emerge each day. The opposite is true as well—old sites "disappear." Keep this in mind as you use this book. Some sites become defunct and are no longer retrievable. Others move without there being a forwarding address—these you can try to track down by using a search engine of your choice. Sometimes URLs (uniform resource locators) change ever so slightly. For these, work your way backwards to the main page URL and see if you can ferret out the particular page from there.

Remember too that what may be available online for free today may cost you a fee in the future and also that site content may have altered somewhat by the time you read this book. In other words, site descriptions here might not match exactly with what you'll find online. If this is the case, just poke around the site, looking for something that sounds similar, and you'll likely find it if it's still there.

Something else to remember is that, while the Internet has a lot to offer, it doesn't have it all. Don't rule out trips to the local library or career center. And don't forget that there are other people you could approach for advice or just to bounce ideas around with. You can get good feedback and support from the people who know you—family members (parents, siblings, grandparents, aunts or uncles) and peers. You have a lot of resources available to you as you plan your future.

Now that you have an overview of the topics covered in the book, you should be ready to go online and see for yourself the wealth of useful career information there is just waiting to be discovered. It's time for you to embark on your very own career exploration on the Internet!

Section I: Self-Exploration and Discovery

CHAPTER 1

THINKING ABOUT YOUR INTERESTS, SKILLS, AND GOALS

Okay, so the book is called *Career Exploration on the Internet*, but what if you don't know what career you want to explore? Not to worry. Whether you are just beginning your quest for a first career or you are researching possibilities for a second or third career, you will find much of interest in this chapter. Featured here are some Web sites intended to give you an overview of ways to begin, questions to ask, and points to consider—in other words, some career guidance.

Many people think that choosing a career means choosing their employer or choosing what type of job they would like to do. But choosing a career means more than just getting and working at a job. Every person has a career whether or not he or she is ever involved in paid employment because career means "path in life." The idea of career management is to choose and direct your own path in life, particularly the part of your life that has to do with working. Career guidance helps people manage their own careers.

You will face career choices throughout your life. These choices may involve decisions such as enrolling in educational programs, enlisting in the military, gaining paid employment, being a volunteer or an intern, starting a business, or moving to accept a new job position. Of course it is impossible for you to know what is going to happen throughout your entire life, so you may wonder how you can choose and plan your career. Career counselors suggest that individuals can be personally empowered to guide their own careers through career guidance, which promotes the process of career development by providing pertinent information and aiding in building skills for career management.

Although there are many different theories in the field of career development, current thinking suggests that a variety of things influence individual careers; however, you can and should be responsible for your own career by practicing career management. *Career management* is the process of developing skills that you use throughout your life to direct your career development. Some of the skills that the various theorists in the field believe are important to career management include self-awareness, planfulness (or ability to plan), personal management, personal marketing, and knowing about the world of work.

Throughout your life you will develop and use the skills outlined here and at the Web sites that follow. Typically, career development counselors suggest that you should approach career decisions by engaging in self-exploration—that is, engaging the skills required in self-awareness—and by learning about the world of work. The skills of planfulness and personal management are used to select occupations that might offer jobs appropriate to your career goals and to determine how to get the training and experiences needed to enter these jobs. To get a job, you must use your personal marketing skills. To keep a job or to determine if another job will offer greater satisfaction, you use your personal management skills and planfulness skills. The idea of career resiliency is improving these skills and using them as needed throughout your life to manage your own career development.

While many skills are required for career management, many of them are also required for success in both formal and informal educational experiences, and many are transferable from other settings. These skills can be developed either on your own or with the help of a professional. References such as the Web sites reviewed in this chapter provide information on the world of work and on the development of other career management skills.

Self-awareness and personal management skills should be used to help identify individual short- and long-term goals. Planfulness skills and knowing about the world of work are used in decision making to develop short- and long-term plans for meeting goals. Knowing about the world of work, labor market trends, and the relationships among occupations will help you maintain flexibility and adaptability in your career goals.

There are many skills required for work that you will not find in a job description. These are skills other than the technical skills required to do the job. They are sometimes called *soft skills* and can be broken down into the categories of *basic skills, personal/interpersonal skills,* or *job-keeping skills.* Many employers consider these skills to be "givens"—that is, they expect anyone applying for a job to have them, which is why they are usually not mentioned in job descriptions. Because soft skills apply to any job, developing them promotes your abilities to do well in whatever job you take, be marketable when seeking a new job, and manage your career.

Soft skills are interrelated and overlapping. Not everyone can excel in all soft skills or be as adept at best applying them in different situations. But then not everyone would be happy in all work environments. Career management involves (a) identifying which soft skills are areas of strength that are enjoyable and advantageous to use (thereby figuring out which soft skills are desired to be developed and which are not) and (b) finding employment that provides a good fit for soft skills already possessed and for developing desired skills.

Modern employers often claim to have difficulty finding workers with the basic skills they require. Your competency in basic academic skills is usually demonstrated by having a high school diploma. There are very few positions available in the job market that do not require the mastery of basic academic skills. Some of the basic skills are communication, computation, technology and information management, and understanding social systems.

Personal/interpersonal skills have to do with personal self-development and getting along with others at work. Such skills have to do with character, manner, initiative, diplomacy, teamwork, leadership, organization, and problem solving.

Job-keeping skills have to do with understanding the normal behaviors your employer expects from you. Keep in mind that different behaviors are often expected from employees whose positions differ and that many of the rules governing what an employer expects might not be written down. Certain job-keeping skills are attendance and punctuality, timeliness, proper attire/personal hygiene, and appropriate participation in the company's organizational culture.

BUILDING BRAND YOU

HTTP://WWW.FASTCOMPANY.COM/CAREER/BRAND.HTML

Fast Company magazine is responsible for this entertaining and useful resource pertaining to you—what it is that makes you who you are and how you can use that to further your career. A wide range of related topics are covered here, including emotions on the job, office politics, decision making, mentoring, handling difficult conversations, and burnout.

Tom Peters helps you explore your own unique talents and qualities that will make you an asset at the workplace in the section "The Brand Called You." You're presented with ideas on how to capitalize on and market your skills as well as how to manage your career.

CAREER DEVELOPMENT MANUAL

HTTP://WWW.ADM.UWATERLOO.CA/INFOCECS/CRC/MANUAL-HOME.HTML

Detailed information on self-assessment and career exploration is presented here by the University of Waterloo Career Services. Six "Steps to Career/Life Planning Success" are outlined. They are self-assessment, occupational research, decision making, employment contacts, work, and career/life planning. Each step has substeps you should read and work through for a better understanding of the process. For example, in self-assessment you will first determine your personality and attitudes before moving on to a discussion of skills and achievements. Then you can go on to knowledge and learning style, values, and so on. For the work step, you will learn something about job offers and acceptance, as well as work success.

CAREER GUIDES
HTTP://WWW.BIO.COM/HR/SEARCH/

Most of the articles in this large collection were written by David Jensen of the recruiting firm Search Masters International, which specializes in placing pharmaceutical and biotechnology professionals. While some articles address industry-specific issues (for example, the biotech job market and employment trends), the vast majority pertain to issues that will appeal to a wider audience of job seekers.

The first section, "Self-Analysis and Personal Mastery," presents articles that should help you to formulate and manage your career path, as well as to survive hardships that may arise once you've entered your profession. The article "Vision: The First Step in Career Management" comments on the usefulness and importance of drawing up a "career vision statement" to help you realize your career goals. "The Seven C's of Career Control" reminds us that we can make choices in certain aspects of our professional lives that we control: the clock, our concepts, our contacts, our communication, our commitments, our causes, and our concerns. "Take Charge of Your Career" explains some of the choices you might have even in situations that appear to be out of your hands.

The second section, "The Job Hunt," includes articles that deal with basic job search tasks and skills: networking, telephone interviewing, creating a resume, negotiating a job offer, writing a cover letter, and conducting a marketing campaign to promote yourself, among others. "Career Skills Improvement" tackles such topics as making oral presentations, charisma, and mentoring a possible successor. Finally, "The Management Track" and several articles on miscellaneous subjects complete the collection.

CAREER PLANIT
HTTP://WWW.CAREERPLANIT.COM/

"Your launching pad to career exploration" is how this resource, from the National Association of Colleges and Employers, describes itself. Indeed, if you are in college, you should find that there is quite a lot to learn here about navigating and designing your future. "Career Planning 101" is a good place to start. There's information about desirable personal characteristics and skills—what you should have and how to develop them. "Making Choices" presents articles that delve into the issue of self-assessment testing or discuss how to turn your hobbies, passions, and interests into a career. Elsewhere you will find guidance on acquiring work experience and selecting a graduate school. For those seeking a bachelor's or associate degree, there are outlines of the steps to take in your career-planning process. Throughout the site, ideas are given on how best to utilize your college or university career center in preparing for your future.

CAREER PLANNING PROCESS

HTTP://WWW.BGSU.EDU/OFFICES/CAREERS/PROCESS/PROCESS.HTML

Bowling Green State University offers this site designed to help you work through those tough career choices you are bound to face. Begin with the "Self Assessment" section, which describes the information you will gather through the process of exploring your abilities, interests, values, and so on. There's a related exercise supplementing this material, which is also the case in several of the other sections. Next is "Academic and Career Options," providing ideas on how you can narrow your search and select an occupational direction. Go on to "Relevant and Practical Experience," where your focus is on gaining actual experience through internships or summer jobs. This will help you determine if your selected occupational direction is the right one. You can then move on to "Job Search and Graduate School Preparation." Learn about how to organize your job or graduate school search. Finally, "Career Change" will help you reevaluate your career.

GETTING REAL!

HTTP://WWW.GETTINGREAL.COM/

Getting Real is a teen's dream. You can meet and chat with other teenagers about career hopes, read message boards, and learn about applying to college. While the site isn't your typical career-counseling or self-assessment resource, what it offers should motivate you to think creatively about who you are, what you really want to do with your life, and how you can get there. Examples of this kind of thinking are exhibited by the teenagers who write about these and other issues in their diaries featured at the site.

There are teen correspondents for a variety of channels, in such categories as art, careers, college, film and video, music, sports, and technology. In their diaries, the teens discuss their opinions, experiences, and hopes in these fields. They also provide witty and opinionated descriptions of an assortment of other teen-related resources. If you want to get in on the action, check out the chat room, where you can talk with teens about their career goals and life's dreams. Or you can post your thoughts on the topic-specific message boards.

GOALMAP
HTTP://WWW.GOALMAP.COM/

This is an entertaining, interactive site where you can create a Goalmap not only to get a clearer idea of what you want to do in business and your career but of what you want to get out of other aspects of your life: for your own self and well-being, home and family, and community and humanity. Discovery steps for each category require you to indicate your level of interest in several activities, how important each activity is to you in the next twelve months, and your commitment to reaching your desired goals in regard to these activities. Upon completion of these three steps, you are to write brief descriptions of your goals for those activities receiving the highest ratings, after which you are to select a colorful image to correlate with each goal. These images along with your goal descriptions will be displayed in your own personalized Goalmap. This tool can make it fun to identify your goals as well as to keep track of your progress in reaching them.

HOW TO DECIDE WHAT TO DO WITH YOUR LIFE

HTTP://WWW.ROCKPORTINSTITUTE.COM/PATHFINDER3.HTML

Do you know what you want to be when you grow up? Do you know where to even begin when you're trying to determine what might be the career of your dreams? If your answer to either of these questions is less than an enthusiastic "yes," then check out this excerpt from Nicholas Lore's book The Pathfinder: How to Choose or Change Your Career for a Lifetime of Satisfaction and Success. The author recommends that you commit yourself to making necessary decisions; break the big questions down into smaller, more manageable questions, and take it from there; put together your career plan one step at a time; take risks rather than settling for comfort; persist no matter what; and finally, celebrate your progress—or even lack thereof.

MANAGEMENT AND TEAMS

HTTP://CONTENT.MONSTER.COM/CAREER/TEAM/

Do you have what it takes to be a manager? If you don't already know, you may find out after visiting this Monster.com site. Here you can read about time management, teamwork, communication, mentoring, and discipline.

MIND TOOLS

HTTP://WWW.MINDTOOLS.COM/INDEX.HTML

This company, located in England, makes software products intended to provide customers with the skills necessary to utilize their minds to a greater extent than before. Several such techniques are described at this site. Among these are brainstorming, decision making, speed reading, memory exercises, stress and time management, effective planning, and communication. Perhaps you are already highly adept in some or many of these skills. But if not you may want to check out this resource as it should help you to fine-tune skills that are important to possess in the workplace environment.

THE SEVEN CHALLENGES: COOPERATIVE COMMUNICATION SKILLS WORKBOOK & READER

HTTP://WWW.COOPCOMM.ORG/W7A1TOC.HTM

Good communication is an essential aspect of workplace relationships. This workbook from Dennis Rivers affords a guide to learning healthier, more respectful communication. Points covered can be applied to any life situation: with family or friends, in the community, and in the workplace. Some of the skills highlighted include responsive listening, conversational intent, clear expression, and acknowledging appreciation. Several exercises are suggested so that you can practice the skills outlined. A list of recommended titles for further reading is available.

TRANSITION ASSISTANCE ONLINE

HTTP://WWW.TAONLINE.COM/

TAO assists military personnel with making the transition to civilian employment. Service members and veterans can submit resumes and search or browse job postings. Topics pertaining to career exploration or the process of reentering the workforce include self-assessment, developing goals, devising a plan of action, general job-hunting and "second career strategies," relocation, and financial considerations. Links to military, career, education, and community assistance sites are available.

CHAPTER 2

ASSESSMENT TESTS

Assessment tests are a type of tool used in career counseling to help enhance your self-awareness. They do this by clarifying values, identifying occupations that match personal interests, suggesting aptitude areas, and ascertaining abilities. Assessment tests also can provide a measure of your career maturity—that is, how ready you are to undertake your career management.

There are many assessment tests, also called standardized assessment instruments or inventories, used in career counseling. They come in either the pencil and paper or computer variety and are typically given by professionals, such as career counselors, who are trained in administration, scoring, and interpretation. The results frequently show how people taking the test compare to other people of their age and backgrounds. Extensive career testing is usually not recommended for students below the junior high school level because their values and interests are not set until they reach their mid-teens. To be effective as a tool in career counseling, the purpose and results of assessment tests must be made clear so that the test taker understands how these fit into the process. Assessment tests—including those administered by career counselors and those found at the sites discussed in this book—are not crystal balls. They are not designed to find you the "perfect" job any more than they can reveal the "true" you. They are usually done as a battery of tests (for example, you may be given inventories measuring your interests, values, and personality traits) so that results from the different inventories can be compared. In this way, the results of the tests taken as a whole can best be weighed and discussed.

Values inventories focus primarily on work values or on lifestyle values. Their results are often related to occupations, so that after you take a values inventory, you can identify jobs you might want to explore. Your responses are scored to determine how they compare to others on values such as achievement, altruism, autonomy, creativity, economic rewards, independence, intellectual stimulation, physical activity, prestige, risk, security, social relationships, and variety. There are no right or wrong answers.

The scaled results of values inventories alone, however, frequently do not reveal values that might be very important to individual career decision making. For best results you must discuss the inventory with your career counselor.

There are a wide variety of instruments that measure values. Some examples include the Work Values Inventory, Values Scale, Survey of Interpersonal Values/Survey of Personal Values, Study of Values, and Work Environment Preference Schedule.

Interest testing, whereby personal interests are matched to occupations, is a method that has been a hallmark of career counseling. You are asked to indicate your level of interest in performing various activities; for example, whether you like, dislike, or don't know if you'd like or dislike to rewire a toaster or write a play, and so on. Some interest inventories ask you to indicate your interest in specific occupations. Results may take the form of lists of specific occupations or clusters or groups of occupations. Some interest inventories compare your responses to interest themes of people employed in specific occupational groupings. There are also inventories that ask you to indicate your level of interest in various leisure activities, which are then related to occupations.

Interpretation of interest inventories includes soliciting your feedback regarding occupational areas of both high and low interest to confirm and explore the reasons behind your interest pattern. People who have not had opportunities to engage in specific activities may rate them as "don't know," resulting in low interest patterns. Younger people may generalize from limited experiences, such as doing poorly in one science class to rejection of items like "working in a laboratory." Interest inventories are not designed to find the occupations that are "right" for you but to identify occupations that match your interests. To get the most out of the test, you must get more information about the occupations that are identified by the results.

Frequently used interest inventories include the Self-Directed Search, Strong Interest Inventory (formerly the Strong Campbell Interest Inventory), Kuder Occupational Interest Survey, USES (the United States Employment Services Interest Inventory), and Career Assessment Inventory (yields only occupations that can be entered with a high school diploma).

Achievement tests measure skills that you have acquired, while aptitude tests measure both acquired skills and the potential you have to acquire a skill. Achievement tests, given in batteries that test a variety of academic areas (such as spelling, reading, math, and science), are frequently used in educational settings. Achievement tests focused on a single subject are used both by employers and by boards that issue professional licenses. Aptitude tests are used to predict the likelihood that the test taker will be successful in an educational program or in the military forces. Typically including broader samples of domains than achievement tests, aptitude tests cover areas such as space relations, mechanical reasoning, form perception, motor coordination, and figure and manual dexterity. There are right and wrong answers on both achievement and aptitude tests. Also, there are often time limits to complete sections. Results are frequently given in standardized scores that compare your performance to the performance of similar individuals.

Both achievement and aptitude tests are used in American society as gatekeeping mechanisms—that is, failure to meet certain standards on these tests may keep you from pursuing certain career paths, such as entering an educational program or the military services, or from receiving a professional license. Interpretation for people who do well usually consists of confirming their likelihood of success in an educational or occupational endeavor. It should be noted, however, that performance on the test does not guarantee success but suggests that, with appropriate application, you are capable of achieving success.

Commonly used achievement and aptitude tests include the Metropolitan Achievement Test, California Achievement Tests, Iowa Tests of Basic Skills, Stanford Achievement Tests, the Scholastic Assessment Test, the ACT Assessment, Graduate Record Examinations, the General Aptitude Test Battery, and the Armed Services Vocational Aptitude Battery.

Some career counselors use personality assessment instruments to explore your preferences and relate them to occupations. These instruments are especially useful for adults who are having trouble with both career and personal concerns. Typically you indicate if test items like "I prefer to stay home and read a book rather than go to a party" are true or false for you. There are no right or wrong answers. Results may be reported in terms of traits such as achievement, affiliations, autonomy, conformity, dominance, emotional stability, friendliness, nurturance, and social adjustment. Results typically compare you to others based on a particular category.

While not a requirement, counselors sometimes sit with you while you are taking the test so they can listen to your comments as you decide how to respond to items. It is not unusual to want items to specify situations or to want to "argue" with items. Your comments can provide insight into your values and identify areas for further discussion in interpretation. Interpretation in career counseling usually involves relating personality profiles to occupation choices and is similar to interpretation of interest inventories.

Personality instruments used in career counseling sometimes include the Myers-Briggs Type Indicator, Edwards Personal Preference Schedule, California Personality Inventory, California Test of Personality, and Sixteen Personality Factor.

Career maturity testing, or career development inventories, measure readiness to undertake career management. Results yield scores for attitudes toward work, planfulness, readiness for explorations, and knowledge of the world of work. Usually these instruments are used with young people in a school setting to measure the effectiveness of guidance programs; however, there are versions appropriate for use with adults as well. Interpretation focuses on areas of both strength and weakness, with the aim to increase understanding of career development and management.

Career maturity instruments include the Career Development Inventory, Career Maturity Inventory, Career Beliefs Inventory, Adult Career Concerns Inventory, and Salience Inventory.

Now that you've seen the many different kinds of assessment tests there are and learned a little about their purposes, let's go online for more in-depth coverage of certain tests and inventories. Some of these tests are sold to career-counseling professionals and others are available for you to take online. Try a couple to get an idea of some career directions you might want to explore.

Miscellaneous

CAREER DECISION MAKING

HTTP://WWW.ANSELM.EDU/STUDENTLIFE/CAREER/DECISION1.HTML

The Career and Employment Services at Saint Anselm College (New Hampshire) offers several self-assessment exercises at this site. The subpages are called "Personal Traits Inventory," "Work Values Inventory," "Influence of Significant Others and Significant Factors," "Interest Inventory," "The 'I Want To Work With People' Exercise," and "Skills—How Do You Know What You Are Good At?"

At each subpage you'll find worksheets to fill in by rating, identifying, or answering questions about your values, your skills, your interests, and outside influences. Use the results to determine a possible career path or to create a resume. You may be wondering how. Well, first off, these exercises should help make you even more aware of your strengths and weaknesses as well as your interests, not to mention what kinds of things you absolutely don't like to do! It should be easier, then, to decide what your college major should be or what field you want to go into. You can also highlight your skills and interests in your resume or cover letter. Plus you can discuss the results with a career counselor.

Interest Testing

THE CAREER INTERESTS GAME

HTTP://WWW.MISSOURI.EDU/ CPPCWWW/HOLLAND.SHTML

University of Missouri's Career Center brings you this "game" based on John Holland's RIASEC model of occupations. To "play," you need to rank the top three groups that appeal to you (based on descriptions provided) out of six groups of people, each group representing one of the RIASEC (realistic, investigative, artistic, social, enterprising, conventional) types. This will give you your Holland Code. For example, if you select the artistic, social, and investigative groups (in that order of preference), your Holland Code is ASI.

Your Holland Code can help you to identify what career path might be suitable for your personality.

When you click on each RIASEC type, you will find lists of pertinent personality traits, likes, and hobbies, as well as career possibilities. In the ASI example, one of the career possibilities listed is writers and editors. If you click on that link, you will discover a job description plus useful information on education and training, employment outlook, and salaries. You will find similar coverage for numerous other job types.

THE CAREER KEY

HTTP://WWW2.NCSU.EDU/UNITY/LOCKERS/USERS/L/LKJ/

Lawrence Jones's Career Key is a vocational test designed to help you explore what career fields you may be suited for. The test can be taken online. You are asked to indicate career fields that appeal to you as well as to rate yourself in various skills, interests, character traits, and values. After you respond to all the statements, you are scored in regard to the six Holland types: artistic, conventional, enterprising, investigative, realistic, and social. Select your top personality type(s) to discover representative occupations, and then choose those jobs that seem most attractive. When you finish you are presented with links—one for each job you selected—to the appropriate page in the Bureau of Labor Statistics' ' Occupational Outlook Handbook, where you can read about the nature of the work, required training, earnings, and employment outlook. If you'd rather, you can print out the Career Key instead. Advice is offered on making career decisions, and links to further information are listed.

NCS CAREER ASSESSMENTS

HTTP://ASSESSMENTS.NCS.COM/ASSESSMENTS/CAREER/CAREER.HTM

National Computer Systems provides assessment tools to professionals in the fields of career counseling, mental health, medicine, and workforce development. While this is a commercial company resource where industry professionals can order assessments, the site also offers descriptions and background information on several tests pertaining to career choice, personality, or other related issues. Visit the site to learn more about the Career Assessment Inventory (vocational and enhanced), Campbell Interest and

Skill Survey (CISS), Interest Determination, Exploration and Assessment System (IDEAS), Sixteen Personality Factor (16PF), Cross-Cultural Adaptability Inventory (CCAI), and Quality of Life Inventory (QOLI).

SELF-DIRECTED SEARCH

HTTP://WWW.SELF-DIRECTED-SEARCH.COM/

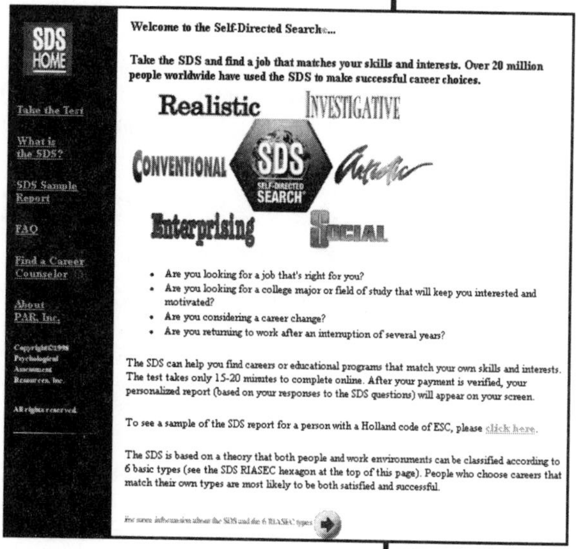

This site from Psychological Assessment Resources provides an overview of SDS, a career interest test, plus information on John Holland, the person who developed it. There are subpages for each of the six RIASEC (realistic, investigative, artistic, social, enterprising, conventional) types. Personality traits are listed for each type, along with related occupations. You can actually take the test at the site, but you must pay a fee if you want to get the results.

Achievement and Aptitude Testing

ACT

HTTP://WWW.ACT.ORG/

This site, for the organization ACT (which used to be called the American College Testing Program), presents materials on career exploration, planning for college, and various assessment tools including the ACT Assessment, a college admissions test taken by high school juniors and seniors.

You'll probably be most interested in gathering information about the ACT Assessment, so follow that link. There you can browse the ACT FAQs to learn more about the test—why to take it, how to prepare for it, what to take along to the test center, and so on. You can also get the scoop on test dates, locations, and registration; look at "Score Reports" for advice on how to understand your test scores; and study the tips and sample questions so you'll be ready to do your best.

Some other site features are mainly for parents and teachers, but feel free to check them out yourself. The section for parents includes a small collection of links, one of which is for the "Best Bookmarks for High School Students," compiled by U.S. News. Definitely worth a visit. There are also descriptions of other career-related assessment tools such as Counseling for High Skills (CHS), DISCOVER, and Work Keys.

ASVAB CAREER EXPLORATION PROGRAM

HTTP://WWW.DMDC.OSD.MIL/ASVAB/

Postsecondary students and those in grades 10-12 participate in this U.S. Department of Defense program, which consists of the Armed Services Vocational Aptitude Battery, an interest inventory, and a work values exercise. The ASVAB assesses verbal, mathematical, and technical ability in ten areas. Brief descriptions are given of each, along with background information on the program, its use in career development, and the role it plays in military recruiting. Participants in this battery of tests needn't necessarily be considering entry into the armed services, although the military, in its recruitment efforts, may use the results to screen those individuals interested in pursuing a military career.

FAIRTEST

HTTP://FAIRTEST.ORG/

The National Center for Fair & Open Testing (FairTest) is an organization concerned with making sure that standardized K-12, college admissions, and employment testing is fair to all participants, regardless of race, ethnicity, gender, or income. You'll find numerous fact sheets dealing with issues such as national testing, SAT myths and misuse, academic standards, grades 1-2 achievement tests, and computerized testing. A large collection of sample articles from Examiner, FairTest's newsletter, is available. If you want to find other similar resources, browse through the related links page.

GRE

HTTP://WWW.GRE.ORG/

Are you thinking about attending graduate school someday? If so, then you'll probably have to take the GRE (Graduate Record Examinations) to gain entrance to the school of your choice. Whether you're interested in taking the paper-based or the computer-based test, you'll find plenty of information about registration, fees, test structure, scheduling conflicts, and so on. Sample questions testing your verbal, quantitative, and analytical abilities—along with instructions—are also presented. There are sections specifically of interest to educators and researchers as well.

KAPLAN

HTTP://WWW1.KAPLAN.COM/

Kaplan has long been known for its test preparation courses, which are intended to help individuals prepare for the PSAT, SAT, and ACT (college), the LSAT, MCAT, GMAT, and GRE (graduate school), and various licensing and specialized examinations. This site contains a wealth of information pertaining to these exams as well as regarding financial aid, career exploration, SCORE! educational programs for kids four to fourteen years of age, the development of study skills, and more.

Among the site's numerous features are test descriptions and dates, background information, practice tests, vocabulary flash cards, and admissions strategies. The career section examines a wide range of topics including various occupational options, cover letters and resumes, networking, job fairs, interviews, placement services, and job success. Supplementary links to other sites are available.

PSAT/NMSQT

HTTP://WWW.COLLEGEBOARD.ORG/INDEX_THIS/PSAT/COUNSLRS/HTML/INDX000.HTML

This site is all about the Preliminary SAT/National Merit Scholarship Qualifying Test. Who should take the test and why? Where can you take the test? How should you prepare for taking the test? How do you interpret your test scores? The College Board (College Entrance Examination Board) explains all of this and more. Read about the types of questions you'll be asked in the verbal, math, and writing skills sections of the test. Then try your hand at several sample questions.

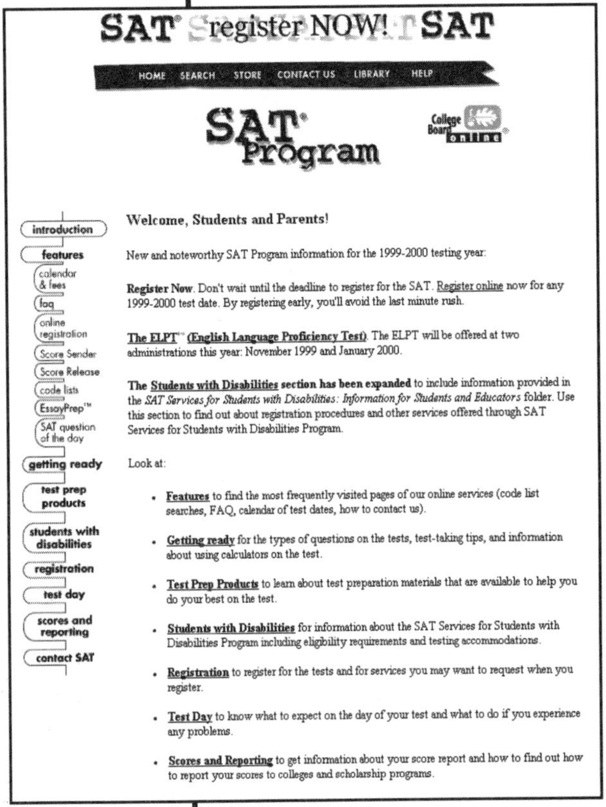

SAT register NOW! SAT
HOME SEARCH STORE CONTACT US LIBRARY HELP
SAT Program
College Board online
introduction
features
calendar & fees
faq
online registration
Score Sender
Score Release
code lists
EssayPrep™
SAT question of the day
getting ready
test prep products
students with disabilities
registration
test day
scores and reporting
contact SAT
Welcome, Students and Parents!
New and noteworthy SAT Program information for the 1999-2000 testing year:
Register Now. Don't wait until the deadline to register for the SAT. Register online now for any 1999-2000 test date. By registering early, you'll avoid the last minute rush.
The ELPT™ (English Language Proficiency Test). The ELPT will be offered at two administrations this year: November 1999 and January 2000.
The Students with Disabilities section has been expanded to include information provided in the SAT Services for Students with Disabilities: Information for Students and Educators folder. Use this section to find out about registration procedures and other services offered through SAT Services for Students with Disabilities Program.
Look at:
Features to find the most frequently visited pages of our online services (code list searches, FAQ, calendar of test dates, how to contact us).
Getting ready for the types of questions on the tests, test-taking tips, and information about using calculators on the test.
Test Prep Products to learn about test preparation materials that are available to help you do your best on the test.
Students with Disabilities for information about the SAT Services for Students with Disabilities Program including eligibility requirements and testing accommodations.
Registration to register for the tests and for services you may want to request when you register.
Test Day to know what to expect on the day of your test and what to do if you experience any problems.
Scores and Reporting to get information about your score report and how to find out how to report your scores to colleges and scholarship programs.

SAT
HTTP://WWW.COLLEGEBOARD.ORG/SAT/HTML/STUDENTS/INDX001.HTML

Here is the place to find everything you wanted to know about the SAT (originally known as the Scholastic Aptitude Test, later called the Scholastic Assessment Test). Everything, that is, except the answers! The College Board (College Entrance Examination Board) offers information on registration, fees, what to bring to the testing center on test day, and test scores and how they're reported to colleges.

Separate sections give details specifically about the SAT I (which measures your verbal and math reasoning skills) and the SAT II (which measures your knowledge in different subject areas). Read about the types of questions you'll find on the tests, get tips to help you do your best, find out whether or not you should bring along a calculator, and more. You can test yourself by answering the question of the day. And if you want to purchase additional preparation materials, you can do that here as well.

STANFORD 9
HTTP://WWW.HEMWEB.COM/TROPHY/ACHVTEST/ACHVINDX.HTM

The Stanford Achievement Test Series (9th edition) assesses skills and knowledge for students in grades K-13. This site, from Harcourt Educational Measurement, is intended mainly to be used by educators. But if you want to learn about this long-standing national achievement test (it dates back to the 1920s), check it out. Read descriptions of the test's multiple choice and open-ended topics, including language, listening, mathematics, reading, science, social science, spelling, and study skills.

Personality Testing

KEIRSEY TEMPERAMENT AND CHARACTER
HTTP://KEIRSEY.COM/

This Web site, about personality typing, contains a lot of information from the books Please Understand Me and Please Understand Me II, written by David Keirsey with (respectively) Marilyn Bates and Ray Choiniere. You will find descriptions of temperament and character as well as two tests used to identify personality types. These are the Keirsey Character Sorter and the Keirsey Temperament Sorter II. Similar to the Myers-Briggs personality inventory, these tests sort individuals into one of four temperaments: the rationals, the idealists, the artisans, or the guardians. Each category is broken down even further into variants, sixteen in all. For example, the idealists group is made up of teachers, champions, counselors, and healers.

You can take the tests online. Just answer the questions and submit your responses electronically, after which you'll be presented with a rough indicator (that is, a good idea) of your temperament and the specific variant. Want to know some of people who make up each category? Famous people representing each temperament type are listed: Albert Schweitzer is identified as a healer idealist, while Eleanor Roosevelt is a counselor idealist.

TEAM TECHNOLOGY
HTTP://WWW.TEAMTECHNOLOGY.CO.UK/HOME.HTM

This company site presents several useful resources pertaining to the Myers-Briggs Type Indicator (MBTI). One section assists you in determining your Myers-Briggs type. Do this by considering your personality in terms of introversion and extroversion, sensing and intuition, thinking and feeling, and judgment and perception. There are 16 different Myers-Briggs types, each being a combination of four of these characteristics (for example, Introverted iNtuition with auxiliary extroverted Thinking [Judgment], or INTJ). A chart and brief descriptions are provided for each type. Additional details are available, including notes on the ways in which each type might contribute to a team environment, attain personal growth, and respond in a moment of crisis or when under stress. An entertaining "slide show" illustrates what is and isn't measured by the MBTI and further portrays various Myers-Briggs types.

Section II: Career Preparation

CHAPTER 3

RESEARCHING CAREER FIELDS AND CHOOSING A MAJOR

After exploring and assessing your interests, skills, and goals in life, it's time to take the next step. It's time to begin researching career fields that you've found to be of interest so that you can determine your educational and training needs. Whether you know exactly what kind of work you want to do, you have only a general idea of the direction you want to take, or you're still feeling a bit clueless, the career and educational guides covered in this chapter should provide you with the background information and guidance required to help you more clearly identify possibilities and formulate plans.

These guides include information on a variety of occupations, allowing you to sample and compare jobs or majors that are alike or vastly different. You saw in Chapters 1 and 2 that there are numerous variables to take into account when selecting a career path. Keep these in mind as you explore the sites in this chapter, asking yourself questions such as the following:

- What educational level do you need to reach in order to enter this profession?
- Do you have the basic skills required to perform the job?
- Do you feel passionate about the career field?
- Will it provide the intellectual stimulation you desire?
- Does work in this field involve physical labor?

- Will you be working with other people or primarily alone? Which is your preference?

- What are the long-term prospects for someone in this field? Is there growth or decline in the industry? (See Chapter 5 for more on this topic.)

In addition to the general guides available, there are a number of government classification systems used to organize labor market information. A tremendous resource for researching career fields, such systems feature specific occupational information detailing

- the industries that employ people in the occupation,

- typical responsibilities and duties of workers in the occupation,

- the work environment and tools used on the job,

- the skills required, the level of education associated with these skills, and any special requirements such as licenses or certifications,

- typical compensation such as wages, salaries, and benefits,

- employment outlooks,

- ways to obtain training and ways to enter the occupation, and

- sources of further information.

You can use labor market information in many ways. If you are starting your career and seeking to enter an occupation, you can (a) identify occupations that match your interests, aptitudes, and abilities, (b) determine if working conditions in specific occupations will match your values, (c) find out how to get training to obtain skills to enter an occupation, and (d) learn about career opportunities the occupation offers. If you are managing a career transition, you can (a) check the potential for job openings in an occupation, (b) determine if skills you possess can transfer to another occupation, and (c) identify specific job openings.

There is so much occupational information available it can be difficult to determine what is relevant to any specific career challenge and to understand what it means. Career counselors are experts in finding and interpreting labor market information. They are familiar with the variety of systems commonly used to organize labor market information. In the United States, data on the labor market is collected and disseminated by the U.S. Department of Labor (DOL). The three major government classification systems used by DOL are the Dictionary of Occupational Titles (DOT), in use since the 1930s; the Guide for Occupational Exploration (GOE), designed to help people explore occupations matching their interests; and the Standard Occupational Classification System (SOC). Beginning in 1999, a fourth classification system—the Occupational Information Network, or O*NET—was added, designed to replace the DOT. In Canada, Human Resources Development Canada uses the National Occupational Classification (NOC) system to provide descriptions for more than 25,000 occupations in the Canadian labor market.

Many students have difficulty deciding on a major field of study when they enter undergraduate studies. They think that they will be able to find a high-paying job when they graduate no matter what their major, seeing that occupations paying more than average frequently require a bachelor's degree. They may think a degree that indicates a broad field of studies, such as "general studies" or "liberal arts," will prepare them to enter a number of occupations. While it is possible to enter many occupations with a liberal arts degree, people who are most competitive for jobs seek out specific courses and experiences to prepare for occupational entry. Some occupations—for example, buyers, insurance claim representatives, and interpreters—employ workers who have bachelor's degrees but their major fields of study may not be specific. If you are uncertain what major area of study will best prepare you to enter your occupation of choice, refer to the sites following to discover what the relevant educational requirements are for various fields. Furthermore, you might benefit from doing information interviewing (see Chapter 4) with employers to inquire about what course work and experiences they consider most important when they hire. And of course consult with a career counselor, who will be able to help you pull together all the information and arrive at some decisions.

Career and Educational Guides

ADVENTURES IN EDUCATION

HTTP://WWW.ADVENTURESINEDUCATION.ORG/

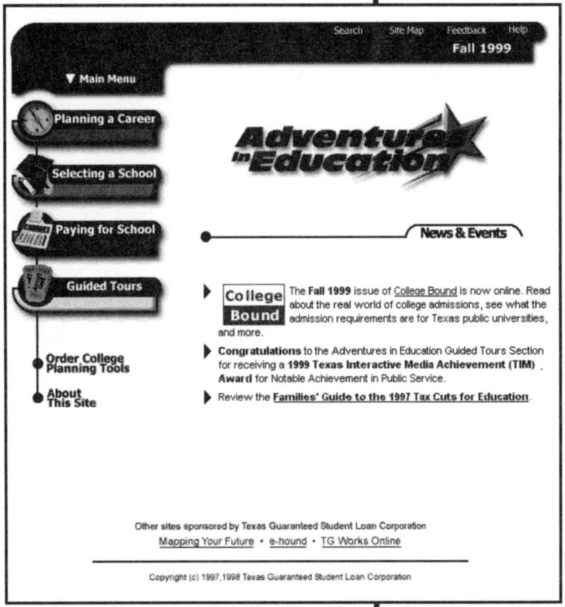

This site, by the Texas Guaranteed Student Loan Corporation, is an excellent resource for researching careers. There's also quite a bit of information about colleges and financial aid. "Guided Tours" are offered for students (in middle school, high school, or college), parents, and counselors and teachers. The section for high school students, for example, covers career planning, includes a planner to help you track your school course schedule and requirements, provides guidance on researching and selecting a college, describes college entrance exams, and discusses the process of applying for college admission as well as for financial aid.

These topics are expanded on in other areas of the site: "Planning a Career," "Selecting a School," and "Paying for School." You'll find more detailed information to help you plan your education and career plus links to additional resources, such as the Occupational Outlook Handbook, where you can research careers.

CAREER DOCTOR

HTTP://ASP.STUDENTCENTER.COM/DOCTOR/DOCTOR.ASP

Do you know what you want to major in—but you're not sure how you can apply that major in today's job market? Or do you know what you like to do—but you're not sure what major is an appropriate match for your interests or skills? Monster.com's Career Doctor has some ideas for you!

Say you've decided to major in English. There's a brief description of such a major, along with lists of marketable skills and career choices. For an English major, your choices might include being an editorial assistant, an adult education teacher, a literary agent, a business writer, or a librettist, among many others. Take a look at the notes for any occupation that looks interesting.

Going about the process in reverse, suppose one of your passions is conducting research. Some of the majors that relate to this interest are anthropology, chemistry, education, history, political science, and sociology. Read the brief descriptions of the major of your choice, then check out the list of marketable skills and links to notes on possible career options. Either way you use the Career Doctor, you'll also have access to contact details for organizations that might be able to provide you with additional information.

CAREER EXPLORATION LINKS

HTTP://WWW.UHS.BERKELEY.EDU/CAREERLIBRARY/LINKS/CAREERME.HTM

This site, from the University of California at Berkeley, is a primo spot for researching and exploring various careers and educational choices. The disciplines covered are agriculture, architecture, arts and letters, biological sciences, business, computer science, education and social work, engineering, environmental, government, health, industry, trades, and services, international, law, media, nonprofit, physical sciences, and social sciences and humanities. Click on your field of choice, and—voila!—you'll find subcategories and links to relevant sites in the field. Each site is marked with a symbol that denotes it as offering occupational information (data about the field, the kind of work involved, working conditions, etc.), educational information (concerning graduate, professional, or other educational programs), and/or information of interest to multicultural populations. Here's an example: select "Environmental," and you'll be presented with the subcategories "General," "Fish and Wildlife Management," and "Forestry." Pertinent links, with applicable symbols, are then listed beneath each subcategory.

EXPLORING OCCUPATIONS

HTTP://WWW.UMANITOBA.CA/COUNSELLING/CAREERS.HTML

Designed to help you determine your career path, this straightforward University of Manitoba site gives you access to loads of information about various occupational groups. Categories are listed, such as economics, geology, journalism and communications, law, nursing, physiotherapy, and travel and tourism. When you go to a specified category, you'll be treated to links covering relevant educational programs, career advice, related organizations, and other helpful resources.

Get job information straight from the horse's mouth when you read the occupational profiles, or interviews with professionals, featured for certain career categories. Some of the professionals profiled include a clinical psychologist, a dentist, and an environmental lawyer. You'll find answers to questions about how their career choices were made, what duties their jobs entail, how much education they completed, and the challenges—and rewards—of their careers.

FUTURESCAN

HTTP://WWW.FUTURESCAN.COM/

This career guide site for teenagers is packed with fun and useful information. You'll find all sorts of articles about different career fields, along with some great job advice. For help in researching career fields, be sure to read the in-depth job profiles covering architecture, the environment, law, and veterinary medicine. Though there aren't many career fields profiled here, the content is extensive. There is information about the industry, the types of jobs available, and necessary schooling, plus links to other resources for further research. Some of the material is presented in a question-and-answer format based on interviews with professionals in the field. There's also a report on management and business administration.

A lengthy feature article discusses the importance of getting real-world experience through internships, volunteering, and part-time jobs. The "Guidance Gurus" section answers career-related questions such as "What are the top 15 careers that will be in demand in the near future?" and "What kind of career information is available for teenagers with dyslexia?" Answers are detailed and sometimes supplemented by links to relevant sites.

INFORMATION ON MAJORS

HTTP://WWW.COLLEGEEDGE.COM/COLLEGE/CM/MAJ/ART/

CollegeEdge's guide to college majors includes a lot of practical advice on the subject. Some of the issues discussed are how to go about selecting a major, what to do if you want to change majors, the pros and cons of liberal arts versus science or business majors, declaring a single or a double major, finding a college with a strong program for your major of choice, and assessment tests.

In the "Inside Scoop on Top Majors," students majoring in various fields respond to several questions relating to their majors. Example questions are "How many hours per week do you devote to school?" "Why would you recommend this as a major?" "On average, how many papers do you write per semester?" and "What kind of work does your major entail?" Their responses should give you a pretty good idea of what you can expect if you decide to pursue a similar educational path.

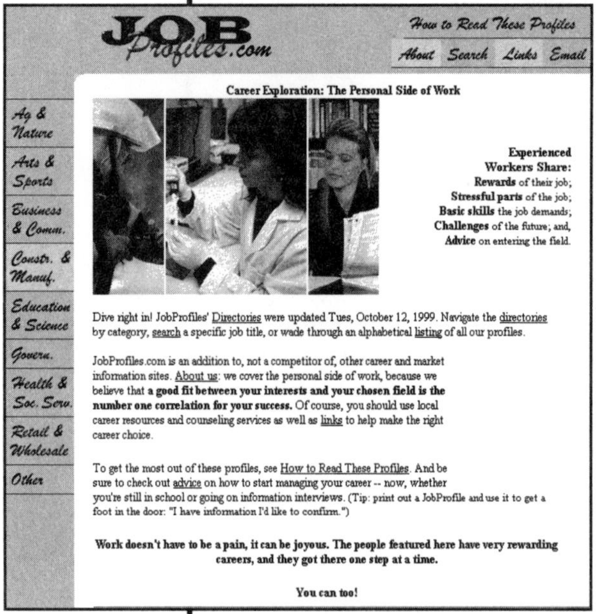

JOBPROFILES.COM

HTTP://WWW.JOBPROFILES.COM/

To learn about the world of work, take a look at this compilation of occupational profiles written by workers themselves. Profiles came from individuals working in various careers who filled out questionnaires in which they summarized their job duties, explained how they entered the field, listed job stresses and rewards, projected the kinds of problems they expected to encounter in their industry within the next five years, identified skills necessary to do their job, and offered tips for newcomers to their profession. Among the wide variety of occupations described are those of auctioneer, cartoonist, florist, obstetrician, professional speaker, special education teacher, welder, and wetlands biologist. Advice is given to assist you in interpreting the profiles. A section covering general information on career management and a small collection of related links round out the site.

LIBERAL ARTS JOB SEARCH

HTTP://RICEINFO.RICE.EDU/PROJECTS/CAREERS/CHANNELS/SIX/LIBERAL/TEXT/LIBERAL.ARTS.HTML

So who told you a liberal arts degree was worthless? This Rice University Web site not only will tell you otherwise but will provide you with plenty of ammunition to back up the claim. There is discussion about the advantages and disadvantages of liberal arts degrees. To ensure that you are prepared for entry into the job market, you are advised to stay aware of your career direction by preparing early and on an ongoing basis.

Examine the "Top 10 Job Resources" (it might surprise you to see that telephone books are listed here) and the "Six Step Successful Liberal Arts Job Search," which includes steps such as "identify your job goal" and "research target employers." Starting salary estimates are listed. And to get an idea of the wide-ranging career options available to liberal arts majors, browse through the brief overviews of sample job fields, such as accounting, advertising, consulting, and merchandising.

ONE-STOP CAREER FIELD SEARCH

HTTP://WNJPIN.STATE.NJ.US/ARCHITEXT/AT-CAREERSQUERY.HTML

Courtesy of the Workforce New Jersey Public Information Network and sponsored through a grant of the U.S. Department of Labor One-Stop Career Center, this straightforward resource is packed with information relating to a wide variety of career fields.

To get to that information, you have to search on a keyword or "words describing a concept." Your keyword and concept searches will turn up slightly different results, each rated to the percentage of confidence that your search term and the resulting category are close matches. Say, for instance, you're interested in a career in music. Some of the closest matches to the search term "music" are musician, musical instrument repairer, recreational therapist, and dancer. Follow the link to any one of these and you get notes on the nature of the work, sample occupational specialties and work activities, worker requirements, related education and training, employment outlook, and sources for further information.

As you scout around this site, you'll likely notice that some of your results might not appear relevant—but don't automatically dismiss these. There's no telling, but you just might find details about some fascinating occupations you never considered before!

WEB EXCHANGE: LIBERAL ARTS CAREER NETWORK

HTTP://OFFICES.COLGATE.EDU/CAREER/WEBEXCHANGE/

This resource offers a unique perspective on career research and exploration. Each of more than twenty colleges and universities has compiled a list of Web sites recommended to be used for exploring a particular career field. The schools all take their own approach to presenting their material, so the visual effect is quite varied, as is the content. Among the career fields covered are advertising, consulting, marine science, multimedia, performing arts, social activism, sports management and recreation, and teaching (public and private schools or overseas). Some of the links are annotated to give you a clearer idea of what you can expect to find if you visit the site. Other links are merely categorized according to subtopics. One thing this site makes clear—there's certainly plenty of resources out there for you liberal arts job seekers!

WHAT CAN I DO WITH A MAJOR IN . . . ?

GOPHER://GOPHER.WUSTL.EDU:70/11/WU_LINKS/CAREER_CENTER/MAJCHOOSE/MAJOR/

This no-frills gopher site from Washington University in St. Louis displays a list of college majors, including art history and archaeology, chemistry, environmental studies, foreign languages, mathematics, philosophy, political science, and so on. Select the major you are interested in to discover lots of useful information about careers stemming from that major. Pick political science, for example, and you'll get a list of ideas for occupations, such as television news producer, lobbyist, and management analyst. This is followed by suggestions of possible internships, whereby you can gain experience and develop necessary skills. Advice on other steps you should take to prepare for a job search plus titles of helpful books and publications are also provided.

Government Classification Systems

DICTIONARY OF OCCUPATIONAL TITLES
HTTP://WWW.OALJ.DOL.GOV/LIBDOT.HTM

The fourth edition of the Dictionary of Occupational Titles (DOT), revised in 1991, is presented here by the U.S. Department of Labor's Office of Administrative Law Judges Law Library. You will find introductory material, detailed explanations of how occupational definitions are created and how occupational titles and codes are arranged, and lists of occupational categories, divisions, and groups, as well as occupational definitions. Certain information is offered in files that can be downloaded and opened using WordPerfect or Word.

INFORMATION BY NATIONAL OCCUPATIONAL CLASSIFICATION CODE
HTTP://WWW.EOA-HRDC.COM/3519/MENU/OCCNOC.STM

Human Resources Development Canada (HRDC) offers here a vast resource combining National Occupational Classification (NOC) materials with those pertaining to Ottawa in particular. NOC's extensive job descriptions are provided, along with numerous Ottawa job opportunity surveys and statistics covering employment by age and gender, occupational outlook, wages, and more. At the "User Guides" page, you can find additional information specifically about NOC (including a downloadable zipped file of occupational titles) and other occupational coding systems, as well as labor market data.

O*NET
HTTP://WWW.DOLETA.GOV/PROGRAMS/ONET

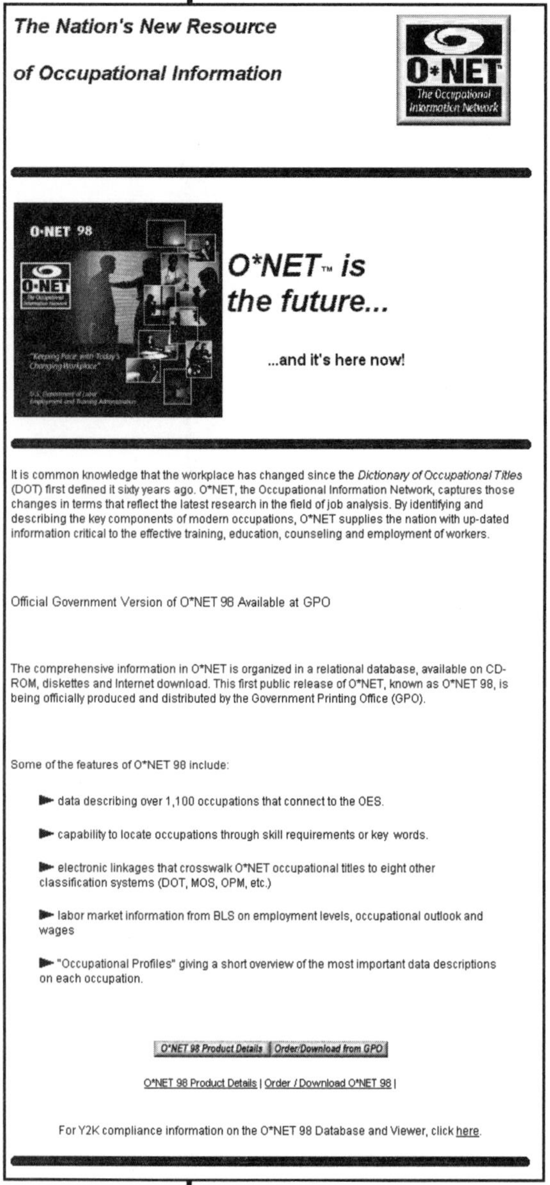

The Nation's New Resource

of Occupational Information

O*NET The Occupational Information Network

O*NET 98

*O*NET™ is the future...*

...and it's here now!

It is common knowledge that the workplace has changed since the *Dictionary of Occupational Titles* (DOT) first defined it sixty years ago. O*NET, the Occupational Information Network, captures those changes in terms that reflect the latest research in the field of job analysis. By identifying and describing the key components of modern occupations, O*NET supplies the nation with up-dated information critical to the effective training, education, counseling and employment of workers.

Official Government Version of O*NET 98 Available at GPO

The comprehensive information in O*NET is organized in a relational database, available on CD-ROM, diskettes and Internet download. This first public release of O*NET, known as O*NET 98, is being officially produced and distributed by the Government Printing Office (GPO).

Some of the features of O*NET 98 include:

- data describing over 1,100 occupations that connect to the OES.
- capability to locate occupations through skill requirements or key words.
- electronic linkages that crosswalk O*NET occupational titles to eight other classification systems (DOT, MOS, OPM, etc.)
- labor market information from BLS on employment levels, occupational outlook and wages
- "Occupational Profiles" giving a short overview of the most important data descriptions on each occupation.

O*NET 98 Product Details | Order/Download from GPO

O*NET 98 Product Details | Order / Download O*NET 98 |

For Y2K compliance information on the O*NET 98 Database and Viewer, click here.

This site comes from the U.S. Department of Labor's Employment and Training Administration, sponsor of O*NET (Occupational Information Network). Along with a brief description and background details, official program information is provided, including news, a project schedule, and answers to frequently asked questions. Links to other DOL/ETA and a wide assortment of career-related resources are also presented.

STANDARD OCCUPATIONAL CLASSIFICATION
HTTP://STATS.BLS.GOV/SOC/SOC_HOME.HTM

This Standard Occupational Classification (SOC) resource, covering 1998 revisions to the 1980 classification system, is offered by the U.S. Department of Labor's Bureau of Labor Statistics. You can search or browse through the major groups or the index of detailed occupations to arrive at occupational definitions.

CHAPTER 4

INFORMATION INTERVIEWING AND NETWORKING

The process of information interviewing is to interview someone in a chosen profession to get information about possible jobs or career paths you can pursue in that profession. While there is a wealth of occupational information available in print, on video, on software, and through the Internet, interviewing someone who works in a field you are interested in can give you a new perspective and more detailed understanding of what it takes to succeed in a job. Information interviewing also helps you develop a network of contacts, which can be important later on when you are ready to look for a job; thus it is just as important to make a good impression in an information interview as it is in a job interview. Information interviewing is more than just talking to people who know something about an occupation, however. In order to get the best results, you must carefully prepare and strategize to get interviews and to get the most from them.

Look at information interviewing as a process rather than as a one-time thing. To do it effectively, you must conduct research to determine what you want to find out and identify people who are likely to lead to your finding that information; you must do the actual interviewing; and you must follow up with what you have learned by pursuing more contacts and doing further research.

Knowing what questions to ask can be very difficult. Remember that you are trying to find out if the job or field you are researching would be right for you. Think about your interests, values, aptitudes, and abilities and ask questions that relate to those. One good question is always, "What was one thing that you did not know when you entered this occupation that you wish you had known?" Also, the last question you ask should always be, "Can you recommend anyone else I should talk to?"

Sometimes it can be difficult to identify the right person to interview. In the process of information interviewing, you usually have to ask others to help you identify the people who can best answer your questions. Some people who might be able to help you include

- career counselors,
- librarians,
- members of local chambers of commerce, and
- friends and family members.

Some of the people you might want to interview include

- workers in the occupation,
- teachers and professors preparing people to enter the occupation,
- leaders of local professional organizations, or
- members of state boards that issue professional licenses or certificates.

Another way to find out about possible jobs and learn about career path options is through networking. Networking, sometimes called personal networking, entails developing a system of contacts through which you can obtain information and find support. Network contacts can help you by

- giving personal and emotional support during difficult career transitions and job searches,
- sharing resources and ideas about personal marketing strategies,
- giving you letters of recommendation,
- being references,
- directing you to other people who might be able to provide information, and
- exchanging information about opportunities and job openings.

Networks are assets for career management across one's lifetime. Most people are involved in networks of some kind. They consist of acquaintances, friends, and family members. Networks that just naturally exist in most people's lives are called informal networks. Networks that are most helpful in career development are referred to as professional networks. Good career management involves actively developing and cultivating members for one's professional network. It is never too late to start developing or expanding your network.

INFORMATIONAL INTERVIEWING TUTORIAL

HTTP://WWW.QUINTCAREERS.COM/INFORMATIONAL_INTERVIEWING.HTML

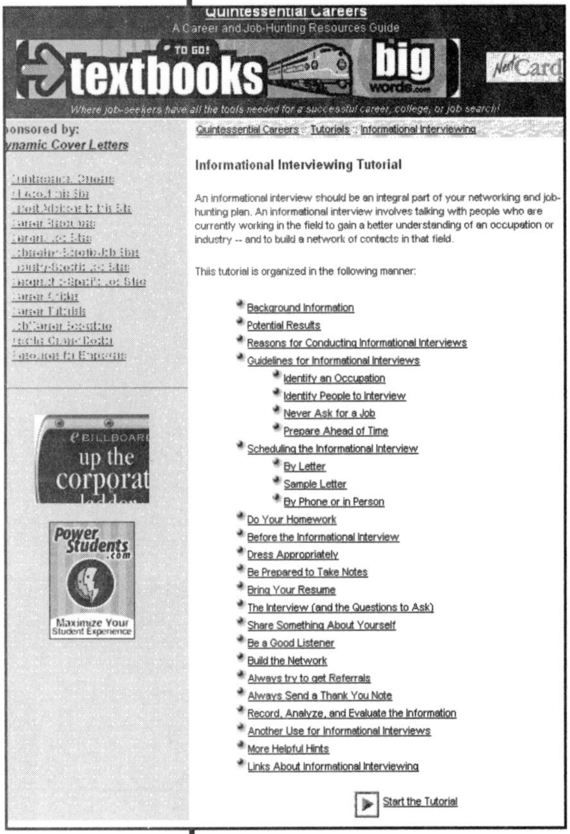

This Quintessential Careers tutorial presents a thorough discussion of the process of information interviewing. You will find here some of the reasons for conducting this kind of interview, suggested guidelines to follow (for example, don't ask for a job when you're on an information interview—wait for the actual job interview), a list of the types of questions you might want to ask, advice on appropriate follow-up and what to do with the information you've gathered, and much more. The step-by-step format is straightforward and will surely give you a good head start on preparing for your information interview. Want to know more? Check out the links to other related resources.

JOB SEARCH NETWORKING: WORTH THE EFFORT!

HTTP://WWW.CAREERMAG.COM/NEWSARTS/NETWORKING/1093.HTML

This article presents a detailed, step-by-step guide to networking. Preliminary steps are outlined first. These include skill assessment; compiling a resume; creating a "job search business card" containing your contact information, job objective, and career keywords; interview preparation; and company research. This is followed by lots of sound advice and questions to ask yourself that will help you figure out which people will likely be of assistance in your job search networking.

Particularly useful are the suggestions for how you can keep track of all the information you gather in this process as well as ideas of how to follow up after you've made contact. Above and beyond everything you'll find here are recommendations of a few Web sites and books where you can get additional material on the topic.

NETWORKING
HTTP://CONTENT.MONSTER.COM/NETWORK/

Here are some ideas about networking from Monster.com, a major career resource on the Internet. You'll read about why you should network, different types of networks (personal, social, and professional), and how to conduct a networking meeting. A few networking scenarios are presented, offering guidelines on how to network with a former colleague, an old boss, or someone you meet at a party or a conference. Information is given on setting the agenda, common networking fears and mistakes, and nurturing contacts.

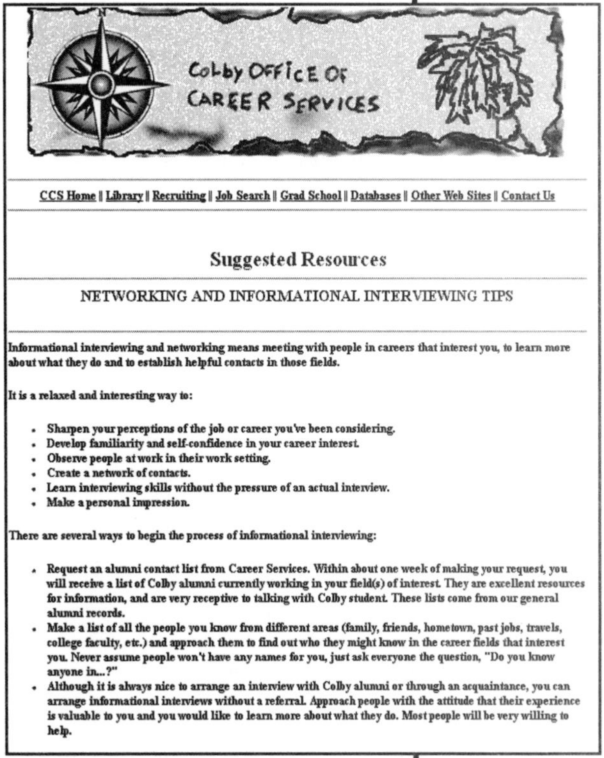

Suggested Resources

NETWORKING AND INFORMATIONAL INTERVIEWING TIPS

Informational interviewing and networking means meeting with people in careers that interest you, to learn more about what they do and to establish helpful contacts in those fields.

It is a relaxed and interesting way to:

- **Sharpen your perceptions of the job or career you've been considering.**
- **Develop familiarity and self-confidence in your career interest.**
- **Observe people at work in their work setting.**
- **Create a network of contacts.**
- **Learn interviewing skills without the pressure of an actual interview.**
- **Make a personal impression.**

There are several ways to begin the process of informational interviewing:

- **Request an alumni contact list from Career Services. Within about one week of making your request, you will receive a list of Colby alumni currently working in your field(s) of interest. They are excellent resources for information, and are very receptive to talking with Colby student. These lists come from our general alumni records.**
- **Make a list of all the people you know from different areas (family, friends, hometown, past jobs, travels, college faculty, etc.) and approach them to find out who they might know in the career fields that interest you. Never assume people won't have any names for you, just ask everyone the question, "Do you know anyone in...?"**
- **Although it is always nice to arrange an interview with Colby alumni or through an acquaintance, you can arrange informational interviews without a referral. Approach people with the attitude that their experience is valuable to you and you would like to learn more about what they do. Most people will be very willing to help.**

NETWORKING AND INFORMATIONAL INTERVIEWING TIPS
HTTP://COLBY.EDU/CAREER.SERV/HANDOUT.INF.INTVW.HTML

This concise outline covering information interviewing comes from the Colby College (Maine) Office of Career Services. It addresses the basics: why you should conduct an information interview, how to conduct one, and what to do with the information you get. A lengthy list of useful sample questions you might want to ask is provided as well.

NETWORKING SKILLS

HTTP://WWW.ANSELM.EDU/STUDENTLIFE/CAREER/NETWORKING1.HTML

This job search tutorial, on networking and information interviewing, comes from Career and Employment Services at Saint Anselm College (New Hampshire). Along with brief descriptions of what networking is and why you should do it is a list of people in your life who you can network with and from whom you can gather names of additional potential networking contacts. Other site features include examples of what to say when you call to arrange an information interview, an assortment of questions you might want to ask during that meeting, and samples of approach letters and a thank you note.

CHAPTER 5

THE FUTURE WORLD OF WORK

One of the most difficult aspects of career management is that it includes planning for an unknown future. Career managers consider questions such as, "If I invest my time and money in training for an occupation, am I likely to get a job that will pay me back?" There are many events in life that you cannot anticipate but which influence your career. Even when you train for and enter an occupation for which you are well suited, your career path may be interrupted by events such as losing a job through downsizing or a disabling accident that keeps you from performing your job. An element of uncertainty is always part of career planning. Awareness of what the job market is now and what it might be in the future helps to take some of the uncertainty out of career planning.

Most forecasters make predictions about the future by looking at the past as well as at the current state of things and by analyzing trends and then extrapolating the trends to make projections.

In the economy of the United States, who is working (or looking for work), occupations, and job opportunities are always fluctuating for a variety of reasons. Changes in people's life roles result in both changes in the labor market and changes in the demand for workers in some occupations. For example, since the mid-1970s there has been a shift in American women's roles from homemakers to wage earners. Since 1976 increasing numbers of women have been joining the labor force. By 2006 it is projected that 47 percent of the labor market will be women. As more women enter into full-time employment, there has been a steadily increasing demand for child care workers (projected growth to 2006: 36 percent).

Another reason for changes in the types of jobs available is new technologies. For example, in the 1980s and 1990s, when technological developments allowed computers to become commonly used tools, demands for workers having technical skills increased. While some occupations were created, others have employed fewer and fewer people, and some become obsolete.

Two perspectives on the future of work come from information about (a) the composition of the labor force and (b) both the types of occupations in demand and the number of openings these occupations are likely to offer. The best source of accurate projections of the U.S. labor market and the occupational opportunities for the labor market is the U.S. Department of Labor, Bureau of Labor Statistics.

BLS looks at the future world of work in the United States by making projections about the labor force and about occupational opportunities. It updates its projections of the future of work in the United States every two years. BLS makes these projections available in a variety of publications including the Monthly Labor Review, Occupational Outlook Quarterly, and Occupational Outlook Handbook (OOH).

Awareness of occupational projections and trends should be a key consideration in your career management. To keep up, be sure to check out the Web sites (covering BLS projections and other information on trends in the U.S. job market) described in this chapter.

AMERICA'S CAREER INFONET
HTTP://WWW.ACINET.ORG/ACINET/

Here you can find information on the outlook of and trends in the U.S. job market and wages. If you click on "General Outlook," you can get data on occupations that are the fastest growing, have the most openings, have the largest employment, are declining in employment, or are the highest paying. For any of these categories, you can specify the level of experience required (work experience, postsecondary training, bachelor's degree). Employment statistics are given for a recent year and then projections are made for a future date.

More specific data is available. Once you select a particular occupation (maybe physical therapists, child care workers, cashiers, photoengravers, or optometrists), you can then indicate a state in order to get data comparing the job market in that state with the national median and midrange. This is supplemented by descriptions of necessary knowledge and skills, prerequisite training and education, and tasks to be performed, as well as numerous links to relevant Web sites where you can get further information.

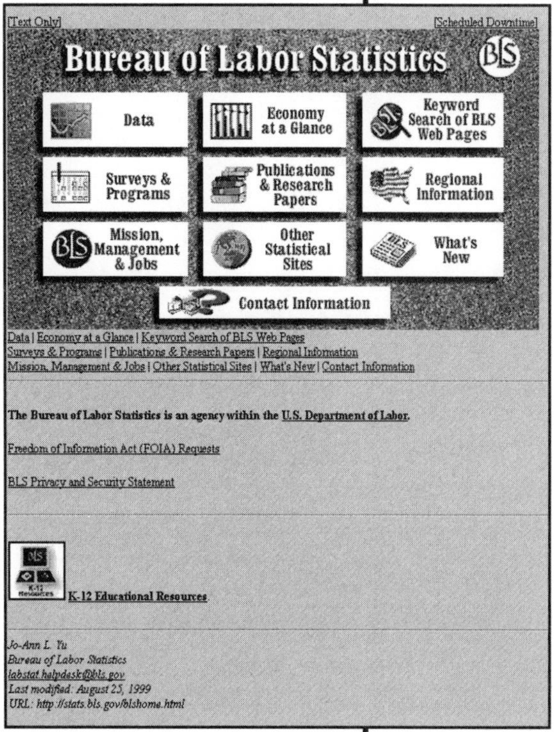

BUREAU OF LABOR STATISTICS
HTTP://STATS.BLS.GOV/BLSHOME.HTML

This U.S. Department of Labor agency provides a vast number of online resources pertaining to national and regional labor economics and statistics of the past, present, and future. Reports, surveys, and statistics offered here deal with such topics as the cost of living, the consumer price index, employment and unemployment, as well as projections, safety and health, foreign labor, and so much more.

You can order BLS publications from the Web site or you can read selections online. Some of your choices are abstracts, excerpts, or full texts of articles or chapters from Monthly Labor Review, Compensation and Working Conditions, Issues in Labor Statistics, BLS Handbook of Methods, and Occupational Outlook Handbook. Some files are presented in HTML while others are in PDF.

Other site features include a list of links to U.S. federal and international statistical agencies, a keyword search page of the entire BLS site or portions thereof, and regional economic analyses.

GARY JOHNSON'S BRAVENEWWORKWORLD AND NEWWORK NEWS

HTTP://WWW.NEWWORK.COM/

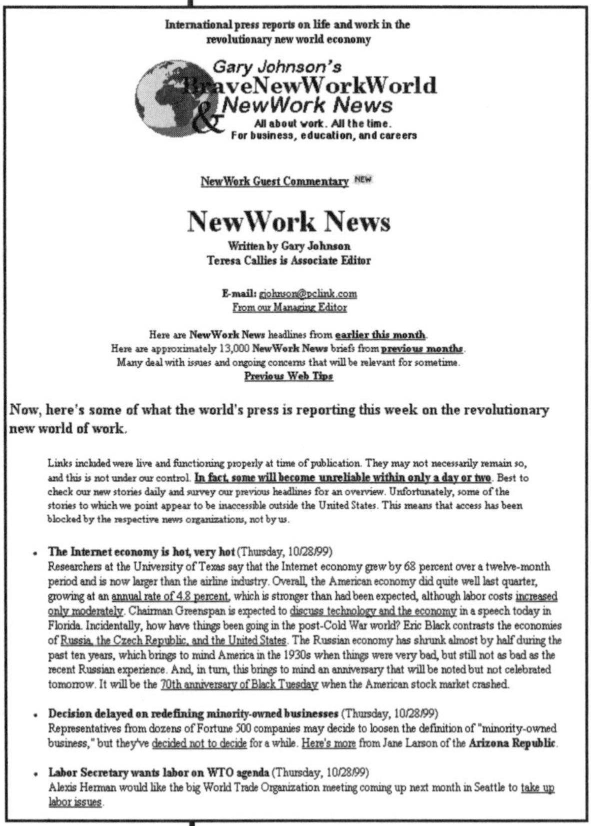
International press reports on life and work in the revolutionary new world economy

Gary Johnson's BraveNewWorkWorld & NewWork News
All about work. All the time.
For business, education, and careers

NewWork Guest Commentary NEW

NewWork News
Written by Gary Johnson
Teresa Callies is Associate Editor

E-mail: gjohnson@pclink.com
From our Managing Editor

Here are **NewWork News** headlines from **earlier this month**.
Here are approximately 13,000 **NewWork News** briefs from **previous months**.
Many deal with issues and ongoing concerns that will be relevant for sometime.
Previous Web Tips

Now, here's some of what the world's press is reporting this week on the revolutionary new world of work.

Links included were live and functioning properly at time of publication. They may not necessarily remain so, and this is not under our control. **In fact, some will become unreliable within only a day or two**. Best to check our new stories daily and survey our previous headlines for an overview. Unfortunately, some of the stories to which we point appear to be inaccessible outside the United States. This means that access has been blocked by the respective news organizations, not by us.

- **The Internet economy is hot, very hot** (Thursday, 10/28/99)
  Researchers at the University of Texas say that the Internet economy grew by 68 percent over a twelve-month period and is now larger than the airline industry. Overall, the American economy did quite well last quarter, growing at an annual rate of 4.8 percent, which is stronger than had been expected, although labor costs increased only moderately. Chairman Greenspan is expected to discuss technology and the economy in a speech today in Florida. Incidentally, how have things been going in the post-Cold War world? Eric Black contrasts the economies of Russia, the Czech Republic, and the United States. The Russian economy has shrunk almost by half during the past ten years, which brings to mind America in the 1930s when things were very bad, but still not as bad as the recent Russian experience. And, in turn, this brings to mind an anniversary that will be noted but not celebrated tomorrow. It will be the 70th anniversary of Black Tuesday when the American stock market crashed.
- **Decision delayed on redefining minority-owned businesses** (Thursday, 10/28/99)
  Representatives from dozens of Fortune 500 companies may decide to loosen the definition of "minority-owned business," but they've decided not to decide for a while. Here's more from Jane Larson of the **Arizona Republic**.
- **Labor Secretary wants labor on WTO agenda** (Thursday, 10/28/99)
  Alexis Herman would like the big World Trade Organization meeting coming up next month in Seattle to take up labor issues.

This extensive resource features a wide assortment of international news, essays, and book reviews pertaining to employment and the economy of the future. Brief synopses are given for current and archived headline news stories, with links to full texts from major news providers. These stories deal with such topics as teen employment, labor issues, the "new economy," women in the workforce, layoffs, unemployment, retirement planning, and much more. Certain articles are given in French as well as English.

As you peruse the site, you will run across numerous recommendations for other sites where you can find additional information similar to that which you'll read about in the news stories and essays. Some of the "best" sites are highlighted in "NewWork News Web Tips."

NATIONAL CURRENT EMPLOYMENT STATISTICS

HTTP://STATS.BLS.GOV/CESHOME.HTM

The National Current Employment Statistics (CES) is a "monthly payroll survey of nonfarm business establishments" conducted by state agencies along with the Bureau of Labor Statistics. The site presents data in several different forms, including news releases, tables, and data sets. You'll find reports addressing such issues as real earnings, the employment situation, and labor strikes and work stoppages. You can access nonfarm payroll statistics dealing with average hourly and weekly earnings, weekly hours, and overtime in various industries (perhaps construction, finance, mining, or retail trade). Through "Most Requested Series" and "Selective Access" you are able to specify exactly or more generally the information you're seeking and how you want it displayed on-screen. If you need some help figuring out how to navigate the site, check out "CES Data Access Tips." For more regional information, follow the link for "State and Area CES Data."

OCCUPATIONAL OUTLOOK HANDBOOK

HTTP://WWW.BLS.GOV/OCOHOME.HTM

Many career research sites refer to the Occupational Outlook Handbook and even use its data. Well, this is the site! Brought to you by the Bureau of Labor Statistics (BLS), this resource has all sorts of information to help you determine a career path. For particular occupations, you can learn about the nature of the work, working conditions, training required, job outlook, and earnings (this section gets pretty specific, by the way). If you need help, there's a section that explains how to interpret the BLS projections and data. Additionally, you can find out about the jobs of tomorrow (for example, which industries expect growth and which expect a decline within the next several years) and read up on financial aid, job search methods, and considering a job offer.

U.S. DEPARTMENT OF LABOR

HTTP://WWW.DOL.GOV/

The DOL deals with practically anything work-related: wages, unemployment, health and safety, equal employment opportunity, child labor, and

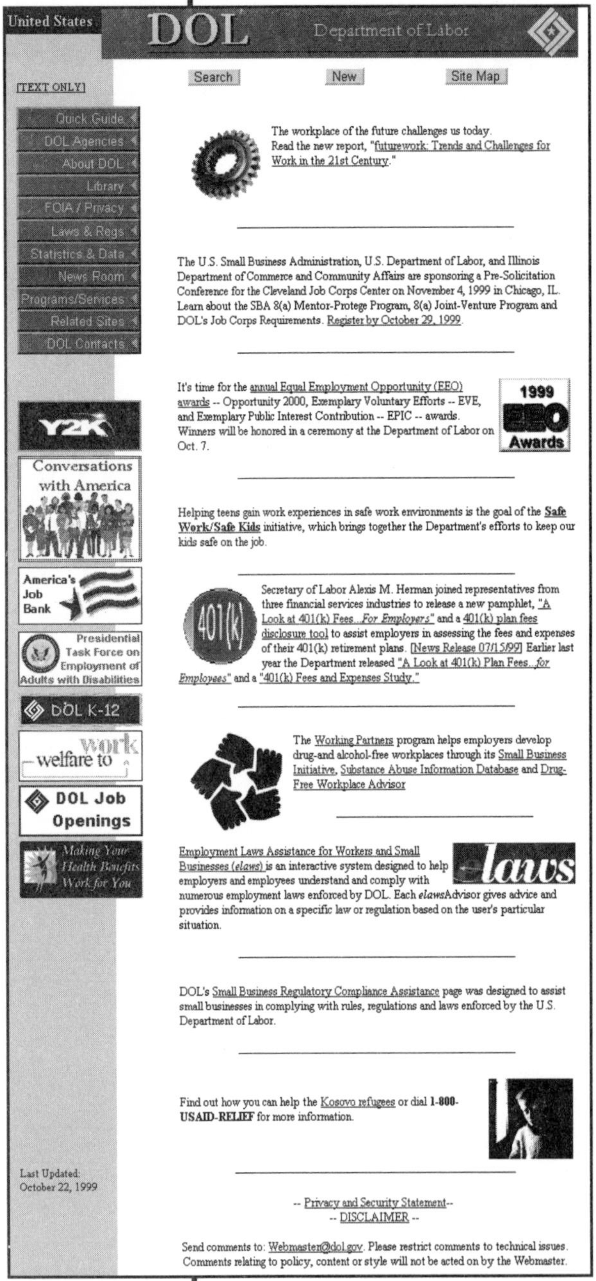

more. The "Quick Guide" gives you a table of contents and there's also a site map with an alphabetical list of contents, either of which should help you figure out where you want to go in this vast resource. Along with background material and a history of the DOL, there's information on laws and regulations, press releases, access to federal statistics and data, and images of workplace posters.

Links to the Web sites of the DOL's many agencies—for example, Bureau of Labor Statistics (BLS), Occupational Safety and Health Administration (OSHA), Office of Small Business Programs (OSBP), Pension and Welfare Benefits Administration (PWBA), Veterans' Employment and Training Service (VETS), and Women's Bureau (WB)—are available as well.

Section III: Education and Training for Job Entry and Career Development

CHAPTER 6

TWO- AND FOUR-YEAR ACADEMIC PROGRAMS AND GRADUATE STUDIES

The majority of jobs in the U.S. labor market can be entered with a high school diploma and require short-term on-the-job training. These positions, however, generally offer the lowest pay and poorest benefits. As a rule, the more training that is required to enter a job, the higher the pay. In today's labor market, most of the jobs that pay above-average earnings require postsecondary training.

Typically, higher-paying occupations that require much training to enter also require successful completion of specific, accredited training programs, while occupations that require less training to enter offer more options in obtaining training, frequently including on-the-job training. You should make certain that the training programs in which you enroll will fulfill requirements for your occupational goals. If you are seeking postsecondary training, you should consider the following:

- What training is considered appropriate for entry into the occupation?

- What are the various options to obtain training for this occupation?

- If there is a license or certification requirement, does the academic program provide the appropriate course work and have the appropriate accreditation?

- Is any further training required to obtain the license or certification beyond the academic degree or certificate of completion of the training program?

Consulting with a career counselor is often an excellent way to learn about training options and financial resources for obtaining proper training. A career counselor can help determine if any given program is likely to provide the appropriate training required by employers in the occupation.

Higher education is educational programming beyond high school. It includes course work from two- or four-year institutions and from graduate schools. People who successfully complete these educational programs receive degrees, either associate's, bachelor's, master's, doctoral, or professional. On average, workers who have earned bachelor's, master's, doctoral, or professional degrees have higher incomes and lower unemployment rates than do workers with less education. Some occupations that require a college degree for entry also require people entering the occupation to obtain a license or to be certified.

An associate's degree is considered a two-year degree, which means that it normally takes two years of full-time enrollment to complete. Some of the fastest-growing occupations that can be entered with an associate's degree include

- paralegals,
- dental hygienists,
- registered nurses,
- health information technicians,
- respiratory therapists,
- cardiology technologists, and

- radiologic technologists and technicians.

An associate's degree may be conferred in Arts (A.A.) or in Science (A.S.) and is sometimes referred to as a technical degree. The course work required to earn an associate's degree typically is focused on specialized knowledge needed for occupational qualification. It is not unusual for associate's degree programming to include an experiential requirement—that is, course work that requires performing job duties in a work setting.

Two-year colleges usually award associate's degrees. Some four-year colleges may also offer associate's degrees. Two-year colleges are often called community colleges, technological colleges, or junior colleges. Many two-year colleges have open admissions policies. This means that if your high school academic performance would not qualify you for regular college admission, you may be admitted to a two-year college if you satisfactorily complete remedial courses. Two-year colleges often have transfer agreements with four-year colleges so that you may enroll in a two-year college to complete your first two years of college course work and then transfer to a four-year institution to complete a bachelor's degree.

A bachelor's degree is considered a four-year degree and is often referred to as an undergraduate degree. It is usually designated as either a Bachelor of Arts (B.A.) or a Bachelor of Science (B.S.), depending on the area of academic study. While it is possible to complete a bachelor's degree in four years of full-time enrollment, today's students are taking on average four to six years to complete their undergraduate degrees. One reason for this is because many students prolong their studies to include internship experiences, which, although not typically required in undergraduate studies, tend to make them more competitive in the job market. Currently, the majority of the fastest-growing occupations in the U.S. labor market require a bachelor's degree for entry. Some of these include

- database administrators and computer support specialists,
- computer engineers,
- systems analysts,
- physical therapists,
- occupational therapists, and
- special education and high school teachers.

Four-year colleges and universities award bachelor's degrees. Given that there is a wide variety of institutions offering numerous divergent educational experiences, high school graduates who are planning to attend college often find that weighing the different options makes it difficult to select a college or university. The degrees offered and the size of the student body are two important considerations in choosing a college or university. Each college and university offers degrees in specific areas and may not offer a program or studies or a degree in other areas. Universities are usually bigger than colleges, having more educational resources and greater student enrollment. They often award graduate degrees at all levels—master's, doctoral, and professional—as well as undergraduate degrees. They do not necessarily offer all levels of graduate degrees in all program areas. Colleges may or may not offer graduate degrees, and if they do offer graduate degrees, they typically do not do so at all levels. Both colleges and universities may be either private or public. Private schools may be affiliated with religious groups. Public schools are state-sponsored. Tuition is usually less at public schools than at private schools, and it's even less for students who are residents of the school's state.

Students who enroll in a four-year institution knowing that the occupation they seek to enter requires a graduate degree should start planning to earn that degree after receiving their bachelor's degree. While some institutions offer programs of study that allow you to progress from bachelor's degree studies to pursuing a master's degree, it is more typical that you must apply for admission into a graduate program. That program may or may not be offered at the institution from which your undergraduate degree was awarded. In fact, an institution that has awarded you an undergraduate degree may choose not to admit you into a graduate program. If you are enrolling in an undergraduate program and anticipate that you will attend graduate school, you should ask faculty members where their program's graduates have continued their education. Acceptance into graduate programs often depends on factors such as (a) what area of study the bachelor's degree was awarded in, (b) the grade point average earned in undergraduate studies, and (c) recommendations from undergraduate faculty members.

Master's, doctoral, specialist, and professional degrees are awarded as graduate degrees. Typically, it takes a student from two to six years of studies after earning an undergraduate degree to earn a graduate degree. Some colleges, universities, and institutes of specialized study are accredited to award graduate degrees. Some programs of graduate study require students to be awarded a master's degree and then seek a doctoral degree, while others will admit students with the intention that they will complete their studies with the award of a doctorate or professional degree.

Programs of study for entry into specific occupations or professions may need to be accredited by professional associations' accrediting bodies. For example, the National Architectural Accrediting Board accredits architectural programs, the American Bar Association accredits law programs, and the American Psychological Association accredits psychology programs. Professional associations will provide lists of colleges and universities that offer accredited programs of study. For graduates to be competitive in the job market, and often to be eligible to obtain licenses or certificates to practice in an occupation, it is essential that they have degrees from programs of study accredited by appropriate professional bodies.

Completing a graduate degree from an accredited program is often only one requirement in the process of obtaining a professional license or certificate. Other requirements may include passing competency tests after graduation and working under supervision in the occupation. If you are seeking entry into a graduate program, you should see yourself as a consumer seeking the best graduate program to meet your occupational goals. It is appropriate to inquire where graduates obtain employment and if the graduate degree is useful in obtaining occupational licensure or certification.

Master's degrees usually require between thirty-six and sixty-four or more graduate semester credit hours to be earned and usually take not less than two years of full-time study to complete. Some of the fastest-growing occupations that can be entered with a master's degree include

- speech-language pathologists and audiologists,
- counselors,
- psychologists,

- librarians,
- curators, archivists, and museum technicians, and
- operations research analysts.

Master's degrees may be conferred in either Arts (M.A.) or Sciences (M.S.), depending on the field of study. Master's degrees may be very specialized toward entry into a specific occupation; others may be awarded after studies that may qualify graduates for entry into a variety of occupations. Some course work may be specified by accrediting bodies or by licensing or certifying boards. Experiential learning components may or may not be required. Completion of either a comprehensive examination or a master's thesis is usually required before graduation.

There are a variety of degrees that may be earned for graduate studies beyond the master's level, such as a specialist degree, as in education specialist (Ed.S.); a doctoral degree, as in philosophy (Ph.D.), education (Ed.D.), or psychology (Psy.D.); and a professional degree, as in doctor of medicine (M.D.), doctor of dental science (D.D.S.), juris doctor (J.D.), or bachelor of laws (L.L.B.). Doctoral studies usually require earning ninety graduate semester credit hours beyond the undergraduate degree. They often take four to six years to complete. Typically, both academic course work and experiential learning components are included in programs of study. Evaluative components may consist of comprehensive examinations and a research project that may involve writing a doctoral dissertation.

ALL ABOUT COLLEGE

HTTP://WWW.ALLABOUTCOLLEGE.COM/

Here's a site that contains links to the home pages of thousands of colleges and universities in the United States and abroad. You can browse through the listings by state or country. Your non-U.S. choices are Africa, Asia, Australia, Canada, Europe, Mexico, and South America. Not only are you given easy access to these home pages, but where available you will also have at your fingertips the e-mail addresses for admissions offices at many of these institutions.

CAMPUSTOURS

HTTP://WWW.CAMPUSTOURS.COM/

This site provides you with access to "virtual excursions of colleges across the United States." First, find a school, alphabetically or by state. You'll then get a list of links for virtual tours, Web cams, interactive maps, videos, campus pictures, and/or home pages of each school. You won't find links for all the features at each school's home page, but what you will find will give you a visual introduction to the schools you're interested in attending. And that's what makes this site different from other directories of college home pages. Here you'll be taken directly to pages with pictures instead of pages simply consisting of text or statistics. Additionally, there's a college admissions message board and plenty of information on financial aid (provided in conjunction with the lender Educaid).

COLLEGE COMPASS: COLLEGE SELECTION

HTTP://WWW.EDONLINE.COM/COLLEGECOMPASS/CHOOSE.HTM

Are you feeling a little overwhelmed by some of the flashy, graphics-intensive, multilayered sites aimed at helping you find a college? Are you looking for some really straightforward steps to follow and questions to consider when selecting a college? Then this might be a good place for you to start. This site prompts you to evaluate yourself in terms of academics ("Are you at your best in practical lab courses, small discussion groups, lecture courses?"), activities and involvement ("Are sports important to you? Movies? Theater? Musical events?"), and goals and values ("What accomplishments are you most proud of in your life so far?"). Then there's a checklist you should use to help decide the kinds of things you're looking for in a college. Do you have feelings about whether or not a school has religious or military affiliations? whether the academic environment is really competitive or not? where the school is situated (rural, suburban, big city)? and so on. This page will give you a head start in assessing pertinent issues involved in school selection, which will better prepare you for talking to your school guidance counselor.

COLLEGE IS POSSIBLE

HTTP://WWW.COLLEGEISPOSSIBLE.ORG/

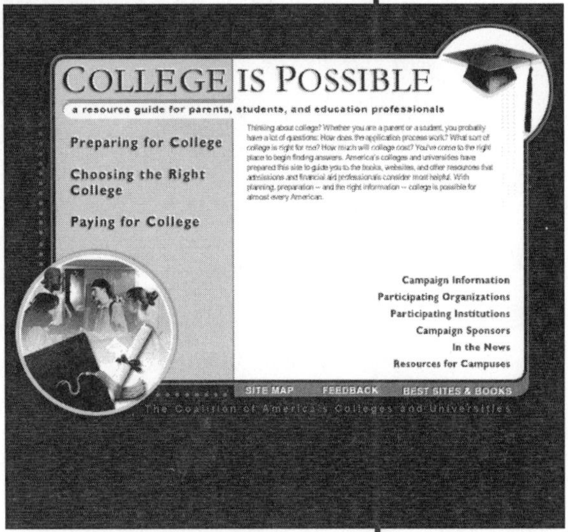

Here is the Web presence for the College Is Possible campaign of the Coalition of America's Colleges and Universities. If you're thinking about going to college one day, you (and your parents) will want to visit this very approachable and worthwhile site. Along with materials specifically about the campaign, there are sections on getting ready to attend college, selecting a school, and paying for it.

"Preparing for College" lists suggestions on the types of classes students should take in middle, junior, or high school. The section "Choosing the Right College" presents a "College Admissions and Financial Aid Calendar" that outlines some of the steps you should take in selecting a college and readying yourself to attend it. Steps include meeting with the school counselor, taking certain entrance exams, attending college fairs, acquiring admissions and financial aid materials, and so on. If you want to research particular schools, take a look at the links to directories of community college, college, and university home pages.

The bulk of the site deals with the financial side of going to college. "Paying for College" features descriptions of various financial aid programs, data on the price of attending college, and FAQs, myths, and realities. All sections are supplemented by resource listings of books or Web sites relevant to the topic at hand.

COLLEGENET
HTTP://WWW.COLLEGENET.COM/

Once you've decided on a school, you might very well be able to apply for admission to that school from this Web site. But we're getting ahead of ourselves a bit. Before the application process comes the search for the right school. At this site you can search for two- and four-year colleges, institutions offering an MBA program, and vocational/technical, business, or medical schools. For most of these options you can then request to display the results in any of a variety of orders; for example, by highest or lowest out-of-state tuition, highest or lowest mean SAT scores, or highest or lowest undergrad enrollment. The results consist of the school's street address, phone number, data on enrollment and tuition, and URL (where available), as well as an icon identifying those schools for which you can enroll online.

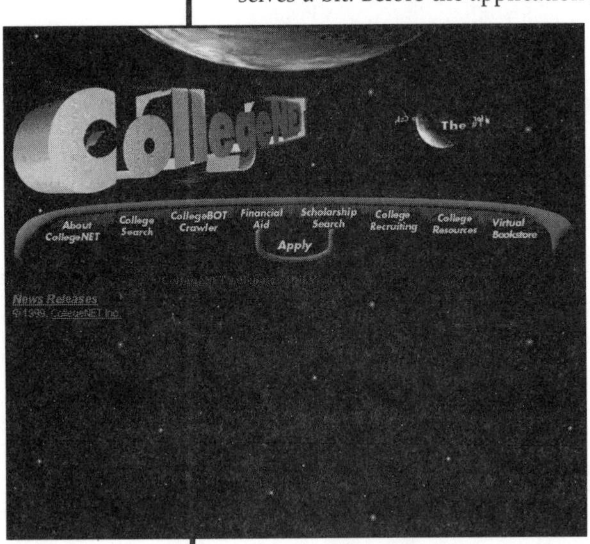

Other site features include CollegeBOT, an education-specific search engine; sections devoted to financial aid and scholarships; and assorted college-related resources. Furthermore, you have the option of creating a Standout profile (for a fee). Your profile goes into a database that is accessible to recruiters and admissions directors from various colleges who might approach you if your profile matches what they're looking for in their particular school's student body.

COMMUNITY COLLEGE WEB
HTTP://WWW.MCLI.DIST.MARICOPA.EDU/CC/INDEX.HTML

If you're thinking about attending a community college, visit this site, where you'll find links to home pages of hundreds of community colleges in the United States and a few other countries. You can search geographically, alphabetically, and by keyword. Also useful is the site's wide assortment of annotated links to further Web resources. Some of the categories are students, employment, organizations, and journals.

COUNCIL FOR HIGHER EDUCATION ACCREDITATION

HTTP://WWW.CHEA.ORG/

CHEA serves as "the voice of the nation's colleges and universities on all matters regarding accreditation." Previously, the Council on Postsecondary Accreditation (COPA) and then the Commission on Recognition of Postsecondary Accreditation (CORPA) had been responsible for evaluating and recognizing postsecondary accrediting agencies. At this site you can read about the process of accreditation plus you can access directories of regional, specialized and professional, and national accrediting organizations, including links to home pages where available.

.EDU

HTTP://WWW.USNEWS.COM/USNEWS/EDU/HOME.HTM

This hefty site, from U.S. News Online, focuses on education, with sections covering colleges, graduate schools, and financial aid. You can find details on specific community and four-year colleges, or you can fill in the interactive form to identify certain criteria that's important to you in your college search. This could include distance from home, region of the United States, school size, student/teacher ratio, campus setting, diversity, academic programs, and extracurriculars. Trying to choose between a few different schools? Click on "Compare Colleges" and enter the names of as many as four colleges to get a "college comparison worksheet," which includes data for each school on its location, academics, cost, financial aid, admissions, and student body. For graduate schools you can get information by looking up a school's name or by identifying the specialty you're interested in (for example, the arts, education, or library science). The section on financial aid enables you to search for scholarships awarded in various categories, calculate your college tuition costs, and compare financial aid offered by as many as four schools of your choice. Pertinent articles, statistics, and links to school pages and other resources round out this site.

GRADUATE SCHOOL GUIDE

HTTP://WWW.SCHOOLGUIDES.COM/

Find a grad school with this searchable directory to U.S. schools offering doctoral, master's, and professional degree programs. Search the database by identifying the particular school name you want to look up or by indicating state and major. Listings include institution name, address, phone number, and (where available) fax number, e-mail address, and Web site address. Before making your final decision, read the "Graduate Questions" section to learn the types of questions to ask on your search for the right grad school. Links to other sites of interest are also provided.

PETERSON'S

HTTP://WWW.PETERSONS.COM/

This massive site from Peterson's, the publishing company that brings you all those college and career guides, is a great place not only to learn about the books the company publishes but also to pick up some advice on selecting a college as well as on conducting career research.

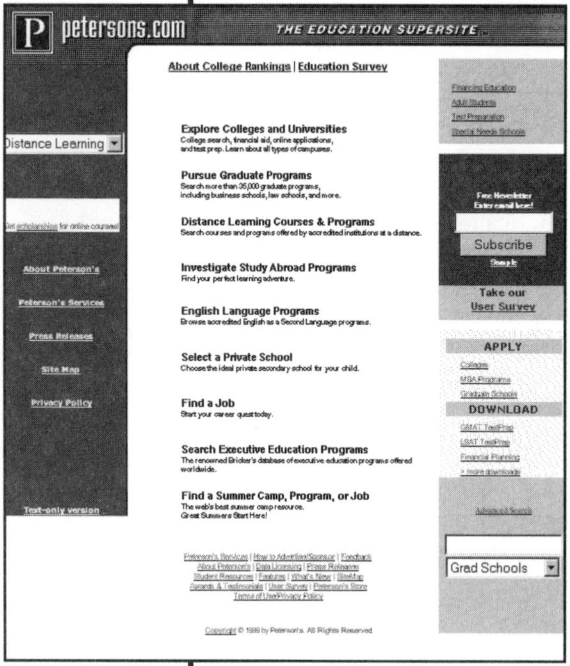

Explore your post-high school options by reading through pertinent sections on colleges and universities, graduate schools, distance learning, study abroad, and summer programs. If you're getting ready to take the SAT, ACT, GRE, or some other assessment test, you'll want to look at the materials on test preparation. Among the site's features are articles, discussion boards, applications, news, search tools, and links to additional resources.

You'll find a variety of other resources at this site. The "Careers & Jobs" section features articles about various careers and issues ("Companies Minority Engineers Want to Work For") as well as an employer database viewable by alphabetical letter or searchable by company name. The database provides a brief overview of the company. There's even information on executive education, on the education of special-needs students, and for international students. Be sure to check out the bookstore for a peek at the latest titles from Peterson's.

POWERSTUDENTS.COM
HTTP://WWW.POWERSTUDENTS.COM/

This is a really fun and educational site that has something for students of all ages—those in high school, college, or grad school—as well as for individuals considering entry into or moves within the workforce.

The section for high school students offers tons of information and advice on researching, selecting, getting into, and paying for college. College students can read all about roommates and settling in, going to class and taking tests, money and scholarships, jobs, and travel abroad. There's plenty of extracurricular materials included as well. These have to do with campus life, dating, entertainment, health, sports, travel, and more.

"Student Diaries" are just what you'd expect: stories and comments written by students about their real-life experiences. For the high school crowd, these might pertain to self-exploration, school involvement, or college visits. College students talk about the transition from high school to college or perhaps about student orientation, choosing a major, or summer break, while grad student diaries might delve into what it's like to pursue various grad school programs (for example, in animation, business, or medicine). All in all, you'll get a pretty good idea of how to embark on the road to college and what to expect once you get there!

If you're ready to hit the pavement and find a job, you'll want to check out the career section. Information on resumes, interviewing, internships, working abroad, and job listings are among the many features to be found here. For the various areas, there are forums, newsletters, member services, and links. All of this only begins to touch the surface of what you'll find on a visit to PowerStudents.com.

STUDY ABROAD DIRECTORY
HTTP://WWW.STUDYABROAD.COM/

If you're interested in attending college outside the United States, then check out this site. You'll find a handbook covering general information pertaining to living abroad, such as differences in culture, safety, how to deal with emergency situations, the costs of studying abroad and other money-related issues, and necessary documents to bring along. A search tool allows you to look for schools that offer international study programs. Select the criteria you want to search by (country, subject, summer programs). Your results page will include links to Web sites, contact information, and/or program descriptions. The "Marketplace" suggests sites where you can learn about financial aid, health insurance, travel agencies, student IDs, and more. There are also a few listings for study abroad opportunities for high school students.

THINK COLLEGE

HTTP://WWW.ED.GOV/THINKCOLLEGE/

This U.S. Department of Education resource has something for everybody. That is, anybody who's considering a college education. There are separate sections aimed at middle school students and their parents ("Think College Early"), students in high school or college ("High School & Beyond"), and adult learners ("Returning to School"). You can read about courses to take in preparation for going to college, long-range planning, and tuition and financial aid. Numerous annotated links supplement the material presented here. Plus there are directories of state grant agencies, guaranty agencies, and postsecondary education resources organized by state. If you're thinking about college, be sure to stop by!

OTHER POSTSECONDARY TRAINING OPTIONS

CHAPTER 7

Currently, numerous varied occupations in the U.S. labor market can be entered without needing a higher education degree. Sometimes training is provided on the job. Training may also be available from a wide variety of programs. Some may feature academic course work and experiential components. Some may combine both academic and on-the-job training. For instance, training to become a hairdresser, hairstylist, or cosmetologist is available in high school vocational classes, postgraduate adult education, private career schools, and apprenticeships.

The length of time spent in training varies depending on a program's requirements and is not necessarily an indicator of its quality, nor does just having a certificate or diploma from a program necessarily make you more competitive in the job market. You should think of yourself as a consumer of educational programming and carefully examine the training options available to help you determine what training program will best match your time commitments, financial situation, learning style, and career goals. It may be helpful to do information interviews (refer back to Chapter 4) with local employers to determine what sort of training programs they prefer their employees to have completed.

Many public school systems sponsor adult education classes that offer course work both to obtain General Education Development (GED) certification and to get vocational training. GED certification is the equivalent of a high school diploma. Students who successfully complete vocational classes usually receive a certificate. These training programs generally can be completed in a year or less. Classes are frequently offered in the evenings and on weekends. The cost of training is usually moderate. The specific vocational classes available vary from school system to school system, but it is possible to obtain training for a wide variety of occupations including

- dental assistants,
- hairdressers, hairstylists, or cosmetologists,
- automobile mechanics,
- heating and air-conditioning technicians, and
- administrative assistants.

The U.S. Department of Labor's Employment and Training Administration (DOL/ETA) sponsors a number of programs that provide placement services. These programs include, among others, Employment Services, One-Stop, Job Corps, and Job Training Partnership Act. Employment Services offices offer services at no cost to any person who can be legally employed in the United States. There may be eligibility criteria to qualify for other government programs. To use Employment Services it is usually necessary to go to one of its offices. At these placement offices, you will typically find an enormous number of resources for the job search. Some of these might include

- printed materials that provide general information about occupations and the skills needed to enter specific occupations,
- workbooks to help with the career management process,

- standardized assessment instruments to identify abilities and aptitudes,

- Internet access and computer-delivered occupational and educational information,

- training seminars and workshops on specific career management and job search topics, and

- support and networking groups for job hunters.

You should realize that it is unlikely that you will walk in and be told where to go to get hired for a job you want. Visits to these offices usually will be most productive if you can initially spend an hour or more without distractions—to take full advantage of all the resources, you may have to visit the office more than once. Prior to your visit, it is advised that you think about what career management objectives you hope to accomplish using the placement service's resources. These might include

- assessing personal skills and identifying matching occupations,

- creating a list of skills developed in previous employment,

- exploring occupational opportunities and learning how to get training,

- identifying local employers and learning about their job openings,

- learning how to complete a job application,

- creating a resume,

- testing to be screened for employment openings, or

- improving interviewing skills.

Trade and technical schools or colleges are usually private, for-profit institutions that offer vocational training. Sometimes they are referred to as private career schools, vocational schools or colleges, or proprietary schools. These schools may be Career College Association (http://www.career.org/) members approved by the U.S. Department of Education (accreditation information can be found online at http://www.ed.gov/offices/OPE/Students/Accred.html). They may be licensed or registered by state boards of education. Typically, their programs of study emphasize training for a specific occupation. Training is commonly offered to enter occupations such as

- automobile mechanics,
- dental assistants,
- desktop publishing,
- food service preparation and management,
- hairdressers, hairstylists, or cosmetologists,
- licensed practical nurses,
- heating and air-conditioning technicians, and
- administrative assistants.

These schools may offer course work similar to that available through adult education courses or at community colleges. Private career schools may also offer instructional programs in occupations that may be entered without specialized training (for example, child care workers). If you are considering these courses you should carefully consider their usefulness in improving your competitiveness in the job market.

Training programs may be completed in a year or two. Students who successfully complete course work usually receive certificates, but some private career colleges are accredited to award associate's degrees.

Many private career schools are accredited and offer both professional instruction and job placement that helps their graduates advance on their career paths. However, because the offering of educational programs and vocational training is not a highly regulated industry, you must be a cautious consumer. Typically, these schools cannot guarantee that after graduation their students will be hired in positions suitable for their training. State Boards of Education and Better Business Bureaus can often provide information to help you choose a private career school. It is appropriate to ask to tour instructional facilities and to ask school representatives questions such as

- What accreditation does this school have?

- How many people graduated from the educational program in the past couple years?

- What are the credentials of the instructors teaching the course work?

- Is job placement service available?

- How long does it typically take graduates to find jobs in their field?

- How many graduates have found jobs in the occupations for which they were training? and

- Where are graduates currently working? In what positions?

Apprenticeships have been a traditional way to enter occupations referred to as skilled trades or blue collar. These include occupations in building trades and construction, such as carpenters, electricians, floor layers, painters and paperhangers, and plumbers. They also include machine trades or industrial trades that employ boilermakers, ironworkers, machinists and tool programmers, millwrights, and tool, die, mold, and pattern makers. Although the majority of apprenticeships to enter the skilled trades pay apprentices wages that are lower than those of more-skilled workers, it is possible for experienced workers in many of these occupations to earn higher-than-average wages, so entry into apprenticeships in these occupations is often very competitive. Apprenticeships have also been a traditional way to learn artisan occupations that are sometimes referred to as crafts. These include occupations such as musical instrument makers, jewelry crafters, and glassblowers. Apprenticeship training can also be available to enter a broad variety of other occupational fields, such as farm and animal workers, health care workers, and human services workers.

Apprenticeships are based on the idea that a skilled worker teaches an apprentice occupational skills and, in exchange for this training, the apprentice agrees to work for the trainer, at lower wages, for a certain period of time. Traditionally, people working in the skilled trades and arts are classified by their level of expertise:

- An apprentice is a beginner who is learning the craft.
- A journeyman is a skilled worker who has successfully completed an apprenticeship.
- A master craftsman is a highly skilled worker who is an expert in the craft.

An apprenticeship is a training program based on a contract made between the trainer and the trainee, usually either between an apprentice and a master craftsman or an apprentice and a business that employs workers at all skill levels. Apprenticeships often combine academic course work with on-the-job experience.

Apprenticeships in sought-after training opportunities are usually competitive to enter. Think of entering an apprenticeship as similar to asking an employer for a job. Having good basic academic skills and being able to talk about why completing the apprenticeship is important to your career goals will make you more attractive to program administrators. Each apprenticeship usually includes a probationary period during which your ability to benefit from the training may be evaluated. The probationary period is a trial period during which either you or your trainer may decide to terminate the apprenticeship. After the probationary period, the apprenticeship contract binds both the trainer and the trainee in obligation to each other, and it becomes more complicated to end the apprenticeship.

Distance learning, or distance education, offers you the availability of educational programming close to home. In fact, you do not have to go to the educational institution to take courses; instead, the academic faculty comes to you via electronic media. There are many different forms of educational opportunities that can be called distance learning.

The oldest form of distance learning is the traditional correspondence course, in which academic course work may be completed by mail. Educational institutions typically provide home study materials such as workbooks, which may be supplemented by texts that you must provide. You mail completed homework assignments to the educational institution for grading. Correspondence courses are usually purchased at a set fee per course. You study on your own and complete courses at your own pace. Completion of a series of correspondence courses usually results in your being awarded a certificate.

Today, the availability of a variety of media has broadened the delivery methods and scope of distance learning. Distance-learning course work is offered via videoconferencing, the Internet, or a combination of the two. Videoconferencing sends audio and video images from a transmission station to receiving stations. This means you have to go to some facility in your community, usually an educational institution or a convention center, to attend distance-learning classes. Videoconferencing is usually two-way, allowing students and teachers to interact. Many educational institutions supplement course work delivered via videoconferencing with Internet instruction. You access course work information and assignments via computer and may correspond with the instructor and other students by e-mail.

Distance-learning opportunities are offered by a wide variety of sponsors, including U.S. government agencies, professional associations, and institutions of higher education. Many colleges and universities offer some course work via distance-learning formats. While it is possible to complete specific courses through distance learning, most colleges and universities require students to attend some on-campus classes in order to complete degree programs that include distance-learning components.

There is great variance in the quality of course work offered via distance-learning formats. Some is provided by accredited institutions of higher education. Other opportunities for education, particularly on the Internet, might be opportunities for being scammed. It is vital that you be an informed consumer and determine if the source of distance learning is legitimate and if the educational program offered will be useful in your personal career development. How do you know if your online educator is on the up-and-up? Distance learning offered by state and national universities is your best bet. Consider contacting—or visiting the Web site of—the Accrediting Commission of the Distance Education and Training Council for a list of accredited institutions (for details, see the DETC review that follows). There are also many Internet discussion groups that focus on distance learning. Get involved with one and ask around to learn more.

Adult Continuing Education and DOL/ETA

AMERICAN ASSOCIATION FOR ADULT AND CONTINUING EDUCATION
HTTP://WWW.ALBANY.EDU/AAACE/

Publisher of three education and training journals—Adult Learning, Adult Education Quarterly, and Adult Basic Education—AAACE is devoted to promoting continuing education opportunities for adults. If you're interested in finding out more about the field of adult learning, head for the links section. Here you'll find descriptions of a large assortment of suggested sites. Some of the topics covered include adult literacy, lifelong learning, workplace education, vocational training, technology education, and professional development. There is also an extensive listing of companies offering adult learning products (books, software, videotapes) and services.

AMERICA'S ONE-STOP CAREER CENTER SYSTEM
HTTP://WWW.TTRC.DOLETA.GOV/ONESTOP/

One-Stop, a program of the Training Technology Resource Center, sponsored by the U.S. Department of Labor's Employment and Training Administration (DOL/ETA), has centers in many states nationwide that offer services relating to employment, education, and training and that help bring together job seekers with employers. In other words, these centers allow you to gain new job skills (or fine-tune old ones), do your career planning, and conduct a job search all at one place—or one stop.

Scout around the site to discover brochures, newsletters, and progress reports that provide more information. You will need Adobe Acrobat Reader to view some. Other materials here pertain to partnership training programs, Job Corps, and the One-Stop Disability Initiative. Do you want to see if there's a One-Stop center in your state? You can find links to center Web sites here as well as names and addresses of people to contact. Additionally, the section for job seekers (back at the DOL/ETA site) presents information on such topics as career exploration, job searching, unemployment compensation, and laid-off workers.

Vocational Training and Apprenticeships

BUREAU OF APPRENTICESHIP AND TRAINING

HTTP://WWW.DOLETA.GOV/BAT/

Administered by the U.S. Department of Labor's Employment and Training Administration (DOL/ETA), BAT is one of two apprenticeship registration agencies (the other being State Apprenticeship Councils [SAC], discussed at this site as well). For an overview of apprenticeships and the role played by the federal government, refer to the FAQs section. If you want to find a program, contact the nearest BAT or SAC office. Street addresses and phone numbers are provided. "Recognized Apprenticeable Occupations" is a huge basic listing of officially recognized occupational titles. Also offered are descriptions of related programs, including School-to-Apprenticeship Programs (for students in their junior or senior year of high school who intend to enter the workforce upon graduation) and Outreach (authorized by the Women in Apprenticeship and Nontraditional Occupations Act).

MY FUTURE

HTTP://WWW.MYFUTURE.COM/

This site offers career-planning advice for high school graduates. One particularly helpful section is "Beyond High School," which is aimed at graduates who do not wish to go on to a four-year college. Here you'll find descriptions of other options, including military opportunities, apprenticeships, internships, and technical and vocational schools. For each option you're given an idea of what to expect in regard to the cost involved, what you'll get out of the experience, advantages and disadvantages, along with additional comments and resources for further data.

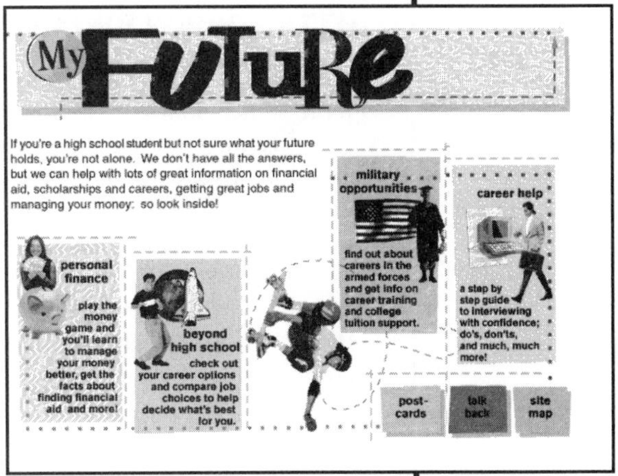

Advice for finding financial aid assistance or buying a used car is offered in the "Personal Finance" section. There's also an entire section devoted to the military. "Career Help" provides guidance on various steps of the job search process. Take the Interest Finder Quiz to determine the type of career you might be best suited for. A resume builder, cover letter dos and don'ts, interview tips, and materials on "hot jobs" round out the site. The information is concise, fun, and quick to read through.

PENNSYLVANIA APPRENTICE COORDINATORS ASSOCIATION

HTTP://WWW.APPRENTICE.ORG/

This organization presents here quite a useful resource for helping you decide if an apprenticeship—and resulting career—in the construction industry is right for you. You'll find information on various occupations: boilermakers, carpenters, cement masons, glaziers, ironworkers, plumbers, roofers, sheet metal workers, and so on. Featured are job descriptions; education recommendations; details on working conditions, terms of apprenticeships, qualifications, and relevant union admission requirements; and links to specific trade union sites where you will have access to further materials. While the contacts are only for Philadelphia or Pittsburgh, the rest of the site is appropriate for anyone considering a future in construction.

RWM VOCATIONAL SCHOOL DATABASE

HTTP://WWW.RWM.ORG/RWM/

Addresses and phone numbers of private postsecondary vocational schools in the United States can be found at this site. First select the state you're interested in, and then choose the category. Among the fields represented are automotive, barbering, business, fashion design, plumbing, telecommunications, and welding. More specific occupations are included under these headings; for example, business comprises accounting, administrative, general office, marketing, secretarial, and so on. If you want to find a book on the subject of vocational and alternative education, click on the Amazon.com links where you can find descriptions of a few titles. Links are also offered for sites with financial aid information and the Bureau of Labor Statistics' Occupational Outlook Handbook.

Distance Learning

THE DISTANCE EDUCATION AND TRAINING COUNCIL

HTTP://WWW.DETC.ORG/

The DETC is a nonprofit association responsible for maintaining a storehouse of information about distance learning. The council sponsors the Accrediting Commission of the Distance Education and Training Council, a nationally recognized accrediting agency. There is a directory of more than seventy accredited institutions. Contact details (including Web site addresses where available) and notes on courses and degrees are featured. The "Useful Resources" section provides links to educational resources, libraries, reference services, and educational agencies that focus on distance learning.

THE DISTANCE LEARNING "GETTING STARTED" BOOKLIST

HTTP://PERSONALPAGES.TDS.NET/RLAWS/

Here you'll find a list of titles (books, journals, and software) pertaining to distance learning. Additionally, you can access the FAQ pages of the newsgroup alt.education.distance. These pages cover everything from choosing a distance-learning program to financial aid to links to colleges and universities with distance-learning programs and other sources.

PETERSON'S LIFELONGLEARNING

HTTP://WWW.LIFELONGLEARNING.COM/

Peterson's, publisher of educational books, offers this database of distance-learning opportunities. According to your interest, you can search by program, course, or school. You can read about distance-learning programs at various institutions. Course descriptions plus information on credits, requirements, cost, and dates are featured. Links to additional Peterson's resources are also included. If you need information on how to pay for your education, Peterson's provides some advice, courtesy of Key Education Resources.

WESTERN GOVERNORS UNIVERSITY

HTTP://WWW.WGU.EDU/WGU/INDEX.HTML

WGU compiles distance-learning course and program listings from a variety of colleges and universities and presents them all together in a single course catalog. You can browse the catalog for courses and program descriptions and take a Distance Learning Quiz to gauge whether or not this type of learning may be suitable for you.

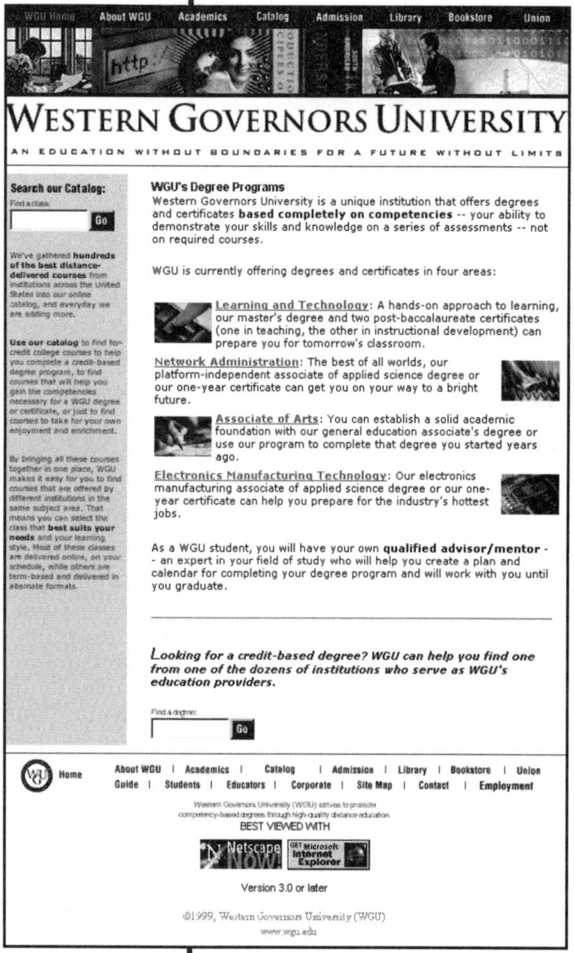

CHAPTER 8

GETTING EXPERIENCE

If you've ever browsed through job listings, you've probably noticed that most say "experience required." Kind of a Catch-22, isn't it? How are you going to gain experience if you can't get the job to begin with? This chapter may offer the solution. Volunteer opportunities, internships, and summer jobs are excellent "no experience necessary" paths to acquiring skills and coming away with something legitimate to put on your resume. They are also the best way to try out certain career fields, which should help you formulate plans about what you want to do with your life. Furthermore, your interactions with other workers might well form the beginnings of your professional network, a system of contacts through which you can get advice and information regarding your career development. So instead of sitting around being bored during the summer or at the end of the school day, why not get out there and do something to gain experience and improve upon your skills so you'll be better prepared for a full-time career when the time comes!

You could try service learning, which means working as a volunteer in a community service agency. Service learning helps you gain a sense of civic and social responsibility as you develop personal, professional, and academic skills by applying classroom learning in a work environment. There are volunteer opportunities in all occupational areas. Volunteers learn about jobs in different occupational fields and can participate in activities that develop skills. Some high schools make service learning a requirement. Many community colleges and some undergraduate colleges include service learning as experiential components in their course work.

Service learning often allows volunteers to work with employees in their work environments. Volunteers learn about the job duties of people in specific occupations and observe people employed in different occupations working together. For example, volunteers in shelters for homeless or abused people may work in close proximity with food preparation workers, such as cooks and kitchen helpers; administrative assistants; janitors and maintenance workers; helping professionals, such as social workers and counselors; and law enforcement officials. Volunteers may also get opportunities to learn how specific activities—say, a political campaign, a criminal trial, a community festival, or a fund-raising event for charity—are organized and carried out. Volunteers can develop skills that make them more marketable, such as learning to greet and help customers, assisting in clerical duties, running meetings, and dealing with the media.

If you are not a student, you may find that volunteering in a service learning format provides you with experiences that will aid you in career transitions or job advancement. Volunteer work may offer an opportunity for you to demonstrate skills and abilities that can be used in employment. Achievements and activities performed in unpaid volunteer work can be legitimately reflected on resumes and job applications.

To enter into some occupations with a bachelor's degree you may be required to complete an internship. For example, people who want to become dietitians should plan on completing a year's dietetic internship in a program approved by the American Dietetic Association. Although many areas of study do not require any experiential components to earn a bachelor's degree, students intending to enter an occupation requiring a bachelor's degree, who want a competitive advantage in the job market after graduation, should seek out opportunities to include experiential learning, such as practicums and internships, in their degree programs. A practicum or an internship affords you an opportunity to perform the job duties expected of an employee in an actual work setting. It provides two advantages: (a) you can determine if you are on the right career path by seeing if you enjoy working in the occupation and (b) you can start developing a professional network of contacts who may be able to help you find employment after graduation. College- and university-sponsored experiential learning programs often have a very high rate of placement of their graduates. You should learn about the possibilities of completing an experiential learning component, either with or without academic credit, by visiting your college or university career placement office.

Among the organizations commonly offering volunteer opportunities are those concerned with the environment, humanitarian causes, or animal rights, while summer jobs can often be found at state or national parks or at day or overnight camps. Even though these areas might not seem relevant to your ultimate career goal, remember that much of the experience you'll gain and the skills you'll learn will likely be transferable to your occupation of choice. At the very least, you should come away better able to follow instructions and relate to your fellow workers, important assets for any job!

Keep in mind that while the reviews listed in this chapter under "Summer Jobs and Jobs for Teens" are just that, you're sure to find summer and teen opportunities in the "Volunteer Opportunities and Internships" section as well (not to mention job listings). And if you know of a company or organization you're interested in but for which you can't locate any internship or volunteer information, contact the business and ask about available opportunities. Need some ideas? Chapter 12 ("Resources to Meet Specific Needs") might be able to point you in the right direction. Or check out your occupational field of interest in Chapter 13 ("Resources for Specific Industries") for names of organizations that might have suggestions for where to find internship or volunteer positions. All that's required is a bit of creative thinking and some initiative on your part!

Before you make any commitments, be sure to use common sense. Find out about a group—its reputation, legitimacy, goals, and practices—before agreeing to volunteer or work for it. Read through the organization's information about volunteering and talk to someone directly, to get answers to your questions, before you sign up. Make sure you have a clear understanding of what will be expected of you. If you are thinking about signing up online, first study the privacy materials presented in Chapter 10 ("Job Searching on the Internet").

Volunteer Opportunities and Internships

ACADEMY OF TELEVISION ARTS & SCIENCES: EDUCATION PROGRAMS
HTTP://WWW.EMMYS.ORG/EPS/IN

Are you looking for a paid internship and willing to live in or near Los Angeles? This site describes the internship program offered by the Academy of Television Arts & Sciences, a nonprofit organization that's been around since 1946 (just a month after network television).

You can apply for any of more than two dozen internship categories, including animation (traditional or computer), art direction, broadcast advertising and promotion, casting, children's programming and development, cinematography, commercials, costume design, editing, entertainment news, episodic series, movies for television, music, network programming management, public relations and publicity, sound, syndication and distribution, television directing (single or multi-camera), television script writing, and videotape postproduction.

Complete instructions are given on what to include in your application. If you're one of the finalists selected, you'll be asked to submit a videotaped interview in response to assigned questions. Interns are paid a stipend for eight weeks of full-time work, plus an additional fee for those who have to travel to Los Angeles from somewhere else.

To get background information on the academy itself, its activities and news, or the Emmy Awards, just click on the appropriate icon.

ADVICE FOR VOLUNTEERS
HTTP://WWW.SERVICELEADER.ORG/ADVICE/

This site offers exactly what its title suggests, in great abundance. It is part of the Volunteerism and Community Engagement Initiatives of the Charles A. Dana Center at the University of Texas at Austin, responsible for a lot of great volunteerism resources. Here you'll find articles that discuss reasons for volunteering, finding a suitable assignment, using the Internet to explore your options, how volunteering can help you in career exploration, how to incorporate your volunteer work into your resume, and much more. Many of the articles were written by Susan J. Ellis, well known in the field of volunteerism and volunteer management. There are a few links to additional related resources, including the Virtual Volunteering Project (reviewed separately in this chapter), another project of the Volunteerism and Community Engagement Initiatives. This is a terrific place to start if you're considering your volunteer options. You'll be sure to come away with many ideas to think about before you accept a position.

ALASKA STATE PARKS

HTTP://WWW.DNR.STATE.AK.US/PARKS/PARKS.HTM

If the call of the wild is music to your ears, you might want to spend some time at this Web site from Alaska's Division of Parks and Outdoor Recreation. Not only can you read about all the state parks in Alaska and link to home pages of individual parks, but you can also find out about volunteer opportunities. How would you like to be a volunteer winter ranger assistant near Fairbanks? An archaeological assistant? How about working on a trail crew? Many of these volunteer positions can fulfill college internship requirements as well.

If you don't have the time to be a full-time volunteer, check out the Volunteers in Parks Program. Read about various short-term volunteer opportunities, such as Adopt-a-Trail (whereby organizations maintain certain trails) and Park Watch (participants take turns watching a park in an effort to deter crime).

AMERICAN RED CROSS

HTTP://WWW.REDCROSS.ORG/

If the thought of donating blood makes you queasy, but you still want to help the American Red Cross, why not volunteer? The American Red Cross provides humanitarian services to needy families all over the world, and volunteers make up more than 90 percent of the workforce. Training is provided for the wide array of volunteer positions available. "ARC Link" is aimed specifically at young people. Here you can read about the experiences of young Red Cross volunteers and about what you can do to help as a volunteer yourself. Some of the areas in which you can find volunteer opportunities are Community Innovations, Disaster Services, and International Services. Many of the volunteer positions are described on the Web site. You can contact your local Red Cross chapter for details about others.

AMERICA'S CHARITIES

HTTP://WWW.CHARITIES.ORG/

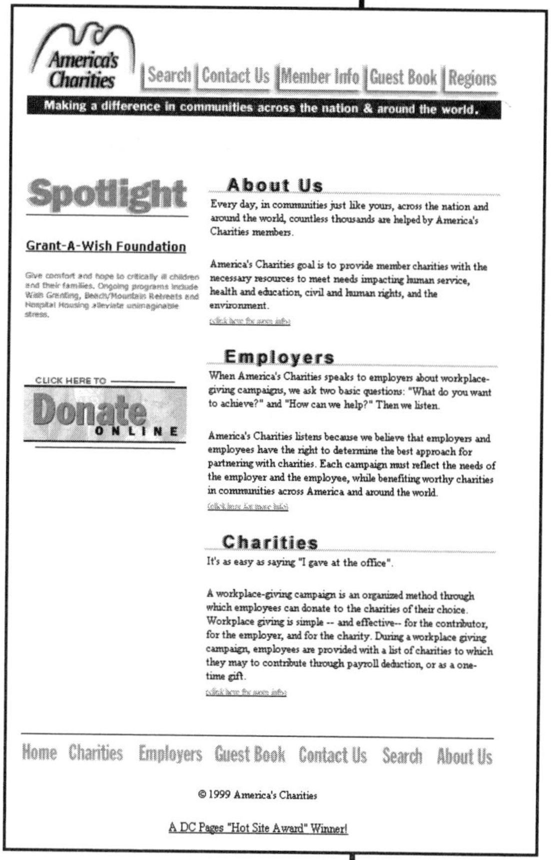

America's Charities represents numerous national charities and offers fund-raising services to employers. Member charities are diverse and are categorized by health, education, environment, human services, and civil and human rights. You'll find listings for such organizations as African Christian Relief, Farm Aid, National Breast Cancer Coalition Fund, Guide Dog Foundation for the Blind, Multiple Sclerosis Association of America, and Amnesty International of the USA, just to name a few. Brief background information is provided, along with links to home pages (if available), where you can learn more about these charities before making donations—or before inquiring about volunteer opportunities. Details are given about becoming an America's Charities volunteer.

AMERICORPS

HTTP://WWW.CNS.GOV/AMERICORPS/

AmeriCorps is a Corporation for National Service program. In exchange for a year of service, volunteers receive help paying for their education. This Web site explains the AmeriCorps programs and the types of services provided by the volunteers. The programs include AmeriCorps*VISTA (Volunteers in Service to America) and AmeriCorps*NCCC (National Civilian Community Corps), which is a full-time residential service program for those eighteen to twenty-four years of age. You may have seen some AmeriCorps*NCCC volunteers working in your neighborhood, providing education and human services or addressing public safety and environmental issues.

Don't miss the section on jobs, fellowships, and internships. Browse through the job openings, and read program overviews and department descriptions. AmeriCorps is a great way to attain new skills while working off a school loan (or saving to finance additional schooling). Links to a few other recommended resources are offered.

ARCHAEOLOGICAL FIELDWORK OPPORTUNITIES
HTTP://WWW.SSCNET.UCLA.EDU/IOA/AFS/TESTPIT.HTML

If digging around rocks and ruins is your idea of fun, you'll surely be intrigued by what's to be found at this Web site. It lists worldwide volunteer fieldwork opportunities, many specifically geared toward high school students. You might get to conduct archival research in Antigua, West Indies, or be involved in the excavation of an ancient Jewish village near the Dead Sea. Sound exciting? Then hurry on over to this Web site and follow the links to get the whole scoop, because this is just a sample of what's available.

THE CARTER CENTER
HTTP://WWW.CARTERCENTER.ORG/

This Atlanta-based nonprofit public policy institute was founded by former U.S. president Jimmy Carter and his wife, Rosalynn. What does the center do? The Web site says it best: "It seeks to prevent and resolve conflicts, enhance freedom and democracy, and improve health." You'll get a better idea of what that really means when you read through the major accomplishments or look at the sections on peace or health programs. The Carter Center has assisted farmers in various African nations; monitored multiparty elections to ensure fairness in Mexico, Haiti, and Panama; and worked in the United States to improve services for those suffering from mental illnesses.

The Carter Center sponsors an internship program for students interested in international and domestic issues. Read through the internship description and application procedures to learn more. Volunteers are also welcome. Just contact the Volunteer Office to get more information.

COUNCIL ON INTERNATIONAL EDUCATIONAL EXCHANGE

HTTP://WWW.CIEE.ORG/INDEX.HTM

If you've ever wanted to go abroad to study, work, teach English, or volunteer, you'll want to pinch yourself when you land on this site. CIEE is a nonprofit organization that offers a variety of programs and services for students from high school through university levels as well as for adults. Explore the Web site to find the opportunity that's right for you! There are separate subsites devoted to CIEE's three operating divisions: Council Exchanges, Council-International Study Programs, and Council Travel.

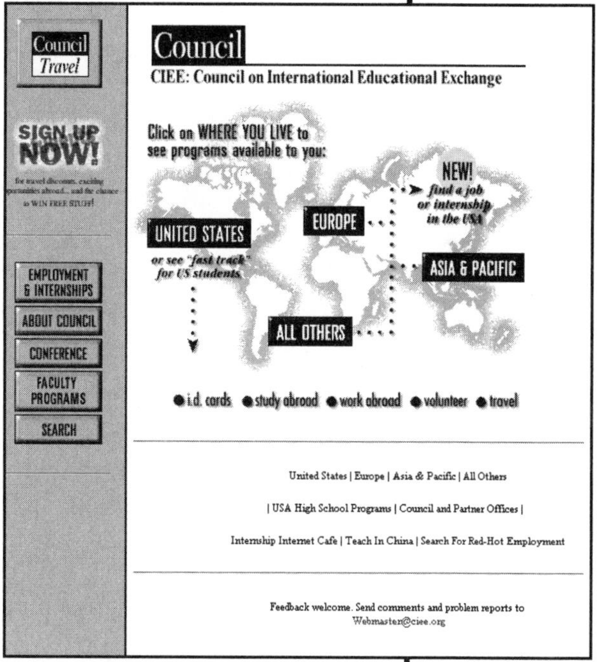

Council Exchanges is where to head if you're looking for volunteer information. Click on "Volunteer" to learn about CIEE's more than 600 International Volunteer Projects in thirty countries. Some of your volunteer options (usually lasting two to four weeks) might include building playground equipment for children in Belgium, participating in agricultural projects in Morocco, or repairing cultural objects in Ukraine. Room and board is provided, but you will have to pay for your own travel and insurance. There is a placement fee as well.

Click on "Study Abroad" to access information on the International Study Programs by country or region. For example, how would you like to go study philosophy in Paris, France? How about studying at a biological station in tropical Costa Rica?

The "Work Abroad" section is geared toward the college student or recent graduate who has up to half a year available for travel and work. Jobs can range from clerical office work and waiting tables to paid internships in more career-oriented fields.

EARTHWATCH INSTITUTE

HTTP://WWW.EARTHWATCH.ORG/

Earthwatch Institute is a nonprofit organization devoted to worldwide scientific field research having the goal to better understand and improve Earth's natural resources and the quality of animal life. The Web site lists all current expeditions, samples of which are tracking the wolves of India, monitoring dolphins in the Mediterranean, examining the environmental degradation of Easter Island, and measuring changes in the reefs of the Bahamas. Sounds rather exotic, doesn't it? Expeditions are usually about a week or two in length, and volunteers must pay for airfare along with a share of the expedition cost.

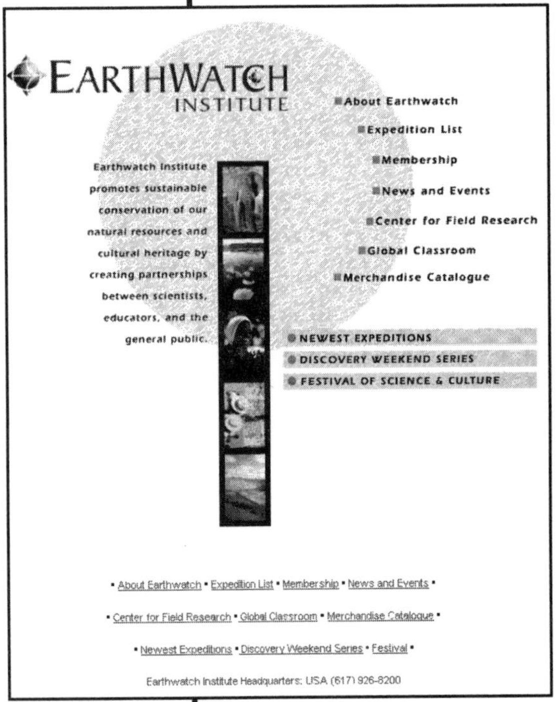

The Student Challenge Awards Program enables select high school students to spend a few weeks conducting research, working in the field (in North America or Costa Rica) with scientists. Full details can be found at the site. Center for Field Research grants are also described.

ENVIROLINK

HTTP://WWW.ENVIROLINK.ORG/

If you care about the environment and want to find out how to get involved, check out EnviroLink, a nonprofit organization that provides environmental resources and information. Projects of EnviroLink include the Animal Rights Resource Site, the Green Living Center, the Sustainable Business Network, and the EnviroLink Library, a listing of organizations, publications, government agencies, and information on dozens of environmental topics. Are you beginning to think that this would be a good place to do some research on environmental issues and possible careers?

If you enjoy gathering information and conducting research, a volunteer position with EnviroLink might just fit the bill. EnviroLink is looking for folks to research issues and organize EnviroLink events all over the world. Contact EnviroLink via e-mail or give them a ring to let them know you're interested.

ENVIRONMENTAL CAREERS ORGANIZATION

HTTP://WWW.ECO.ORG/

Founded in 1972 as an experimental internship program in Massachusetts, ECO has developed into a national nonprofit organization offering career advice, career products, and numerous environmental internships across the United States. If you're looking for a paid environmental internship as a water quality engineer, an assistant park planner, a sediment information assistant, an environmental compliance intern, or a greenhouse assistant, for example, this is the place to go.

The site provides a quick glimpse at the organization: its history, its various programs (including an annual conference on career opportunities), and a detailed list of available internships. Lasting from a few weeks in the summer to more than a year, the internships are mostly for college students or graduates. You can apply for internships electronically. Just follow the instructions for the specific internship you're interested in.

While the site is well suited for people with a college education who know what they're looking for, the descriptions of internships will help high school students plan their future. Also available are links to other career pages and environmental organizations.

EXERCISE SCIENCE, FITNESS/WELLNESS, AND HEALTH PROMOTION INTERNSHIP INFORMATION

HTTP://WWW.NAU.EDU:80/HP/PROJ/RAH/INTERN/INTERN.HTML

If fitness is your game, you'll be jumping for joy when you hit this Web site, which lists internship opportunities in the fitness and exercise science fields. Browse by location to find internships as fitness specialists for corporate fitness centers and exercise science specialists for cardiac facilities, to name a few. There are several links to fitness-, internship-, and career-related sites as well.

GLOBAL VOLUNTEERS
HTTP://WWW.GLOBALVOLUNTEERS.ORG/

Global Volunteers is a nonprofit organization developed to promote and maintain world peace through humanitarian services. Volunteers sign on for stints of as many as three weeks to work on human and economic development projects in Africa, Latin America, Europe, the United States, or Asia. This might entail teaching English, digging wells, planting community gardens, or providing professional services (don't worry—you won't be asked to do anything you're not qualified to do).

You can read volunteer testimonials, project descriptions, and the philosophy of Global Volunteers, plus you can download an application form at the site. You do have to pay a program fee, but this is tax-deductible (okay, so if you're a student this might not really matter to you) and covers most of your expenses.

GREENPEACE INTERNATIONAL
HTTP://WWW.GREENPEACE.ORG/

You may be surprised to find that Greenpeace does more than just "save the whales." The organization's goals are to end all nuclear threats; prevent pollution of the ocean, land, air, and freshwater; protect biodiversity in all its forms (this would include saving the whales); and promote peace, nonviolence, and global disarmament. Greenpeace's Web site offers press releases and information regarding the group's latest toxics, nuclear, atmosphere, and biodiversity campaigns. You can also read up on what's happening on Greenpeace ships.

To learn about volunteer, internship, activist, or work opportunities with Greenpeace, you will need to go to the home page of the Greenpeace office in your country. The U.S. Greenpeace Web site, located at http://www.greenpeaceusa.org/, lists jobs with Greenpeace.

HABITAT FOR HUMANITY INTERNATIONAL

HTTP://WWW.HABITAT.ORG/

Habitat for Humanity is a nonprofit volunteer organization dedicated to eliminating substandard housing by building affordable housing with and for underprivileged families. Fact sheets provide answers to questions about how the homes are built (volunteer labor and tax-deductible donations), who is eligible to purchase a Habitat home (families in need must apply), and more.

There are Habitat for Humanity chapters on college campuses across the nation and elsewhere. This is a great way to get involved if you're in school. Check for your school in the "Campus Chapters and Youth Programs" section. You might also look into the Collegiate Challenge, a program whereby high school and college students work during school breaks. You can look for the home pages of affiliates near you by searching through the affiliate database. The database includes campus chapters as well as regular affiliate offices.

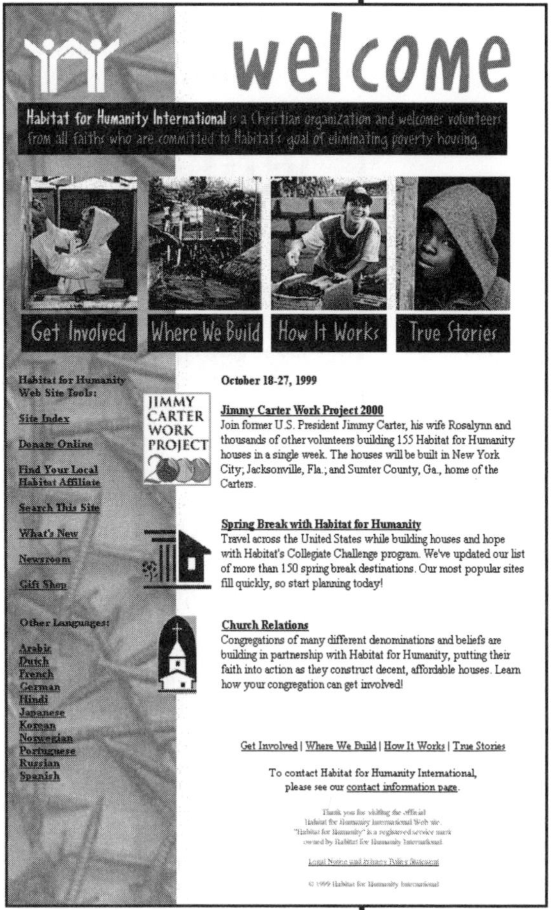

If you want to learn about Habitat for Humanity, you can certainly do it at this Web site. Read through "True Stories" for some touching and inspirational tales from volunteers and new homeowners. How about the eighty-year-old woman who bought her first home from Habitat for Humanity? There's also plenty of information about former U.S. president Jimmy Carter's involvement.

IDEALIST

HTTP://WWW.IDEALIST.ORG/

If you are interested in researching jobs, internships, or volunteer opportunities in the nonprofit sector, this resource from the organization Action without Borders is a great one. The "Nonprofit Career Center" features an international directory of information on more than 15,000 nonprofit groups worldwide, with links where available. The database is searchable by many variables, including country, area of focus, and mission keyword. If you don't want to use the search form, you have the option to view everything. You also can browse through the links to other Web sites containing tips for nonprofit job hunters and details on academic programs that might lead to a career in the nonprofit sector, along with much more.

Information is available for those looking for volunteer situations as well. Some of the categories covered are disaster relief, housing and homelessness, and wildlife and animal welfare. You'll also want to check out "News Updates from Around the World," which lists online publications focused on nonprofit news. Titles are sorted by those updated daily and those updated weekly. Follow the links to get your news.

INTERACTION

HTTP://WWW.INTERACTION.ORG/

InterAction is a coalition of nonprofit organizations advocating humanitarian aid to impoverished countries. The group is involved with disaster relief, sustainable development, and public policy. At the Web site you can read about InterAction programs, including the Africa Liaison Project, the Commission on the Advancement of Women, the Middle East Working Group, and Migration and Refugee Affairs. InterAction publications are also available and cover gender integration in programs, global solutions to local problems, and other topics.

"Volunteer Opportunities" lists Web sites that offer international volunteer opportunities. Don't miss the volunteer profiles and InterAction's "Guide to Volunteer Opportunities." The guide lists organizations that accept clothing donations, collect books for overseas schools, pack medical kits, participate in student exchange programs, or provide technical support. You'll also find organizations that need volunteers with medical skills, agricultural knowledge, or teaching experience. This site is pretty global—stick with it and you're sure to find an opportunity that suits you.

INTERNSHIPPROGRAMS.COM
HTTP://WWW.INTERNSHIPPROGRAMS.COM/

This growing database of some 200,000 positions in 2,600 programs is for students seeking internships in a variety of fields. You can search for an internship by selecting a category (for example, architecture firms, arts and humanities, news and media, or sports teams and organizations) or a region of the United States where you want to work. Pick an internship that sounds appealing and you'll be given contact details (phone and fax numbers plus street and Web addresses) so that you can pursue the lead. Where available, there are also links that will take you directly to the company's internship program page. There not only will you find out about potential internship opportunities but current job openings as well.

INTERNSHIP RESOURCES ON THE WEB
HTTP://WWW.CC.COLORADO.EDU/CAREERCENTER/SUMMERJOBSANDINTERNSHIPS/INTERN.HTML

The Colorado College Career Center has compiled this basic yet useful directory of links to point you in the right direction if you want to explore the Internet for internship information or opportunities. You'll find links to sites in such general categories as summer or seasonal jobs or for more specific areas such as art and entertainment, computer technology, engineering, nonprofit, education, science, the environment, law, and government. There are select international resources represented here too.

NONPROFIT CAREER NETWORK

HTTP://WWW.NONPROFITCAREER.COM/

This site lists job and volunteer opportunities with nonprofit organizations. You'll have to pay an annual registration fee if you want to post your resume, but you can peruse the job listings at no cost. You can search by job type, computer skills, or region; if you specify no preferences, all available jobs will appear. Some of the jobs you might find include bookstore clerk, emergency recruitment administrator, and development officer. To find out more about the nonprofit organizations that post openings at this site, go to "Corporate Profiles." The separate volunteer database contains information on organizations offering volunteer opportunities. Some of the organizations represented at the site are Christmas House, Debt Counselors of America, National Group Rides and Designated Drivers, People for the Ethical Treatment of Animals, Special Olympics International, UNICEF USA, and VISTA.

PEACE CORPS

HTTP://WWW.PEACECORPS.GOV/

If you've ever thought about joining the Peace Corps but weren't sure what it really entailed, you'll love this Web site because it's loaded with all sorts of details. You'll learn about the history and goals of the Peace Corps, programs and countries the Peace Corps is currently involved in, and the people of the Peace Corps.

The "Volunteer" section offers pages upon pages of in-depth information about how to become a volunteer. You will learn about the application and selection process, and you can read about the career, educational, and financial benefits of becoming a Peace Corps volunteer. Look at the regional pages to get descriptions of some of the countries where Peace Corps volunteers serve along with overviews of Peace Corps programs implemented in these countries. Types of volunteers frequently requested by host countries include agriculturists, educators, nurses, businesspeople, and natural resource workers. The FAQ page answers such questions as "Can I choose the country where I'll serve as a volunteer?" and "Do I need to speak another language to get into the Peace Corps?"

Learn about other Peace Corps programs, such as World Wise Schools, a program designed to acquaint students in grades three through twelve with various countries. Additionally, there are sections presenting volunteer stories, resources aimed at returned Peace Corps volunteers, and press releases and fact sheets about the Peace Corps. Some interesting statistics are given about the Peace Corps too, such as the percentage of volunteers over age fifty (about 7 percent), the number of countries served to date (more than 130), and the percentage of volunteers with bachelor's degrees or higher (about 80 percent).

For further information about the Peace Corps and its departments, refer to the section on regional offices. Addresses and phone numbers of all Peace Corps recruiting offices are listed here, as are dates for and details on area Peace Corps events.

PEOPLE FOR THE ETHICAL TREATMENT OF ANIMALS

HTTP://WWW.PETA-ONLINE.ORG/

This international animal rights organization says in its mission statement that "animals are not ours to eat, wear, experiment on, or use for entertainment." To find out how PETA is working toward this end, read about the activist group's activities and campaigns. Some of the areas of focus are fur, circus animals, fishing, and vegetarianism. The action alerts explain how you can get involved. There are sections specifically aimed at kids and college students. If this sounds right up your alley, then you might want to check out year-round internship opportunities with PETA. Brief details are provided at the site—you'll have to contact PETA directly to find out more as well as to get an application.

PRESIDENT'S STUDENT SERVICE CHALLENGE

HTTP://WWW.STUDENT-SERVICE-AWARDS.ORG/

Have you spent at least 100 hours in a one-year period as an active volunteer in your community—perhaps at a local hospital, homeless shelter, or nursing home? If so, your volunteer work could add up to a $1,000 scholarship toward your education.

This Web site will clue you in on the President's Student Service Scholarships program, which is a way for schools and communities to recognize young people for outstanding volunteer service and help them to continue their education. High school juniors and seniors who have performed 100 hours of community service in a year can be nominated for a $500 Corporation for National Service scholarship, to be matched with another $500 by a local organization.

The people initially involved in the selection process include the student's principal, counselor, or teachers, who work with a representative of the community organization where the student volunteered. Complete details and a printable application are available at the site.

PROJECT AMERICA
HTTP://WWW.PROJECT.ORG/

Project America organizes Project America Day, an annual volunteer event in which thousands of people across the nation participate in various community-oriented activities. The Web site is quite extensive and gives you all the information you'll need to get involved in Project America; for example, the project's historical background (can you believe it was created by two high school students?), highlights from the last Project America Day, press clippings, and more. Are you interested in finding out what some of the projects are? How about planting trees throughout a city, holding a fund-raiser to benefit a local AIDS outreach center, or collecting canned goods for the hungry, for starters.

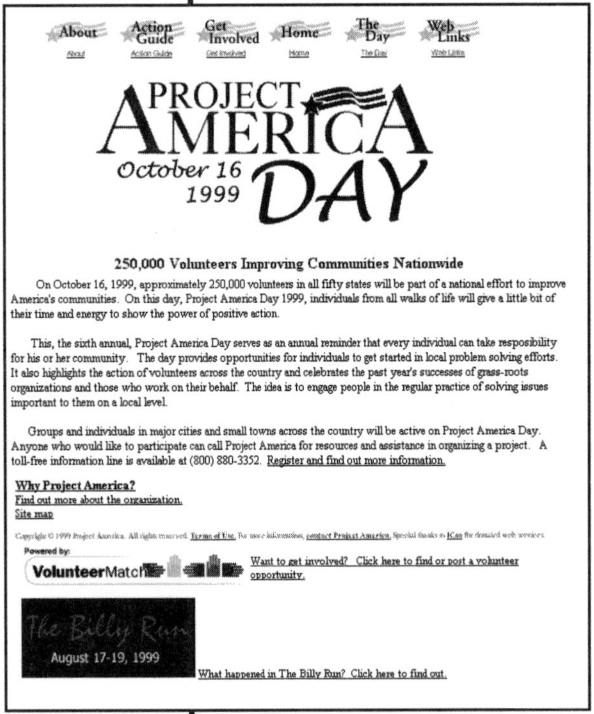

The "Action Guide" suggests ways for getting involved in your community. You can read about project ideas and how to develop your own project. If you're not quite ready to take on a whole project from start to finish yourself, head straight for the "Getting Involved" section to find out what it takes to be a volunteer and find volunteer opportunities. This is a great spot to find out how to learn more about community service organizations. You'll discover tips on locating national, state, or local community service organizations, as well as suggestions on how to find a volunteer opportunity that is right for you, your skills, and your schedule.

RAINFOREST ACTION NETWORK
HTTP://WWW.RAN.ORG/

RAN's dynamic, colorful home page draws you in with its sense of urgency. You don't merely have to visit the site—you can make a statement while you're there. For instance, click on "Action Alert" to learn about current issues affecting the rainforest. But don't just read about the issues—show your support by sending an e-mail to legislators right from the site, using RAN's sample letters as is or customized as you wish.

There are descriptions of RAN's ongoing campaigns, including the Beyond Oil Campaign, the Old Growth Campaign, and the Protect-an-Acre Program. The "Victories" section keeps track of RAN's successful campaigns all the way back to 1987.

If spending time at this site only whets your appetite for more and you live in San Francisco—or you're ready to spend some time there—check out the numerous volunteer and internship possibilities that are listed online.

SECOND HARVEST
HTTP://WWW.SECONDHARVEST.ORG/

If you want to help eradicate hunger while gaining some valuable work-related skills, check out the Second Harvest Web site. Having close to 200 food banks, Second Harvest serves the needy in soup kitchens, senior centers, day care centers, and other facilities all over the United States and Puerto Rico. You can volunteer your time to help sort or serve food, organize canned food drives, or provide some administrative help. See if there is a food bank near you on the U.S. regional map or contact Second Harvest for additional information. While you're at the site, you can read research study findings about the state of the hungry in the United States, browse through Second Harvest's Update magazine, and scan the latest press releases.

STUDENT CONSERVATION ASSOCIATION

HTTP://WWW.SCA-INC.ORG/

Dedicated to "changing lives through service to nature," SCA presents a Web site that features numerous listings of volunteer and internship positions across the country. One opportunity is SCA's High School Conservation Work Crew Program, which offers youths aged sixteen to nineteen a chance to work in teams on month-long projects for the National Park Service and other agencies. This site makes it almost too easy: you can access a list of current positions, read information about sample projects and eligibility, and request an application, all online.

Subscription details are available for EarthWork, a publication on conservation issues, as well as for Earth Work's JobNet, a popular environmental and conservation jobs listing. Several other resource guides and books can also be ordered online.

TEACH FOR AMERICA

HTTP://WWW.TEACH-FORAMERICA.ORG/

Teach For America, a national teaching corps, allows recent college graduates an opportunity to teach for two years in rural or under-resourced urban public schools. This is a comprehensive site with all the information you could ever want about the program. You can download the application form and find out about the rigorous hiring process. You must have a bachelor's degree to apply, but no teaching experience is necessary. Urban sites to which you may be assigned include Baltimore, Houston, and

Los Angeles. The rural areas include Mississippi, North Carolina, and Louisiana. Compensation is about comparable to a first-year teaching salary, but the contributions you make toward educating America is the real bonus.

Definitely look over the Q&A section to get more details about the program. You'll find answers to pressing questions such as "Is Teach For America only for recent college graduates?" and "Why doesn't Teach For America actively recruit education majors?"

U.S. STATE DEPARTMENT INTERNSHIPS INDEX

HTTP://WWW.STATE.GOV/WWW/CAREERS/RINTERNCONTENTS.HTML

Maybe you're an avid reader of Tom Clancy novels, or maybe you really have a keen passion for international affairs. Whatever the case, the Department of State offers internships to qualified students who are interested in international affairs. You can work in Washington, D.C., or at a consulate or an embassy overseas. Most internships are unpaid and available throughout the year, to coincide with a school semester or quarter or with summer break. A very small percentage of internships are paid. Make sure you read the internship Q&A section—you'll learn details about the security clearance process and the types of tasks you may be assigned.

VIRTUAL VOLUNTEERING PROJECT

HTTP://WWW.SERVICELEADER.ORG/VV/

Originally begun by Impact Online, this unique project is part of the Volunteerism and Community Engagement Initiatives of the Charles A. Dana Center at the University of Texas at Austin. What's it all about? Well, to be a virtual volunteer means to conduct volunteer work (in whole or only partially) in cyberspace, via the Internet. Such work might involve providing some sort of technical assistance (for example, performing online research or advocacy, designing a logo or database, or translating a document) or direct contact (perhaps supervising or moderating a company's chat room or mailing list, participating in an online support group, or training others as part of a distance-learning program). You can read all about the idea at this Web site.

Not sure where to start? There's advice on how to approach organizations with the idea of doing virtual volunteer work for them, whether or not they've already instituted the practice! The challenges of virtual volunteering are addressed in detail. "Seeking and Promoting Involvement of People with Disabilities in Virtual Volunteering Programs" is quite an extensive treatment of this pertinent subject.

VOLUNTEERMATCH

HTTP://WWW.VOLUNTEERMATCH.ORG/

A project of the nonprofit organization Impact Online, VolunteerMatch serves to match individuals with volunteer opportunities in their community. Check out "CityMatch" to see what's available in cities throughout the United States. Pick a city, enter your zip code, indicate how far you're willing to travel and how soon you want to volunteer, select the type (one time or ongoing), and designate a category (for example, animals, disabled, legal aid, race and ethnicity, religion, women, or everything). Click on "Find," and your results will be displayed. Select a volunteer job title to see details about the position.

Another great feature of the site is a searchable directory of nonprofits. To get a list of organizations, simply fill in the boxes to indicate such search parameters as zip code, travel radius, volunteer category, and sort criteria (alphabetically, categorically, geographically). Check out their descriptions to find something of interest. Sign up for Impact Online's newsletter to receive news about site updates and upcoming activities.

VOLUNTEER ORGANIZATIONS ON THE WEB

HTTP://WWW.COLLEGEBOARD.ORG/FEATURES/SERVICE/HTML/ORGS.HTML

The College Board (College Entrance Examination Board) assembled this annotated directory of volunteer groups having an online presence. Listings for human rights, health services, environment and conservation, horticulture, animal rights, rehabilitation, urban planning, social work, political, substance abuse, and communications organizations are included. Each is briefly described. Once you've found a group that looks like a good match for you, follow the link to its home page, where you will find more in-depth information (such as a mission statement, organizational history, and news on current projects). And, of course, details on volunteer opportunities!

Summer Jobs and Jobs for Teens

COLLEGE PRO PAINTERS (U.S.) LTD.
HTTP://WWW.COLLEGEPRO.COM/HOME.HTML

Want to paint during your summer break? College Pro Painters is a painting company that recruits summer painters from college campuses across the nation. Employees run their own painting businesses during summer breaks and can earn internship credit as well as money. The job is more than a painting job—employees are franchise managers and must handle the marketing, hiring of personnel, and quality control.

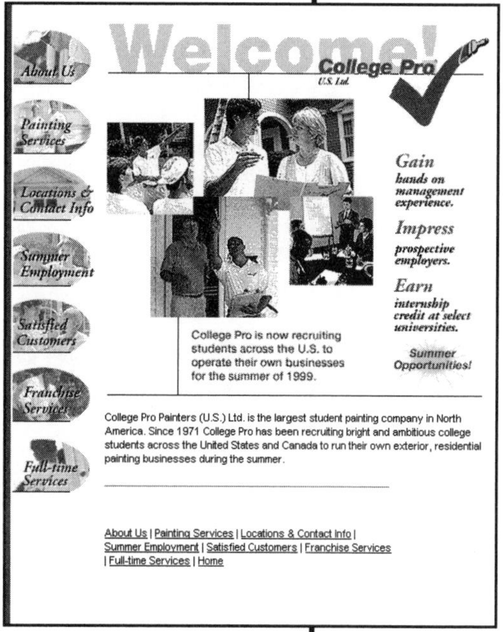

The "Summer Management Opportunities" page outlines the job requirements and responsibilities. It also details the training involved. Learn more about the possibility of earning college credit through College Pro on the "Other Summer Opportunities" page. Profiles of former College Pro managers are included so you can see how the job helped them in their current careers. A summer with College Pro is intended to supply you with experience in the areas of business planning, marketing, sales, accounting, and personnel management, not to mention paint systems. If that appeals to you and you're ready to take the plunge, just fill out the online application form.

COOL WORKS
HTTP://WWW.COOLWORKS.COM/

Can you picture yourself saddling up mules at the Grand Canyon or working as a tour guide at Mount Rushmore this summer? If you've always been interested in working at a park or recreation area, you'll be thrilled to find this Web site boasting more than 70,000 job listings, with links to facilities' home pages where available. Cool Works quickly links you up to a mass of information about seasonal employment at dozens of national and state parks, preserves, monuments, and wilderness areas. There are also listings of jobs and volunteer opportunities at ski areas, private resorts, cruise ships, and summer camps. Pick a category to see what's in store for you here!

Specific job descriptions can also be accessed by clicking on a location that interests you on the U.S.A. Job Map. The map links to comprehensive descriptions of the park's attractions, facilities, and jobs currently available. You can also check out where recruiters for some of the larger parks and resorts will be holding job fairs. If planning ahead isn't your forte, look to the "Help Wanted Now!" listings for immediate job openings. Most of the national and state jobs require that applicants be eighteen years or older. While only a handful of jobs allow you to apply directly online, many have downloadable application forms.

GREAT SUMMER JOBS
HTTP://GSJ.PETERSONS.COM/

This site, by Peterson's and the American Camping Association, lists jobs at summer camps. It's a great resource with information about why you should work at a summer camp (a major bonus is that you get to be outside), the kinds of skills camp directors are looking for (it helps if you get along with kids!), and what you might earn. The types of jobs available at summer camps range from activity instructor to counselor to lifeguard. Great Summer Jobs starts listing jobs for the next summer in November, so that's when you'll want to start visiting the site on a regular basis.

KIDS' CAMPS
HTTP://WWW.KIDSCAMPS.COM/

If you loved camp when you were growing up, here's your chance to return to the campfires and outdoors. Among the many features to be found at this site, Kids' Camps has numerous listings for camp jobs, most of them in the United States. You can search for jobs by location or by position type, such as counselor, activity specialist, or administration and support staff. Job titles can range from kitchen staff to computer instructor to pool director.

You can also research camps on the Web site. Camps are listed by category, such as residential camps, sports camps, special needs camps, family camps, art camps, academic camps—you name it! The list is pretty extensive. Under art camps you'll have a choice of art, performing arts, film, photography, music, or other. After you select one, you can search by state, country (United States, Canada, or certain other countries), region, and session length. Leave your options set at "No Preference" if you want a complete listing. If in the jobs section you didn't find a job opening for any of the camps you're interested in, you can at least get phone numbers and links to home pages (where available) here so you can contact the camps directly and let them know you're available.

NATIONAL SCHOOL-TO-WORK LEARNING & INFORMATION CENTER

HTTP://WWW.STW.ED.GOV/

The School-to-Work Opportunities Act of 1994 was developed with the intention of better enabling high school students to develop essential job skills through real-world work experience in combination with school-based learning, the goal being to assist as many young people as possible to successfully enter today's competitive job market. With the training received as a result of the program, high school students should with confidence be able to make a smooth transition to their postsecondary options, including two- or four-year college, technical training, or skilled entry-level employment in the workforce. You'll read about how this program involves and benefits people at all levels: students, employers, educators, and state and local officials. Extensive details are provided at the site. For your particular state, you can access information on opportunities available as well as listings of grant representatives. Also presented are reports and guidelines, a calendar of events, grant deadlines and other important dates, and links to numerous related sites.

PART-TIME JOBS FOR TEENAGERS
HTTP://WWW.BYGPUB.COM/BOOKS/TG2RW/PART-TIME.HTM

Straightforward advice on issues pertaining to part-time employment for teenagers can be found in this online resource supplementing Marshall Brain's book titled The Teenager's Guide to the Real World. While just going out and getting a job, perhaps at a fast-food restaurant, might be feasible for some, other kids might not have access to regular transportation or might not have regular hours available to devote to work. What are some other part-time job options? If you want to know, then hurry over to this site. After you read this article, you may want to check out some of the other related resources offered, including several sample chapters from the book. And if you still want more, you can order the book online!

PETERSON'S: THE SUMMER OPPORTUNITIES CHANNEL
HTTP://WWW.PETERSONS.COM/SUMMEROP/

Your commitment to a brilliant academic future might waver when you visit this site. Along with some great information about academic and career-focused summer programs, you'll be tantalized by summer camps that revolve around activities that are less mentally rigorous—like white-water rafting or touring Switzerland on a bicycle. There's no rule that says you can't have the best of both worlds, especially during your summer break! So don't miss this resource, which offers good tips on assessing any summer program or camp you might be considering and directs you to seasonal employment openings as well.

Finding a program that suits your interests is easy enough at this site—just search the database of academic, travel, and camping programs. Type in the keyword "science," for instance, and you'll bring up a list of links to more than 200 summer programs, including ActionQuest, Space Camp and Aviation Challenge, Sail Caribbean, and Yale University summer programs. Then click on a specific program or camp for a quick overview description. In some instances you'll get a more in-depth description, along with photographs, applications, and online brochures. If you need to limit your search to your home state, that's easy enough too. You can sift through the database by geographic region (United States, Canada, or all the rest) or alphabetically.

SEASONALEMPLOYMENT.COM
HTTP://WWW.SEASONALEMPLOYMENT.COM/

Looking for a job to tide you over before school starts up in the fall? Want to spend time in the great outdoors working at a national park or resort? Then you'll want to stop here for details about seasonal employment opportunities. Listings include (where available) street and e-mail addresses, links to home pages, phone and fax numbers, and data about hiring season, elevation, and climate. There are several ways for you to track down pertinent information, so take your pick: summer or winter employment, jobs by U.S. state or in Canada, or company listings.

SUMMER JOBS
HTTP://WWW.SUMMERJOBS.COM/

This colorful site could be your ticket to a great summer job! There are some international summer jobs, but the majority are in the United States. Conducting a location search is the easiest way to find what you're looking for if you know where you want to work this summer. You can do a search by keyword, but the location search is easier to navigate in that it lists the number of available jobs in each country—and then, for the United States and Canada, by state or province. The jobs are quite varied, with everything from apple picker to hot air balloon ground crew to water safety instructor to cashier to Web services intern. There's something for everybody here! Job descriptions include a summary of responsibilities and requirements, hours and dates, and contact information.

If it all sounds too good to be true, drop by the "Success Stories" section and read about people who found summer jobs through this site. You can add your own success story if you have one. And if you can't find what you're looking for at this site, hop on over to the links page and peruse the many links to other job search sites.

USA JOBS: SUMMER

HTTP://WWW.USAJOBS.OPM.GOV/A7.HTM

Here at this subsection of the U.S. Office of Personnel Management's main jobs page you will find—you guessed it—information about summer jobs in the United States. Since this is a government site, the job openings are with various federal agencies. Begin your search by designating geographic area. You can rule out older postings if you limit your search to jobs added sometime within the last week. Results are listed with minimal details: location, hiring agency, and end date of open period. Click on a job title that looks interesting in order to view the listing in full. Among the jobs you might find here are lifeguard, interpreter, forestry technician, and clerk. Some of the hiring agencies include the U.S. Army Test and Evaluation Command, Navy Field Offices, and the USDA Forest Service.

CHAPTER 9

TUITION AND FINANCIAL AID

An important thing to keep in mind as you're considering your postsecondary education options is how much it's going to cost you and how you're going to pay for it. Tuition and fees are typically lower at two-year colleges than at four-year institutions. Also, tuition is generally less at public schools than at private schools, and even less for residents of the school's state. And tuition costs at trade or technical schools may be equal to or exceed that of community colleges.

Different programs' options have varied requirements in terms of tuition. If the school is approved, it may be possible to receive financial aid in the form of loans to pay for tuition. In addition to student loans, some of your other options might be grants or scholarships, military aid, and work-study opportunities. Your last choice would probably be paying for your education in full!

Certain financial aid options must be repaid, in terms of money or in an exchange of your time. You are expected to repay student loans over a period of time, whereas military aid and work-study opportunities involve a commitment of time on your part. Grants and scholarships, which do not need to be repaid, are awarded based on any number of different factors—financial need, athletic prowess, academic achievement, artistic ability, musical talent, religious affiliation, and so on. Another way you can pay for your education is to get a summer job. As discussed in the preceding chapter, this is also a great way for you to gain relevant work experience and make networking contacts.

Many of the Web sites you've already looked at—or that you have yet to check out—present some useful information about tuition and financial aid. This chapter includes listings of sites that are primarily or even exclusively devoted to the subject. In order to receive financial aid information online, you may first have to submit some personal data: name, address, phone number, educational background and goals, and so on. Before you post anything of a personal nature online, be sure to check out a site's legitimacy and its privacy policy. Read the fine print. Sometimes these sites will offer to share the information you post with educational institutions or other organizations. And sometimes this will be the default option, so if you don't uncheck a box, your information might automatically be passed along. Also be sure you understand the terms and your obligations before you sign up for any kind of financial assistance. Do your research—compare your various options, looking at the short-term as well as long-term benefits and repercussions. (If you have to repay a student loan, when must you begin? How much time do you have before it must be repaid in full?) For advice on how to determine a site's legitimacy, see Chapter 10 ("Job Searching on the Internet"). You can also talk with your school guidance counselor or a librarian about this and about any questions you have concerning the pros and cons of your assorted financial aid options.

FASTAID.COM
HTTP://WWW.FASTAID.COM/

This terrific guide to scholarship research on the Internet, an offshoot of Project FAST (Financial Aid for Students Today), is from Daniel J. Cassidy, author of The Scholarship Book. The site is very user-friendly and highly readable. You're sure to learn a lot here.

There's a glossary of common terminology, a step-by-step outline of the process, discussion of scholarship facts and myths, descriptions of the six federal programs (Pell, Supplemental Education Opportunity Grants [SEOG], Work-Study, Perkins, Stafford, and Parent Loans for Undergraduate Students [PLUS]), lots of links, and much more. Once you've read about the various forms of financial aid available, how about searching for the money? You can do that here as well.

FASTWEB
HTTP://WWW.FASTWEB.COM/

Before you start digging for specifics, you might want to get an overview of college admissions, scholarship, job, career-planning, money, and financial aid issues. If so, visit the "fastFOCUS" section and browse through the articles there.

When you're ready to search for scholarships, venture on over to "fastSEARCH." You'll have to sign up to use the scholarship search tool. Be prepared to answer questions about your interests and extracurricular activities, academic achievements, memberships in various organizations, work and military experience, top college choices, and intended majors. You'll also be asked a few questions about your parents' background, so you might want to complete this form when they're nearby. It'll probably take longer for you to fill out the form than to get your personalized results! Once you have your results, click on the links to get details about each award. Check your fastWEB mailbox often because new awards are regularly added to the site's database. And when any of these match your criteria, they will be added to your mailbox.

The college directory is designed for conducting financial aid research. After you've selected the state you're interested in, you'll get a list of colleges and universities there. The list contains links to school home pages, as well as separate links (where available) for financial aid, admissions, and application information for that school. (You can also look up schools by name.)

Need a break from all this financial research? Then check out "fastLIFE," which features current news, weather, and astrology.

FINAID

HTTP://WWW.FINAID.ORG/

Subtitled "The SmartStudent Guide to Financial Aid," this site offers an abundance of resources that should help you figure out how you're going to pay for your college education. The various financial aid options are described, plus there are numerous links to appropriate sources and/or contact details.

You might want to begin by looking at the question-and-answer section. Here you can read the answers to such questions as "I probably don't qualify for aid. Should I apply for aid anyway?" and "Do I have to reapply for financial aid every year?" The student's financial aid checklist is also useful.

Education loans—student, parent, and private loans—are discussed in full, as is the consolidation loan. FinAid suggests several preferred lenders for each type. There are also sections devoted to various other kinds of aid. Descriptions and links to further resources are provided. Some of the categories include military veterans; disabled, women, minority, older, or gay, lesbian, or bisexual students; graduate, business, law, or medical school; grants; and sports and athletics. Scholarships are briefly discussed, with further information to be found at the Web site of FinAid's partner fastWEB.

If you need help with the math, be sure to try out one or more of the many custom calculators available. You and/or your parents might find use for the College Cost Projector, Financial Aid Estimation Calculator, or Loan Payment Calculator.

FINANCIAL AID 101

HTTP://WWW.SALLIEMAE.COM/CONSUMER/FA101/CONTENT.HTML

This primer, presented by the Student Loan Marketing Association (Sallie Mae), covers the topic of—you guessed it—financial aid. If you're looking for a concise introduction to the subject, you should drop by. The material is presented in the form of lessons, each one ending with a quiz (automatically graded online). You will find a definition of financial aid, discussion of financial aid qualification and application, notes on follow-up procedures, and information on what to do if you need a student loan.

What will you learn here? You'll discover that not all scholarships or loans are based on financial need, get advice on steps to take in applying for aid and how to stay on top of everything, see the questions to ask yourself before accepting a financial aid package, and learn about some of your options if you need more money. Links to other loan and scholarship resources are provided. Additionally, you can find out all sorts of other financial aid information by visiting the Sallie Mae home page. In fact, some of the lessons will refer you back to pertinent Sallie Mae pages.

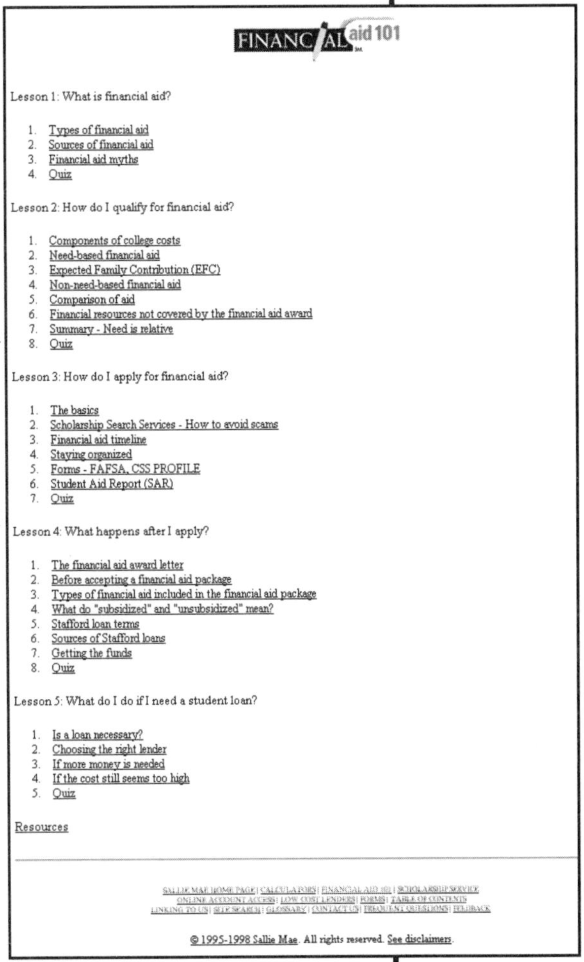

FINANCIAL aid 101
Lesson 1: What is financial aid?
1. Types of financial aid
2. Sources of financial aid
3. Financial aid myths
4. Quiz
Lesson 2: How do I qualify for financial aid?
1. Components of college costs
2. Need-based financial aid
3. Expected Family Contribution (EFC)
4. Non-need-based financial aid
5. Comparison of aid
6. Financial resources not covered by the financial aid award
7. Summary - Need is relative
8. Quiz
Lesson 3: How do I apply for financial aid?
1. The basics
2. Scholarship Search Services - How to avoid scams
3. Financial aid timeline
4. Staying organized
5. Forms - FAFSA, CSS PROFILE
6. Student Aid Report (SAR)
7. Quiz
Lesson 4: What happens after I apply?
1. The financial aid award letter
2. Before accepting a financial aid package
3. Types of financial aid included in the financial aid package
4. What do "subsidized" and "unsubsidized" mean?
5. Stafford loan terms
6. Sources of Stafford loans
7. Getting the funds
8. Quiz
Lesson 5: What do I do if I need a student loan?
1. Is a loan necessary?
2. Choosing the right lender
3. If more money is needed
4. If the cost still seems too high
5. Quiz
Resources
© 1995-1998 Sallie Mae. All rights reserved. See disclaimers.

STUDENT FINANCIAL ASSISTANCE PROGRAMS

HTTP://WWW.ED.GOV/OFFICES/OSFAP/STUDENTS/SFA.HTML

Here you'll have access to information on the U.S. Department of Education's student aid programs. The student guide offers extensive coverage of federal loan, work-study, and grant programs. Topics discussed include eligibility, financial need, dependency status, the application process, special circumstances, and deadlines. Materials pertaining to other federal and state financial aid opportunities are available as well. If you require further information, be sure to check out some of the links.

Section IV: General Career Exploration and Planning

CHAPTER 10

JOB SEARCHING ON THE INTERNET

Still hungry for more? Expand your career exploration by looking for job information using search engines. Search engines generally utilize a spider, or robot, program, which as it travels the Internet picks up Web pages to be added to the search engine's database. Often site owners can submit their sites to be included in search engine databases. When you use these search engines, you're searching their databases. To help you find sites most closely matching your criteria, most search engines offer an advanced search option, which allows you to fine-tune your search (using words in combination, excluding certain terms, and so on). Methods by which to do this vary, so be sure to read the site's instructions. Search results tend to be rated by relevancy, with the "best" hits presented first.

In regards to career exploration, you might want to start your search using keywords like "resume," "jobs," "career," and "work." Another strategy is to try searching on a specific field that interests you, perhaps "computer animation." Or look for a particular company, such as "Ferguson Publishing." There are also directories that list Web sites arranged according to topic. Directories provide descriptions (either picked up from the site or written specifically for that directory) of the sites. You can save a lot of time by using a directory, which guides you to specific sites that respond to your needs and interests. Simply browse through the directory by clicking on topics that appeal to you.

What were once basic search engine sites have by and large grown to include numerous other features, such as specialized channels, free e-mail, personalized options, stock data, weather information, and so on. It's not uncommon for a search engine site to also offer a browsable directory. This is an area of the Internet that is constantly developing—with so many similar services competing for your "business," changes and enhancements can be expected regularly, as far as what is being offered, who is providing what tools, and who's partnering with whom. You'll find that while various search engines will generate some of the same results and feature the same kinds of added services, there will be subtle and sometimes not-so-subtle differences. So you might want to use a combination or choose to stick with whichever one you prefer. Some of the more popular search engines are described in this chapter.

How do you sort through the overwhelming amount of information on the Internet? If you do not know specifically what you want to find, you can become bogged down looking at lots of sites without learning what you want to know. Following are a few guidelines to keep in mind as you conduct career research online.

- For starters, be selective. You do not have to go to every site to get a good general picture of career management information from the Web. If you enjoy surfing the Web, go ahead and do it. You will find that there are many interesting places to visit. Don't think that you need to explore every career site on the Web, however—that if you don't see every career site you might miss that one piece of information that will magically transform your career management. There are a lot of good career-exploration sites out there. Visit several and, from those, pick a couple that especially appeal to you, for whatever reasons. Then just stick with them and learn what there is to learn. If at some point these couple of sites don't meet your needs, check a few more in order to find new favorites. Because most career sites will give you the same basic kind of career guidance, your time will probably be better spent digging through a couple good sites, absorbing pertinent information, than looking at dozens upon dozens of sites.

• Next, be sure to consider the source. Anyone can post information online. Information from sites sponsored by government agencies, colleges and universities, and large employers is usually considered more reliable than information from an individual. (Unless you're looking for information on that particular individual, that is!) Because many sites provide links to other sites, however, it can be easy to move from site to site and become confused as to where information originated (or what site you are on). Double-checking any information with sources outside the Internet is a good idea. Remember that even though a site may use a name that sounds reputable, that does not mean it is necessarily credible. When in doubt, you might want to ask a librarian.

• Protecting yourself and your privacy is of vital importance. Even on the Internet there are people who are looking to take advantage of others. When you are job seeking, you are looking for an opportunity, and that can make you vulnerable. Before allowing charges to be put on your credit card, you should always check the legitimacy of the claims, products, or services being offered. Also examine the site's level of security and privacy guarantees. An example of a common Internet scam is the sale of information about high-paying, "hot" job openings—that is, for a charge on your credit card, you will be sent via e-mail a listing of twenty to thirty job openings. Of course, there is no way for you to be sure these are legitimate openings for which workers are being sought. If after reading all the fine print you still feel uneasy about a site's claim or offer, your best bet would be simply to move on and look elsewhere for the information or service. Better safe than sorry!

Chat rooms on the Internet provide forums for discussion and support about careers and job search experiences. It is again important to protect your privacy and to carefully consider how much personal information you feel comfortable about sharing as well as about what you are being offered. Remember that Internet postings are not private. Frequently you have no way to control the many possible destinations of information that you post. So while it is a good idea to look for a job when you already have one, you may not want to let your current employer know you are looking for another job—and on the Internet, there's a chance your employer might see information you post.

• It helps if you know your field. Consider how employers in your occupational area advertise their openings. It is unlikely you will have much success if you think you will log on to the Internet and find the right job for you without being aware of where job listings in your occupational field are usually located. Many occupational fields have very traditional media (most often print publications) via which openings are advertised, and some of these charge fees for Internet access.

• Consider your personal job search desires. Using the Internet, you can research many companies. Getting a job with one of these employers might well require you to make a geographic move. If you are unwilling to leave the area you are currently living in, it will probably be a more fruitful use of your time to go to your local chamber of commerce and learn about local employers than to explore job opportunities, or to post your resume, on the Internet. But if you are willing to move to work for a particular employer or if you want to live in a particular city, you can use the Internet to learn about openings with that employer or look at the classified ads in the major newspaper in that city.

• Use the Internet along with other resources. The Internet is a good place to explore and to use as one of the tools of career management. Job openings on the Internet are bound to be very competitive because the Internet is a worldwide tool. You may be one among thousands of applicants for a job posted online, whereas a job opening advertised even in a major metropolitan newspaper may attract only hundreds of applicants. It is important not to neglect other job search tools, like your personal network, placement office, or local library. Much of the information posted on the Internet about businesses and employers is self-generated, so naturally it will have a positive slant. Reading how a business represents itself on the Internet is valuable prior to interviewing with that employer. But before accepting an offer with that employer, you might also want to talk to some of the company's employees as well.

Search Guidance and Privacy Issues

BBBONLINE
HTTP://WWW.BBBONLINE.COM/

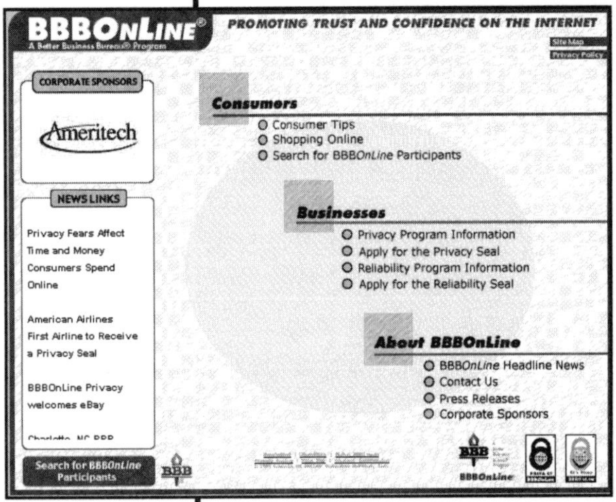

Having the goal of "promoting trust and confidence on the Internet," this subsidiary of the Council of Better Business Bureaus awards seals to legitimate businesses with good online privacy policies in place. You can learn about this system as well as search the Better Business Bureau company database. There's also useful, succinct information on passwords, online purchases and other commerce issues, cookies, privacy policies, and kids online.

CAREER EXPLORATION ON THE INTERNET
HTTP://WWW.UTC.EDU/CAREERED/HSBHOM.HTM

The Center for Community Career Education at the University of Tennessee at Chattanooga, through funding by the Education Edge Office of the Tennessee Department of Education, has compiled a directory of links to assist you in your Web search for career information. Each link is briefly described to give you a good idea of what you'll find if you visit the site.

You can follow links to sites about career planning and offering general career materials. Discover self-assessment tests, explore your different occupational choices, get advice about creating resumes and portfolios, learn about internships, and more. Other sections are devoted to career research for girls and minorities. There are also links to help you find a useful search engine and evaluate the authority and value of a Web site.

"Career Clusters" features selected sites where you can read about certain specific career fields: arts and communications, business and marketing, health care, hospitality and tourism, human services (for example, legal, military, ministerial, and psychology professions), manufacturing, construction, and transportation, and science and technology.

CDT'S GUIDE TO ONLINE PRIVACY
HTTP://WWW.CDT.ORG/PRIVACY/GUIDE/

The Center for Democracy & Technology (CDT) presents this guide to online privacy issues. "Top Ten Ways to Protect Your Privacy Online" describes several things you can do that will ensure greater online privacy. Among the suggestions offered are that you should double-check to be sure that online forms are secure, reject unneeded cookies, and use encryption. Privacy as discussed in the U.S. Constitution, Fair Information Practices, and legislative protection are covered in other sections. Several legal and Internet terms are defined in a glossary. This is just a small part of the CDT site. If you want to find out more about the organization's goals and activities, click on the home page link and browse from there.

CONDUCTING RESEARCH ON THE INTERNET
HTTP://WWW.ALBANY.EDU/LIBRARY/INTERNET/RESEARCH.HTML

Although this University at Albany Libraries site doesn't deal specifically with Internet-based job searching, it suggests many useful techniques that can be incorporated as part of your online job search. You can read about several different ways to find information on the Internet, including e-mail discussion groups and newsgroups, URLs, browsing, subject directories, and search engines. Not only are detailed descriptions offered, but links to further resources are featured as well.

Additionally, you can learn how to compose queries utilizing Boolean logic and get some advice on fine-tuning a search. Access is provided to other University at Albany Internet tutorials; for example, "A Basic Guide to the Internet," "Evaluating Internet Resources," "Boolean Searching on the Internet," and "How to Choose a Search Engine or Research Database."

GUIDE TO JOB-HUNTING ON THE INTERNET

HTTP://WWW.QUINTCAREERS.COM/JOBHUNT.HTML

You will discover that the Web has a lot to offer in the way of job search-related resources as you explore this Quintessential Careers guide, which walks you through the process of conducting an online job search. Follow the steps to get information on or go to recommended sites dealing with such topics as general career exploration, company research, online networking, internships and summer jobs, posting a resume on the Web, job offer negotiations, salary calculators and surveys, and relocation.

ICYOUSEE: T IS FOR THINKING

HTTP://MEMBERS.AOL.COM/XXMINDYXX/EVALUATE/QUESTION.HTML

It's important to remember that anybody can create a site on the Web—meaning that not all information to be found online will be authoritative. Subtitled "The ICYouSee Guide to Critical Thinking about What You See on the Web," this site (created by John Henderson, a reference librarian at the Ithaca College Library) discusses some of the criteria to consider when evaluating a site's value as a research tool. This is supplemented by links to additional sites dealing with Web site evaluation.

There are even more links included, to recommended sites in a wide assortment of categories. You'll find suggested resources in music theory and composition, history, international business, philosophy and religion, recreation and leisure studies, and more. Some of these could in fact be helpful to you in your career exploration.

PRIVACY IN CYBERSPACE

HTTP://WWW.PRIVACYRIGHTS.ORG/FS/FS18-CYB.HTM

This fact sheet, from Privacy Rights Clearinghouse, a Utility Consumers' Action Network program, examines various forms of online activities and services (private, semiprivate, and public). E-mail and Web site privacy issues are discussed. Recommendations are given for protecting your privacy. This includes advice and/or cautions concerning newsgroup participation, selecting a password, anonymous remailers, and encryption.

Other site features are a glossary of Web terminology, contact information and URLs for organizations involved in online privacy issues, and links to relevant sites where you can find further information on some of the topics covered.

TRAVELING IN CYBERSPACE? BE SAVVY!

HTTP://WWW.FTC.GOV/BCP/CONLINE/EDCAMS/CYBRSPCE/INDEX.HTML

The Federal Trade Commission has compiled a few privacy-related resources to help surfers safely travel the Internet. Basic guidance is offered on how to be "Web ready." The article "Site Seeing on the Internet" suggests privacy travel tips to keep in mind as you explore the Internet. A supplemental glossary explains pertinent terms. Advice is given on traveling the Internet with kids. Other topics discussed include fraudulent online business ventures and junk e-mail solicitations. Furthermore, there are links to other FTC privacy-related materials. Instead of being dry, this important information is presented in a very accessible and entertaining manner.

USING THE INTERNET IN YOUR JOB SEARCH

HTTP://WWW.DBM.COM/JOBGUIDE/JOBSRCHW.HTML

This helpful resource, a subsection of the Riley Guide (see Chapter 11), is from librarian Margaret F. Dikel (formerly Margaret F. Riley). Straightforward guidance is given on how to decide which of the many directions to take when exploring online what career options you have.

You can read about reasons why you might want to conduct an online job search. Also offered is advice on coming up with keywords specifically designed to make your Web search more productive, to yield a greater number of hits. Further tips are presented on how best to find what you're looking for on the Web, how to research potential employers, and how to scout

out information about wages, employment trends, relocation, and general career topics.

Other sections cover locating job postings and recruiter sites, deciding how and where to do your networking online, posting a resume online, determining which online resources are most suitable for your purposes, and managing your online schedule. Links to further materials supplement topics discussed.

Search Tools

ALTAVISTA
HTTP://WWW.ALTAVISTA.COM/

This mammoth search engine looks through Web pages for occurrences of the keywords you enter. In addition to its search functions, AltaVista has expanded to include several content and service platforms. One of these is the LookSmart Directory, which in partnership with various career sites features articles and resources of interest to job seekers.

ASK JEEVES
HTTP://WWW.ASKJEEVES.COM/

This Internet search tool is quite unique in the way it presents search results. First off, the idea is to type in a question (in other words, to ask Jeeves!) rather than a search term (although that approach will work too). Be sure that the question contains relevant keywords. Your question is submitted to the Ask Jeeves database, which consists of "answers" (that is, links to Web sites) to millions of commonly asked questions. Answers are pooled not only from the Ask Jeeves database but from several different search engines as well. Results are displayed in drop-down list boxes that serve to complete various questions similar to yours. These questions, while perhaps not exactly matching yours, incorporate several of the keywords from the question you asked and therefore are meant to lead you to an answer that closely corresponds to the information you're seeking. So for the best results, select the question that most closely matches your original question, scrolling through the drop-down list boxes to look through other possible answers. If you need clarification, check out the extensive "Help" section. Ask Jeeves can certainly be a fun way to look for information!

DEJA.COM
HTTP://WWW.DEJA.COM/

Dedicated to the "exchange of user-generated information, knowledge and opinion," this site makes it easy for you to contact other users in some 40,000 newsgroups. Newsgroups are a great way to meet others with similar interests and to learn more about possible careers—just ask somebody! To learn how to navigate the site, your best bet is to check out the "User Tour." You can search or browse through the thousands of current discussion threads or communities to track down conversations having to do with subjects of interest, perhaps choosing a college or career exploration—or entertainment, money, sports, or travel.

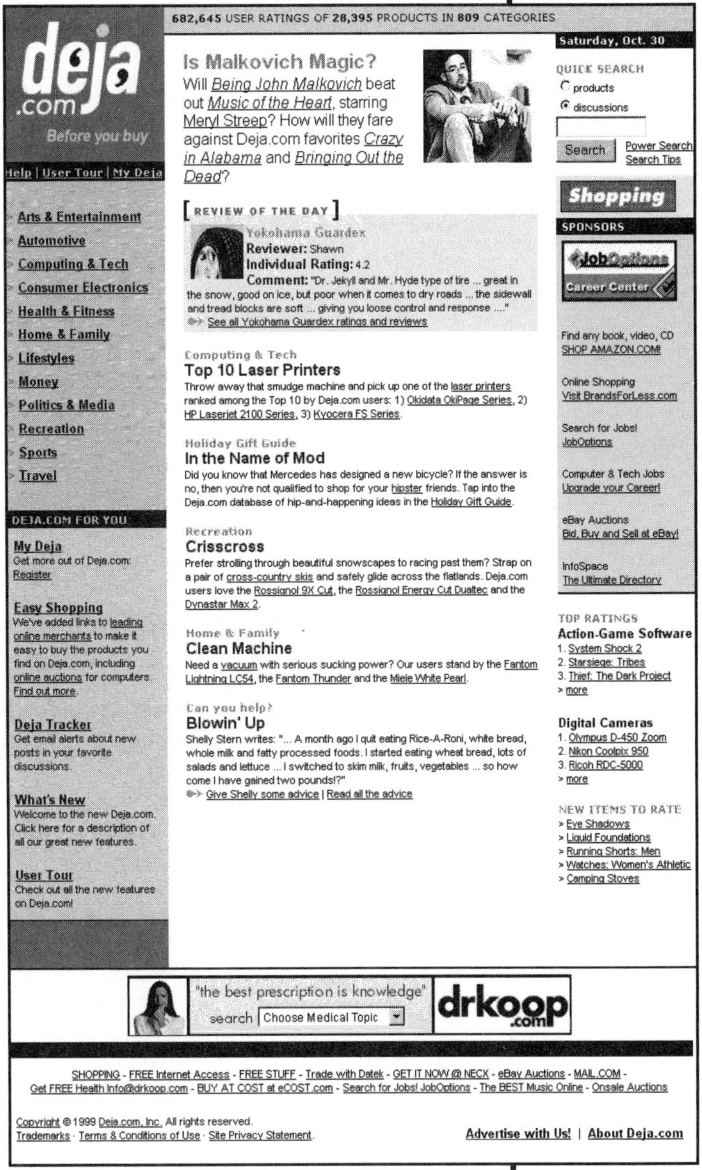

EXCITE
HTTP://WWW.EXCITE.COM/

Excite offers both a search engine and a directory of links. The directory is categorized into sections such as careers, education, health, news, and real estate. Excite communities give users a chance to interact with others sharing similar interests. Several shortcuts will give you quick and easy access to popular categories like stock quotes, an airline and hotel reservation service, movie showtimes, a job finder, maps and directions, and more.

GO NETWORK
HTTP://WWW.GO.COM/

GO Network, from Infoseek Corporation teamed up with the Walt Disney Company, features a search engine powered by Infoseek, which allows you to enter a topic of interest. With the advanced search, you can specify if you want to search the Web or search specifically for companies, news, stocks, or shareware. The site also offers a directory, online communities featuring chat rooms and message boards, and direct links to partners including Disney, ABC, and ESPN.

HOTBOT
HTTP://WWW.HOTBOT.COM/

HotBot is Wired Digital's search engine. (Other Wired Digital properties include HotWired, Webmonkey, and Wired News, all available through links at the site.) In addition to its search engine, HotBot gives you direct access to other resources through its directory. Here you will be able to find education- and career-related resources. There are also special search services for FTP and discussion groups.

LIBRARIANS' INDEX TO THE INTERNET
HTTP://SUNSITE.BERKELEY.EDU/INTERNETINDEX/

LII is a subject directory of more than 5,000 Internet sites selected for inclusion by librarians. You can search by keyword or browse through the directory for subjects that interest you. Each site is described. If you use the search mechanism, only those relevant resources that are part of the index appear (that is, it isn't going to generate results from the entire Internet). The section on jobs and careers will point you toward recommended sites dealing with employment laws, job hunting, resumes, wages, job opportunities, and more.

METACRAWLER

HTTP://WWW.METACRAWLER.COM/

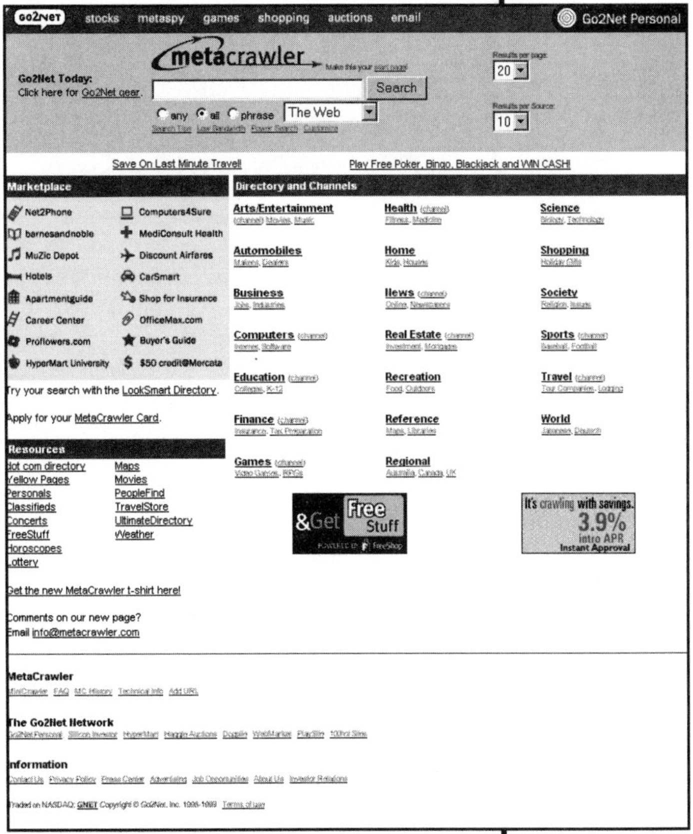

Known as a multi- or meta-search engine, MetaCrawler compiles results generated from other popular search engines and directories, including AltaVista, Excite, Infoseek, WebCrawler, and Yahoo! This is a great asset because it means you don't have to go from one search engine site to another to another. Results are presented in order of relevance, and databases where results were found are named. This serves to give you an idea of which search tools are pulling in the best hits. If you wish, you can designate which of the available search engines you want to use for your searching. As with most of the other search engines, MetaCrawler offers various other Internet services, such as channels for computing, education, finance, news, and shopping.

SEARCHIQ

HTTP://WWW.SEARCHIQ.COM/

Here is a resource that describes and rates (by IQ) various Internet search tools. You'll find information on specialty search engines (covering, for example, business, crafts, education, jobs, government, special interest, sports, and travel), multi- and meta-search engines (which use several different search engines to pull in results), and general search engines. There are links to a lot of really useful sites explaining the ins and outs of Internet searching. Definitely don't miss this site!

YAHOO!

HTTP://WWW.YAHOO.COM/

You can search the Internet (including Web sites, discussion groups, and e-mail addresses) with Yahoo! or you can browse its massive directory of indexed sites. Yahoo! offers numerous special features, among them separate sections devoted to careers, finance, local resources, entertainment, Internet events, and much more. If you're new to the Internet or want to know more about surfing the Web, HTML, or other topics, be sure to visit the "Yahoo! How-To" section. Yahooligans! (a kids' version of Yahoo!) is also available.

GENERAL CAREER RESOURCES

CHAPTER 11

If you prefer one-stop career shopping instead of searching for career sites using the search engines discussed in Chapter 10 or visiting the more focused, topic-oriented career sites covered in the rest of the book, then you'll keep plenty busy perusing this chapter's selections. The sites here could by and large be described as either mega-sites or clearinghouses. In other words, they offer you pretty much everything you'll need in the way of Internet career-related resources, gathering together much of what you've seen already and what you have yet to explore in the space of a single, vast Web site. Each site will contain wide-ranging career information or will consist of a comprehensive collection of career-related links.

What can you expect to discover on your travels here? How about some or most of the following—and then some—at a single site?

- college selection advice,
- discussion forums about starting a career,
- career-preparation tools covering resumes, cover letters, and interviewing,
- resources geared toward minorities,
- company profiles,
- links to employer home pages,
- job listings and resume databases,

- career articles concerning such issues as harassment and employee benefits,
- virtual bookstores and bibliographies of reference materials for further reading, and so on.

To learn about the value these individual resources can add to your career-exploration process, be sure to check out the chapters in this book dealing with them specifically. For example, Chapter 6 addresses college selection; Chapter 12 features material for minorities; resumes, cover letters, and interviewing are discussed in Chapters 14, 15, and 17 (respectively); Chapter 19 leads you to data on specific companies; employee benefits are explained in Chapter 22; and harassment is one of the topics explored in Chapter 25. Now just imagine having access to most or even all of this and more at one site!

The fact that there's so much to be found at each of these sites may lead you to wonder how you can know which site is "best." Well, it's actually a matter of opinion and personal preference. Some of the factors you may want to consider are the site's

- accuracy, depth, and comprehensiveness of content (or content being linked to),
- ease of navigation,
- presentation,
- authority,
- currency (when was the last update? how often are updates made?),
- organizational structure, and

- loading/response time.

Use the site assessment tools you learned about in Chapter 10 to help you determine the value of these resources. Keep in mind that all of these sites are worth a visit. Which ones you return to will depend on how they rate according to the criteria you've established, according to your priorities and needs. So why not start with those that sound most appealing and work your way through the chapter, bookmarking the ones you like best and find to be most useful. Happy shopping!

ARGUS CLEARINGHOUSE
HTTP://WWW.CLEARINGHOUSE.NET/

This online library should be helpful when you're researching careers. You can find information on a number of categories, such as arts and humanities, computers and information technology, education, engineering, health and medicine, and recreation. Go to the category you're interested in, say health and medicine, and you'll find subcategories, including disabilities, diseases and disorders, and fitness and nutrition. If you check out fitness and nutrition you'll find even more subcategories! This time there's diet, fitness, nutrition, and vegetarian. Let's try fitness. Now there's a listing of guides to relevant Web sites. Each guide is rated on a scale of one to five. Select a guide and you'll find a more detailed rating (given for resource description, resource evaluation, guide design, etc.), along with a link to the site.

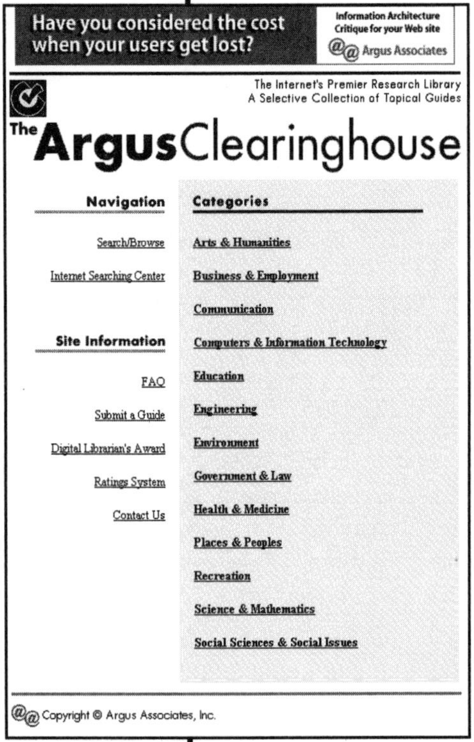

CAREERBABE
HTTP://WWW.CAREERBABE.COM/

CareerBabe is a user-friendly site with career advice and all sorts of employment information. If you need some direction, CareerBabe may be able to show you the way. Don't let the title mislead you—the information here is appropriate for men as well as women.

"Top Career Sites" has links to dozens of useful job sites. They are categorized by type, such as employment data, resume writing, job fairs, and salary information. If you have a question for CareerBabe, send it to her! Select letters are posted for public viewing, but the sender's name is not listed. Subjects for questions range from career counseling to problems on the job to Internet job leads. Take CareerBabe's resume tutorial if you are a little rusty on your resume-writing skills. It's informative and even kind of fun. There are several overall rules to keep in mind, followed by detailed steps to guide you through creating a killer resume.

Other helpful information at this site deals with generating leads, wage and unemployment data, and the "Acid Test for Job Security."

CAREERBUILDER
HTTP://WWW.CAREERBUILDER.COM/

This site is like a candy store—there are lots of different options on the front page and it's hard to decide where to go first. This is an excellent resource for researching careers and companies.

"Getting Hired" might be a good first stop. This section offers a lot of articles suggesting what you should do to commence your job research. There are also "how-to" guides on interviewing, resumes, cover letters, and job offer negotiation, supplemented by links to sites providing additional reference tools.

Continue your research under "Communities," where you'll find information directed at college students and entry-level job hunters. There's additional materials here on resumes and interviewing, as well as guidance on starting out on your career path.

In the section devoted to finding a job, you can search for vacancies by specifying certain criteria. This includes job description and location (lists supplied); contract, temporary, full-time, or part-time; keyword; salary; and which Web job sites are to be checked (choices include CNET, USA Today, CareerPath, and others). A wide variety of jobs, such as validation engineer, family service worker, Web developer, photographer, network administrator, or director of finance, may crop up.

There are plenty of articles about various other career-related topics. Some are devoted to working women, self-employed workers, and human resources. Others deal with workplace issues, getting ahead on the job, career transitions, and balancing work and family.

CAREERCITY
HTTP://WWW.CAREERCITY.COM/

On a visit to CareerCity (which is sponsored by Adams Media Corporation), where do you start? In "Career Planning" you can find some of the more introductory career-planning information, such as about various occupational choices, self-assessment, and career management. "Salaries & Job

Searching" offers detailed resume advice (for example, visual impact, resume bloopers, what to include—and leave out), along with sample resumes. This section also gives advice on how to network, how to negotiate for a good salary, and how to compose a cover letter. What can you expect from an interview and how can you prepare? There are plenty of interviewing tips given, including guidance on dressing for the interview, handling the stress interview, how you should follow up after an interview, and more. The advice gets very detailed and should answer most questions you might have about interviews.

You say you're ready to look for a job now? CareerCity lets you search for jobs in a number of ways. You can search member company job listings by category or state. (Member companies register with CareerCity for the opportunity to post their job openings.) Other choices are to look through the job listings posted on any of thousands of company home pages or to pursue leads from industry resources. And this only touches the surface of the resources and information you'll discover at CareerCity.

CAREERLINK

HTTP://WWW.SANDIEGO-ONLINE.COM/FORUMS/CAREERS/

This site is from San Diego Magazine. Yes, you can browse the magazine to find out about good restaurants in San Diego, but here what you get is a great career reference section! Created by certified personnel consultant Barbara Walter—not to be confused with Barbara Walters the newswoman—this site does more than just scratch the surface. There are CareerLink interviews with professionals regarding their industries and their jobs, a Q&A section, and employment articles that offer advice about finding the right company, how to get the most out of a job fair, what recruiters can do for you, and more. "Working Lifestyles" explores the more personal side of the job search. You'll find material dealing with such topics as "Life As a Temp—Insiders' Perspectives" and "Working for Yourself."

CAREER MAGAZINE

HTTP://WWW.CAREERMAG.COM/

Career Magazine's massive Web site has all the features popular in job search sites and more! There are directories of recruiters (listing executive recruiting firms by job category) and consultants (listing consulting firms that want to hire as well as consultants for hire), links to other career Web sites, a resume database, and a mailing list that will notify you when the site is updated. You can read current and archived articles from Career Magazine or discuss career issues through the bulletin board.

Employers and recruiters pay to post jobs with Career Magazine. If you want to see who the member companies are, click on "Employers." To search the job listings, you can specify location, skills, title, and keyword.

Diversity issues in the workplace are given coverage as well. There are discussion boards devoted to working women, discrimination, older workers, and diversity programs. Career Magazine articles and related links provide additional information of interest.

CAREERMART

HTTP://WWW.CAREERMART.COM/

CareerMart is sort of like a shopping mall—lots of places to shop around for different sorts of career goodies! If you want to conduct some research on colleges, stop by the "College Info-Center." There are links upon links to the home pages of universities, colleges, and community colleges, as well as a schedule of on-campus recruiting fairs.

Need a little career advice? That's what the "Advise Tent" is for. Included here are articles on such topics as "hot jobs," trends in various industries, and employment statistics. The "Newsstand" features links not only to career-related resources but to assorted publications covering college issues, computers, entertainment, government, news, sports, and more.

Or perhaps you want to head straight for the job search. You can search by state, region, or country. You can also specify the job category. Or look through the company index for background information and/or job listings. Hundreds of companies are named here, so there's a lot of opportunities to consider. Post your resume to the resume database and/or sign up for the E-Mail Agent matching service.

CAREERMOSAIC

HTTP://WWW.CAREERMOSAIC.COM/

This comprehensive site features not only online job fairs, a resume database, and job listings but also links to jobs pages of hiring companies. The jobs database allows you to search by job title, company, city, and other criteria. The number of employers represented is quite immense. You can also go through the Usenet newsgroup search page, where thousands of job postings from various newsgroups are indexed.

CareerMosaic's "College Connection" area assists college students and recent graduates in making educational decisions, conducting a job search, and finding entry-level employment. Link to college career centers and university home pages, internship information, and assorted reference materials (financial aid resources, salary scales, tips on networking, researching companies, and more). The "Resume Writing Center" presents just what you'd expect—advice on resume writing. Refer to the list of action verbs to avoid using the same old tired verbs over and over, study the proofreading checklist to help you spot common mistakes before it's too late, and examine the section on electronic resumes to make educated decisions on how to put one together.

CAREERS & JOBS

HTTP://WWW.STARTHERE.COM/JOBS/

If you're not one to be bothered by categories and multilayered sites, this is the resource for you. This meta-list lists all the links right there on one page. There are no descriptions or ratings. The only distinction is between job sites and resume service sites.

CAREERS.WSJ.COM

HTTP://CAREERS.WSJ.COM/

From the Wall Street Journal and the National Business Employment Weekly, this large site contains a wide variety of career-planning resources. There are articles on career focus, resume tips, navigating the job hunt, interviewing, networking, trends in employment, workplace diversity, salary negotiation, finding a job overseas, and starting a business. For those of you thinking farther ahead, you can read about planning for retirement. "Who's Hiring" features links to home pages of prominent companies plus a searchable jobs database. Job descriptions and details on required education and experience are provided. There are also links to online resources regarding employment law, women and minorities, career and industry profiles, and relocating. Given the diversity of information to be found throughout, you won't want to miss this site.

COLLEGE GRAD JOB HUNTER
HTTP://WWW.COLLEGEGRAD.COM/

Aptly subtitled "Your Link to Life after College," this site presents Brian Krueger's book College Grad Job Hunter plus other career materials. This is a tremendous resource that will be a great help in planning out your career if you are a college student or recent graduate—all the information is tailored to meet your needs.

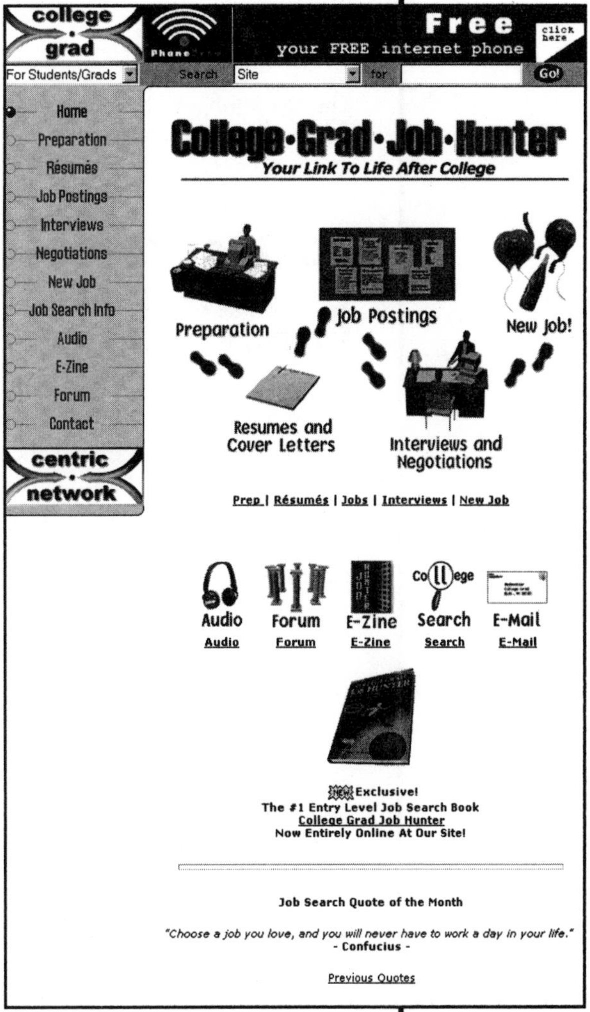

Start your journey with "Preparation," the section that will help you get the ball rolling. Ask the Hiring Manager is an online career discussion forum. Questions are submitted by visitors and answered by Krueger. You'll probably find answers to questions you've already been wondering about, such as "Who do you address a cover letter to when no contact person is given?" and "An employer was initially interested in me, but now I cannot get them to return calls. Why is this happening?" In this section you can also read articles from the "Job Hunter" e-zine column, including making an irresistible resume, handling illegal interview questions, posting your resume online, and using the library in your job search.

Once you feel prepared enough to move on, get some advice about resumes and cover letters as well as job search strategies. Then go ahead and browse the job postings. You can conduct an entry-level job search, an internship search, or an employer search.

The sections pertaining to interviewing and negotiations offer advice to help you ace your interview and get what you're worth. There are dozens of interview tips for different aspects of an interview: dressing for the interview, job fair success, on-campus interviewing, mastering the interview, and phone interview success. You'll also find out what follow-up steps to take after an interview, how to evaluate your benefits package, and what to do if you don't get that job offer.

The "New Job" section features guidance to help you get ready for work and make a smooth transition. Some of the advice? Get your offer in writing and make sure you understand all the conditions of employment.

COLLEGE OF WILLIAM & MARY OFFICE OF CAREER SERVICES

HTTP://WWW.WM.EDU/CSRV/CAREER/INDEX.HTML

This site is loaded with helpful links. Select a focus (employment, graduate school, internships, or career choice) and then find the links organized according to category. Employment categories include general resources, job opportunities, career fairs, employer listings on the Web, and building a personal network. These categories are further subdivided (for example, general resources has links for help guides, career directories, and relocation materials).

If you are thinking about continuing your education, take a look at the section on graduate schools, which lists links for general resources, graduate schools on the Web, and financial aid sites.

Want to get some real-life experience before committing yourself to a career? Check out the internships section with its links to internship resources as well as to summer and postgraduate job sites. Some of the internship resources are Alaskan State Parks, the National Assembly of Health and Human Service Organizations, and Smithsonian Institution internship opportunities.

The section on career choices offers links to the Occupational Outlook Handbook and other sites with information on interest and skills testing, career-planning resources, and ideas of what kind of work you might do with particular college degrees.

COLLEGEVIEW CAREER CENTER FOR CAREER PLANNING
HTTP://WWW.COLLEGEVIEW.COM/CAREERS/

What you'll get at this site is an interesting array of resources to help you with your career search. There are dozens of categories with advice and links to relevant sites where available. You'll find advice on and links pertaining to career planning, assessment tools, education and training, internships, resumes, cover letters, and more. There are sections listing declining fields (including bank tellers, farmers, and typists) and growing fields (for example, business services, medicine, and recreation).

1ST STEPS IN THE HUNT
HTTP://WWW.INTERBIZNET.COM/HUNT/

The Internet Business Network (IBN), the same company that brings you the Electronic Recruiting News, presents here the latest in news and technology to assist you with your job search. Feature articles, which are updated almost daily, are about such topics as career marketing, jobs in Asia, and women and work. There are also links to a few thousand company job sites plus tools, lots of tools. You'll find sites offering resume advice, information on how to conduct your job search, job guides, job ads, matching services, newspapers and other publications, recruiting assistance, and job-related newsgroups. You can also sign up for a related newsletter.

JOBHUNTERSBIBLE.COM
HTTP://WWW.JOBHUNTERSBIBLE.COM/

This sizable resource serves to supplement the popular job-hunting book What Color Is Your Parachute? by Dick Bolles. The material presented is wide ranging, covering everything from the basics (how to use a search engine) to the specifics (the place of religion in a job search and how to deal with being fired).

Links in abundance are waiting to be discovered. Resumes, job-hunting manuals, assessment tests, jobs databases, resources for minorities—they're all covered. One question remains: Where do you start? You can take your lead from the accompanying detailed, opinionated annotations to decide which links to follow first. Fairy Godmother Reports, which precede each of the major site sections, express the author's feelings about what one would hope to find online, what can actually be found online, and the effectiveness of what is found online.

Then there are all sorts of career articles to be read on-site. Titles include "The Three Dangers of Resumes," "The Characteristics of Jobs Today," and "How Long Should You Wait for Your Dream?" This is but a brief glimpse into a vast resource—a definite must-see!

JOB-HUNT.ORG

HTTP://WWW.JOB-HUNT.ORG/

An excellent starting point, NETability's Job-Hunt.Org is a meta-list of resources useful to the job seeker. Numerous job search Web sites are listed here—all you have to do is click on a link and you will automatically be taken to the appropriate home page.

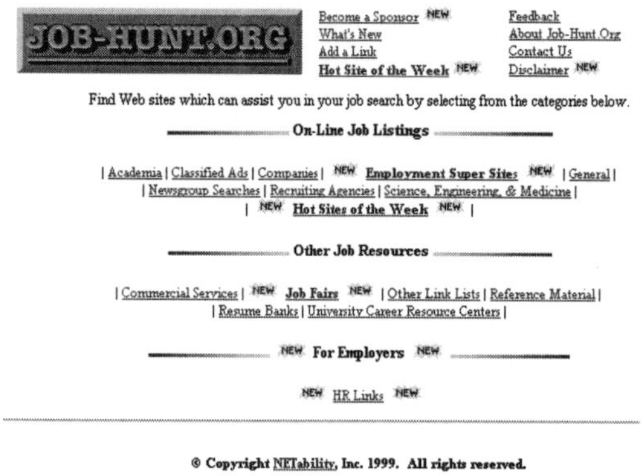

Job listings are organized by academia, classified ads (print ads), companies with job listings, general, newsgroup searches, recruiting agencies, and science, engineering, and medicine. Each listing is accompanied by a brief description. Sites considered to be outstanding job resources are noted by a smiley face. Additionally, there are links to commercial services, other meta-lists, resume banks, and university career resource centers.

Large and loaded with a wealth of resources, Job-Hunt.Org is easy to navigate and not loaded down with graphics. Bookmarking this site is highly recommended.

JOBNET

HTTP://WWW.WESTGA.EDU/COOP/

This State University of West Georgia site is a meta-list of job search resources on the Web. There are links to sites dealing with job search strategies, trends and statistics, resume banks, employment opportunities, and research systems (where you can research companies). The jobs section allows you to explore professions by region or by subject.

JOBOPTIONS
HTTP://WWW.JOBOPTIONS.COM/

Here you can search an employer database of more than 6,000 companies to find current openings as well as links (where available) to home pages. But the site's highlight is its top-notch collection of career resources. Among these are links to other sites covering the usual career-planning fare: self-assessment, resumes, cover letters, salary, relocation, job fairs, interviewing, employment trends, and so on. Then there are resources you're not as likely to find at most other career sites: materials pertaining to online continuing education and a section directed at working parents, to aid them in balancing family life with a career.

JOBWEB
HTTP://WWW.JOBWEB.ORG/

JobWeb, sponsored by the National Association of Colleges and Employers and partnered with more than 1,700 universities and colleges, is an indispensable tool for mapping out career possibilities. Check "Jobwire" for job openings currently posted in NACE's newsletter Spotlight, read through the employer profiles (by keyword, alphabetical, or location), or follow links to recommended minorities resources. Then there's Job Choices Online, which features numerous career-planning articles. And definitely don't miss "Catapult," the career-planning information section containing links to graduate schools, sites to help you with career choices, job listings, professional associations, relocation resources, Internet search tools, and more. Career-development professionals can discuss industry issues via the JobPlace discussion forum.

KRISLYN'S STRICTLY BUSINESS SITES
HTTP://WWW.KRISLYN.COM/SITES/EMPL.HTM

Another meta-list, this one features links to general job-related sites plus links categorized by profession, including accounting, health care, legal, and retail. There are also a few international listings. A brief description is provided for each link. Employment book titles are listed along with a link to Amazon.com, so if you're interested, you can place an order.

MONSTER.COM
HTTP://WWW.MONSTER.COM/

Monster.com is a monster-sized career site with something for job seekers at all stages of the job search. Because of its size, it may be a bit challenging to navigate, but given that it's jam-packed with information and fun to boot, Monster.com is definitely worth your while.

Jobs are posted by a vast number of employers. To get an idea of who is posting jobs and what their line of business is, check out the company profiles. There are various avenues by which to search the job listings. You can conduct a nationwide, an international, or a company search, specifying appropriate keywords as desired. Listings are plentiful, detailed, and up-to-date. You'll have to register if you want to create a resume online. Registration will give you access to additional site features as well.

Certain major sections of Monster.com are known as "zones." These deal with different career stages or industries, such as entry-level and midcareer workers, health care, international employment, entrepreneurship, human resources, and technology. If you are interested in any of these categories, be sure to visit the appropriate section. For example, go to the health care zone and you will find an assortment of articles discussing health care, including education and jobs in the field. There are also many links to other useful Web sites covering professional organizations, education, advocacy groups, management and administration, children's health, and more.

Among the general resources to be found at the site are tools and information to help you get your job and career search on track. Get answers to and advice about many of your career concerns: how to start your job search, getting the top jobs, networking and interviewing, writing your resume, volunteer jobs, relocation, online education, and much more. Interactive possibilities abound here too. To interact with your computer, take a self-assessment test or a quiz. If you'd rather interact (virtually) with other human beings, check out the many scheduled job-related chats or the message boards dealing with career issues.

NATIONAL BUSINESS EMPLOYMENT WEEKLY
HTTP://WWW.NBEW.COM/

National Business Employment Weekly is a career guidance publication from the publishers of the Wall Street Journal. The Web site offers articles and news from recent issues. While you may not get a step-by-step list of how to organize your career research, the featured articles cover pertinent issues related to the process of job searching and the world of work. For example, the "Best of NBEW" section has included such titles as "Make Sure Your Resume Is a Scannable Document," "Selling Yourself like a Product," and "Can I Really Find a Job by Using the Internet?"

The "Managing Your Career" section offers some insight on what may be in store for college graduates. The articles are not only informative but entertaining as well. You might find subjects such as internships, interviewing, and job offer negotiation.

You can view the table of contents from the current issue. Be sure to take a look at Weddle's "Web-Site Review," which gives you the lowdown on some job search sites. Descriptions are concise and provide information on the sponsors of the Web site, the number of job listings with the top three fields and salary ranges, a list of other resources available at the site, and details on the resume database, including the number posted, length of posting period, and any fees involved. This is a great place to get an overview on a large assortment of career Web sites.

PRINCETON REVIEW ONLINE: CAREER
HTTP://WWW.REVIEW.COM/CAREER/

This impressive site by Princeton Review Publishing, publisher of career books and college guides, boasts dazzlingly detailed information. You'll have to register (for free) to view or use certain site features, such as the career search function or the Birkman Method Career Style Summary, a questionnaire that helps determine what careers might be suitable for you. The career search function utilizes a database containing extensive profiles of hundreds of careers. Simply enter a career (such as writer) and the database will return high-confidence hits (writer) and low-confidence hits (actor, agent, editor, journalist, and so on). You can then click on the desired job title to generate additional data, covering what a typical workday might entail ("A Day in the Life"), necessary training, associated careers (if you want to branch out), the future of such a career, and the quality of life you can expect in that career. You'll also find some statistics concerning the career, major employers, the types of publications read by people in that career field, and more.

There are assorted career-related articles to assist you in your exploration and planning. Topics that you might read about include long-distance job searching, networking, resumes, cover letters, and interviewing. To hear what others have to say, participate in an online discussion about various career issues.

QUINTESSENTIAL CAREERS
HTTP://WWW.QUINTCAREERS.COM/

This multifaceted site, by Dr. Randall S. Hansen of Stetson University, incorporates an enormous amount of career information and reaches out to all sectors of the job-search population. "Career Resources" provides the tools necessary to get your job search in gear. You'll find a marketability test (self-assessment tool) and materials on or links pertaining to resumes, cover letters, interviewing, and salary negotiation. Much of the information is presented in an easy-to-follow step-by-step tutorial format. In the "Jobs & Career Sites" section, you'll find many links (yes, more links!) specifically for minorities and women, college students, and teenagers, as well as for sites arranged by job type, industry, and location. The bookstore steers you toward helpful books in various categories, which you can buy from Amazon.com if you follow the links.

THE RILEY GUIDE
HTTP://WWW.DBM.COM/JOBGUIDE/

The Riley Guide, compiled by librarian Margaret F. Dikel (formerly Margaret F. Riley), coauthor (with Frances Roehm, and Steve Oserman) of The Guide to Internet Job Searching, was one of the first online guides to job resource sites. (Read about its history and evolution if you want the details.) Intentionally graphics-free so as to be usable by everyone, this is a giant clearinghouse of helpful sites to aid you in exploring your career or conducting your job search. You will find links to free sites (sites accessible at no charge to job seekers) only.

Click on "Work Opportunities" to find links to sites falling under the category "General Recruiters and Location/Population-Specific Resources" or "Resources for Specific Industries and Occupations." Examples of sections under the first category include "Finding Local U.S. Opportunities," "Resources for Women, Minorities, & Other Affinity and Diversity Groups," and "Online Resume Databases." The second category covers such specific occupational areas as agriculture and forestry, sales and marketing, and building, construction, and mining.

Back at the main page, the "Researching Careers, Employers, etc." link offers help in researching your career choices. There are sections like "Where Is My Job Going?" and "Maybe I Need More Education or Training?" The section called "I'd Like Some Guidance" has links to sites dealing with counseling, support groups, self-assessment, and so on.

Need help with the Internet or with structuring your online job search? Read about how to prepare your resume for the Internet, how to navigate the Internet, and how to use the Internet in your job search.

There is so much more to be found here that you most likely won't be able to explore the entire site on one visit. Bookmark it and check back frequently!

VIRGINIA TECH CAREER SERVICES
HTTP://WWW.CAREER.VT.EDU/

Virginia Tech's thorough site is a great place to research job possibilities and plan your career. Although some of the material is primarily applicable to Virginia Tech students, all of the information is usable. For instance, the site lists the different majors offered at Virginia Tech, which might not seem like it would do you much good if you're not a student there. But you can study the guide to majors at Virginia Tech—to learn more about the types of classes offered, the kind of work entered by graduates having that degree, what to expect regarding employment trends are in the field, and so on—and then search for something comparable at another school.

The "Job Search" section will arm you with ample resources for managing your job search. There are discussions of using the telephone as part of your job search, how (and why) to research employers, pros and cons of various ways to conduct a job search, job fairs, how to send your resume via e-mail, procuring and using employment references, how to dress for an interview, sending follow-up letters, negotiating a job offer, relocating, and so much more. This is terrific information! You're sure to find enough to keep you busy for some time to come. And then to supplement the material here, there are plenty of links to related sites, including the Occupational Outlook Handbook, where you can research various professions.

Section V: Narrowing Your Focus

CHAPTER 12

RESOURCES TO MEET SPECIFIC NEEDS

This chapter introduces you to career sites catering to specific audiences, such as workers with disabilities, minorities, or women. Other sites have a U.S. regional, a federal, or an international focus. If any of these categories apply or appeal to you, then you'll want to check out the relevant sites to get support and encouragement, background information, and direction to help you realize your career dreams.

You will notice that many of the sites described in the following pages offer the standard job search fare: information on required education and training, resume databases, job listings, career advice, relocation resources, and so on. The difference between these sites and sites described elsewhere in this book are that the ones here are generally narrower in focus and scope. This will be helpful to you if you have a more specific idea of what you're looking for and would prefer not to wade through several mega-sites in order to find it.

Among the regional sites you'll see that many are really classified ad sites, straight from publications and newspapers. Browsing these classified ads could give you a sense of where in the United States certain industries are more prevalent. While every state probably has at least one Web site devoted to careers or job opportunities in that state, not every state is individually represented here—and not every state even has equal coverage on the Internet. A state's representation on the Internet will depend on a number of variables. In California, for example, there are a great number of businesses in the high-tech industry (including new media, such as the Internet), which will invariably lead to its having a highly visible presence on the Internet. This might not be the case for some other states. If you don't find what you're looking for in a particular region, check out the general directory sites, where you will uncover links to many more state job sites than there is room for in this book! Although this book predominantly covers U.S. career resources, several representative Canadian and international sites have been included for those of you wishing to venture elsewhere to pursue your career goals.

Workers with Disabilities

JOBACCESS

HTTP://WWW.JOBACCESS.ORG/

Employers dedicated to recruiting qualified disabled workers post job openings at this site. Search for a job opening by keyword, location, or category. When you get your results, check the dates for current listings and then indicate which search results you want to see in full. For these you will get a job summary covering job title, location, duties, qualifications, physical demands, work environment, and contact information. You are given the option of applying online by compiling a resume at the site. If you're looking for information on the Americans with Disabilities Act, this would be a good place to check. Full text of the law can be found here, along with FAQs, tips, and news.

JOB ACCOMMODATION NETWORK

HTTP://JANWEB.ICDI.WVU.EDU/

The mission of JAN, located at West Virginia University at Morgantown, is to assist employers in hiring and promoting individuals with disabilities in the workplace and to help companies to realize their accommodation options. On the flip side, JAN provides disabled workers with resources for finding such organizations and other sources of support. Examples of job accommodations are given, discussing, for instance, what a company might have to do to enable an injured employee to return to the workplace. Employers and workers alike can post concerns to the site's bulletin board. There is a wide selection of reports, fact sheets, and tips that you can read using Adobe Acrobat Reader.

"Points of Interest" offers numerous links pertaining to disabilities, covering legislation and general resources. There are disability-related employment sites listed, which should lay some groundwork for you on where to look for a job. Also, JAN has compiled a number of employment tips, outlining strategy for your job search. The Americans with Disabilities Act is given in-depth treatment, including a Q&A section and links to guidelines, assistance manuals, and compliance information.

NEW MOBILITY
HTTP://WWW.NEWMOBILITY.COM/

Based on the print magazine of the same name, this site is intended to be an online interactive community for people with disabilities. Some of the interactive features are a message board and a chat room. You will be able to view the magazine's table of contents as well as read select articles. If you're wondering about career resources, then you'll be pleased to discover that there is a searchable jobs database. Tips on resumes and job interviews are also presented. To round out the site, there's a nice selection of disability-related links on such topics as coping skills, empowerment, parenting, research, sports, travel, products, and companies.

PRESIDENT'S COMMITTEE ON EMPLOYMENT OF PEOPLE WITH DISABILITIES
HTTP://WWW50.PCEPD.GOV/PCEPD/

This federal agency has the goal to increase and improve job opportunities for individuals with disabilities. At this site you can read about the progress being made by the organization. Project reports and press releases are available, as are fact sheets that should be of interest as you explore your career options. Among the topics covered are self-employment, affirmative action, workplace laws, job accommodations, and insurance and benefits. Many of the documents are aimed at employers, but it doesn't hurt to know what's being discussed on the other side of the employment fence! To top it off, there's a long list of U.S. employers actively looking to hire qualified people with disabilities. Street and Web addresses are provided, along with phone numbers. Check out a company home page to see if there are any current job openings.

UNIVERSITY/EDUCATION DISABILITY RESOURCES

HTTP://WWW.ESKIMO.COM/ JLUBIN/DISABLED/UNIVERSI.HTM

If you're disabled and trying to figure out how best to pursue your educational goals, don't miss this resource. This very basic site lists links in such categories as financial aid, education resources, job training and placement, and university resources. Follow the links to read about special education, distance learning, scholarships and employment opportunities for disabled people, and other services. For more disability-related information, check out the main page, where you'll have access to sites covering newsgroups, publications, products and services, medicine, politics, and more.

Minorities

AMERICAN INDIAN SCIENCE & ENGINEERING SOCIETY

HTTP://WWW.AISES.ORG/

Offering educational programs to students in middle school through graduate school, this nonprofit organization is dedicated to the professional development of American Indians and Native Alaskans, especially in the fields of business, engineering, science, and technology. The site contains information on AISES programs including internships, contact details for college chapters, news and announcements, notes on scholarships and awards, a message board, a resume posting service, and links to "friends of AISES" and other resources.

THE BLACK COLLEGIAN

HTTP://WWW.BLACK-COLLEGIAN.COM/

Self-described as being a "career site for students and professionals of color," this is the Web complement of the magazine having the same name. Look through the magazine and read about current workplace and career issues relevant to African Americans, or visit the excellent "Graduate/Professional School" section, which discusses steps to take in preparing to attend graduate school, how to succeed in graduate school, and opportunities for the MBA. There's also a listing of graduate schools committed to increasing the minority pool and organizations offering fellowships or scholarships.

Definitely check out the "Career Related" section. You'll find information about career planning and how to conduct your job search, as well as articles such as "Using Newsgroups in Your Job Search" and "The On-Campus Interview." Study the industry and career reports to find out about fields you're interested in (perhaps accounting, electronics, entertainment, hospitality, military, pharmaceuticals, or retail). The job opportunity listings feature the names of various companies, the types of jobs typically available, and the majors desired for those jobs, which can help you plan your education.

There's also a searchable jobs database, for which you can designate keyword and/or state or specific employer. You may find jobs such as purchasing specialist, landscape architect, or accountant. You can add your resume to the resume database as well.

BLACK VOICES CAREER CENTER

HTTP://WWW.BLACKVOICES.COM/CAREER/

This section of a larger African-American online community offers resources for job seekers. Not only is a free resume posting service provided, but you can check out the up-to-date job listings by typing in a keyword. You'll get full job descriptions along with information on how to apply. If you want to know more about companies posting these jobs, you can read background material on select companies. Learn about the importance of diversity in the workplace as well as company benefits. Where available, links to home pages are given. The site also includes feature articles that deal with workplace issues, career advice, and profiles of successful black businesspeople. When you're ready to take a break from thinking about your career options, be sure to browse through the rest of the site. There are sections devoted to news, entertainment, chat, money, events, and much more.

DIVISION OF INDIAN & NATIVE AMERICAN PROGRAMS

HTTP://WWW.WDSC.ORG/DINAP/

This resource provides information about the U.S. Department of Labor's Job Training Partnership Act (JTPA), specifically Section 401 Indian and Native American Program. The intent of the act is to provide a job training program for people who otherwise would likely face major obstacles in the way of successful employment in the workforce. If you want to read the act in its entirety, you'll find it here. A brief, more manageable introduction to the program is also available. The 1998 Workforce Investment Act is presented in full as well, with the section devoted to Native American programs given separately for easy access. This act also deals with employment and training activities. Yet another section addresses the Indian and Native American Welfare-to-Work Program. And finally, there's a small collection of links to related resources and government sites.

GAYWORK.COM

HTTP://WWW.GAYWORK.COM/

Aimed at GLBT (gay/lesbian/bisexual/transgender) job seekers, this site presents job listings posted by equal opportunity employers, most having nondiscrimination policies and many offering domestic partner benefits. To search the database, you can indicate profession, state, experience, salary, education, and terms of employment (full-time, part-time, internship, summer, or temporary). The more specific you are, the fewer results you will get, so you might want to start out with a broader search. Employer profiles are searchable based on select criteria such as benefits, industry, and state.

Do you want more than just to find a job? Then take a look at the great collection of links to other resources dealing with GLBT workplace issues.

GOLDSEA CAREER SUCCESS CENTER
HTTP://GOLDSEA.COM/CAREER/CAREER.HTML

Part of a mega-site devoted to all things Asian American, this career resource contains articles, survey results, and links to further sites. First off, you can read articles on workplace stereotyping and how to get on—and stay on—the management track, as well as articles pertaining to women in the workplace. Then there are survey results listing fifty of the best employers for Asian Americans. Employers are listed for such categories as aerospace, biotech, computing and communications, defense and international relations, financial services, and media and entertainment. Each employer is given a brief overview, along with a link to the company's job page. There's also a similar list of the twenty worst employers. If you are looking for more career information, you're sure to find something of interest from among the many links that round out this page.

MINORITIES' JOB BANK
HTTP://WWW.MINORITIES-JB.COM/

Developed by Black Collegiate Services, publisher of Black Collegian magazine, this is a valuable career resource—and then some. The searchable jobs database features listings from companies dedicated to workplace diversity. Type in a keyword and specify a U.S. state to get a list of job openings. You'll need to register if you want to post your resume.

Career and other information is presented via several "villages," each for a different minority: African Americans, Asian Americans, Hispanic Americans, Native Americans, and women, as well as underrepresented minorities. The villages offer numerous interesting articles that address a wide assortment of workplace issues. Some of the titles include "How to Conduct Yourself during a Business Meal," "Courtesy Counts" (about the practice of sending thank you notes after an interview), "Networking with Your Peers," "Artistas, Empower Thyselves," "Starting Over" (about homemakers entering the workforce), and "60 Percent of U.S. Corporate Boards Now Have Ethnic Minority Directors, but Where Are the Native Americans?"

But that's not all. There are other articles on art and culture, education, politics, business and finance, harassment and discrimination, and family and lifestyle, plus news, events listings, and more. This is a vast resource that you won't want to miss.

NATIONAL ASSOCIATION OF ASIAN AMERICAN PROFESSIONALS

HTTP://WWW.NAAAP.ORG/

NAAAP is a network of U.S. organizations focusing on the advancement of Asian-American professionals. The site provides you with a basic overview of the NAAAP. Additionally, you will have access to street addresses and phone numbers of NAAAP chapters and affiliates, as well as links to home pages where available. At these Web sites there is much more specific information on a local level. Coverage varies but may include event listings, program descriptions, bulletin boards, and job opportunities.

NATIONAL BLACK MBA ASSOCIATION

HTTP://WWW.NBMBAA.ORG/

If you're pursuing a career in communications, finance, human resources, information systems, general management, or marketing, don't miss the jobs section at this site. To pull up a list of openings, you can designate whichever of these fields appeals to you and then specify the U.S. state or country where you want to work. Check off listings of greatest interest to get full job descriptions and application details. Of course there's also a lot of information here on the organization itself, including NBMBAA chapter listings, program descriptions, and mailing list details.

NATIONAL SOCIETY OF BLACK ENGINEERS

HTTP://WWW.NSBE.ORG/

For those considering or already in the engineering field, the NSBE offers a huge amount of information at its Web site. Along with the material for NSBE members, there is some aimed at precollege students, college students, and technical professionals. Read about awards, projects, scholarships, conferences, and NSBE publications.

If you're in the market for an engineering job, you'll be happy to know there's an extensive jobs section here. It's called the W.O.O. (Window of Opportunity) Zone. You'll have access to job listings in the areas of information technology management, hardware and software engineering, other engineering (such as aerospace, chemical, civil, industrial, nuclear), administration, technical support, sales and marketing, operations, and training. Links are given for a large number of employers (who are NSBE advertisers) in the engineering field, so you can visit their Web sites and conduct further research if interested.

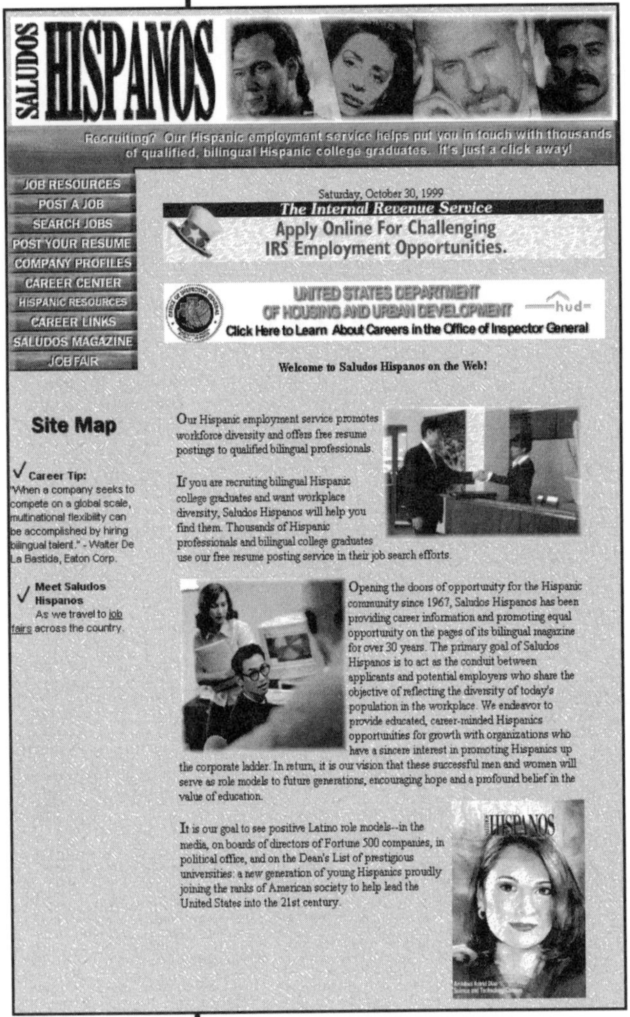

SALUDOS HISPANOS

HTTP://WWW.SALUDOS.COM/

Sponsored by the magazine of the same name, this site (in English) is devoted to promoting the careers and education of members of the Hispanic community. Your first stop should be the "Career Center," which is designed to help you define your job interests. The job listings are searchable by state, job category, and company. Along with job descriptions, you'll get links to home pages of employers who recruit Hispanic workers. Career articles offer informative and fun mentor and organization profiles. You can read about the careers of a financial advisor, musicians, an aquarist, and others. There are also articles on various industries, including animation, forensic science, and oceanography.

To expand your exploration, check out the "Hispanic Resource Center," which provides links to sites that serve the Hispanic community. You'll find mailing lists, newsgroups, and Web sites covering career resources, job listings, and resume databases. Another useful site feature is the company profile section. Here you'll get background information on employees at companies that are interested in workplace diversity.

TODOLATINO CAREER CENTER

HTTP://WWW.TODOLATINO.COM/CAREERCENTER/

The main TodoLatino ("Everything Latino") page is a searchable and browsable directory of links to Latino-related sites. Categories include business, culture, education, entertainment, government, health, news, organizations, politics, sports and recreation, and travel—plus careers, which is the page under discussion here.

There's a selection of links to Web resources dealing with self-assessment, interviewing, cover letter and resume writing, and salary negotiation. Sites are briefly described and rated. These are supplemented by a list of suggested book titles, with links to order information. Are you actively seeking a job? Then you'll want to follow the links to the job boards offered by recommended sites geared toward diversity in the workplace. If you venture over to the "Development Center," you can ask questions of the TodoLatino management consultant, "El Consejero," or participate in a discussion forum.

TRIBAL EMPLOYMENT NEWSLETTER

HTTP://WWW.NATIVEJOBS.COM/

Aimed at a Native American audience or companies dedicated to diversity in the workplace, this site is used by job seekers and recruiters alike. Jobs are posted in such areas as administration, business, education, information technology, legal, and national resources. Job descriptions, contact details, and sometimes links to Web sites are presented. A small collection of related resources is offered as well.

Women

ADVANCING WOMEN
HTTP://WWW.ADVANCINGWOMEN.COM/

This site offers several sections that will be of use to women seeking career information. "Workplace" contains articles and links aimed at many segments of the female population; for example, "grrls," teens, Hispanic women, and women in real estate, the arts, and education. In the "Career Center," you can search the jobs database, which is offered in conjunction with CareerMosaic. There are links to additional resources as well.

If networking is what you're looking for, then check out that section. There you'll have access to chats, message boards, and community (that is, Advancing Women) events listings. Does your job require you to do any computer or Web work? Then don't miss the "Web & Hi-Tech Women" articles for some timely commentary, reports, and tips.

FEMINIST MAJORITY FOUNDATION ONLINE
HTTP://WWW.FEMINIST.ORG/

Packed with information for and about women, this site affords a forum where you can learn about issues the Feminist Majority is involved with, keep up-to-date on the latest feminist news, discover ways to take action, read about girls and women in sports ("Empowering Women in Sports"), or enjoy a chuckle at the humor page. The "Feminist University Network" section provides links to universities with women's studies programs and women's centers as well as a Feminist Student Network—a database of students you can search through to find others with similar interests.

The "Feminist Career Center" lists job and internship opportunities with progressive and feminist groups. Representative organizations include Asian Immigrant Women Advocates, Center for Reproductive Law & Policy, Democratic National Committee, National Organization for Women, and Planned Parenthood Federation of America, just to name a few. Click on the organization you are interested in and you will jump to a page with an outline of the main goals of the organization, contact information, and a description of job responsibilities or internship details.

INDEPENDENT MEANS

HTTP://WWW.ANINCOMEOFHEROWN.COM/

This company, having a home office in Santa Barbara, California, is devoted to helping teenage girls achieve financial independence through the development of business and leadership skills. While the company's products and services are advertised here, the site by itself nevertheless has a lot to offer young girls. Focus is placed on teaching girls about managing money and inspiring them to follow their dreams and goals.

Women entrepreneurs discuss their business enterprises and offer advice in response to specific questions in a Q&A section called "Just Ask Her!" You might learn about how these women conduct their business day to day, as well as their achievements and struggles in the process. Articles in "Independence Hall" concern things like steps to achieving independence, ways to make—and save—money, and how to really relax on your time off.

IVILLAGE CAREER

HTTP://WWW.IVILLAGE.COM/CAREER/

The Web site iVillage is an online network for women. It offers many varied resources covering such areas of interest as books, food, money, parenting, pets, shopping, travel, and careers. What will you find in the career section? For starters, there are columns by the experts: the "Burnout Counselor," the "Confidence Coach," the "Management Guru," and the "Office Politics Coach," to name a few. Click on any one of these in order to read about on-the-job experiences and get some helpful tips in coping with certain situations. The "Tools" section, for members only, is meant to help you assess your skills and interests. (Registration is free, and with it you can access many members-only sections of iVillage.) Then there are the "Features," covering such topics as interview skills, job changes, inspiring women, advancing on the job, and time management.

You'll find message boards galore here! They deal with a wide variety of pertinent subjects like workplace rights, African-American women in the workplace, computing, business travel, and continuing education. If you are looking for other ways to interact virtually, check out the scheduled chats. Several are held weekly. There's plenty of activity at this site, so you'll probably want to drop by often!

ONLINE WOMEN'S BUSINESS CENTER
HTTP://WWW.ONLINEWBC.ORG/

The U.S. Small Business Administration's Office of Women's Business Ownership has joined with an assortment of corporations to sponsor this site, which features a wealth of information for women wanting to start a business. A collection of more than 1,000 articles deal with starting, growing, and expanding your business, as well as key components of running a business, including management, finance, marketing, and technology. You might find inspiration in the numerous success stories presented, plus there's information on welfare to work. Much material is offered in Spanish.

Local women's business centers throughout the United States are listed, along with contact details. There's also a directory of resources covering accounting, financial assistance and loans, licenses and permits, taxes, and more. Entries may consist of phone numbers, street addresses, descriptions, or Web site addresses. The most useful tool for finding additional information, however, is the vast collection of business-related links. These are organized under such categories as banking and finance, international business, office tools, regional information, and women's associations and business. As you can see, there's a lot here even for those of you who aren't thinking about going into business for yourself!

WEBGRRLS INTERNATIONAL
HTTP://WWW.WEBGRRLS.COM/

Webgrrls, founded by Aliza Sherman (president of Cybergrrl), has the goal to provide a "supportive and nurturing environment where women can learn from other women about technology." Members represent all areas of the new media industry—content developers, Web designers, online editors, site developers, digital artists, programmers, new media technical recruiters—you name it, someone does it! In addition to the standard membership information, chapters in the United States and abroad are listed, with links to home pages where available. Chapter pages offer a variety of resources, often a calendar of events, a mailing list, educational details, and a links list. Sound good? Then go ahead and locate a chapter near you, join up, sign on for the mailing list, talk tech, network, learn and share, and have fun!

WOMEN'S CAREERS AND PROFESSIONAL ORGANIZATIONS
HTTP://FEMINIST.COM/CAREER.HTM

Feminist.com has compiled an important collection of links having to do with women in the workforce. The sites listed here will inspire and challenge women in pursuit of a career or in transition, as well as women firmly situated in a job. As you page through these sites, you might find a worthwhile organization to join. What you'll definitely find is an enormous amount of information covering a wide variety of career fields. You'll have access to materials from such organizations as American Agri-Women, the Association for Women in Mathematics, Black Career Women, the National Association for Female Executives, the Society of Women Engineers, the U.S. Equal Employment Opportunity Commission, the Women Chef's Resource Center, Women in Film, and others. Some general career links are interspersed with the organization listings. If you're still in the mood to browse some more after all this, there are plenty of other resources for women, though not necessarily career-related, elsewhere at the Feminist.com site.

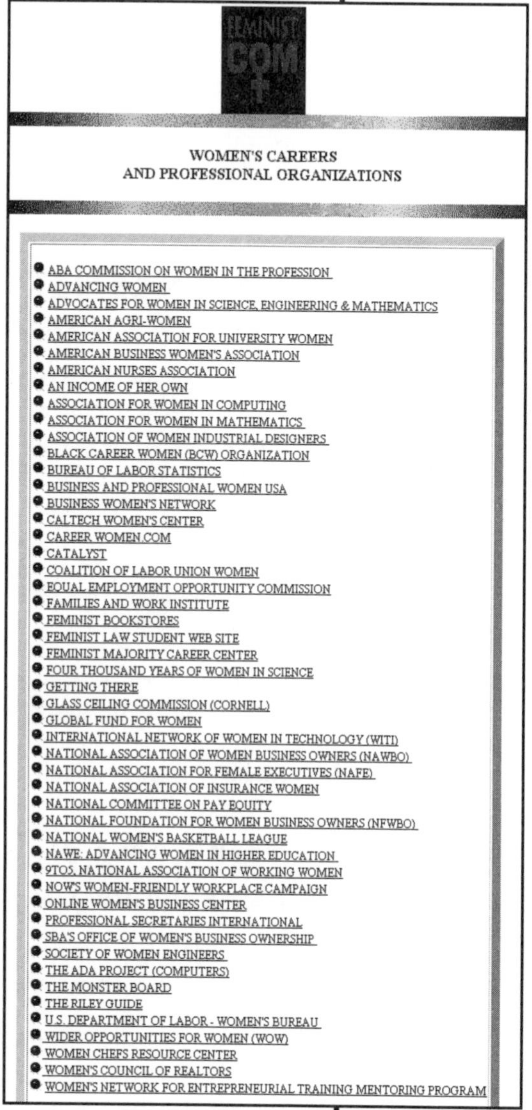
FEMINIST COM

WOMEN'S CAREERS
AND PROFESSIONAL ORGANIZATIONS

- ABA COMMISSION ON WOMEN IN THE PROFESSION
- ADVANCING WOMEN
- ADVOCATES FOR WOMEN IN SCIENCE, ENGINEERING & MATHEMATICS
- AMERICAN AGRI-WOMEN
- AMERICAN ASSOCIATION FOR UNIVERSITY WOMEN
- AMERICAN BUSINESS WOMEN'S ASSOCIATION
- AMERICAN NURSES ASSOCIATION
- AN INCOME OF HER OWN
- ASSOCIATION FOR WOMEN IN COMPUTING
- ASSOCIATION FOR WOMEN IN MATHEMATICS
- ASSOCIATION OF WOMEN INDUSTRIAL DESIGNERS
- BLACK CAREER WOMEN (BCW) ORGANIZATION
- BUREAU OF LABOR STATISTICS
- BUSINESS AND PROFESSIONAL WOMEN USA
- BUSINESS WOMEN'S NETWORK
- CALTECH WOMEN'S CENTER
- CAREER WOMEN.COM
- CATALYST
- COALITION OF LABOR UNION WOMEN
- EQUAL EMPLOYMENT OPPORTUNITY COMMISSION
- FAMILIES AND WORK INSTITUTE
- FEMINIST BOOKSTORES
- FEMINIST LAW STUDENT WEB SITE
- FEMINIST MAJORITY CAREER CENTER
- FOUR THOUSAND YEARS OF WOMEN IN SCIENCE
- GETTING THERE
- GLASS CEILING COMMISSION (CORNELL)
- GLOBAL FUND FOR WOMEN
- INTERNATIONAL NETWORK OF WOMEN IN TECHNOLOGY (WITI)
- NATIONAL ASSOCIATION OF WOMEN BUSINESS OWNERS (NAWBO)
- NATIONAL ASSOCIATION FOR FEMALE EXECUTIVES (NAFE)
- NATIONAL ASSOCIATION OF INSURANCE WOMEN
- NATIONAL COMMITTEE ON PAY EQUITY
- NATIONAL FOUNDATION FOR WOMEN BUSINESS OWNERS (NFWBO)
- NATIONAL WOMEN'S BASKETBALL LEAGUE
- NAWE: ADVANCING WOMEN IN HIGHER EDUCATION
- 9TO5, NATIONAL ASSOCIATION OF WORKING WOMEN
- NOW'S WOMEN-FRIENDLY WORKPLACE CAMPAIGN
- ONLINE WOMEN'S BUSINESS CENTER
- PROFESSIONAL SECRETARIES INTERNATIONAL
- SBA'S OFFICE OF WOMEN'S BUSINESS OWNERSHIP
- SOCIETY OF WOMEN ENGINEERS
- THE ADA PROJECT (COMPUTERS)
- THE MONSTER BOARD
- THE RILEY GUIDE
- U.S. DEPARTMENT OF LABOR - WOMEN'S BUREAU
- WIDER OPPORTUNITIES FOR WOMEN (WOW)
- WOMEN CHEFS RESOURCE CENTER
- WOMEN'S COUNCIL OF REALTORS
- WOMEN'S NETWORK FOR ENTREPRENEURIAL TRAINING MENTORING PROGRAM

Federal

FEDERAL JOBS DIGEST
HTTP://WWW.JOBSFED.COM/

If you want to work for Uncle Sam, you might want to stop by the electronic version of the Federal Jobs Digest. Loads of federal jobs are listed here under such occupation groups as science and math, education and foreign affairs, communications, blue collar, transportation and aviation, and many more. (Need some background information about the various categories? Check out the "Job Descriptions" section.) Select a category and up comes a list of job titles and the number of listings currently in the database (updated daily). If you find a job title that appeals to you, click on it for open dates, location, and resources for further details, including how to interpret the listings, salary charts, a description of the codes used in the job descriptions, and addresses for Offices of Personnel Management all over the country. Full details (including contact name) are available to registered users only. Additionally, there is a section devoted to federal employee benefits, where you're sure to find a lot of useful information.

FINANCENET
HTTP://WWW.FINANCENET.GOV/

Operated by the National Science Foundation, this site offers a wealth of links to government job sites. It also lists government asset sales of federal surplus and unclaimed property, which can be a bit distracting if you feel like shopping for postal equipment, public land, or noncombatant ships instead of looking for a job. But don't tempt yourself! Just click on "Jobs" or "Training."

The "Jobs" page has a long list of federal employment resources from around the United States. Many have a focus on the finance industry. There are links to federal as well as state or local government job sites. You'll also find links to general job search sites. Under "Training" you'll have access to quite a number of sites where you can get information on government-related education or training. These include online courses, course catalogs of graduate schools, training facilities, and so on.

THE GREAT AMERICAN WEB SITE
HTTP://WWW.UNCLE-SAM.COM/

This site, by a nongovernmental research firm, makes the jumble of federal agencies a bit more accessible. It's not exactly a job search site, but it's a great place to conduct research in order to find out more about the federal government and all its branches. Speaking of branches, there are links to offices and agencies of the executive branch, the legislative branch, and the judicial branch, as well as to executive departments and independent agencies. And don't worry if you can't remember anything from your high school civics class because everything is defined and explained.

You'll also find lists of popular sites in "10 Most Visited Sites" (would it surprise you to know that the CIA gets quite a few hits?), "Our Favorite Sites," and "Our 'Ten Best' Lists" (covering various categories such as statistical sources or business research), along with "Weekly Highlights" spotlighting various federal Web sites.

INTERNET CAREER CONNECTION
HTTP://WWW.ICCWEB.COM/

This general job search resource, which also has a site on America Online, is sponsored by career guidance agency Gonyea & Associates. The gem of the site is its federal government employment page. It is packed with useful information about federal jobs and how to get one. You might want to start with the "Introduction to Government Service," which gives an overview of federal employment. The section on how to apply for federal jobs features a job hunter's checklist as well as information on civil service exams and the job application process.

"Resources for Locating Federal Jobs" provides details on books, computer software, computer bulletin boards, job hotlines, and Web sites. Contact information for personnel offices and federal employment information centers is provided. There are some in-depth articles on specialized areas of employment, such as the U.S. Postal Service, overseas opportunities, and student employment. You can also learn about the various branches of the government or read articles about federal employment (for example, "Jobs in Air Traffic Control" or "Health Care Jobs with Uncle Sam").

INTERNET JOB SOURCE
HTTP://WWW.STATEJOBS.COM/

An amazing resource if you want to work for the government, this site lists hundreds of links for federal, state, city, or county jobs. Among the various federal agencies listed here are the Central Intelligence Agency, the Department of Agriculture, the Executive Office of the President, the International Trade Commission, the Library of Congress, and the National Park Service. If you prefer the corporate world to the federal one, you'll be happy to know that there are also links to more than 200 major corporations in the United States. Furthermore, there are links to newspaper and other career sites.

PLANNING YOUR FUTURE . . . A FEDERAL EMPLOYEE'S SURVIVAL GUIDE

HTTP://SAFETYNET.DOLETA.GOV/

From the U.S. Department of Labor's Employment and Training Administration (DOL/ETA), this site is intended to help federal employees with career transition. It packs in a lot of information about career exploration and how to go about a job search, so even if you're not in job transition, this site could be very handy.

"Starting a New Career" presents quite a few resources for conducting a successful job search. There are plenty of links to other job-related Web sites and college and training sites. You'll also find sites to help you choose a career, hone your interview and resume-writing skills, and research the job market (market research and industrial outlook).

The site also has information on federal retirement issues, resources for career transition professionals, and documents addressing things employees should know about reductions in force.

USA JOBS

HTTP://WWW.USAJOBS.OPM.GOV/

This is the U.S. government's official site for jobs and employment information, brought to you by the U.S. Office of Personnel Management. The jobs are organized by category, such as "Entry Level Professional," "Senior Executive," and "Trades and Labor." Requirements associated with the categories are supplied. Once you select a category, you can search the database by job type, experience, salary, and region. An easy-to-use form is provided to facilitate the search. When you find a job to your liking, you can fill out the online application form.

Don't miss the "General Information" page because here you'll find information on how to apply for federal jobs as well as on student employment and intern programs. The section on student employment includes a handy page titled "Federal Jobs by College Major." It lists various college majors along with the federal jobs you might be qualified for if you study that particular subject. For instance, if you study journalism, you might be able to get a federal job as a public affairs specialist or an agricultural market reporter.

Miscellaneous

EQUAL OPPORTUNITY PUBLICATIONS
HTTP://WWW.EOP.COM/

Equal Opportunity Publications publishes career magazines for minorities, women, and people with disabilities. You can browse through sample articles from the magazines, which include Woman Engineer, Minority Engineer, Equal Opportunity, Careers & the disABLED, and Workforce Diversity for Engineering and IT Professionals. Details are given for subscribing, which is free if you fall into the category covered by that publication. Names of companies actively recruiting minorities, women, or people with disabilities are listed.

RESOURCES FOR WOMEN, MINORITIES, AND OTHER AFFINITY GROUPS AND AUDIENCES
HTTP://WWW.DBM.COM/JOBGUIDE/DIVERSE.HTML

Here's another very useful Riley Guide page from Margaret F. Dikel. This collection of annotated links will point you in the right direction if you're looking for general information in the categories of women, military personnel, affinity and diversity groups, or the disabled. While the site itself isn't specifically career- or job-related, you're sure to find much relevant material at those sites that are suggested.

General Regional

AJR NEWSLINK: NEWSPAPERS
HTTP://AJR.NEWSLINK.ORG/NEWS.HTML

From American Journalism Review and NewsLink Associates, this site gives you direct access to about 5,000 newspapers in the United States and abroad. Just think of all the job classified sections you'll have at your fingertips as a result! You can look for a newspaper of your choice by state or continent. The publications are also listed by category: major metros, dailies and nondailies, business, alternative, and specialty. Campus papers can be found here as well. The links take you to the front page of the newspaper's online edition. From there you'll have to look for the classified section to see if there are job listings available.

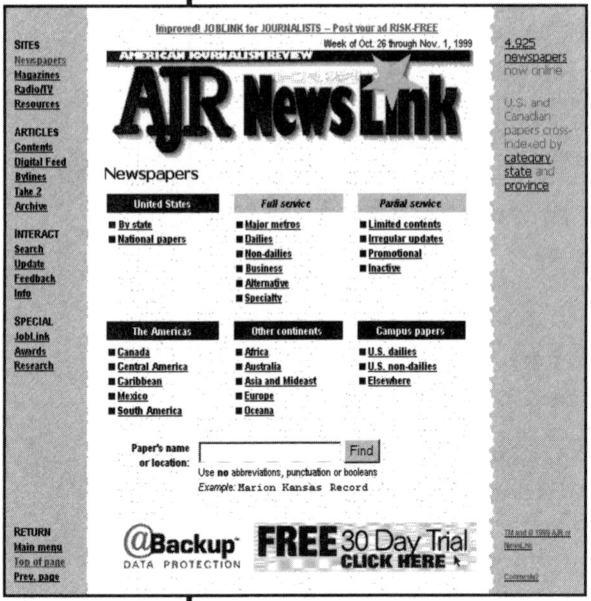

BONA FIDE CLASSIFIED
HTTP://WWW.BONAFIDE-CLASSIFIEDS.COM/

Newspaper classifieds bearing the Bona Fide Classified mark are from Newspaper Association of America (NAA) members. At this site you can easily find these newspapers' real estate, auto, and employment classifieds. Simply select a state or type in the name of a U.S. city or newspaper. Then indicate which classifieds you want to view: real estate, auto, or employment. Take your pick from the resulting list of newspapers to look for a job (or a car or an apartment) in your desired location. This is a great way to find job listings for whatever city or state you're interested in.

HOW TO RESPOND TO HELP WANTED ADS

HTTP://WWW.SMARTBIZ.COM/SBS/ARTS/IRISH3.HTM

This brief essay offers some useful advice on what steps to take when you are ready to respond to a job advertisement. Some of the key points to remember are to reply promptly and then to follow up shortly after this initial response. Also, there's an explanation of how you can try to read between the lines to determine which companies may be hiring for positions not yet advertised.

JOB RESOURCES BY U.S. REGION

HTTP://CDC.STUAFF.DUKE.EDU/STUALUM/EMPLOYMENT/JOBRESOURCES/JREGION.HTML

From the site title, it's pretty apparent what you can expect to discover here. And you won't be disappointed! Pick a region where you want to work—Southeastern, Northeastern, Midwestern, Southwestern, or Western United States—and then browse the annotated site listings to find something of interest. Many job resources are represented here: Internet job banks, job sites in education and human services, government listings, and newspapers. Sites for summer jobs and internships are also described, as are job resources by specific career fields (including archaeology, business, nonprofits, religious, and sports).

As if all of that wasn't enough, Duke University's Career Center has even compiled an assortment of career-related resources, such as on resumes, cover letters, interviews, salary, and relocation. Plus there are directories of job resources listed as well.

LOCAL U.S. WORK OPPORTUNITIES

HTTP://WWW.DBM.COM/JOBGUIDE/LOCAL.HTML

As you've already seen, the Riley Guide (from Margaret F. Dikel) is an up-to-date career resource having wide-ranging scope. Here is a three-part presentation on U.S. regional job searching on the Internet. First off you get numerous links listed by state. Some of your choices will be newspapers, newsgroups, and government or other sources. Most of the "other sources" are annotated, which will give you a clue about what you can expect from those sites. In addition to specific state resources, "More Resources for Finding Local Opportunities" will point you toward the mega-sites and directory sites where you'll get lots more pertinent job search information. If you're thinking about international employment, you'll be happy to know that from here you can access the separate Riley Guide section devoted to just that.

NEWSGROUPS GETAJOB

HTTP://WWW.GETAJOB.COM/NEWSGRPS.HTML

This is a great resource for finding job-related newsgroups, another way to search for jobs on the Internet. You can hook up with newsgroups by going through the geographical listing. You'll find U.S. states and some international listings, such as for the United Kingdom and Bermuda. Newsgroups are also categorized by industry or as "uncategorized."

In addition to newsgroups, you'll have access to other career-related resources through other areas of the site. You'll find articles of interest, links to human resources pages of potential employers, and descriptions of suggested book titles for further information.

United States: Northeast

BOSTON.COM CAREERS

HTTP://CAREERS.BOSTON.COM/

Looking for a job in Boston? Boston.com is the online edition of the Boston Globe, and this is the career section. You can scan through all the classified ads from the Sunday Globe by category. Be sure to specify the week(s) you want to search. Additional ads are posted online only, so you'll have access to these as well.

Boston.com offers more than just the classified ads. You can read profiles of employers that advertise in the Boston Globe and take a peek at their job listings (if any). Browse through the job resources section, which features education and training materials, job-hunting information, and a salary calculator. There are career-related events listings, with details about participants. You can also dig through the Boston Globe's article archives if you wish to research companies.

CAREERPOST

HTTP://WWW.WASHINGTONPOST.COM/WP-ADV/CLASSIFIEDS/CAREERPOST/FRONT.HTM

CareerPost is the Washington Post online job site, but it is much more than just the classified ads. In addition to the jobs database, you'll get loads of advice and helpful tips for finding a job.

The job search area allows you to browse by category, featured employers, location, or keyword. There are extensive featured employer listings, with links to company home pages and direct access to each company's CareerPost job listings. An interesting section called "Job Matrix" charts various career fields, the number of jobs currently open in those fields, and distribution by city (the cities are in the Virginia, District of Columbia, and Maryland regions, with miscellaneous postings categorized as "Other"). This affords you a variety of ways to view job ads. In addition to these regional resources, you can access national career resources from CareerPath.com.

JOBFIND

HTTP://WWW.JOBFIND.COM/

Jobfind was originally launched by the Boston Herald newspaper. Job listings are mainly centered on the Northeast, but there are listings for other areas of the United States as well. You can search by location and category. Choices are listed in a scrollable box. From your results list, you can select those you're interested in and see complete job details. In "Corporate Profiles" you'll find background information on dozens of Jobfind clients. Here you can read about the employer's history, products and services, and benefits. Where available, there are links to company home pages.

NEW ENGLAND OPPORTUNITY NOCS

HTTP://WWW.OPNOCSNE.ORG/

This regional online edition of Opportunity NOCs (nonprofit organization classifieds), a biweekly recruitment newsletter, lists jobs in the nonprofit sector of the New England area. Opportunities are listed under the categories of jobs, volunteer, and internships. Some of the types of jobs you'll find listed include business administrator, volunteer coordinator, clinician, public relations coordinator, library docent, and grants associate. Additionally, there are useful links to other nonprofit organizations and sites posting job opportunities in the nonprofit and other industries throughout the United States.

PENNSYLVANIAJOBS.COM
HTTP://WWW.PENNSYLVANIAJOBS.COM/

If you call Pennsylvania home and you're looking for a job, this may just be the ticket. You can search for job openings by typing in keywords or check out job opportunities for featured employers in such fields as real estate, technology, food services, home furnishings, finance, and utilities. While numerous companies are represented in the job listings, only a small percentage are directly accessible as featured employers.

"Pennsylvania Places" is a small collection of articles about the business, culture, or lifestyle of Pennsylvania, intended to give readers a taste of the diversity and attractions of the state. Also available are dates and locations of job fairs and other career-related events throughout the state. To supplement the materials here, links are offered to sites dealing with tourism, education, government, real estate, and weather—not to mention jobs.

SILICON ALLEY JOBS
HTTP://WWW.SILICONALLEYJOBS.COM/

Are you looking for a high-tech job in New York? How would you like to find employment as a site editor, a producer of interactive content, a Web designer, an online sales coordinator, or a technical development director? Well, those are the kinds of jobs that are posted here, and most of them are for positions situated in or around New York City. Select the job category of your choice, in the areas of design, marketing and sales, management, internships, editorial, programming and tech, or support staff. There are links to plenty of additional materials (having to do with commerce, technology, downloads, news, and more) at affiliate sites @NY and internet.com. If you require some feedback on a career concern or question, you can post to a career-related bulletin board.

SMARTDOG
HTTP://WWW.SMARTDOG.ORG/

Self-described as a "matchmaker" service, this imaginatively presented resource has the goal of finding a "SmartDog a good home." In an attempt to line you up with a job in the high-tech field, the site gives you access to job listings with some 1,700 companies located in and around Rochester, New York. Addresses and phone numbers are given for representative companies. You have the options of searching or browsing the jobs database. Among the categories of jobs you'll find here are computer graphics, engineering (hardware, software, Web, intranet), information systems (client/server, database administration, network), quality assurance, and technical marketing, sales, training, and writing.

Want to know more about the Rochester area? Check out "A Better Job" to read about Rochester's growing high-tech industry or "A Better Life" for information on climate and lifestyle. Join in on the discussion groups to learn even more.

TOWN ONLINE WORKING
HTTP://WWW.TOWNONLINE.COM/WORKING/

This is the online version of Working, a publication from the New England publisher Community Newspaper Company. If you're looking for a job in eastern Massachusetts, this is a good place to start. You can browse through all the listings or by specialty, or you can search by keyword. Fill out the registration form (free) and upload your resume; Job Agent, the matching service, will find jobs matching the criteria you specify.

Also available are New England-area company profiles, job fair listings, and a discussion group. "Career Resources" leads you on a detailed path to finding the right job. You'll find job search tips, information about hot industries in Massachusetts, discussions on various workplace issues, and articles about continuing education programs and their benefits. There's a lot to absorb, so take your time.

TRI-STATE JOBS

HTTP://WWW.TRISTATEJOBS.COM/

If you want to work in Connecticut, New Jersey, or New York, this site may be able to offer some assistance in your job search. To search the database of some 20,000 jobs, first identify pertinent keywords, state (or all three), ad date, job type (permanent or contract), and job function. The last item gives you such choices as accounting, consulting, creative, education, finance, health care, legal, operations, retail, scientific, and service, among others. Job duties plus required education and work experience are described, and contact information is provided. You may also be given links to company home pages, where you can conduct your own research before applying online. A unique feature of this site is the option to forward job ads to a friend who might be interested. You can even include a message of your own.

VTJOBS

HTTP://WWW.VTJOBS.COM/

This Vermont job site comes from the employment service firm Personnel Department Incorporated. Jobs are listed in a variety of categories, including accounting, computers, contract work, drafting and design, engineering, manufacturing, and trades. Seasonal and miscellaneous positions are also featured. Job duties and minimum requirements are described. If something strikes your fancy, contact PDI directly. A small collection of links to Vermont-related sites is also available.

United States: South & Southeast

ARKANSAS EMPLOYMENT REGISTER
HTTP://WWW.ARJOBS.COM/

AER is a Little Rock newspaper devoted to employment. Here at its Web site you will have access to job fair details, career articles, profiles of Arkansas employers, and job listings in the categories of office support, medical, professional, technical, or general. If you prefer, you can enter a search term to find suitable listings. Company profiles arm you with founding date, number of employees, and information about apprenticeship opportunities, rate of turnover, promotion from within, and more. The links page gives you direct access to recruiting firms and other employment resources.

CAROLINA'S PREFERRED JOBS
HTTP://CAROLINA.PREFERREDJOBS.COM/

The bulk of the North or South Carolina jobs you'll find here are in the technical field. Search job listings by category and/or keyword as well as other variables. In addition to these you will be able to search technical or nontechnical jobs in other states. Brief company profiles are provided. Enter or edit your resume online at the Job Search Workstation. Your resume is available to paying employers who visit the site. If you find a job you're interested in, you can automatically send in your resume.

Not only can you look for a job here, but you can conduct some career research of your own as well. Check out the links to salary surveys in assorted career fields, read about select internship programs offered nationwide, access information about diversity issues, or find out what all is involved if you have to relocate. Job-related newsgroups are listed, and career advice is presented ("Career Advocate").

HAMPTON ROADS CAREERCONNECTION

HTTP://WWW.PILOTONLINE.COM/JOBS/INDEX.HTML

This resource, from the Virginian-Pilot, offers job listings for the Hampton Roads (Virginia) area. This includes Chesapeake, Gloucester, Hampton, Newport News, Norfolk, Portsmouth, Suffolk, Virginia Beach, and Williamsburg. Type in a keyword and/or specify a job category. Choices are varied and feature accounting, advertising, care giving, chemistry, counseling, driving, environmental, hotel, Internet, merchandising, operations, publishing, recreation, security, shipping, travel, and word processing. Selected hiring employers are profiled. If you find one that appeals to you, go ahead and view the job openings. For career advice, read the collection of pertinent articles and helpful tips. And if you are considering settling in one of these communities, work your way back through the site to the Hampton Roads community guides, where you'll find much of local cultural interest.

HERALDLINK EMPLOYMENT CLASSIFIEDS

HTTP://WWW.HERALD.COM/MAX/EMPLOYMENT/CONTENT.HTM

Here is the online version of the Miami Herald's employment classifieds. Simply choose a category—perhaps aviation, city/government, domestic, engineering/technical, medical/health care, personal services, sales, or self-employment—and/or type in a keyword to view job listings. Select the maximum number of ads to be displayed. Then browse to your heart's content!

United States: Midwest

CENTRAL INDIANA.COM CLASSIFIED ADS

HTTP://WWW.CENTRALINDIANA.COM/CLASSIFIEDS.HTML

From this site you can access classified advertisements from newspapers that are part of the Thomson Indiana group. Among the newspapers represented are the Greensburg Daily News, Anderson's Herald Bulletin, the Kokomo Tribune, Logansport's Pharos-Tribune, the Rushville Republican, and Terre Haute's Tribune-Star, as well as suburban Indianapolis papers. Simply select the newspaper of your choice and then click on its employment icon. Search or browse job listings as appropriate. In addition to employment classifieds, you will be able to view other classifieds (merchandise, pets and animals, real estate, and so on), not to mention the online newspaper in full.

CHICAGO TRIBUNE CAREERPATH

HTTP://CHICAGOTRIBUNE.COM/MARKETPLACES/CAREER/

The Chicago Tribune's online offering is affiliated with CareerPath.com, a national job site. Not only will you have access here to CareerPath.com's national job listings, but you will have direct access to the Trib's classified ads. You can go through the ads by designating any of a wide range of categories (for example, assembler, drafting, floral designer, horticulture, journalism, nursing, plastics, sales, or transcriber) or you may indicate search words.

If you want to research particular companies, look at the "Featured Employers" section. Here you'll get links to company home pages along with details on current job openings. There is a "News & Advice" section that keeps you informed about what's going on in the Chicago job market. Within this section you'll find "The Job-Seekers Guide," the advice area that will help you explore your career options, whip up resumes and cover letters, gear up for job hunting, and ace those interviews. If you're ready to put those skills to the test, look at the events calendar to see what career fairs and conferences are coming up. "Silicon Prairie" gives you the latest on Chicago's high-tech industry.

IOWA: THE SMARTCAREER MOVE

HTTP://WWW.SMARTCAREERMOVE.COM/

There are a few ways for you to utilize this Iowa Department of Economic Development site to search for a job in Iowa. Check out the links to home and employment pages of participating companies, which are also briefly described. Or enter a keyword (examples are given) to pull up a current listing of openings. Submit a career profile in order for SmartCareer Mail to deliver (via e-mail) details to you on new job postings matching your specified criteria.

Here you can also learn about the growth of business in Iowa. Sections are devoted to manufacturing, technology, and service. Information is also given on living and playing in Iowa. Some of the categories covered are arts, communities, education, recreation, sports, and tourism. Links to additional state and local resources expand on the materials presented here.

MICHIGAN WORKS!

HTTP://WWW.MICHWORKS.ORG/

This Web site supplements the career services offered by Michigan Works Agency centers statewide. To find the office nearest you, check out the listings of local MWA centers by county. In the meantime, use the site to search for jobs in Michigan. Select counties or regions and then specify an occupational category or a job title. Job descriptions and application instructions are provided. Additionally, extensive labor market information is available, and links to a few related state and career sites are included.

MINNESOTAJOBS.COM
HTTP://MINNESOTAJOBS.COM/

MinnesotaJobs.com, a division of the Trumor Company, has the goal of bringing together job seekers and hiring employers. Listings are offered for companies and placement firms in the areas of business and management, medical, or technical, as well as for organizations offering training opportunities, with links to home pages where available. To search jobs, enter a keyword or select a job category (most of which are of a technical nature).

Other resources include a large collection of articles and helpful tips. Sample titles are "How to Increase Referrals," "Climbing the Career Ladder," and "Hire Me!" There are also links to related sites of interest.

OHIO CAREERS RESOURCE CENTER
HTTP://WWW.OHIOCAREERS.COM/

This Ohio employment resource focuses on jobs in the engineering and information technology industries. To search the jobs database, enter appropriate search terms. Among the jobs you'll find here are programmer/analyst, application engineer, business technical consultant, usability specialist, and corporate banking representative. Details on job duties, requirements, responsibilities, and location are given. More useful material can be found by following the links to other career- or Ohio-related sites.

WISCONSIN JOBS ON-LINE
HTTP://WWW.WISJOBS.COM/

This state employment and recruiting resource offers job seekers numerous ways to fine-tune an online job search. From drop-down list boxes, you can identify a particular employer, location, job category, and job class. Results will be listed, from which you can access more detailed information on job duties and application procedure. You will find jobs posted in all areas of the workforce, such as for chemists, food service packagers, purchasing managers, reservations agents, security guards, systems engineers, technical architects, and word processing operators, just to name a few. Sign up to have matching job openings sent directly to you by e-mail. Interview and resume tips plus links to other related sites can be found here as well.

United States: Southwest and Mountain Region

CAREERSCOLORADO
HTTP://WWW.CAREERSCOLORADO.COM/

Services geared toward Colorado employers as well as job seekers are offered at this site. If you are looking for a job, one of your options is to view openings by way of the company listing. Click on a company name to see what jobs are currently available. Profiles are provided for select companies. Read these to learn about the company's history, benefits packages, work environment, and more. Another way to find a job here is to search the database. Type in a keyword and/or choose a skill category. (Choices run the gamut and include child care, graphic arts, human resources, insurance, mechanical, and retail.) You can also designate your level of education. Career-related tips, event listings, and links complete this site.

JOBSOK
HTTP://WWW.JOBSOK.COM/

This CareerPath.com site provides you with direct access to job listings from the Oklahoman. Look through the daily or Sunday classifieds to find job openings in fields that are of interest to you. Business news and employment-related feature stories from the Oklahoman are offered for your perusal. If you decide to expand your job search, you will be able to look through CareerPath.com's national job listings as well.

MONTANA JOB SERVICE
HTTP://JSD.DLI.STATE.MT.US/

The Montana Department of Labor and Industry presents this career resource. Search the jobs database by keyword, job category, or job title, specifying a region or city of Montana as well as minimum salary. Results feature a brief job description along with posting and closing dates, job title and location, hours, wage information, and contact details. Jobs can be found in such categories as clerical and office, community and social services, education and training, farming, health and science, mechanics, military, production and manufacturing, sports and recreation, and transportation.

TEXAS-JOBS.NET

HTTP://WWW.TEXAS-JOBS.NET/

You will have access not only to job listings for Texas here but for all of the United States as well as certain other locations worldwide. But the focus is on Texas—mostly Dallas, Houston, and Austin—so let's start there. When you visit the site, there will likely be dozens of new Texas job postings. Click on the employer's name to read the company profile, to browse all job opportunities with the company, and to get a link to the company's home page. Or click on the job title to read that specific job description. You can add desirable job postings to your own in-box. If you want to apply online, you will first have to build and post a resume at the site. There's a separate employer directory, which you can view according to your own specifications. You can also search the company directory.

Unless you specify otherwise, the jobs database covers openings nationwide or even internationally. So if you're only interested in Texas jobs, be sure to indicate that. Links to all sorts of other Texas job and company sites are included, as are links to sites of local interest plus various relocation tools.

UTAH'S CAREER CENTER

HTTP://KSL.TOPJOBSUSA.COM/

Salt Lake City's KSL Television & Radio sponsors this career site. When you go to search the jobs database, the default setting is Utah—but you can also search for jobs in other states as well. You can elect to view your search results as full-text job descriptions or as a geographical listing. A searchable company database offers profiles and contact details. The site also features articles discussing resumes, networking, marketing oneself, interviewing, and stress management. "The Inside Job" covers Utah job trends and current career-related events. And of course you can find out what's on the air by going back to the KSL home page. Here too you can track down local information that might be of interest if you're considering relocation.

WORKAVENUE.COM: PHOENIX

HTTP://AWORKAVE.STARNEWS.COM/CGI-BIN/TEXIS/CODE/WORKAVENUE/

WorkAvenue.com matches job seekers with hiring employers. This particular site is presented in conjunction with the Arizona Republic and serves people and companies in and around Phoenix. Take a tour to discover what all is waiting to be found here and at similar affiliated pages for the Twin Cities of Minneapolis and St. Paul, Minnesota; Indianapolis, Indiana; and Orange County, California (all accessible from the WorkAvenue.com main page).

As a job seeker, you can browse company listings (including recruiting agencies) and search job openings. Some of the job categories covered are architectural, auto industry, computer and information systems, government and military, hospitality, legal services, real estate, science and research, and the trades. Select any or all and type in your keywords. To zero in on just the right job, be sure to make use of some of the several fine-tuning options offered.

United States: Pacific Coast

ALASKA JOBS CENTER
HTTP://WWW.ILOVEALASKA.COM/ALASKAJOBS/

This site presents a varied collection of links to resources having to do with employment in Alaska. You'll have access to education pages, vocational training and rehabilitation programs, government sources, job classifieds, volunteer and seasonal listings, and Alaskan businesses, corporations, and organizations, as well as national career directories. Assorted classifieds (for automobiles, furniture and appliances, garage sales, pets, and more) are to be found at the site as well.

BAY AREA JOBS
HTTP://WWW.BAYAREACAREERS.COM/

Created by a San Francisco Bay area realtor, Bay Area Jobs is a useful and extensive resource for those interested in settling—and working—in the San Francisco Bay area. This is not a membership-based site, nor are there any job listings, but there are links aplenty.

Links to just about any site that lists jobs in the Bay area will most likely appear here. You can find employer sites by region: North Bay (Marin County area), San Francisco, Peninsula (just south of San Francisco), East

Bay (for example, Berkeley, Fremont, and Oakland), 680 Corridor (Concord, Pleasanton, Walnut Creek, and others), South Bay (San Jose area), Santa Cruz, and Sacramento. If you're unfamiliar with these areas, you'll want to glance at the available area maps. While many of the employer sites are listed at the Bay Area Jobs site, some regions have separate Web sites of their own, in partnership with Bay Area Jobs. Just follow the relevant links to find information on whatever area you're interested in.

In addition to company pages, there are links to dozens of other informative sites, such as classifieds, newsgroups, and general job-hunting resources.

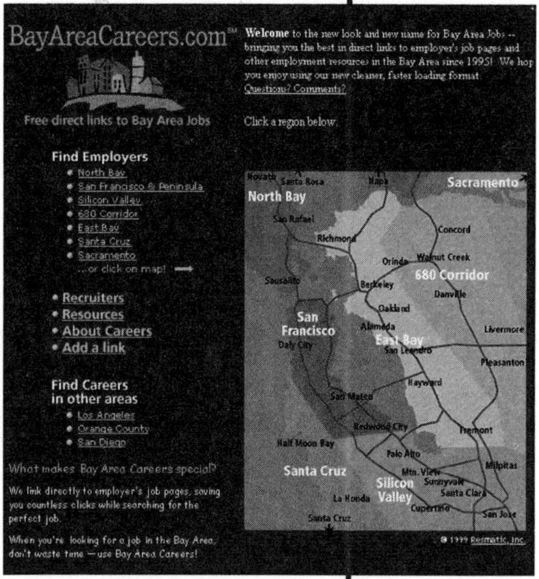

JOBHUNTER

HTTP://CLASSIFIEDS.SJMERCURY.COM/CLASSIFIEDS/JOBHUNTER/INDEXNOJAVA.HTML

Here's another California site, but this one has job listings. JobHunter lets you search the classified ads from the San Jose Mercury News and Contra Costa Times. Look through today's newspaper or papers dating back thirty days. You can search by keyword or by selecting a category (for example, administrative, driver, grocery, machinist, nursing, printing, security, or telecommunications). Using CareerPath.com, you'll have access to national listings as well.

But this site is more than just the classified ads. JobHunter is packed with career articles, job fair dates, dates for meetings of clubs and professional associations, and assorted company profiles. In the story archive you can read about telecommuting, how to build a better team, or women in the high-tech workplace. There are also interviews with notable businesspeople in Silicon Valley.

JOB SEARCH
HTTP://WWW.JSEARCH.COM/

This site is limited to the southern California region, but it sure packs a wallop. Job Search maintains a database of more than 40,000 companies, 3,000 resumes, and 5,000 active job vacancies. The jobs database is searchable by keyword. A sample search using "engineer" as the keyword may generate a few dozen current openings, with such titles as mechanical engineer, software engineer, structural engineer, and compliance engineer.

Check out the self-evaluation tests, which are intended to determine if you suffer from job burnout, if you are a workaholic, or if you're stressed out. They're all free and results are immediate! Links to other career-related sites are listed, with ratings and brief annotations.

You can also search a database of southern California companies by specifying various criteria (industry, location, commute distance, company size). A summary report is available at no charge, but to see complete listings (including current job openings), you'll have to pay a registration fee. Registered users can also add a resume to the database.

JOBSHAWAII
HTTP://WWW.JOBSHAWAII.COM/

If Hawaii is your ultimate destination, be sure to pay a visit to this site to discover what's in store for you there. Search jobs by keyword or browse openings by company. Recently added jobs are listed separately, so if you're a regular visitor you might want to check here first. To be notified of jobs matching criteria you specify, just sign up for the CareerAgent e-mail notification service.

Additional career resources are plentiful. Get data on Hawaii's job outlook; find out about grants, scholarships, fellowships, and graduate assistantships; track down numerous placement agencies; participate in an online job forum; and follow links to access even more information.

JOBSTAR
HTTP://JOBSTAR.ORG/

You could and should spend a considerable amount of time at this extensive Web site if you want to land a job in California. Partners include Sacramento public television station KVIE and the Wall Street Journal. Maintained by the Bay Area Library and Information System, JobStar is not only easy to navigate but fun too.

JobStar's emphasis is on career counseling. You can read about constructing a resume, study the salary scales, and learn how to explore the hidden job market, in which employers don't advertise positions but you look for the employer. JobStar also offers advice about how to research careers and companies. An excellent resource is the "Career Guides" section, which includes links to useful sites categorized by specific industries. Are you interested, for example, in the field of anthropology? You'll find a link to a career guide from University of California at Berkeley's Department of Anthropology. Other fields represented in "Career Guides" include culinary arts, law, military, and psychology, to name a few.

If you already know the city where you'd like to find a job, you might want to visit one of the sections devoted to Los Angeles, Sacramento, San Diego, or the San Francisco Bay area. You'll find links to local and national classified ads, area job banks, Internet job search resources, company directories, and area job hotline phone numbers. JobStar has lists of career centers, libraries, and training centers, as well as job fair information. This may all sound overwhelming, but JobStar is well-organized and unintimidating. If you're looking for something about employment in southern California and you can't find it at JobStar, you may not find it anywhere!

LOS ANGELES TIMES
HTTP://WWW.LATIMES.COM/CLASS/EMPLOY/

The classified ads from the L.A. Times can be searched at this Web site. You can look through the Sunday listings or those for the current day. Or you can search through the job listings posted by specific companies in southern California or nationwide. But be sure not to miss the site's career advice segments: "Job Search Tips," "Career Columnist," "Career News," and "Career Counselor." All have articles that are intended to help you land that great job you want. The articles are not only informative but entertaining and engaging as well. You'll find articles dealing with such issues as internship and volunteerism, getting ahead, workaholism, employment trends, retirement plans, and salary.

SF GATE: WHO'S HIRING?

HTTP://WWW.SFGATE.COM/CAREERSEARCH/

For those of you looking for employment in the San Francisco Bay area, this is the place to be! Browse through the classifieds from the San Francisco Chronicle and the San Francisco Examiner, from the Sunday paper or from any other day of the week. You can also specify search criteria if you don't want to go through the entire employment section. KRON-TV/BayTV job listings are available as well.

But there's more than just job listings here. Read through the career-related articles for tips and commentary. You'll also find information on regional job fairs, dates and descriptions of special events, and a list of "Job Hotlines" (phone numbers of area employers).

SOBA.NET

HTTP://WWW.SOBA.NET/

This independent job search resource came into being when its creator happened to be looking for a job in the Seattle, Washington, area. As a result, it offers a unique perspective on the job market. There's a large directory of local employers. Each listing is very briefly described, and links to home or employment pages are provided. This is true also for area recruiting and placement firms. Back to the company directory—you can view the list alphabetically or by industry, including accounting, aerospace, arts and culture, banking, design, education, engineering, government, health care, legal, marine and maritime, media, retail, software, and telecommunications. Check out listings on the local job boards for the arts, business, marketing, health, or tech. More job listings can be found when you follow any of the number of links to classified sites on the Web. Furthermore, employment news and events (such as job fairs) are detailed.

TODAY'S CAREERS
HTTP://WWW.TODAYS-CAREERS.COM/

Aimed at job seekers in the Pacific Northwest and more specifically Seattle, Washington, and Portland, Oregon, this Trader Publishing Company employment newspaper site features a jobs database that is both searchable and browsable. Type in a keyword to describe what you're looking for, or browse jobs alphabetically by job title or by category (health care, high tech, or sales). Links to numerous other employment-related sites enable you to broaden your job search.

YOUTH WORK
HTTP://WWW.YOUTHATWORK.ORG/

This site is an employment service for job-seeking youth (ages fourteen through twenty-four) in San Mateo and Santa Clara counties in California. Along with links to sites dealing with labor market information, educational institutions, career exploration, and employment regulations, there is a searchable jobs database. You can search by designating such criteria as full-time or part-time job, job category (drop-down list provided), location, type (apprenticeship, internship, work experience, and so on), and age. Many of the jobs are in food service, retail sales, recreation, and customer service.

Canada

CAREERMOSAIC CANADA
HTTP://WWW.CANADA.CAREERMOSAIC.COM/

This career resource is focused on Canada but features materials that will be useful to job seekers around the world. Before looking for a job, you might want to conduct some general career planning, so let's start at the "CampusConnection," which is aimed at students considering their educational and career options. Annotated links to sites dealing with the basics of career exploration are included, as are links to college career centers throughout Canada and pages where you can learn how to gain relevant work experience.

In the "Career Resource Centre" you'll discover other career management tools. "Stay Tuned to Your World" suggests sites you can visit to stay on top of news pertaining to Canada's workforce, economic conditions, and industry news. "Connect with Your Industry" offers links to sites having more focused industry-related content in the areas of business, diversity, finance, high tech, and hospitality. There are also sections on improving your writing skills, compiling a resume, and relocating.

All of this plus a searchable jobs database. Specifying any number of criteria, you can search for jobs in Canada or around the world. Do your research before applying by studying the employer profiles of select hiring companies.

JOB BANK OF CANADA

HTTP://JOBBANK.HRDC-DRHC.GC.CA/

Job Bank is brought to you by Human Resources Development Canada. The job listings are from employers who place their listings with the HRDC. You can search specified Canadian regions or cities for designated occupational keywords, or you can view jobs posted in the last forty-eight hours. Details are given on experience required, salary, and who to contact.

In the "Quick Search" section you can try to find job listings appropriate for students. To do this, include the word "student" in your search terms.

This basic site does not supply any career advice. It is, however, a valuable resource for finding job vacancies in Canada.

WORKINFONET

HTTP://WWW.WORKINFONET.CA/

This is a massive directory of career resources covering all of Canada, with information also specifically devoted to individual Canadian provinces and territories. Some of the sections are titled "Jobs, Work and Recruiting," "Occupations and Careers," "Learning, Education and

Training," "Workplace Issues and Supports," and "Financial Help and Issues." You can view lists of fully annotated links for Canada or you can designate a specific province or territory and view links relevant to it.

It might be difficult to decide where to start, since there are so many topics represented here: volunteer opportunities, career planning, professional associations, apprenticeships, continuing education, starting a business, workplace regulations, student scholarships, business loans . . . the list goes on! "Quick Reference" is designed to give you "rapid access to some selected resources," so this might be the way to go. You won't find job listings at the site, but you will have access to jobs posted at various other Canadian Web sites. If you want to check out a specific province or territory—say, British Columbia—then you can go to its very own WorkinfoNET site. Most provinces and territories have one. Interested in practicing your French? WorkinfoNET information is given in French as well as English. If you work in Canada or are planning to do so, this is an excellent place to begin or continue your career exploration process.

International

ASIA-NET
HTTP://WWW.ASIA-NET.COM/

This site is great for those of you who wish to go east—far east, that is. Asia-Net lists job opportunities for those who are bilingual in English and Japanese, Chinese, or Korean. Actually, some of the jobs you'll find here are based in the United States.

Scan through the current job vacancies by language, category (technical, business, new hire/intern, administration, education), and/or source (company ad or executive search). Then click on those results you're interested in so you can get details about the company, responsibilities, and qualifications. To get an idea of how this would work, if you select business as being the category, Japanese as the language, and company ads being the listing source, you may generate listings such as financial analyst, executive secretary, event coordinator, industrial engineer, or system sales specialist.

If you want to keep up with new job postings or changes to the Web site, you can sign up for the free mailing list. Asia-Net's message board lets you network with other bilingual job seekers. The "Salary Tracker" lists (anonymously) members' salaries, along with job titles, years on the job, location, and languages.

CAREERS ONLINE
HTTP://WWW.CAREERSONLINE.COM.AU/

Want to go down under? Careers OnLine may be able to help. It offers job resources for Australia. You might want to make your first stop the "Job Seeker's Workshop," which will help you organize your job search and offer you hints on where to start looking for jobs. "Choosing a Career" gives you a chance to look within yourself to do some self-assessment. Topics covered include past experiences, abilities and interests, and rewards from work. When you're done here, this might be the time to go to the "Virtual Careers Show" section, where you'll have access to about 1,000 job descriptions sorted by category.

Move on to "Job & Course Info," which discusses deciding on an actual career and how to go about securing a job. Be sure to take a look at "Education Levels," "Job Study Page," and "Jobs Which WON'T Suit You." Here you can also study industry and occupational groups.

The site has a resume builder to help you write a winning resume, interview tips, and a section to help guide you through tricky application forms.

Last but not least, you can access job listings for Australia or even worldwide or you can search or browse Careers OnLine listings. Some of the categories available for browsing are hospital/medical, agricultural, tourism/leisure, and community services. And once you find a job, you'll need to look at the section (linked from Australia's Department of Immigration and Multicultural Affairs) regarding Australian immigration.

EMPLOYMENT INFORMATION
HTTP://WWW.PSC-CFP.GC.CA/INTPGM/EPB6.HTM

This site, by the Public Service Commission of Canada, might not look like much, but it offers a wealth of resources for an international job search, listing direct links to job listings and other employment information posted by international organizations. Representative organizations include the African Development Bank, the World Health Organization, the European Bank for

Reconstruction and Development, the United Nations Development Programme, the Asian Development Bank, and the International Trade Centre.

ESCAPE ARTIST

HTTP://WWW.ESCAPEARTIST.COM/

The world is your oyster, and this Web site is the pearl. Escape Artist features dozens of resources to help you not only get an overseas job but also learn everything about moving and living abroad. This site is jam-packed with information!

The first stop is the "Overseas Jobs" page. There is no jobs database, but you can search for job links by selecting the country you're interested in. Some of the countries listed are Africa, Norway, Hungary, Luxembourg, and Slovenia. For example, the Norway area lists links to sites in or pertaining to Norway. A short description indicates whether the site is in English or Norwegian. Informational sites about the country itself are also listed.

The "Moving Overseas" section presents perhaps all the resources you'll need to assist you in moving abroad. This area has links to telecommuting resources, embassies of the world, emigration and immigration information, worldwide moving companies, expatriate resources, and much more.

JOBSERVE

HTTP://WWW.JOBSERVE.COM/

If you hanker for bangers and mash (British for sausage and mashed potatoes) and you've got some technical skills, JobServe might serve you well. This Web site lists an enormous number of computer industry jobs, most in the United Kingdom with a smaller percentage in other countries worldwide. The jobs, both contract and permanent, are in the fields of engineering, computer science, banking, and more. The site claims to be used regularly by "over 1,800 IT [information technology] recruitment agencies to advertise more than 140,000 new contract and permanent vacancies every month."

Search through the job listings by keyword, skills, or preferred location. The "Instants" page lists all the newest job openings—they are posted immediately upon receipt. You might find vacancies for Delphi developers or help desk operators. If you wish, you can download database files containing job listings for later viewing.

JobServe also offers a matching service that will send you a daily e-mail with vacancies tailored to your skills and preferences. Be sure to check out the links to U.K. business home pages to get an idea of JobServe's clientele.

JOBSITE

HTTP://WWW.JOBSITE.CO.UK/

Job openings in the United Kingdom are posted here by major companies and recruitment agencies. Personalize "My Jobsite" to suit your needs (skills, desired location, part-time or full-time). You'll have access to thousands of job listings each month. Industries represented include aviation, construction, information technology, logistics, media, purchasing, sales, and travel and hospitality.

OVERSEAS JOBS EXPRESS

HTTP://WWW.OVERSEASJOBS.COM/

If somewhere other than here is where you want to be, then try this international jobs database site. You'll find vacancies all over the world. You can browse job openings by category. The categories are diverse—for example, architecture, environmental engineering, information technology, marine, nanny and au pair, seasonal, transportation, and many more—and each indicates the current number of vacancies. All jobs for that category are displayed, no matter the country. If you want to personalize your results, then use the "Quick Search Form." Here you can specify keyword, country, and category. There are links to other job search sites, as well as an annotated list of career- or job-related books that can be ordered.

PROSPECTS WEB

HTTP://WWW.PROSPECTS.CSU.MAN.AC.UK/

This extensive site's purpose is to help college graduates explore careers in the United Kingdom and Ireland. There is much to see here, including detailed descriptions of recruiting firms with links to their home pages (where available) and a database of law firms and chambers offering training internships. The jobs section gives you access to a jobs database where you can find vacancies in the areas of administration, engineering, finance, information services, manufacturing and processing, social and pastoral care, and others. From "Employer Search" you can specify criteria for the type of work, desired location (worldwide), and your major. Your results won't actually be job openings but descriptions of companies that frequently hire graduate entrants. Some of the details given deal with training, benefits, and application procedure.

So much more than just a job database, the site includes a section called "Career Choice," which offers help with your job search. Profiles of hundreds of occupations are provided, plus there are tips on how to start your search. Furthermore, you'll find suggestions on what you can do with a degree in various subjects. There's information on jobs that are directly related to your degree, jobs where that degree would come in handy, types of companies that might employ graduates with that major, and postgraduate study.

If you're not ready to go out into the "real world" and find a job, how about graduate school? The section devoted to postgraduate opportunities has information on research opportunities in various areas of study, details on some 10,000 courses, studentships, and funding.

RECRUIT MEDIA
HTTP://WWW.RECRUITMEDIA.CO.UK/

Interested in landing a creative-technical job in the United Kingdom? You might want to stop by Recruit Media's straightforward site. Jobs are divided into the categories of freelance, permanent, or executive. Some of the job listings are in the areas of multimedia and the Internet, business information, design for print, and editorial. Company names are not given, but brief company profiles and job descriptions are supplied. Recruit Media is a recruiting agency, so you must apply to Recruit Media if you find any interesting positions.

REEI EMPLOYMENT OPPORTUNITIES
HTTP://WWW.INDIANA.EDU/ REEIWEB/ INDEMP.HTML

This site, put together by Indiana University's Russian & East European Institute, lists internships and job openings, many of them in Russia and

Eastern Europe. Search for vacancies by nonacademic or academic opportunities. The nonacademic jobs can be quite diverse, including program coordinator in Ukraine, office administrator in Moscow, editor of Romanian business books, Russian specialty cook, and assorted other positions in Belarus, Kyrgyzstan, Uzbekistan, and elsewhere. Internships are categorized as paid internships or unpaid internships and volunteer positions.

The links page is worth looking at for its wide array of Russian and East European resources. You'll find links to other centers focusing on the study of Russia and East Europe, library collections, and country, language, travel, and business resources.

TEACHING JOBS OVERSEAS
HTTP://JOYJOBS.COM/

Perhaps this site should be renamed "Everything you need to know about teaching abroad." If you are thinking about taking some time to travel and work abroad in the future, stop here before you begin your journey. The friendly and intimate site was created by Pamela Campbell and Igor Smirnoff, teachers who went abroad to work. They share their experiences in great detail and offer advice and resources to those who are considering following in their footsteps.

Suggestions are given on finding jobs abroad and attending an international job fair. You can have conversations or pose questions in the chat area, or you can post to the bulletin board. Links to other international teaching Web sites are included. If you're curious to find out more, you may wish to purchase Campbell and Smirnoff's information package, which supplements and expands on the materials presented here.

Section VI: Learning More about Assorted Career Fields

CHAPTER 13

RESOURCES FOR SPECIFIC INDUSTRIES

'In this chapter you'll be able to browse through a wide array of pages to discover information about your career field of choice. Associations, educational resources, publications, job banks, and Web directories for specific industries make up the bulk of the sites reviewed.

While most of these sites feature career-related materials—perhaps suggestions on how to enter the field, notes on required education and training (and where to find it), or descriptions of assorted occupations in the industry—other sites will be the more basic Web presence of professional associations. Even without specific career or job sections, these sites can be immensely useful. Read up on industry news, find out about upcoming events, track down a representative in your area and see about conducting an information interview. Well, you get the picture! There's plenty to learn from these resources, to give you an idea of whether or not the field appeals to you enough to make a commitment, which you might do by joining an organization, attending a school offering relevant educational programs, or pursuing a job in the field. Keep in mind that certain information at these sites may well be available to members only. Are you already committed enough to that career path to join and take full advantage?

It is not the intent here to cover every industry conceivable, though a great many are represented so as to give you a solid overview of what's waiting to be discovered on the Internet. So don't be mislead into thinking that this is all there is. There's still plenty more! If you're unable to find a specific industry, try looking at something related. For example, the broader sites listed under health care might feature coverage of an assortment of health-related fields, perhaps including dentistry or even veterinary medicine. Also, you can expect some overlap in the areas of hospitality, restaurants, and travel and tourism as well as in computers and the Internet, seeing that these fields are somewhat related. And of course don't miss the association directories. These will lead you to hundreds of other organizations' Web sites. If your interest lies in the areas of humanitarian, environmental, or nonprofit work, be sure to check out the listings of volunteer and internship sites in Chapter 8 as well.

Association Directories

ASAE GATEWAY TO ASSOCIATIONS ONLINE

HTTP://WWW.ASAENET.ORG/GATEWAY/ONLINEASSOCSLIST.HTML

This directory of associations is from the American Society of Association Executives. You can search the database by typing in a keyword, picking a category from A to Z, and/or designating a location, U.S. or international. Some of the numerous categories represented here include appliances, bar associations, ceramics, communications, dairy, fuel and energy, hardware and tools, housing, libraries, manufacturers, metals and mining, minorities, pest control, religion, sanitation, statistics, travel, utilities, and veterans. Search on your criteria to get search results displayed as a list of links. Then follow the links to visit association home pages.

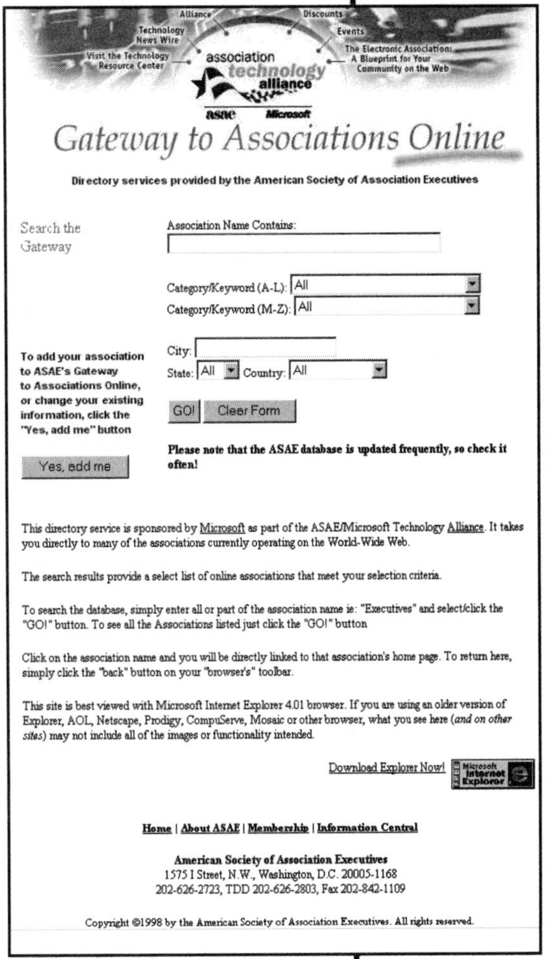

IPL ASSOCIATIONS ON THE NET

HTTP://WWW.IPL.ORG/REF/AON/

The Internet Public Library originated as a graduate project at the University of Michigan's School of Information and Library Studies (now the School of Information), so it is a library of sorts, only it's online and not down the street! And it's quite a large library at that. After you look here for associations of interest, you might want to go to the "Reference Center," where you can browse the entire IPL collection.

But for the moment let's get back to this section of the library. The IPL has compiled more than 1,100 links to association home pages, available here for your searching or browsing pleasure. Type in a keyword, select a subject area, go straight to a more specific subcategory, or pick a letter of the alphabet to browse by title. Some of the subject areas are the arts, humanities, and culture; business; computers and the Internet; industry; law and politics; and social science. You are given the choice of viewing either the short or the long version of a page. What's the difference? The short version gives you the name of the association as a hyperlink—and that's it. Whereas the long version supplies that along with full descriptive annotations to give you a better idea of what the association is all about and what you'll find at its Web site.

SCHOLARLY SOCIETIES PROJECT

HTTP://WWW.LIB.UWATERLOO.CA/SOCIETY/SUBJECTS_SOC.HTML

A terrific resource, the Scholarly Societies Project will direct you to all sorts of wonderful information that you can use as part of your career exploration. Links to about 1,500 scholarly societies worldwide have been gathered together by the University of Waterloo Electronic Library. They are organized according to subject area; for example, agricultural and food sciences, archaeology, area and time-period studies, astronomy, classical studies, drama, earth sciences, education, geography, language and linguistics, mechanical engineering, pharmacology, political science, religious studies, vision science, and women's studies.

The URL-Stability Index is a unique feature of this site. What is that? Well, you know how sometimes you follow a link only to find that the site's gone? The URL-Stability Index tracks that kind of thing. In short, it gives you an idea of how stable, or permanent, the links are for a particular subject area. The higher the percentage, the more stable the links in that subject area. If you're interested in this sort of thing, check out the section that describes it. You'll get the full details there, including a good discussion of domain names. A URL-Stability Rank is assigned to each URL. There's a page explaining this too, along with some useful notes on permanent URLs.

Accounting

ACCOUNTEMPS CAMPUS
HTTP://WWW.ACCOUNTEMPS.COM/CAMPUS/

If you've already decided on a career in accounting, this site (from financial staffing specialist Robert Half International) may be your next move. Some of the resources include tips on finding a job and conducting company research. Once you've found a job you want, you've got to land it. So more tips are given, on composing cover letters, compiling a resume, and conducting yourself in an interview. Links to related accounting or finance organizations and software developers are provided.

Ready to search for a job? You can do that at this site too. If you register with Accountemps, you'll get even more personalized service, such as updated information on job opportunities matching whatever criteria you selected.

ACCOUNTING & FINANCE JOBS
HTTP://WWW.ACCOUNTINGJOBS.COM/

Interested in pursuing a career in financial services? Brought to you by CareerMosaic and AccountingNet, this easy-to-navigate site focuses on resources and job openings in finance and accounting.

The "Resources" section, divided into career, recruiting, accounting, and finance resources, is a great place to research the industry. Some of the areas include "CPA Link," a directory of CPA firms, and "Forum," a discussion forum where you can chat about what's happening in the finance industry. You can read financial news and consumer credit information or browse the "Research Library," which contains links to government, international, and educational sites. Learn about banking, investing, mutual funds, and taxes. If it has to do with money, chances are it's here!

You can search the jobs database by job description or title, company name, or location. The resume database allows you to post your resume by completing a detailed form. The listing will appear in the resume database for ninety days.

The "Employer Index" lists a handful of featured employers, with links to their home pages so you can learn more about the companies, including benefits offered, stock options, and company history.

NATIONAL SOCIETY OF ACCOUNTANTS
HTTP://WWW.NSACCT.ORG/

NSA's large resource offers a wide range of accounting-related information accessible to members and visitors alike. Among the site's features are industry news, a schedule of events, details on NSA meetings and conferences, and coverage of pertinent legislative issues, as well as sections on accreditation, scholarships, financial calculators, and member pages. Some articles in the jobs section offer general career-planning ideas and advice, while others address industry-specific topics (for example, starting salaries in accounting and finance).

Advertising and Marketing

ADVERTISING AGE
HTTP://ADAGE.COM/

If you're always thinking up catchphrases like "just do it" or "got milk," then maybe advertising is the career for you! To learn about the advertising business, check out this online version of Advertising Age magazine. Catch up on industry news or find out when and where pertinent events and conferences are being held.

"Job Bank," created in conjunction with Monster.com, offers job listings in the advertising industry. You might find jobs posted for marketing, copywriting, photography, or public relations. Or fill out an online profile to have a job search agent scout out available jobs based on your specified criteria—use keywords to indicate your occupation of choice and select your desired location worldwide. Results will then be sent to you daily by e-mail.

COMMUNICATION ARTS
HTTP://WWW.COMMARTS.COM/

This inspiring site is aimed at the creative community working in print or digitally, in advertising and other fields. If you're looking for a job, you should start with the "Career" section. There you can view available jobs by U.S. region or state or you can view all listings by date. Results include a brief job description and contact details. Just a handful of the kinds of jobs you'll unearth here include graphic designer, interactive art director, user interface designer, and video animator.

Several discussion forums provide you with a place where you can talk with other creative students or professionals about freelancing, portfolios, software, Web design issues, and more. The "Creative" section features online exhibits and design articles. In the archives there is a timeline documenting the relationship between design and advertising for forty years. Also found at the site are details of design awards, reviews of (with links to) Web sites of the week, columns addressing creative topics like design technology and legal affairs, notes on upcoming conferences and seminars, and an impressive collection of related links for art schools, creative organizations, and creative directories, jobs databases, and recruiting firms.

MARKETINGJOBS.COM
HTTP://WWW.MARKETINGJOBS.COM/

This straightforward site features marketing job openings, a resume database for registered users, and industry news. So if marketing is your gig and you want to explore potential jobs, this site might help.

Conduct a job search by entering a keyword and specifying a U.S. state—or all of them, if location isn't important . Entering the keyword "marketing" may generate listings such as marketing analyst, marketing director, marketing brand manager, marketing research coordinator, or product manager. Your search results also indicate the job posting date, company name, and state. You can view further details (covering job requirements and contact information) for all the jobs you select. Then if the job is of interest to you, go ahead and submit your resume.

To get further industry information, click on "Associations" for a list of links to marketing-related associations and organizations. And for advertising, marketing, and financial news—you guessed it!—click on "News."

Aerospace

AMERICAN INSTITUTE OF AERONAUTICS AND ASTRONAUTICS

HTTP://WWW.AIAA.ORG/

AIAA is an organization of people working in or interested in the aerospace industry. If that sounds like you, then you'll want to be sure to stop by and take advantage of the wealth of materials and resources offered at this extensive site.

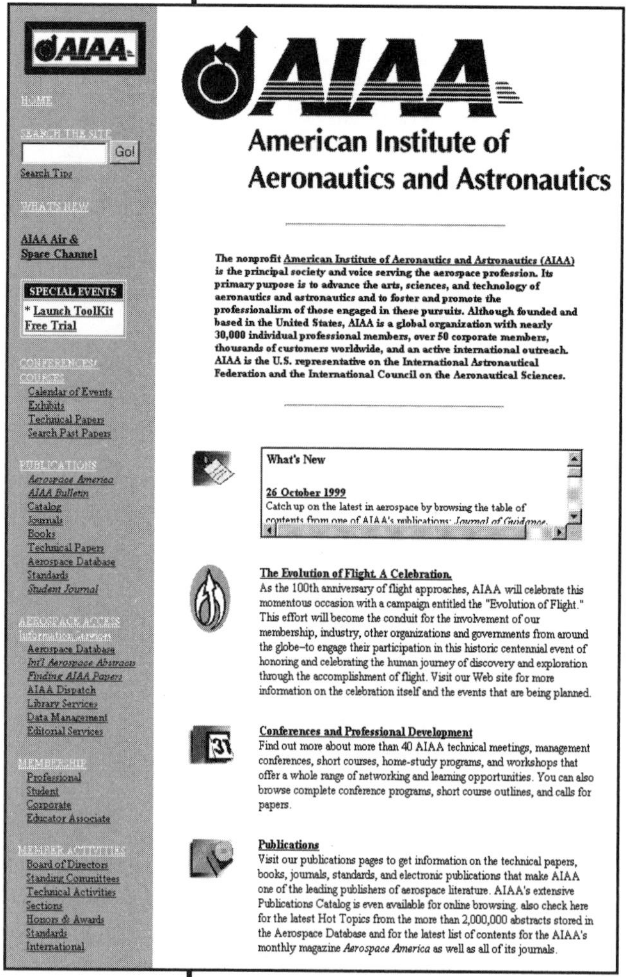

There are plenty of ways to keep up with the goings on in the field. The AIAA Bulletin keeps you apprised of news and events in the industry. Committee activities are described, and public policy and media issues are discussed. You can even subscribe to a weekly e-mail information update.

The bulk of "Career Planning & Placement Services" is available to members only. If you're not a member, what will you be missing? For starters, a searchable job listing, a resume database, a professional career timeline, a membership directory, and other career-related resources for the aerospace industry. A separate section is devoted to student AIAA branches, with contact information and links to pertinent home pages where available.

Agriculture

AG-BIZ.COM
HTTP://WWW.AG-BIZ.COM/

Are you looking for a job in agriculture? Well, that's what this site is all about. Jobs! Select a shortcut to find jobs falling under such categories as academic, commodity trader, crop protection, dairy cattle production, economist, equipment sales, grain operations, livestock pharmaceuticals, management, plant breeding, soil consultant, and vegetable production. Or use the advanced search function, which allows you to designate keywords, state, or state plus job category.

AGRICULTURE ONLINE
HTTP://WWW.AGRICULTURE.COM/

An interactive online community of agriculturists, this site is affiliated with Successful Farming magazine. Click on "Talk" to go straight to the discussion forums. Some of the topics covered include careers, machinery, farm business, crops, women in agriculture, computing, wildlife, and specialty farming. This is quite a busy area! To keep current with what's happening in the industry, you can read market news, get futures prices, and access options data. There's worldwide agriculture news here too.

If all of this sounds right up your alley, then head over to the classifieds section to see what job opportunities await you. Not only can you browse the job ads here, but you can view classifieds for farm machinery and supplies, livestock, real estate (farms and ranches), hay and feed, irrigation, farm buildings, tractors, trucks, parts, and more. Just pick the category you're interested in.

AMERICAN SOCIETY OF AGRONOMY
HTTP://WWW.AGRONOMY.ORG/

Here you'll have access to a multitude of agriculture-related materials, seeing that you are presented not only with ASA resources but with those from the Crop Science Society of America (CSSA), the Soil Science Society of America (SSSA), the Agronomic Science Foundation (ASF), and the

Certified Crop Adviser (CCA) program, all of which are linked from this site. You'll of course find plenty of information directed at members, but there's much of interest to folks considering a job in agriculture.

Speaking of jobs, you can find vacancies listed by going directly to "Career/Placement." You can search through job listings from the newsletter Crop Science-Soil Science-Agronomy News. Jobs are listed by category, including supervisory, private, public government, and assistantships. You may find titles such as agronomy educator, corn breeder, dryland farming systems specialist, forage agronomist, plant pathologist, or soil scientist. If you don't find what you're looking for here, you might want to check out the extensive collection of online job listing resources. You can order a free copy of a career resources booklet to learn more about various career options in agriculture.

Just to back up a moment . . . if you are not quite ready to get a job but are thinking about where to study agriculture, be sure to look at ASA's links page. You'll have access to home pages of college and university agronomy, soil and crop science, horticulture, and agricultural economics departments, among others.

Airlines

CYBERAIR AIRPARK

HTTP://WWW.CYBERAIR.COM/

It will be worth your while to download RealAudio and RealVideo when you visit this site, which aims to give you a full-sense aviation experience. (Okay, maybe not the sense of smell!) The site was put together by pilots and aviation buffs, and it's a refreshing combination of educational and safety-related information and plain old fun stuff.

Click on the home page's graphic of a landing runway to be taken to pages that will let you simulate flight on a United Airlines Boeing 777 or eavesdrop on O'Hare Airport air traffic controllers on the Chicago Approach frequency. There's a map online to help you track the airports that you'll hear mentioned in the transmissions.

Be sure to visit the section devoted to aviation safety, where there is lots of information from the Federal Aviation Administration (FAA), plus the section called "I Want to Be a Pilot." Here you can read the FAA's "Flying Start" guide, which walks you through how to become a pilot and what it's like learning to fly.

FLIGHT ATTENDANT CORPORATION OF AMERICA

HTTP://WWW.FLIGHTATTENDANTCORP.COM/

This site will clue you in on what it takes to become a flight attendant. FACA's "Frequently Asked Questions" is a good place to start exploring this site. Here you'll learn about average pay rates, flight benefits, and typical training. Be sure to check out the minimum requirements if you're wondering whether you're old enough, tall enough, or educated enough. You'll be pleasantly surprised to learn that the airlines no longer have the stringent requirements they had in the past.

There's also a list of the various major, regional, charter, and commuter airlines that are currently hiring. Once you've lined up an interview, you'll appreciate another section that dishes out sample interview questions (and the answers that the airlines will likely want to hear). The "Flight Attendant Resource Center" has links to employment-related pages at the Web sites of several airlines.

Alternative Health Care

AMERICAN HOLISTIC HEALTH ASSOCIATION

HTTP://AHHA.ORG/

Are you interested in practicing nonconventional, or alternative, health care? Or do you want to learn more about it before deciding which direction to take in your educational path? AHHA presents some introductory background material on the definition and practice of holistic medicine. Sample newsletter articles should provide a clearer picture of what to expect if you pursue a career in this area of medicine.

Among the site's resources is a section devoted to career considerations. Other holistic associations are listed here. Some of the practices represented include acupuncture, aromatherapy, biofeedback, chiropractic, herbalism, homeopathy, hypnotherapy, massage, midwifery, and naturopathy. The list contains addresses, phone numbers, and URLs (where available), so if you need additional information, you can follow up with one or more of these organizations.

Animals

AMERICAN VETERINARY MEDICAL ASSOCIATION
HTTP://WWW.AVMA.ORG/

The AVMA presents a wealth of material to look through if you're thinking about a career in veterinary medicine. "NetVet" includes background information on the field and career choices, as well as descriptions of the different roles a veterinarian may play in such areas as education and research, public health, and regulatory medicine. Check out the list of specialty organizations to get an idea of just how many options you have in the field of veterinary medicine. You'll find contact details for groups dealing with veterinary anesthesiology, critical care, dermatology, preventive medicine, radiology, toxicology, and so on. If you're trying to decide which college to attend, follow the links to schools of veterinary medicine worldwide and read about their programs. There's also a list of veterinary technology programs, with notes on the accreditation status of each.

Press releases, reports on public health issues, and certain features from the organization's journal are available to nonmembers. Plus there's advice on purchasing a pet, information on companion animal health care and safety, pet stories, and so much more.

AMERICAN ZOO AND AQUARIUM ASSOCIATION

HTTP://WWW.AZA.ORG/

Under "Publications," AZA presents a few useful articles—"Zoo & Aquarium Careers," "Training Marine Mammals," "Careers in Aquatic and Marine Science"—that are sure to help you in assessing your career options in this area. You'll get brief descriptions of tasks performed by curators, aquarists, aviculturists, herpetologists, mammalogists, veterinary technicians, volunteer coordinators, operations and development directors, and so on. The AZA Schools for Zoo and Aquarium Personnel programs are described, as are available grants and scholarships.

Be sure to check out the organization's publication Communiqué, where you can keep up with what's happening at zoos and in the industry; for example, news, activity reports, births and hatchings, events, exhibits, and awards. You'll have access to job listings here. Zookeeper (of reptiles and amphibians, large or marine mammals, fish and invertebrates, and the like), veterinary technician, volunteer coordinator, falcon keeper, and population biologist are among the positions you'll discover. Internships are listed there as well. If you want to get some hands-on experience before taking the plunge, head for the section called "Support the Zoo & Aquarium Community," where you'll find brief details on volunteering. You can then contact local zoos and aquariums (listed at the site under "Members") for specific guidance. The "Members" section also features a large assortment of other related links, enabling you to continue your online exploration.

Automotives

AUTOCAREERNET
HTTP://WWW.AUTOCAREERNET.COM/

Looking for a job in the automobile industry? This resource intends to help match job seekers with hiring companies. Search the jobs database by category (for example, suppliers of services, parts and accessories retailers, new car dealerships, OEMs [original equipment manufacturers], rental/leasing and used vehicles), keyword, and/or U.S. location. Results include job descriptions and offer you access to other job openings with particular employers. There are other ways to search for information here. You could simply select a category to view contact details for pertinent companies, along with (where available) brief company descriptions and perhaps even access to a more extensive profile, a listing of current job openings, and a link to the company's home page. Find companies by state or by picking a letter of the alphabet.

Other resources include links to automotive industry and trade association home pages, related publications, career advice, and a wide assortment of relocation-related services, covering colleges, city ratings, cost of living, moving and storage, real estate or renting, and weather.

Banking and Financial Services

AMERICAN BANKERS ASSOCIATION
HTTP://WWW.ABA.COM/

Founded in 1875, the ABA is a major player in the banking industry. Read the ABA press bulletins to learn about areas of interest. The "Conference and Education" section provides information on the ABA's educational programs including online courses. Separate treatments are given the American Institute of Banking (offering continuing education courses) and the Institute of Certified Bankers (offering certification programs).

"Executive Career Services" affords a place for executive-level job seekers to look for employment. You can browse listings by date posted, organization, or job type. Or you can search the database. Check it out to see what you have to look forward to sometime on down the road. Can you see yourself as a risk manager, a chief financial officer, a corporate marketing manager, a senior lending officer, or even a bank president?

The site contains plenty of relevant links pertaining to finance (commercial and personal), government, news, and banking associations that can assist you in your quest for banking information. Browse around and expand your career exploration!

BUSINESS JOB FINDER

HTTP://WWW.COB.OHIO-STATE.EDU/ FIN/ OSUJOBS.HTM

If being a credit analyst, an investment banker, or a product manager sounds appealing, but you're not quite sure what they do, check out this Web site. Brought to you by Ohio State University's Fisher College of Business, this site is chock-full of resources for you to use to explore a wide assortment of business careers in the areas of accounting, finance, management, and marketing and nonprofit.

If you want to know what is involved in the field of corporate finance, go to that section and you'll find an outline of the skills required to work in corporate finance, details of some of the key job areas, lists of print and Internet resources where you can conduct further research, typical salary ranges, facts and trends, and names of top corporations. Sound too dry? Actually, the information is presented in a very direct and often entertaining fashion. In the area of corporate finance, for example, you'll find comments such as "Puzzle-lovers Wanted" and "Are You a Forrest Gump Type?" which will help you decide whether the field is right for you. If it's not appealing, check out the other areas, where you'll discover similar sorts of materials that should help you to narrow down your options.

Once you've geared up for your career of choice, move on to the career reference section. There's an extensive link list of sites with business job openings and employer home pages. You can see what types of jobs are out there and research potential employers.

Biology

AMERICAN INSTITUTE OF BIOLOGICAL SCIENCES
HTTP://WWW.AIBS.ORG/

AIBS has been around since 1947. You can read all about the organization at its Web site. Current events and AIBS news are presented in great detail. You will be able to peruse select articles from BioScience magazine (subscribers have full access), as well as view the tables of contents of online issues. Court rulings and other government issues are discussed in the section called "Washington Watch." As you can see, there's plenty here to help you keep abreast of goings-on in the field of biology.

If you want some information specifically about a career in the biological sciences, then you're in luck. There's a section that describes various jobs biologists have. These include positions in research, health care, the outdoors, and education. Required education and training is discussed, as is the future of life science careers. For more focused information, check out the links to AIBS member societies. You'll find Web pages for organizations in the areas of economic botany, mathematical biology, ornithology, parasitology, tropical biology, and many more.

BOTANICAL SOCIETY OF AMERICA
HTTP://WWW.BOTANY.ORG/

The BSA's online brochure Careers in Botany provides a commendable introduction to the field. It includes a definition, discusses current issues (such as biotechnology), outlines specialized areas (plant biology, applied plant sciences, organismal, and other), and provides overviews of educational requirements, employment opportunities, and salary. Want to read about what's in store for the field of botany in the future? Botany for the Next Millennium examines just that.

Back to the present, "Botany in the News" gives you access to botany-related news articles from other sources. Another way to keep up with issues in botany is to read articles (abstract or full text) from the American Journal of Botany and the Plant Science Bulletin. There's a manageable collection of related links covering such topics as employment, kids, images, organizations, gardening, universities, funding, and publications.

EXPERIMENTAL MEDICINE JOB LISTING

HTTP://WWW.MEDCOR.MCGILL.CA/EXPMED/DOCS/JOBS.HTML

This is the job listing site of the Canadian Society of Biochemistry and Molecular & Cellular Biologists, presented in conjunction with Montreal's McGill University Division of Experimental Medicine. In addition to the job listings, the site also offers a tremendous number of useful links to other pertinent resources.

The jobs are all listed on one long page. Most openings are in academia. You'll find them divided by Canadian provinces, United States, Europe, and more. Graduate, postdoctoral, research assistant, scientist, and technician positions can be found in such areas as bioinformatics, cell culture, molecular genetics, peptide chemistry, synthetic chemistry, virology, and X-ray crystallography.

Move on to "Other Job Resource Links" where you'll find links to other experimental medicine-related and career sites. Sites the society deems to be excellent are noted with a star. Definitely stop by "Career Information, Statistics and Advice." You'll be treated to general information and statistics sites, science policy sites, and the usual resume and cover letter sites. Many of the links are useful for students and those considering a career in the sciences.

SCIENCE PROFESSIONAL NETWORK

HTTP://RECRUIT.SCIENCEMAG.ORG/

Brought to you by the American Association for the Advancement of Science and affiliated with Science magazine, this is a huge career exploration site for scientists of all kinds.

View the job ads by date posted or search vacancies using the handy form. Main categories are sciences and life sciences, with disciplines listed beneath. You'll find biochemistry, cell biology, genetics, molecular biology, oncology, physics, and many more. Just check the box next to the disciplines you'd like to search. You can narrow your search further by U.S. or international region, position (for example, clinical, faculty, management, postdoctoral, researcher), or organization (academic, government, industry, medical, foundation). The jobs database contains a formidable number of jobs, all with detailed descriptions.

The "Career Corner" is a good spot to research the science industry and see if it's the right career path for you. "Academic Connections" has a list of graduate programs in science, with links to universities and colleges. "Advice & Perspectives" features Science magazine articles on career opportunities in science. You might find articles on European career opportunities for scientists or on careers for women in biotechnology. Follow the link to the affiliated site Science's Next Wave, an electronic network for the next generation of scientists. You'll find all kinds of articles about science jobs and career transitions, the latest science news, and discussion forums covering career and job search issues and more.

Book Publishing

PUBLISHERS WEEKLY
HTTP://WWW.PUBLISHERSWEEKLY.COM/

The magazine Publishers Weekly is a leader in the book publishing industry, and its online edition affords you a way to stay on top of things. The news section is extensive and up-to-date. Feature articles cover book fairs, examine sales and trends in book publishing, and discuss categories such as hobbies, religion, cookbooks, and so on. If your interest is in children's or international publishing, then you'll want to explore those sections.

Also available are various best-seller lists: hardcover fiction and nonfiction, children's, religion, computer, mass market and trade paperback, and audio fiction and nonfiction. Plus you can read selected author profiles. And speaking of authors, stop by "Authors on the Highway" to learn the dates and places of book reading and signing events.

Ready to look at your job opportunities? The site offers an assortment of classified listings, including those for literary agents, books wanted, publications, publishers wanted, Web services, positions open, and more.

Broadcasting

AIRWAVES MEDIAWEB
HTTP://WWW.AIRWAVES.COM/

This radio broadcasting resource features a wide variety of job listings nationwide. If you want to be on the air, you might find something of interest here. Some of the jobs include news director, salesperson, sportscaster, radio chief engineer, and air talent. You also have the option of posting a listing for yourself.

There's other radio-related information here as well. If you want to look up call letters and frequencies for AM or FM radio stations in the United States or Canada, you can do it using the FCC (Federal Communications Commission) database search engine. To hear about and discuss what's happening in the industry or the way programming used to be, take a look at the Airwaves Radio Journal and Old Time Radio Roundtable Digest discussion forums.

BROADCAST EDUCATION ASSOCIATION
HTTP://WWW.BEAWEB.ORG/

BEA's mission is to prepare students for jobs in the industry and provide useful information for professors as well. Academic and industry job openings are posted, and information on or links to sites on broadcasting scholarships and grants can be found here as well. Elsewhere at this site you can read about past and future BEA conventions, where students are often active participants and speakers, and the various BEA interest divisions (for example, on communication technology, gender issues, multicultural studies, and news).

BROADCASTERS TRAINING NETWORK
HTTP://WWW.LEARN-BY-DOING.COM/

If you've been spinning your wheels about how to get started as a broadcaster, this site might be just what the doctor ordered, given its tag line as being "the most effective way to begin a career in radio broadcasting."

The key is BTN's apprenticeship program, for students fresh out of high school. The program matches each student with an instructor already working at a local radio station. For instance, if you want to become a news reporter, disc jockey, or sportscaster, you'll work with someone who's currently doing that job with a radio station in your area.

This site thoroughly explains how the program works, complete with testimonials. The careers described in greatest detail are disc jockey, news reporter, talk show host, sportscaster, and production engineer. Apprentices, receiving one-on-one training, pay a hefty placement fee to participate in the program, which lasts about four to six months.

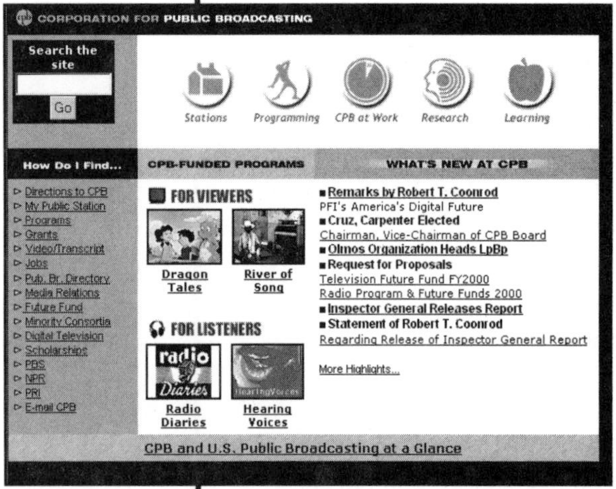

CORPORATION FOR PUBLIC BROADCASTING

HTTP://WWW.CPB.ORG/

Did you watch Sesame Street when you were growing up? Do you try to catch every episode of NOVA? Perhaps you've listened to the radio program All Things Considered. Public television and radio seems to be a part of every American's life. Here's where you can learn more about what goes on behind the scenes—and perhaps even become involved. The CPB Jobline offers a huge list of job vacancies. Detailed job descriptions, outlining requirements, salary, application procedures, and deadlines, are provided.

ELECTRONIC FIELD TRIP TO KENTUCKY EDUCATIONAL TELEVISION

HTTP://WWW.KET.ORG/TRIPS/KET/HIGH.HTML

The point of this site is to make middle and high school students aware of the large variety of television broadcast career options there are to choose from. The site gives information on the skills and educational requirements for each job, plus links to colleges and universities with broadcast degree programs.

The field trip is broken into three main sections: "Pre-production," "Production," and "Post-production." Under each section, you'll see a list of job titles, many of which overlap from one section to the next. Click on a specific career—say, broadcast engineer—to learn if and how that title is further divided into more specific positions. In this example, broadcast engineering encompasses the three jobs of video engineer, videotape engineer, and maintenance engineer. For each job, there are brief entries about general responsibilities, kinds of equipment used, job skills required, and typical starting salaries. Photos add to the feeling of being on a field trip and provide an idea of the work environment to be found in the field of television broadcasting.

NATIONAL ASSOCIATION OF BROADCASTERS
HTTP://WWW.NAB.ORG/

If you're a junkie for all things about broadcasting, this is a site you'll have to visit. Keep in mind, however, that the site was designed for someone already working in the industry, so if you're a fledgling broadcaster you may find some of the topics too esoteric. This might include the sections that focus on legal and regulatory issues or on science and technology, as they relate to broadcasting.

The section on careers allows you to search (using keyword and identifying location) current job listings. If your results aren't what you'd hoped for, you also have the option of browsing all current postings. Some of the jobs you might find would be engineering technician, news photographer, on-air announcer, and station manager.

Other career resources include addresses and URLs (where available) for state broadcasting associations, pointers for getting a job in the field, notes on upcoming events, and links to other related sites. Details are given for NAB research grants and the NABEF (National Association of Broadcasters Education Foundation) summer fellowship program.

TELEVISION AND RADIO NEWS RESEARCH

HTTP://WWW.MISSOURI.EDU/ JOURVS/

Vernon Stone, a former professor at the renowned Missouri School of Journalism, created this site that offers a behind-the-scenes glimpse at television and news broadcasting. Most of the material is compiled from Stone's print publications or national surveys.

Seeming more like a book than a Web site, this resource features a ton of valuable career information. The text looks honestly at varied aspects of the industry. For instance, one section studies how broadcast news salaries have kept up with 1990s inflation. Other sections consider the insufficiency of staff benefits at U.S. television and radio stations, examine how minorities and women have fared in the television news workforce in the 1990s, and report on the operations of television and radio newsrooms.

You'll definitely want to check out the section devoted to the pros and cons of broadcast careers, which includes information that should help you decide whether this is the right career path for you. Here you can compare your personality traits and career values to the results from a survey of people working in the field.

TV JOBS

HTTP://WWW.TVJOBS.COM/INDEX_A.HTM

Here you'll find scads of information about the television broadcasting industry and how to get a job in it. Job listings are up-to-date and cover a wide range of broadcasting positions, including general sales manager, meteorologist, news anchor, photojournalist, sports director, tape librarian, and videotape editor. To have full access to the job listings, however, you must register and pay a subscription fee. There is also a fee to post your resume to the database. In fact, there's a whole tier of fees depending on the type and duration of service. To get an idea of what's in store if you do subscribe, you can register as a guest and see a portion of what regular subscribers have access to.

Not to fret, though, if you don't subscribe because there's plenty of free information that you should find useful. For example, the site offers an extensive database of television stations across the United States, with links to home pages and to the station's job listings where available. Don't miss the "Pet Peeves" because it offers great job search tips for the broadcasting industry from members of the broadcasting industry. There are pet peeves from news directors, operations managers, photographers, and others on hiring committees. One pet peeve is about receiving a cover letter addressed to "Dear Sir or Madame"—when the recipient's name could easily be determined! Another is about receiving sample videotapes beginning with a music or video montage—when that is irrelevant to the position being pursued! Read more pet peeves and you'll definitely be enlightened.

And that's not all. TV Jobs also features networking opportunities, success stories from users who found employment using TV Jobs, links to sites offering scholarship or internship information as well as to broadcasting schools, and even weather radar links.

Business

INTERNATIONAL ASSOCIATION OF ADMINISTRATIVE PROFESSIONALS
HTTP://WWW.IAAP-HQ.ORG/

IAAP is a professional association that's been around since 1942, when it was founded as the National Secretaries Association. "Research and Trends" presents a number of pertinent articles about administrative positions. Start here to learn more about job titles, career advancement, occupational outlook, salaries, and technology. Links are given for international IAAP affiliates and other unaffiliated organizations.

If you want to look for an administrative position in the United States or Canada, you can do so through "Career Opportunities," which leads you to a job search site hosted by OfficeTeam, an administrative staffing firm. Some of the vacancies will be for legal secretary, executive assistant, human resource manager, inventory clerk, receptionist, and staffing manager.

THE ONLINE MBA
HTTP://WWW.COLUMBIA.EDU/CU/BUSINESS/CAREER/LINKS/

This Columbia University Business School site provides links to assorted MBA resources. Even if you aren't an MBA student or are a long way from thinking about graduate school, you'll find some valuable information if you're interested in the business world.

The many links cover such areas as business school listings; internship resources; business-related publications; company databases; job search or recruiting resources such as MBAjob.com, the MBA Employment Connection Association, and the MBA Enterprise Corps; international sites; and more. There are also links to MBA alumni sites and a meta-list of general career sites.

Chemicals

AMERICAN INSTITUTE OF CHEMICAL ENGINEERS
HTTP://WWW.AICHE.ORG/

AIChE's career section presents a brief description of what it is that chemical engineers do, along with a list of specialty areas (for example, agricultural chemicals, petrochemicals, polymers, and synthetic fibers, textiles, and films), a workplace overview, names of colleges and universities offering accredited chemical engineering programs, details on internships and summer research programs, profiles of individuals in the field, and notes on AIChE products that can be ordered for further information. Additionally, job openings posted in Chemical Engineering Progress are available, as are all sorts of job search tips and resource listings, including links to home pages of companies that employ large numbers of AIChE members.

Aside from all these career resources, there's AIChE and industry news to catch up on, a schedule of meetings and conferences to check out, and select Chemical Engineering Progress articles to peruse. Don't miss the current and back issues of ChAPTER One Online, a publication geared toward undergraduate chemical engineering students.

CHEMISTRY & INDUSTRY

HTTP://CI.MOND.ORG/

Here is Chemistry & Industry magazine's home page. The jobs database is updated regularly and is searchable by region (North America, Europe, or the rest of the world) and sector (government, academia, industry, or other). You can check the field in which you're looking for a job, such as physical chemistry, polymers and materials, food and agriculture, or environment. These employment types are further broken down to help you choose the correct category. Sign up for a mailing list that will notify you by e-mail when new jobs have been added to the database, or check out the job-hunting guide for chemists, which lists numerous resources for finding a job.

In addition to using this as a job search resource, you can also browse through Chemistry & Industry articles to keep abreast of current issues or you can search for meetings and conferences in your area.

Computers

ACM SIGGRAPH

HTTP://WWW.SIGGRAPH.ORG/

The computer graphics SIG (special interest group) of the Association for Computing Machinery, SIGGRAPH has been around for more than thirty years. This Web site documents some of its history and provides current materials such as details on conferences and workshops, a directory of SIGGRAPH chapters worldwide, and a newsletter. Newsletter topics include the computer gaming industry and interactive three-dimensional graphics. Ideas for further reading can be found in the GRAPHBIB database, which is linked from the site. It contains more than 17,000 bibliographic citations pertaining to computer graphics, some with URLs or abstracts.

You're in luck if you're looking for something about a computer graphics education or career. SIGGRAPH's education committee has compiled some really great materials in this area. "Choosing Computer Art As a Major in College" is a good place to start. If you're intrigued by what you read here, you might want to track down a school. So go ahead and check out the international education directory. Then there's a career handbook plus the "SIGGRAPH Five-Minute Career Mentor," a handy introduction to computer graphics careers. It discusses job opportunities, education, resumes, and other resources. To see what others in the industry have done, stop by the online computer graphics gallery.

If you're interested in other areas of computing, be sure to venture over to ACM's main page (http://www.acm.org/), where you'll of course find information about ACM as well as have access to materials on many other SIGs.

DICE.COM

HTTP://WWW.DICE.COM/

This resource is geared toward the serious high-tech job seeker. There's no fluff or hand-holding here! What makes dice.com unique is its immediacy. You can register your skills on a questionnaire, but only if you are currently available for a job or will be in the next three weeks. Job openings are posted by subscribing companies and recruiting firms. Links to clients' home pages are offered (where available) along with the job postings.

The job seeker can pursue other avenues here in a search for job opportunities. Not only is there the massive searchable database, but there are metro search pages for major U.S. cities as well as a job search agent that will deliver job listings to you via e-mail. If you're still conducting research in the field, take a look at the career links, where you'll find listings of general career materials, high-tech organizations, programming resources, and more.

So if you're curious about jobs in the areas of technical writing, hardware engineering, data processing, quality assurance, computer programming, systems administration, then dice.com is a must-see site.

THE INFORMATION PROFESSIONAL'S CAREER PAGE
HTTP://WWW.BRINT.COM/JOBS.HTM

This Web site directory is your guide to planning a career in information systems (IS) or management information systems (MIS). You'll find a variety of articles on the current state of the industry, as well as links to sites with job surveys and occupational outlook data.

First you might want to take a look at "W(h)ither MIS? Trends & Controversies in IS Practice and Research" to see if this is the industry for you. There are links to articles that discuss the trends and controversies of the MIS industry from different perspectives and voices. The industry is growing rapidly and changing just as quickly, so you'll want to get a feel for where it's headed.

Also featured here are links to salary surveys, jobs databases (not all computer-related), and sites of professional organizations. You'll be able to track down career resources intended to help you improve your interview skills and polish up your resume.

JOBENGINE
HTTP://WWW.JOBENGINE.COM/

The online recruiting service iSearch brings you this job search site for workers in the computer industry. You can look for a job by perusing the vast company directory or you can search by specifying certain criteria, among them location (U.S. or international), job title or description keywords, and job type (full- or part-time, contract, internship, or consultant). Some of the job vacancies will be for programmers, systems administrators, computer operators, data and applications architects, technical project managers, Web application developers, quality assurance technicians, and artificial intelligence engineers. When you search by specifying a location, a list of represented employers in that area will display along with job search results. This enables you to elect to see all job postings with a particular employer in your selected location.

SEMICONDUCTOR.NET
HTTP://WWW.SEMICONDUCTOR-INTL.COM/

Aimed at technicians, managers, and suppliers in the semiconductor industry, this site is a joint venture of Semiconductor International and FabLink. Content is pretty technical and consists of news, feature articles, product information, details on events and training, and statistics. There's a searchable directory of industry associations, with descriptions and links to home pages. Several other areas are searchable as well, and throughout you will find links to additional relevant resources.

STC REGIONAL AND CHAPTER INFORMATION
HTTP://STC.ORG/

The Society for Technical Communication membership includes technical writers and editors, graphic designers, multimedia artists, engineers, scientists, and more. In the employment section you'll find lists of jobs by region (locations where STC has chapters). The Silicon Valley region generated an enormous page of openings, mostly for technical writers and editors.

Plenty of useful links are featured as well, for schools where technical writing and communication programs are offered, for related professional organizations, and for sites about desktop publishing, graphics, HTML, indexing, and writing. And of course you can find out more about STC chapters and SIGs (special interest groups).

Construction

AMERICAN INSTITUTE OF ARCHITECTS
HTTP://WWW.AIAONLINE.COM/

This site is really for members of the AIA, but if you yearn to be an architect, chances are you'll someday become a member, so why not get a head start? You can read news from the AIA Digest, find out about upcoming conferences and workshops, and get details for continuing education courses offered. Certain articles and features are available to members only.

The section on career resources includes job listings and a resume database. "Career Decision Strategies" offers articles regarding planning your career (discussing internships and the advantages and disadvantages of large and small firms) and taking those first steps (self-assessment, researching firms, applying and interviewing). There are also sample cover letters, a job search checklist, and brief descriptions of architecture-related fields, such as landscape architecture, lighting design, architectural history, and environmental research.

Local AIA chapters and schools with accredited architecture programs are listed, with links to home pages where available. Furthermore, there's a searchable database of thousands of AIA-member firms. If you want to conduct even more research, you might want to explore the AIA bookstore.

ENR

HTTP://WWW.ENR.COM/

This McGraw-Hill Companies site, the online version of Engineering News-Record magazine, is a top resource for the construction industry, appealing to practicing or future architects, contractors, engineers, suppliers, and so on. Not only will you be able to read ENR features, but you can keep up with current industry issues. This includes news covering buildings, finance, power, technology, transportation, and more. There's also an extensive calendar of industry events for upcoming conferences.

"Career Opportunities" leads you to a searchable jobs database. The jobs are from issues of ENR. To get an idea of some of the powerhouses in the industry, take a look at the select company profiles and ENR's "Top Ranked Firms," listing design and environmental firms as well as contractors. Links to home pages are provided where available. This is a great tool for researching companies!

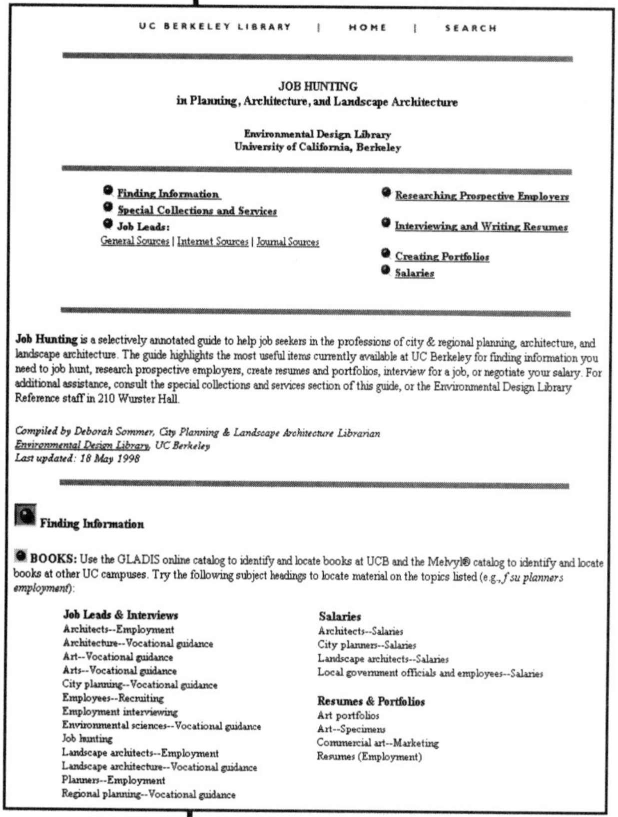
UC BERKELEY LIBRARY | HOME | SEARCH

JOB HUNTING
in Planning, Architecture, and Landscape Architecture

Environmental Design Library
University of California, Berkeley

- Finding Information
- Special Collections and Services
- Job Leads:
  General Sources | Internet Sources | Journal Sources
- Researching Prospective Employers
- Interviewing and Writing Resumes
- Creating Portfolios
- Salaries

Job Hunting is a selectively annotated guide to help job seekers in the professions of city & regional planning, architecture, and landscape architecture. The guide highlights the most useful items currently available at UC Berkeley for finding information you need to job hunt, research prospective employers, create resumes and portfolios, interview for a job, or negotiate your salary. For additional assistance, consult the special collections and services section of this guide, or the Environmental Design Library Reference staff in 210 Wurster Hall.

Compiled by Deborah Sommer, City Planning & Landscape Architecture Librarian
Environmental Design Library, UC Berkeley
Last updated: 18 May 1998

Finding Information

BOOKS: Use the GLADIS online catalog to identify and locate books at UCB and the Melvyl® catalog to identify and locate books at other UC campuses. Try the following subject headings to locate material on the topics listed (e.g., *f su planners employment*):

Job Leads & Interviews
Architects--Employment
Architecture--Vocational guidance
Art--Vocational guidance
Arts--Vocational guidance
City planning--Vocational guidance
Employees--Recruiting
Employment interviewing
Environmental sciences--Vocational guidance
Job hunting
Landscape architects--Employment
Landscape architecture--Vocational guidance
Planners--Employment
Regional planning--Vocational guidance

Salaries
Architects--Salaries
City planners--Salaries
Landscape architects--Salaries
Local government officials and employees--Salaries

Resumes & Portfolios
Art portfolios
Art--Specimens
Commercial art--Marketing
Resumes (Employment)

JOB HUNTING IN PLANNING, ARCHITECTURE, AND LANDSCAPE ARCHITECTURE

HTTP://WWW.LIB.BERKELEY.EDU/ENVI/JOBS.HTML

If you're interested in architecture or planning and want to conduct some research, this is a good place to start. From the University of California at Berkeley's Environmental Design Library, this site offers links and lists of resources to help you find out as much as possible about architecture and planning—and perhaps even land a job in the field.

"Finding Information" gives pointers for conducting library research. Suggestions are given for appropriate subject headings to search under and the journal indexes to look in for articles on architecture and on specific firms and organizations. "Job Leads" lists book titles on career opportunities and finding jobs. Names of academic journals and magazines that might be of use are also provided.

Additionally, you will find ideas for researching potential employers and bibliographies of helpful publications pertaining to interviewing, resumes, portfolios, and salary guides. Numerous links point to relevant Web sites where you can further explore the field of architecture and planning.

RIGHT OF WAY

HTTP://WWW.RIGHTOFWAY.COM/

This site provides resources for the right-of-way profession. Drawing a blank? Any land on which infrastructure (be it a highway or an airport) is built requires right of way. Those involved in the right-of-way profession include appraisers, property managers, surveyors, engineers, and others. Take a look at the job descriptions on the employment page to get a better idea of what the right-of-way profession encompasses.

For further research, there are links to pages for government agencies, railroads, pipelines, publications, property rights, transportation, utilities, and organizations. There's also a directory of right-of-way professionals broken down into categories such as acquisition and negotiation, environmental services, and relocation assistance. The bibliography section can assist with your research by pointing you toward some recommended books.

Cosmetology

AMERICAN ASSOCIATION OF COSMETOLOGY SCHOOLS
HTTP://WWW.BEAUTYSCHOOLS.ORG/

If you're trying to decide which school of cosmetology to attend, the AACS has a list of member schools that just might help. There's also a section devoted to Cosmetology Educator of America, the educational branch of AACS; convention and events details; and a wide array of links covering such areas as aromatherapy, education, equipment and supplies, publications, and nails, cosmetics, hair care, and skin care companies.

Dance

DANCEART.COM
HTTP://WWW.DANCEART.COM/

This resource is devoted to dance art as well as the world of dance. There's actually dance-related clip art and wallpaper (for your computer, that is!) available. But our focus here is on the other stuff—the articles about dance careers and choreography, interviews with dance professionals, dictionary of ballet terms, audition notices, and searchable directories of dance organizations and schools. Not to mention the message boards, of which there are many. You'll find message boards concerning all facets of dance, including adult students, choreography, costumes, eating disorders, injuries, partnering, and residency programs, along with "way cool" dance-related Web sites. There are message boards too that focus on particular types of dance, such as ballet, ballroom, jazz and hip-hop, modern, swing, and tap. Lots to talk about and lots of folks to talk with. Check it out!

DANCE MAGAZINE
HTTP://WWW.DANCEMAGAZINE.COM/

Here is the online counterpart of the magazine of the same name. Not only can you read select articles from the print publication, but you'll have access to dance reviews, a bulletin board, a collection of dance-related links, and an immense calendar of international dance events, covering performances, festivals, workshops, exhibitions, competitions, and media (for example, scheduled online chats). "How to Choose a College" discusses the basics as well as some specifics aimed at dance students. Photo and audition dos and don'ts are featured. If you need help finding and selecting a college or university dance program, you might want to consider ordering the Dance Magazine College Guide.

Dental Care

AMERICAN DENTAL ASSOCIATION
HTTP://WWW.ADA.ORG/

The ADA offers an impressive assortment of career materials here. Under "Dental Practice," check out the dentistry brochure, which presents definitions of the eight recognized specialized areas of dental practice: dental public health, endodontics, oral and maxillofacial pathology, oral and maxillofacial surgery, orthodontics and dentofacial orthopedics, pediatric dentistry, periodontics, and prosthodontics. Other brochures deal with dental hygiene, dental assisting, and dental laboratory technology. A large collection of links will point you toward colleges and universities offering dentistry programs, as well as to other association and organization sites. Ready to look at the jobs? Job opportunities posted in the Journal of the American Dental Association are available for viewing. If you're serious about dentistry, then you won't want to miss the ADA's news updates, position statements, and clinical reports, which will keep you abreast of current issues in the industry.

CAREERS IN DENTISTRY
HTTP://WWW.DENT.UNC.EDU/CAREERS/

The School of Dentistry at the University of North Carolina at Chapel Hill presents this in-depth introduction to the various career choices open to you in the field of dentistry. The section titled "Traditional Private Practice" addresses such topics as solo, group, and solo-group practice, outlining pros and cons of each, required preparation, job opportunities, and salaries, while "Alternatives to Traditional Private Practice" similarly treats dental health maintenance organizations, retail dentistry, and consultation dentistry. Other sections feature formats that are pretty much the same. There are separate sections detailing the career paths of dental hygiene, assisting, and laboratory technology. The section on specialties is very long. That's because it covers all eight recognized specialized areas of dentistry. Also covered is academic dentistry, dentistry in research and industry, military dentistry, hospital dentistry, and much more. Suggestions for further reading and other references are offered. Plus there's an extensive list of graduate programs, some of which are affiliated with dental schools and others not, with links where available.

Earth Sciences

GEOLOGICAL SOCIETY OF AMERICA
HTTP://WWW.GEOSOCIETY.ORG/

If you're wondering what kinds of career options there are available for geologists, check out the classified job listings from GSA Today. You'll find postings for asbestos lab analysts, environmental geologists, fluvial geomorphologists, and Quaternary geologists, as well as numerous faculty positions. Career brochures are available by request—you just have to fill in and submit a form online.

For further information, be sure to browse the links. There are a lot of them! Some of the sites listed are about dinosaurs and fossils, volcanoes and earthquakes, and water, climate, and atmosphere, while others are for internship, scholarship, and summer program details. Plus there are links lists of schools offering geoscience programs, not to mention all the sites for related organizations. As if all of that wasn't enough to keep you busy, there are links to even more job sites.

GEOSCI-JOBS
HTTP://WWW.ESKIMO.COM/ TCSMITH/MAIL/ GEOSCIJ.HTML

This site offers subscription information for the GEOSCI-JOBS mailing list, which posts geoscience job opportunities. Jobs are in the areas of geology, seismology, petroleum engineering, mineralogy, hydrology, oceanography, and the like. Links at the site provide easy access to similar pages presenting subscription details for three other mailing lists, in the fields of civil engineering, GIS and remote sensing, and meteorology and atmospheric science. Archives of past listings are available for viewing.

Also offered is a fee-based employment service. USENET newsgroups and Web sites are scoured for job opportunities, which are then sent to you via e-mail (or you can access the data at the Web site with a password). Finally, there's a resume database available for subscribers.

Education

ACADEMIC EMPLOYMENT NETWORK
HTTP://WWW.ACADEMPLOY.COM/

This is a great site if you want to work in the world of education. It's loaded with links to various teaching-related resources and information, including teacher certification requirements by state. The job ads, for positions in all levels of academia, are usually posted for thirty days and are listed by state. Nestled among teaching jobs you'll find listings of other education-related positions, such as for coaches, aftercare coordinators, or residential shift supervisors. Also useful is the site's discussion forum.

THE CHRONICLE OF HIGHER EDUCATION
HTTP://CHRONICLE.MERIT.EDU/

Do you envision yourself as a professor? This site, which includes contents of the current issue of The Chronicle of Higher Education (available to subscribers), is one of the best resources for finding a job in higher education. So if that appeals to you, start acquainted with it now.

There are great articles about employment in the academic world, making a career change, and scholarly publishing, as well as links to educational sites. Browse the "Bookshelf" for an annotated list of books related to the academic job search, or join an online discussion forum (Colloquy) concerning issues in academia.

The jobs are updated weekly and can be browsed by discipline (humanities, social sciences, science and technology, professional fields) or can be searched by keyword and region. Faculty and research, administrative, and executive positions are listed. The current week's job listings can be viewed only by subscribers, whereas the previous week's job listings are accessible to all visitors to the site.

DAVE'S ESL CAFE
HTTP://WWW.ESLCAFE.COM/

Dave Sperling, an ESL instructor at California State University at Northridge, has pulled together an enormous amount of materials for teachers or students of ESL (English as a Second Language) or

The Chronicle
of Higher Education

Weekend, October 29 - 31, 1999

SEARCH THE SITE
SITE MAP

TODAY'S NEWS
INFORMATION TECHNOLOGY
THIS WEEK'S CHRONICLE
PUBLISHING
MONEY
GOVERNMENT & POLITICS
NEW GRANT COMPETITIONS
COMMUNITY COLLEGES
CAMPUS LIFE
INTERNATIONAL
PEOPLE & EVENTS
OPINION & ARTS
COLLOQUY
INFORMATION BANK
ISSUES IN DEPTH
ON-LINE MARKET
JOBS

About The Chronicle
How to register
How to subscribe
Subscriber services
Change your user name
Change your password
Forgot your password?
How to advertise
Privacy policy
Corrections
Feedback
Help

Today's News

House approves 15% budget increase for the N.I.H. -- but with a hitch

College Board looks to investors to finance $30-million commercial Web site

Stanford president pulls the plug on ailing hospital merger

U. of Vermont spurns federal direct-lending program

U. of North Carolina trustees propose tuition increase to raise faculty salaries

$50.5-million bequest to Georgia Tech is largest ever to a sports program

Updates on 10 capital campaigns

PREVIOUS DAILY NEWS REPORTS

Information Technology

N.S.F. grant aims to improve networks at black, Hispanic, and tribal colleges

Bill Gates looks ahead to the era of "Generation I"

■ Links to Internet resources for higher education

Also New Today

■ Everything you ever wanted to know about 4 artists' life work
MAGAZINE AND JOURNAL READER

■ Fellowships for the study of religious and ethical values in the humanities and social sciences
NEW GRANT COMPETITION

■ Should virtual universities be accredited? Can on-line education be the equal of traditional higher education? With new responses.
COLLOQUY

■ A controversial task force on higher education called, in 1973, for vastly increased flexibility in access to, and financing and accreditation of, postsecondary education in America.
HISTORY

■ More than 1,390 openings, in and out of academe, from the November 5 issue of The Chronicle
JOBS

In This Week's Chronicle

Courtesy Grimmer for The Chronicle

ASSESSING VIRTUAL UNIVERSITIES
Two Opinion articles argue both sides of the issue. James Perley and Denise Marie Tanguay, of the American Association of University Professors, write that accrediting new institutions that operate entirely on line risks robbing higher education of its basic values. But Steven Crow, executive director of the North Central Association of Colleges and Schools, which recently accredited such an institution, says that traditional standards can, once more, be adapted safely to a new trend in education. And you can join the debate, in Colloquy.

A FRESH LOOK AT 'GATSBY'
The impending publication of an early version of the novel by F. Scott Fitzgerald offers a look at how a literary classic can evolve.

'MOVEMENT WITH MARTHA'
Fitness centers add hip-hop, jazz, and salsa dance steps to their aerobics routines, but the practice risks depreciating the discipline, writes Gus Solomons jr, who teaches dance at New York University, in an Opinion article.

SEEKING EMILY DICKINSON
A Mount Holyoke College class at the poet's home, in Amherst, Mass., is an occasion to explore the reclusive, prolific poet "in the light of her own fire."

HIGHLIGHTS
COMPLETE CONTENTS
BACK ISSUES
RELATED DOCUMENTS

EFL (English as a Foreign Language). The ESL Cafe is a fun and wide-ranging resource—like a community of sorts—with plenty of information about finding jobs teaching ESL or EFL and more.

From the "Job Center" you can explore ESL career opportunities. There are a few job boards, where job openings are listed and where job seekers can post their resumes and details on what they're looking for. The "Job Links" page presents career-related links by geographic area and other categories. You'll find sites for Africa, Asia, Europe, Latin America, and the Middle East, as well as sites pertaining to education, volunteerism, and general information.

Other site features include numerous discussion forums (for ESL/EFL teachers and students), book recommendations with links to Amazon.com for purchase, an "Idea Cookbook" (with recipes for teaching grammar, helping students improve listening comprehension, using the Internet, and so on), pages devoted to idioms and slang, a chat room, a "Help Center" where students can post questions to be answered by an ESL/EFL teacher, and much more.

EFLWEB

HTTP://WWW.U-NET.COM/EFLWEB/HOME.HTM

A great resource for those of you wanting to be an EFL (English as a Foreign Language) instructor, this site's FAQ section answers questions such as "What English teaching qualifications are there?" and "What is EFL, TEFL, TESL, and TESOL?" Once you have that down, you can check out the other goodies EFLWEB has to offer. The articles by teachers of EFL are especially helpful if you want to get a feel for what it might be like to be an EFL instructor. You can read about teaching experiences in Hungary, Japan, Korea, and more.

EFL events and conferences are listed here. Other resources include a directory of English language teaching schools in Britain, information on British accrediting organizations, a resume database, a bulletin board, and related links.

Electronics

IEEE-USA

HTTP://WWW.IEEEUSA.ORG/

IEEE-USA, which represents the interests of U.S. members of the Institute of Electrical and Electronics Engineers, offers here a site that's absolutely bursting with information for engineers. Some of the material is specific to IEEE-USA, while some is accessed through the main IEEE Web site. As you follow the links, you'll certainly cover a lot of IEEE territory!

To begin with, there's plenty of news, a "Legislative Action Center" where you can contact members of Congress regarding key industry issues, IEEE-USA conference information, and a "Public Policy Forum" where engineers can keep up-to-date on—and become involved in—what's happening in Washington.

Some of the site's educational offerings include a listing of precollege volunteer opportunities in math and science, the career guidance brochure Your Career in the Electrical, Electronics, and Computer Engineering Fields, links to home pages of IEEE student branches, and details on internships and contests.

The section on employment features "Entry Level Resources" for students and recent grads. Here you'll have access to links to sites that are helpful to the entry-level job seeker (for example, job search sites and career counseling sites), as well as links to select company job pages. Take a peek at the job fair listing to see what's happening next. Then if you're ready to look for a job or you just want to get an idea of what's out there, you'll want to search through the "electrotechnology and information technology-related jobs" database, specifying either your technical specialty or your desired location. You have to be an IEEE member in order to post a resume through Resumé-Link. But you need only visit the IEEE-USA site to have access to dozens of links to even more electrical and electronics engineering career resources.

Energy

ENERGY INFORMATION ADMINISTRATION
HTTP://WWW.EIA.DOE.GOV/

EIA is a statistical agency that's part of the U.S. Department of Energy. Its site is a vast resource containing data on energy of all types. Among the topics covered are biomass, coal, electricity, energy consumption, ethanol, geothermal, hydroelectric, naphtha, nuclear energy, renewables, solar, uranium, wind, and wood energy. But this is only a start. What you'll find here is one vast treasure trove of energy-related materials, a most welcome discovery if this is the field of your dreams!

If you're still trying to make that determination, take the online energy quiz. And if you're already looking for work or want to get an idea of availabilities, check out the EIA job vacancy details. Or you can try to dig up some leads scouring the links section. Here are links to energy companies, trade associations, and numerous other energy-related sites, as well as links to pages for universities, state energy agencies, DOE laboratories, and more.

THE UTILITY CONNECTION
HTTP://WWW.UTILITYCONNECTION.COM/

This directory features a few thousand links to electric, gas, and water and wastewater utility sites. The site map presents an outline of the categories covered. Take a look to see what all is available here. You've got a job bank; municipal, cooperative, and international utilities; magazines and news; financial resources; state agencies; U.S. and international associations; and much more. As you've already learned, the association sites are likely to provide you with some relevant career and educational materials, so you'll want to visit those in the area of most interest to you.

Engineering

AMERICAN SOCIETY FOR ENGINEERING EDUCATION
HTTP://WWW.ASEE.ORG/

ASEE's precollege section (called "Engineering: Your Future") supplies exactly the information you precollege engineers will be looking for. Much of the content is presented in a great question-and-answer format, with questions touching on a wide range of topics, including the diversity of jobs within engineering, the high school courses you'll need to take to get accepted into a good engineering institution, and the SAT or ACT scores you should shoot for.

In case you're wondering whether you'll be able to handle those engineering courses in college, you can assess your interest and aptitude by answering a handful of questions. If you make it past this hurdle, read through the advice on picking the right engineering school and secrets on getting admitted. For details about particular institutions, there are profiles of a few hundred U.S. colleges and universities that offer strong engineering programs. Of course, you'll need to pay for college, and ASEE has thought of that too with its links to the Web sites of the Department of Education and various federal loan, grant, and work-study programs.

And this is only the beginning. There's so much more to explore at this hefty site. Be sure to stop by if engineering is in your future!

A CAREER PLANNING CENTER FOR BEGINNING SCIENTISTS AND ENGINEERS
HTTP://WWW2.NAS.EDU/CPC/INDEX.HTML

If you're looking for guidance on career choices in the sciences, you'll want to explore this resource. The publication Careers in Science and Engineering: A Student Planning Guide to Grad School and Beyond, from the National Academy of Sciences, the National Academy of Engineering, and the Institute of Medicine, is loaded with information—just take a look at the contents page and you won't be let down. Topics covered include career goals, planning a career, evaluating possible careers, the skills necessary to succeed in the sciences, the education required to achieve your career goals, and finding a job. There are numerous links to sites featuring details about undergraduate science education, related organizations, and employment or internship opportunities.

NATIONAL SOCIETY OF PROFESSIONAL ENGINEERS

HTTP://WWW.NSPE.ORG/

Future engineers, this site is packed with information for you. Although some of the areas are open only to NSPE members, there's plenty to go around even if you aren't a member.

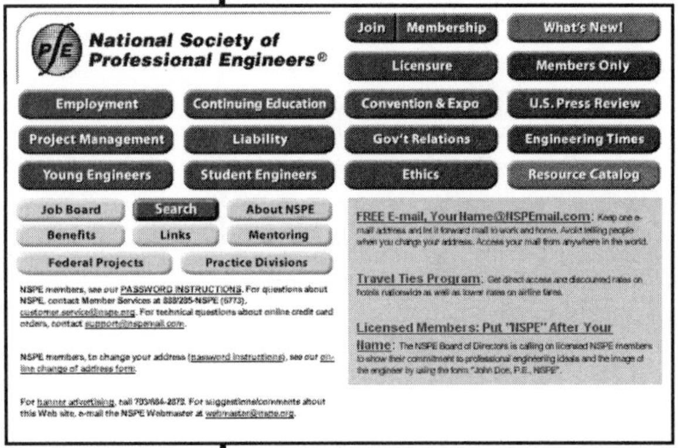

Your first stop should be the "Student Engineers" section. It's designed to help you learn about the engineering industry and what it takes (education and skills) to become a professional engineer. "A Career for You?" gives background information on what engineers do and lists the classes you should take in high school to prepare for an engineering career. You'll also find definitions of different types of engineering (chemical, civil, mechanical, and electrical). Furthermore, the guide discusses what you should study in college and offers ideas for funding your education.

Other areas in "Student Engineers" are directed more toward the college graduate. You can check on scholarship availability or follow links to several student engineering sites. "Welcome to the Engineering Profession" has a checklist to use when applying for engineering jobs—it should help you to compare the pros and cons of different firms you interview with. There's also information about the process of becoming licensed as a professional engineer.

Environment

EE-LINK
HTTP://EELINK.NET/

This environmental education site is packed with links to resources that will surely be useful to you if you're exploring a career having to do with the environment. There are classroom resources covering such topics as air and climate, wildlife and biodiversity, waste and toxics, and rainforests. Professional resources include links to pertinent publications and to schools offering environmental programs, mailing list details, and more.

Looking for work already? Browse the employment listings to follow up on such jobs as associate naturalist, environmental education coordinator, and aquatic resources education specialist. You'll also find information on environmental conferences and workshops, environmental grants and awards, and books and other publications on environmental education.

ENVIRONMENTAL SITES ON THE INTERNET
HTTP://WWW.LIB.KTH.SE/ LG/ENVSITE.HTM

To acquaint yourself with the wide range of environmental careers you might want to research on the Web, spend some time with this meta-list of environmental sites worldwide. Links are organized by subject and range from the general (biotechnology, conservation, energy) to the more obscure (arid lands, ecopsychology, solvent alternatives). There's also a searchable index if the long list of categories seems too unwieldy!

There are no job listings or career advice sections directly on this site, but the links are impressive and afford an invaluable tool for researching possible environmental careers.

WWW VIRTUAL LIBRARY: ENVIRONMENT

HTTP://EARTHSYSTEMS.ORG/ENVIRONMENT.SHTML

At this meta-list of environmental resources, you can view the succinctly annotated links by subject (general, atmosphere, biosphere, hydrosphere, lithosphere, or civilization) or by alphabetical order. There's also a "List O'Lists," which is—you guessed it—a list of directory sites containing even more links to environmental resources. Links are given for other similar subject directories covering energy, environmental law, landscape architecture, and oceanography, among other topics.

Fashion

THE INTERNET FASHION EXCHANGE

HTTP://WWW.FASHIONEXCH.COM/

If you're into fashion and retail (and no, this doesn't simply mean that you enjoy shopping!), the Internet Fashion Exchange is for you. You can submit your profile to the resume database, making it available to potential employers who visit the site. Or you can search job listings in the fashion world. To search the jobs database you must enter job titles of positions you are interested in, or at least keywords—for example, design or sales—that will get you moving in the right direction.

Film

THE FILM, TV, & COMMERCIAL EMPLOYMENT NETWORK

HTTP://WWW.EMPLOYNOW.COM/

This site is for those of you who want to be in the entertainment industry, whether it's in front of the camera, on the stage, or behind the scenes. Browse the job postings, where you'll find a list of job titles and the locations (mostly U.S., some international) where these positions are currently available. You might find listings for cinematographers, directors, film developers, lighting technicians, production assistants, reporters, scriptwriters, and stage managers, among others. Many of the jobs are with television stations. If you can't find the job you want, go to the "Job Hotlines" section and jot down some of the phone numbers. There are hotlines for actors and for crew members.

There is a resume database of sorts. "Crew Now" has sections listing crew members (makeup artists, costume designers, producers), and "Actors Now" lists actors. To be included in one of these sections, you'll have to pay a fee. Also at this site are sections devoted to casting calls and to stand-up comedy, plus you can purchase books on employment in the entertainment industry as well as a screenwriting guide.

SCREENWRITERS & PLAYWRIGHTS HOME PAGE

HTTP://WWW.TELEPORT.COM/ CDEEMER/ SCRWRITER.HTML

Charles Deemer's site is a major online resource for screenwriters and playwrights. There are no job listings, but there are tons of links and loads of concrete information. If you want to learn how to write screenplays or plays—or what to do once you've written them—this is the place to find out. The main page features a drop-down, scrollable box you can use to jump quickly to a topic of interest. Some of the topics are dramatic structure, screenplay format, online classes, and pitches and query letters.

The site's three main sections are "Resources for Screenwriters," "Resources for Playwrights," and "General Writing Resources." The screenwriter and playwright resource sections present information and links under such categories as "Nuts and Bolts" (the mechanics and business of writing), "Networking," "Film Reviews," "Tips from the Pros," and more. Learn about screenwriting technicalities, marketing your script, finding an agent, newsgroups where you can chat with folks about your craft, and deadlines for contests. General resources include miscellaneous links to all sorts of writing sites, such as the Women Writers Network, Poets & Writers magazine, Inkspot, and a zip code finder.

SHOWBIZJOBS.COM
HTTP://WWW.SHOWBIZJOBS.COM/

This site is your source for job vacancies in the world of entertainment, including the film, television, recording, and attractions industries. You can search by job category, including accounting, animation, film, interactive development, legal, marketing, and theme park design, just to name a few. Or you can search by location, posting date, or company. If you find a position you're interested in, you can apply directly with the subscribing company. There is a resume database, but it comes with a price tag. Resumes are kept in the database for six months.

Fire Fighting

NATIONAL FIRE PROTECTION ASSOCIATION
HTTP://WWW.NFPA.ORG/

Founded in 1896, NFPA presents an abundance of materials that will be of interest to anyone pursuing a career in fire protection. Under "Education," the section "Professional Development and Certification" features a booklet detailing the Fire Inspector Certification Program, covering the application, examination, and recertification process. There's also an entire section devoted to the process of becoming a Certified Fire Protection Specialist. Rules and procedures for the examination are outlined, and a study guide plus sample questions are included.

U.S. and international conferences, meetings, and seminars are listed in the events calendar. Don't miss the research area, which offers numerous links to sites covering fire-protection history and education, fire departments, fire and safety organizations, forest fires and wildfires, and related topics. Select articles, bulletins, and Fire Technology abstracts are among the other research services you'll discover at the site.

Food Processing

FOOD PROCESSING MACHINERY & SUPPLIES ASSOCIATION
HTTP://WWW.FPMSA.ORG/

What would we do without manufacturers of food processing and packaging equipment? We wouldn't have that salad mix in a bag or orange juice in a plastic container. This site is a great place to research the industry and the companies involved. There are searchable databases (from the Blue Book Buyers' Guide) of suppliers and processors so you can learn what the different companies do. You can search by commodity (anything from baby food to extracts and flavorings are listed in the drop-down box) or product (for example, blending/mixing machinery, brewery equipment, dehydrators, filter equipment, pulpers, shrink wrapping machinery). You might also want to take a look at the publications section, where you can peruse past issues of the World of Food and Beverage newsletter.

INSTITUTE OF FOOD TECHNOLOGISTS
HTTP://WWW.IFT.ORG/

The self-study online course Introduction to the Food Industry presents an excellent overview of the food science industry. Some of the topics examined are milk and food processing, quality assurance, nutrition, packaging and labeling, the use of computers in the manufacturing process, food transport, product marketing, food production at home, and much more. Each step along the way is described, supplemented by a glossary of terms and suggested book titles for further reading.

Among the other educational materials IFT provides are details for awards, scholarships, and fellowships; descriptions of universities offering graduate programs in food science; and a section on the IFT Student Association. The organization publishes several titles to help you in your job search. Check out the site for specific details.

A large collection of links will direct you to resources for further exploration. These cover U.S. and international food science sites, as well as university food science and technology departments. The Web sites of some of the various IFT divisions, including Carbohydrate, Food Chemistry, Food Laws and Regulations, Product Development, and Refrigerated and Frozen Foods, will afford you even more information.

Government

AMERICAN PLANNING ASSOCIATION
HTTP://WWW.PLANNING.ORG/

While APA's site has a lot of information useful to professionals involved in urban and regional planning, it also serves as a noteworthy introduction to the field of planning. The "Public Information" section features a definition of planning as well as of zoning terms, along with a list of assorted acronyms used in planning, a chronology of planning throughout American history, and a sampling of criteria used in a number of communities for determining off-street parking requirements for auditoriums, churches, colleges, hotels, shopping centers, and the like.

Does this whet your appetite for more? Then you'll want to move ahead to "Educational Opportunities & Careers in Planning." Here you'll get more details on what planning is, what planners do, and what skills are required. Plus there are lists of accredited university and Ph.D. planning programs. For help in choosing a program, be sure to read "9 Tips for Selecting a Planning Program." Notes on scholarships and internships are also available, as are numerous other helpful materials. And there's even a jobs database.

JOBS IN GOVERNMENT

HTTP://WWW.JOBSINGOVERNMENT.COM/

Federal job vacancies as well as job openings in the public sector are listed here. Job seekers, after registering for free, can add their resumes to the database and sign up for the matching service, through which they will be notified (by e-mail) of jobs that match their identified qualifications. The jobs database is searchable by job category or browsable alphabetically. If you decide to search by job category, you'll be presented with a form where you can designate location (U.S. state or Canadian province), salary range, and keyword. Plus there's an extensive list of categories to choose from. These include airport management, city administration, economic development, grants and contracts, highways, housing, neighborhood preservation, parole, public works, sanitation, and utility management, among many others. Select city administration, for instance, and you may generate listings such as labor relations officer, city assessor, budget manager, and deputy city attorney.

The resources section provides various tools for you to research federal career possibilities. There is a diverse listing of links to association pages that might be of help in your job search. You will find organizations in such areas as education, fire fighting, parks and conservation, and waste management. Also available are the names and descriptions of government-related publications, information about employment trends in government and the public sector, and links to local and federal government agencies.

POLICY.COM

HTTP://WWW.POLICY.COM/

Do you want to pursue a career in government and politics? If so, you'll probably want to make this vast public policy resource one of your customary stops. Content—in the form of analysis, news briefings, and position papers—comes from think tanks, advocacy groups, and the government, all of which number among its regular users. Some of the topics you'll find discussed here include health care, regulatory reform, the budget, food safety, IRS reform, race issues, global warming, foreign aid, education, welfare, technology, immigration, and gun control. There's even a glossary of terminology commonly used in discussions concerning such topics.

Interactive opportunities abound here. Debate affirmative action, education, foreign policy, health care, social security, or tax issues with others through the site's bulletin boards. "Virtual Congress" presents in-depth coverage of pending and past legislation, including statements from both supporters and opponents. You can express your opinions to your representative by going to the "Legislative Action Center."

The "Student Union" affords students a chance to explore educational and career options relating to government and politics. There are descriptions of and links for civic education and study abroad programs, scholarships, and internships. Also listed are public policy institutes, campus political publications and newspapers, student political organizations, and student activism resources. You don't want to miss this one!

Grocery Stores

NATIONAL GROCERS ASSOCIATION
HTTP://WWW.NATIONALGROCERS.ORG/

If you're thinking about getting into the grocery business, you'll probably want to head for the "Career Opportunities" section. Here you can explore your career options and learn about NGA programs and services. There is a list of universities that offer bachelor's degrees or graduate programs in food marketing. Scholarship opportunities are outlined. Most of the rest of the site's materials (for example, association news, a schedule of events and meetings, and information on family-owned businesses, food safety, government issues, labor relations, and marketing) will likely be of greater interest to industry professionals.

Health Care

AMERICAN ASSOCIATION OF COLLEGES OF NURSING
HTTP://WWW.AACN.NCHE.EDU/

The AACN describes itself as "the national voice for America's . . . nursing education programs," and at first blush this site may seem too academic, given the emphasis placed on government affairs and college accreditation. But delve into the right sections and you'll see that it contains some precious nuggets for students considering a future in nursing. In fact, one of this site's most useful tools is specifically aimed at nurses-to-be. Go to the education area and, once there, the section "Your Nursing Education." Here you'll find a lengthy, informative article that debunks some misconceptions about the field and that explores shifts in the job market. There's also a financial aid fact sheet and a directory of AACN's more than 500 member schools, with links where available.

This site also includes a schedule of upcoming conferences and seminars. "CareerLink" lists job openings. If academics is your thing, go ahead and read AACN's newsletter and other related publications (position statements, issue bulletins, news releases) online. Keep in mind that the intended reader is probably a nurse working in a teaching environment.

AMERICAN MEDICAL ASSOCIATION
HTTP://WWW.AMA-ASSN.ORG/

The AMA is an authoritative voice in the field of medicine. Among its many contributions are the American Medical Accreditation Program, the publication Journal of the American Medical Association, and its public health advocacy work. Having much of value to offer physicians, medical students, and consumers, this huge resource features articles (abstracts or full texts), a wide assortment of consumer health guides, and advocacy information. You will find, however, that certain materials are available to members only.

There is little at the site that specifically focuses on general career exploration in regards to medicine, so you may want to venture over to the MedCareers site (linked from the section described next) or elsewhere for that. But the AMA does provide details on medical programs and teaching institutions. From the education page, go to the section on FREIDA (Fellowship and Residency Electronic Interactive Database) to search on a medical specialty or subspecialty of your choice (including anesthesiology, dermatology, forensic psychiatry, internal medicine, musculoskeletal radiology, obstetrics and gynecology, oncology, pediatric surgery, pulmonary disease, sports medicine, and thoracic surgery, to name a very few). Residency and workforce statistics and data are also available. This should leave you with plenty to digest as you're considering your educational options.

AMERICA'S HEALTHCARESOURCE
HTTP://WWW.HEALTHCARESOURCE.COM/

This site provides a lot of information about the health care industry. Yes, you'll find job openings, but you'll also find lists of colleges and universities with medical programs (in various fields) as well as professional associations, with links where available, plus details on seminars and events.

ASSOCIATION OF SCHOOLS OF PUBLIC HEALTH
HTTP://WWW.ASPH.ORG/

If you have any interest in the field of public health or are curious and want to learn more about it, check out this informative and detailed site. You might want to start with ASPH's definition of public health, which includes a list of comparisons drawn between the general fields of public health and medicine. The section on career opportunities presents an in-depth discussion of the state of the public health industry and the positive aspects of pursuing a graduate degree and career in public health. There's an overview of the industry and where it's headed, along with information on what you can do with a degree in public health. Career opportunities exist in administration/management, education, community practice, research, and policy. Go to the section on education, for instance, and you'll find lists of possible job settings (wellness programs, colleges, federal and state health agencies), job titles, key issues, and job trends in public health education. To get a better idea of the kinds of jobs available, follow the "Public Health Employment Connection" link to access a job listing from Emory University's Rollins School of Public Health.

HEALTH CARE JOB STORE
HTTP://WWW.HEALTHCAREJOBSTORE.COM/

In this "store," you can shop around for health care jobs in anesthesiology, assisted living, cardiology, emergency medicine, gastroenterology, general practice, health education, mental health, neurology, obstetrics, pediatrics, podiatry, and so much more. Check out the searchable jobs database, or go directly to the link dealing with your specified field of choice. If it looks like a good match, then apply according to the instructions in that particular job listing. Or you could let a job search agent do the checking for you. Specify criteria covering job title, category, location, and type of work (full-time, part-time, consulting, etc.). Matches will be sent to you via e-mail. For free, you can post your resume or career profile to the site's databases. Simply complete the detailed form and paste in relevant sections from your resume. If you haven't created a resume yet, take a quick look at the resume tips to get you started.

HEALTHWEB

HTTP://HEALTHWEB.ORG/

An impressive collaborative effort of more than twenty health sciences libraries, the HealthWeb project is a heavyweight of medical resources and information. Among the many topics covered are AIDS and HIV, cardiology, dentistry, geriatrics and gerontology, minority health, mortuary science, nursing, optometry, physical therapy, radiology, transplantation, and veterinary medicine. You can use the HealthWeb search engine to find what you're looking for. Or you can go straight to the subject pages, which are immense resources of information on their own.

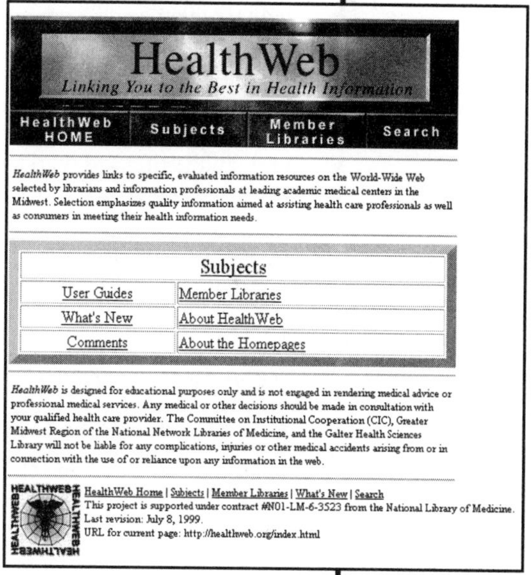

To give you an idea of the range of materials you can expect to find when you go to these topic pages, let's look at nursing as an example. Under the mantle of "Career Information," you can link to the Occupational Outlook Handbook in its entirety, or you can just click on the nursing sections (for registered or licensed practical nurses) already plucked out for you. These sections cover working conditions, employment, training, job outlook, earnings, and related occupations, among others. You might be encouraged to read here that employment of registered nurses is expected to grow rapidly well beyond the year 2000, with many of the new jobs in home health, long-term, and ambulatory care.

In the "Communication" section, you'll find information and e-mail addresses for a number of online nursing discussion groups. If there's a particular field of nursing that triggers your interest, the specialized discussion groups are a good place to gain insight into the field. The "Education" section has links to international and U.S. nursing schools on the Internet. Other sections will link you to nursing school newsletters and nursing journals, professional nursing organizations, and plenty of research sites. If you're the kind of person who believes there's no such thing as too much information, you'll love the HealthWeb site.

THERAPEUTIC RECREATION DIRECTORY
HTTP://WWW.RECREATIONTHERAPY.COM/

Are you interested in a career in the therapeutic recreation industry? This site features articles addressing therapeutic recreation issues plus several bulletin boards and a chat room where you can discuss work or career topics with others in the field. National and international therapeutic recreation organizations are listed, with links to home pages where available. The same is true for colleges and universities offering therapeutic recreation programs. Additional resources include materials on internship opportunities, job listings, and events and workshops.

Home Furnishings

FOUNDATION FOR INTERIOR DESIGN EDUCATION RESEARCH
HTTP://WWW.FIDER.ORG/

FIDER membership is made up of an assortment of professional interior design groups interested in upholding and promoting high standards in interior design education. This site includes information on FIDER's accreditation process, a list of accredited programs with links to home pages where available, a description of what an interior designer does, and a list of professional associations.

Hospitality

AMERICAN HOTEL & MOTEL ASSOCIATION
HTTP://WWW.AHMA.COM/

AH&MA, a powerhouse in the hospitality industry, provides communication, governmental affairs, marketing, hospitality operations, educational, convention, risk management, technology, and member relations services for hotels, motels, and lodging facilities. These are benefits you'll appreciate later once you embark on your career in hospitality.

But for now, just follow the link to the Educational Institute, through which AH&MA offers hospitality training programs. By browsing the synopses of book and video titles sold to EI students, you'll get a clear picture of the many career choices you have in the field. There's food and beverage, general management, guest service, housekeeping, maintenance, marketing, and security, just to name a few. "Student Resources" in the EI academic section includes career-planning advice, covering self-assessment, cover letters, resumes, interviewing, and more. You can learn about classes offered as well.

Back at AH&MA you can find links to schools with hospitality programs, hospitality-related organizations, and hospitality publications.

As you can see, AH&MA together with the Educational Institute give you a lot of useful and interesting material to digest in your search for information on a career in hospitality.

DEPARTMENT OF HOSPITALITY MANAGEMENT AT THE UNIVERSITY OF NEW HAMPSHIRE
HTTP://ORBIT.UNH.EDU/DHM/INDEX.HTM

If you're searching for a university or training program to help you with your career in hospitality, you might want to look here. While there are probably hundreds of schools shopping their wares online, this site stands out for its thorough course descriptions and unbiased advice on choosing a school. To read those course descriptions, as well as to find out what UNH thinks is special about its program, click on "Program Highlights." From here, you'll find a description of the four-year bachelor's degree that prepares students for management spots in hotels, resorts, restaurants, and other tourism-related businesses. There's even nitty-gritty information about course requirements and placement services.

Where do you go to find that unbiased advice? This would be found in the section called "Hospitality Education." It's a primer for high school students on how to compare one degree program to the next when choosing a college.

The faculty has also pulled together an impressive index of hundreds of sites on the Web. Some of the categories represented include food and beverage publications, food service associations, hotel chains, serving equipment—the list goes on! UNH may or may not be the college for you, but you'll certainly want to bookmark this site for its hospitality-related information.

HOSPITALITY JOBS ONLINE

HTTP://WWW.HJO.NET/

Here's a site featuring employment, educational, and internship opportunities for the hospitality industry. The site offers a couple of encouraging industry tidbits that bear repeating here. Did you realize that the hotel industry in North America employs more than two million people? Or that travel industry employment has grown twice as fast in the past decade as all other U.S. industries?

To find some of those jobs, go to the section for job seekers. From here you can pull up an alphabetical list of employers in the hospitality industry, each briefly described. You'll find listed here everything from an elite Hollywood hotel to a resort in Phoenix to a nationwide travel agency. When you see something that interests you, click on its name to learn about current opportunities and how to apply for a job. You can also access similar information by first selecting a state and narrowing it down from there. The classifieds section lists job descriptions of other available management positions.

HOSPITALITY NET
HTTP://WWW.HOSPITALITYNET.ORG/

You will find out what's happening in the hospitality industry when you stop by this up-to-date resource. There's all sorts of industry news that you can browse through, including archived reports from the past few years. If you know which part of the industry you want to focus on—say environment and food safety, human resources, marketing and sales, or technology—pick that category. Read press releases from or concerning various hospitality organizations. Some of the groups featured are the American Hotel & Motel Association, the Council on Hotel, Restaurant and Institutional Education, the Hospitality Sales & Marketing Association International, and the World Travel & Tourism Council. There are brief descriptions of these and other organizations, along with links to home pages. Other happenings, such as conferences and exhibitions, are covered in the events listing.

Want to know about hospitality jobs available right now? Then click on "Job Exchange," where you can browse employment opportunities in the areas of accounting, banqueting, food and beverage, front office, housekeeping, management, and others. The job titles are quite varied, with everything from restaurants manager in Guam to director of housekeeping in Pennsylvania. If you like, you can add your resume to the "Job Demands" database. If all of this information is making your head spin and you feel like settling down with a few books, snag some suggested titles off the "Bookshelf" and continue your career exploration from the comfort of an easy chair.

INTERNATIONAL HOTEL & RESTAURANT ASSOCIATION
HTTP://WWW.IH-RA.COM/

The IH&RA has provided resources and a global network for people in the hospitality and restaurant business for several decades. This Web site expands on what the organization has traditionally offered throughout its history. The "Newsroom" features press releases, current and archived newsletters, and articles covering hospitality industry news. Elsewhere you can learn about hospitality events and workshops past and present, read industry regulation documents on various topics (for example, flexible working conditions and traveler safety), or order industry-related publications (some are free of charge).

Human Resources

SOCIETY FOR HUMAN RESOURCE MANAGEMENT

HTTP://WWW.SHRM.ORG/

SHRM represents those in the human resource profession. Although the material here is geared toward HR professionals and some areas of the site are accessible only to SHRM members, non-HR folks can glean a lot of useful information from this site.

Current HR job openings are listed and described. The database is browsable by location (U.S. and international), job title, or date of posting, or you can search all the listings. Sample openings are compensation analyst, HR consultant, labor relations manager, and recruitment specialist. Entry-level and new positions are indicated. SHRM members can sign up for a free e-mail notification service that sends an e-mail a few times a week when there are new vacancies.

There's a section aimed at students studying HR management. You can read about financial aid (including scholarships and grants), how to get started in HR, and SHRM student chapters, which exist across the United States. There are also links to sites where you can find graduate programs in HR management.

Speaking of links, there are plenty of them. "HR Links" has links to other HR resources. These are categorized as "Diversity," "Education & Training," "Recruitment & Career Planning," "Safety & Health," and more.

Other items of interest include details about SHRM conferences and featured articles from HR Magazine. You'll find articles on such topics as benefits, recruitment, retirement, and software. "Buyers' Guide" has descriptions of and links to all sorts of HR tools in the areas of career development, skills testing, software, and others.

Information Services

AMERICAN LIBRARY ASSOCIATION
HTTP://WWW.ALA.ORG/

If you're considering a career in library science, ALA's site will prove an invaluable tool in your career exploration. The education and employment pages offer an abundance of pertinent materials for perspective students and job seekers. Refer to ALA's directory of accredited master's library and information studies programs, which includes details on such programs along with a guide to selecting a program. Read about accreditation, general versus specialized studies, admission requirements, financial aid, and placement services. Notes on scholarship opportunities are also available.

Job vacancies originally posted in ALA publications American Libraries and College & Research Libraries News are presented, along with late adds to the Web site only. You can also check out the job vacancies from the Library & Information Technology Association, a division of ALA. Yet another guide documents employment sources in the library and information professions. And of course the site also features ALA news, activities, events and conferences, and membership issues.

AMERICAN SOCIETY FOR INFORMATION SCIENCE
HTTP://WWW.ASIS.ORG/

ASIS is one of those groups whose members come from a variety of different fields, among them computer science, education, librarianship, linguistics, and management. Members share a common interest in how information is retrieved, assessed, maintained, distributed, and so on. The catalog of ASIS courses should give you a pretty good idea of the diverse topics studied in information science; for example, copyright, computer and network security, multimedia publishing, legal issues and the Internet, intranet development, management issues, and artificial intelligence. Certain ASIS publications are available in full or in abstract format. You might want to utilize the listings of special interest groups (SIGs) or local and student chapters to make contact with someone in the business of information science.

LIBRARY JOB POSTINGS ON THE INTERNET

HTTP://TOPCAT.BRIDGEW.EDU/ SNESBEITT/ LIBRARYJOBS.HTM

This site, compiled by reference librarian Sarah L. Nesbeitt, presents a comprehensive set of links to job listings for librarian jobs of all sorts. There are jobs to be found in federal libraries, academic libraries, special libraries such as medical or law libraries, and, of course, public libraries. Librarians can also find work in archives and records management or as school library media specialists. Look for jobs by field or by region (U.S. and abroad). You can also view all listings for all types.

Insurance

INDEPENDENT INSURANCE AGENTS OF AMERICA

HTTP://WWW.IIAA.ORG/

IIAA presents its materials in separate sections for consumers, industry professionals, and IIAA members. In the consumer section is a discussion of having a career in insurance. After you look at that, drop by the industry section. There you can read current and archived feature articles from the magazine Independent Agent. One of the site's highlights is its wide-ranging collection of related links. You'll have access to resources in the areas of agency management, disaster and safety, government, insurance regulation, professional organizations, publishers, and risk management. Among the miscellaneous resources are sites dealing with careers, employment, news, legal issues, and property and casualty. Stop by the members area to find out about IIAA activities and programs, the benefits of membership, and how to join.

NATIONAL ASSOCIATION OF PROFESSIONAL INSURANCE AGENTS

HTTP://WWW.PIANET.COM/

There are some interesting brochures available at this site. One is all about careers in the insurance industry. Occupational choices include actuary, adjuster, agent, broker, loss control specialist, risk manager, and underwriter. The other brochures discuss consumer topics like homeowner and auto insurance, workers compensation, natural disasters, and property protection. These afford good overviews of the insurance business for someone thinking about entering the field. If you're getting serious about it, you'll want to read the news coverage, which is quite extensive. Links come in many shapes and sizes, featuring state and regional affiliates, state legislatures, state insurance departments, and insurance publications and organizations.

Internet

ASSOCIATION OF INTERNET PROFESSIONALS

HTTP://WWW.ASSOCIATION.ORG/

AIP is an international organization of professionals in the Internet industry. Here you'll have access to quite an extensive jobs database, listing vacancies for Web architects and developers, product editors, executive site producers, media services managers, copy editors, Internet systems developers, senior system engineers, visual design managers, and the like. To learn more about the organization, read press releases past and present. Also, visit chapter home pages to find out what's happening near you.

CNET WEB BUILDING JOBS
HTTP://WWW.BUILDER.COM/RESOURCES/JOBS/

A leading new media information company, CNET is responsible for numerous Web sites as well as television programs having to do with the high-tech industry. This particular online resource targets those individuals who are interested in a career in building Web sites.

To get an idea of some of the different directions you can go in the field, click on "Real Web Builders Speak Up" to read the profiles of industry personnel (representative job titles include technical publications specialist, senior programmer, Web developer, production manager, director of interactive marketing, and Webmaster). What do you think? Are you ready for more? If so, check out the section called "How to Build Your Online Career." Here you'll find more details about possible job opportunities, as well as guidance on landing the job you want, getting ahead, and being paid what you deserve. Also available are sections covering necessary Web-building skills, freelancing, and salaries. Plus, you can participate in Web-related discussion forums on career change, freelancing, and job hunting. From these you'll have access to additional forums pertaining to Web authoring, programming, graphics, servers, and business.

If you're in the mood for the basics, downloads, tips and how-to resources, and the like, you might want to wander back to CNET's main Web Building page. Or you might simply want to browse other CNET pages not specifically related to Web building. There sure is plenty to explore!

INTERNATIONAL WEBMASTERS ASSOCIATION
HTTP://WWW.IWANET.ORG/

Do you already have a Web site of your own? Might you be interested in a career of managing Web sites? Designing, creating, and updating them? If so, IWA's site should be on your list of sites to visit. Despite its name, IWA membership extends beyond Webmasters to include graphic designers, programmers, multimedia specialists, and others involved in Web site maintenance and management. Known for its Web certification and education programs, IWA presents information at the site concerning its certification programs as well as its Authorized Training Facilities and Testing Centers. Ready to get involved? Check out individual chapter listings to see the kinds of activities there are going on in your area.

Before moving on, be sure to stop by the resource section. Here you can read articles from the e-zine WebProfession, visit "Experts Exchange" to ask questions (or find answers) regarding dozens of high-tech topics, search for a job through the affiliated VirtualJOBS site, find out about IWA volunteer opportunities (which provide good experience as well as networking potential), and explore additional Web sites in such areas as authoring, databases, education, Mac Webmastering, multimedia, networks, security, and server technology.

Law

FINDLAW
HTTP://WWW.FINDLAW.COM/

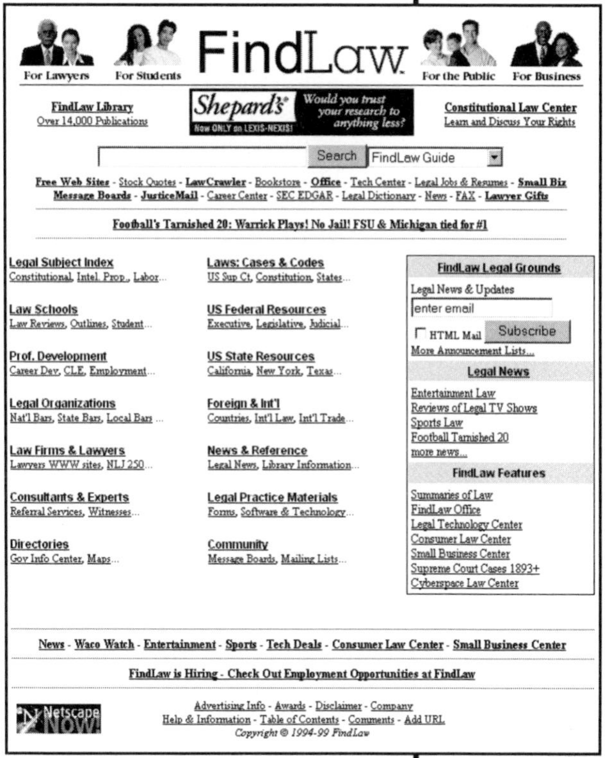

This comprehensive law directory features a multitude of resources. Some are organized in sections devoted specifically to lawyers, the public, business, or students. The last-named section is where you'll want to start if you're considering a career in law. There under "Professional Development" you'll have access to numerous sites pertaining to continuing legal education, employment (including jobs databases, publications, organizations, and mailing lists), and articles discussing self-assessment, selecting a law school, evaluating a job offer, and law career opportunities.

Do you like what you've read so far? If so, then perhaps it's time to look at your law school options. As you can probably imagine, there are plenty of law school links to help you with this. Other links in this area are for course materials in bankruptcy law, civil procedure, contracts, criminal law, environmental law, intellectual property, litigation, torts, and the like. Then there are links pertaining to the bar exam. Visit state bar association home pages to read up on the state where you'll be practicing. Further resources are study guides, publications, financial aid ideas, discussion forums, academic law reviews and journals, and employment sites. And this is only the student section!

LAW NEWS NETWORK
HTTP://WWW.LAWNEWSNETWORK.COM/

If you want to be a lawyer, you'll want to head on over to this resource, which brings you up-to-date news on the legal industry and articles relevant to a variety of practice areas, compiled from an assortment of American Lawyer Media publications distributed across the United States. Links are provided for affiliated regional and national sites of some of these publications.

Job listings are browsable by region, and within a region by practice area (litigation, corporate, intellectual, and property, to name a few). You can also search job openings posted by legal search firms. In "Law Firm Central," conduct your industry research by searching the law firm index, which lists some of the nation's leading law firms. And definitely take a look at the practice areas listing, accessible through "Briefing Papers." While the practices don't come with a definition, you'll have access to pertinent articles, news, recent cases, and related links. More than twenty areas of law are listed, including bankruptcy, environment, real estate, and technology and the Internet.

Literary Arts

INKSPOT
HTTP://WWW.INKSPOT.COM/

There's something for every writer here, whether your genre of choice is business, children, horror, journalism, mystery, poetry, romance, science fiction and fantasy, screenwriting, or technical. Each genre section presents annotated links to relevant resources, which include articles, newsgroups, organizations, publications, publishers, workshops, and other pertinent sites. With all that's to be found here, where does one begin?

Perhaps a good place to start would be the "Beginning Writers' FAQ," which can be found from Inkspot's site map, an easy way to navigate this huge resource. Some of the questions asked—and answered—here are "A publisher's guidelines say 'query first'. What does this mean?" and "What rules apply to copyright on the Internet?" There's also a FAQ section for freelance writers that addresses such questions as "Do we need to bother with a contract?" and "How can I get those first clips?"

If you're not sure where you should submit your writing, head over to "Market Info for Writers." The classifieds section contains listings of paying and nonpaying markets. Subscribe (for free) to the newsletter Inklings to receive (via e-mail) current market news, articles, industry advice, and more. There are plenty of opportunities for connecting with other writers through Inkspot bulletin boards and chats. Wherever you are in this site, you'll have access to links galore. And you're sure to find something new at every visit, so visit often!

NATIONAL WRITERS UNION JOB HOTLINE

HTTP://WWW.NWU.ORG/

If you are interested in becoming a professional writer, this site is a great resource. You'll be amazed at how much you can do with a writing background—you don't just have to be a novelist, though you do have that option, of course! Just look through the job listings to read about the various career choices a budding writer has. How about being a ghostwriter for a book on a famous personality? Or how about a freelance writing job with a music trade publication? And there are plenty of opportunities in technical writing and public relations too.

There's no charge to you just to view the job descriptions. But you must be an NWU member to see the full listings. Also, if you locate a job through this service, you must pay a finder's fee. To search the job listings, select either contract or staff positions. Many of the contract listings are off-site, which means you can telecommute, or work remotely from your home.

NWU offers a lot more than just job listings at its site. "Writer Alerts" provides notification of grievances against publishers, book packagers, and other companies. More information on grievances can be found in the section by that name. Other site features include materials on contracts, details about NWU's various divisions, a discussion of writers' health and safety (dealing specifically with repetitive strain injuries), and a large collection of links to sites covering dictionaries, grammar and style, investigative reporting, related organizations, writing conferences and workshops, miscellaneous writing resources, and much more. NWU members have access to even more.

POETS & WRITERS
HTTP://WWW.PW.ORG/

Here you'll have at your fingertips select content from Poets & Writers magazine—as well as its precursor, Coda—and much more. Along with the classified job listings, there's a section devoted to publishing information, which discusses copyright, freelance and children's book writing, and literary agents, among other topics. Speakeasy is a place for visitors to discuss issues of interest and relevance to writers. A portion of A Directory of American Poets and Fiction Writers can be searched online. To keep up with what's happening, be sure to look at "News from the Writing World," featuring current and archived news stories. There are plenty of links to pages where you can find even more resources in the field, such as for literary organizations, writing references, university writing programs, and contests.

Machining and Machinery

INDUSTRIAL DESIGNERS SOCIETY OF AMERICA
HTTP://WWW.IDSA.ORG/

So, just what does an industrial designer do? If you are wondering this very thing, you're in luck—the IDSA offers a creative introduction to industrial design, by way of a textual definition and a gallery of images. (Basically, industrial design involves the planning and designing of a wide range of products, requiring, on the part of the designer, particular attentiveness to such details as functionality, configuration, and appearance.) If this kindles your interest, you may want to visit the site's chronology of design to get a grasp of its history.

Now that you've been initiated into the process of industrial design, you may be ready to explore career possibilities. Student resources include a mentor directory, a list of schools offering undergraduate and graduate programs in industrial design (with links where available), and details on awards, competitions, grants, and scholarships. Representative job postings are for designers in such diverse areas as footwear, lighting, electronics, sporting equipment, automobiles, and digital products.

INSTITUTE OF INDUSTRIAL ENGINEERS

HTTP://WWW.IIENET.ORG/

In addition to membership information, events listings, and news, IIE's site includes a section devoted to careers. Here you'll get an overview of industrial engineering. You'll also have access to jobs posted in IIE Solutions. These might be for a variety of settings, such as a retail distribution center, manufacturing company, small package processing facility, or university.

Brief descriptions of IIE's assorted societies, divisions, and interest groups will give you a clearer idea of what IIE members are involved in. Certain site features (for example, IIE Solutions online and forums for various interest groups) are available to members only.

Manufacturing

NATIONAL ASSOCIATION OF MANUFACTURERS

HTTP://WWW.NAM.ORG/

NAM's site is geared toward the organization's members, with much information available to members only. But you can learn a lot about the manufacturing industry through some of the site's free features. The Facts about Modern Manufacturing discusses the effect of manufacturing on U.S. economy, technological advances, and the global marketplace, as well as employment-related topics like training, health care benefits, and wages. Read the success stories outlining notable company efforts in the areas of education and training, "merging business and environmental goals," and trade. Also accessible are current and archived NAM news releases.

Another feature is a section that highlights "100 Years of Manufacturing Achievements." This timeline covers such manufacturing achievements as the safety razor with disposable blades (1895), the Harley-Davidson motorcycle (1903), interchangeable socket wrenches (1919), man-made insecticides (1924), cortisone (1949), frozen TV dinners (1954), the countertop microwave oven (1967), soft contact lenses (1971), and the Intel Pentium chip (1993).

If you didn't know before, you should have a clearer picture of what the manufacturing industry holds in store for you if you decide to venture in that career direction. And if you decide to join NAM, you'll have access to even more materials (for example, details about relevant federal legislation and regulations, coverage of key industry issues, and links to pertinent Web sites) to help you in your career exploration.

Mathematics and Physics

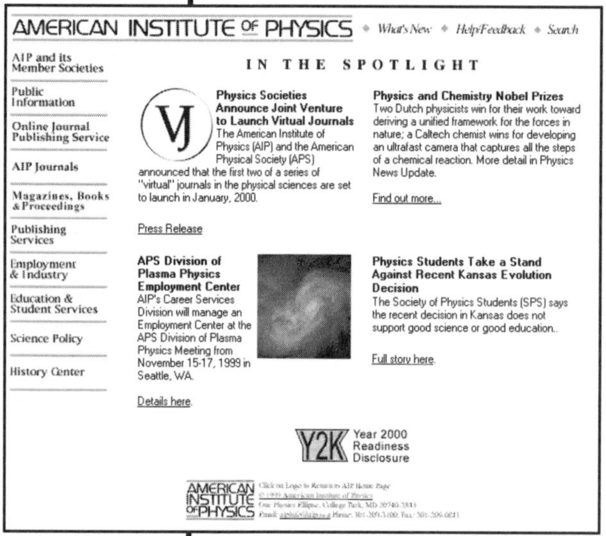

AMERICAN INSTITUTE OF PHYSICS

HTTP://WWW.AIP.ORG/

Planning a career in physics? AIP hosts this comprehensive Web site where you can research employment opportunities, find out about schooling, and locate physics resources.

Physics Is for You, an introductory brochure for junior high and high school students, discusses what physics is and what you can do with a career in physics.

The history section features an Einstein exhibit and the Emilio Segrè Visual Archives, where you can view photos of renowned scientists. There are physics success stories that stress the importance and contribution of physics to society with stories such as "Physics Connects the World—Telecommunications" and "Physics Clears the Air—The Environment." Take a look at these to see how you can use your physics background for tangible real-world gains. For more on what you can do with physics, check out the section called "Education and Employment Trends." Here you can learn about the state of high school physics in the 1990s, common career choices made by physics graduates, and employment and salary data.

"Job Seeker Services" allows you to search for jobs by keyword or browse the classifieds by category (academic, government, industry). New job vacancies are posted frequently. The links section has science-related links, including company and organization pages, as well as general job search links.

AMERICAN MATHEMATICAL SOCIETY

HTTP://WWW.AMS.ORG/

Are you wild for square roots and derivatives? Then check out e-MATH, the AMS's Web page. Here you'll discover a wide range of math resources suitable for professional mathematicians, graduate students, or anybody else having an interest in the mathematical sciences.

If you're a mathematically inclined college-bound high school student, you definitely don't want to miss all the helpful information in the "Careers in Mathematics" section. It helps define different aspects of math (pure versus applied mathematics) and offers questions to think about when you're selecting a college. The section also goes over scholarships, fellowships, and graduate programs and provides links to associations and other math-related sites.

Job listings are accessible either by searching for a specific area of math or by browsing through them. There is a resume database of sorts where job seekers can add their names to a list, which is only active from April to September.

For those of you who want to teach math—or think you will want to in future—be sure to read the pamphlet The Academic Job Search in Mathematics. It's full of lots of good ideas on how to prepare a curriculum vitae (kind of like an expanded resume), what sources to check first for jobs in academia, what to expect in the campus interview, how to handle a job offer, and all the steps in between.

INSTITUTE OF PHYSICS
HTTP://WWW.IOP.ORG/

This is an amazing resource for those of you fascinated by physics. There are links to journals and magazines, including New Journal of Physics, Physics World, Astronomy & Geophysics, and Scientific Computing World. Jobs are listed in Physics World, where you can view job vacancies by the most recent or all the openings, or by using search criteria. You'll find both academic and private sector jobs, in the United States and abroad.

If you just can't get enough physics, go to "Physics for Researchers" and check out the Physics Express Letters, featuring the full text and abstracts of all Letters and Rapid Communications from several IOP academic journals. Read about "heat-kernel coefficients for oblique boundary conditions" and so much more.

THE INTERNET PILOT TO PHYSICS
HTTP://PHYSICSWEB.ORG/TIPTOP/

This site provides many physics-related resources, including a student forum where you can talk shop with other physics students. Also provided are links to student and physics organizations and to schools offering graduate programs, as well as a list of Ph.D. studentships and the student conference calendar. If you're ready to look for a job, you can search through job vacancies and sign up for e-mail notification of updates.

"Physics Around the World" is a major listing of links to educational, media, computing, and reference sites. There are also links to companies and organizations. One of the sections under education is "Undergraduate Programs," which gives links to universities all over the world that offer physics programs.

The "Virtual Laboratory" is for the true physics buff. There are links to physics-related Java applets on the Web. You'll find applets on projectile motion, wave motion, reflection and refraction, gravitation, and more.

Metals

IRON & STEEL SOCIETY
HTTP://WWW.ISSOURCE.ORG/

The ISS is a professional association for workers in the iron and steel industry. This site contains materials—such as descriptions of various ISS divisions, continuing education courses, and publications available for purchase—that will be relevant primarily to those workers. Students who are interested in a career in the iron and steel industry should investigate the benefits of student membership. Details are given about student chapters worldwide as well as about grant and scholarship programs. If you need help finding something, try the site's internal search engine.

Military Services

MILITARY CAREER GUIDE ONLINE
HTTP://WWW.MILITARYCAREERS.COM/

This guide offers a handy introduction to various military career opportunities. The search page includes links to enlisted occupations (for example, human services, media and public affairs, construction, transportation, combat, and precision work) and officer occupations (mainly the same as those for enlisted). Select an occupation of interest and you'll be presented with a further list of career categories. Enlisted media and public affairs includes interpreters and translators, broadcast journalists and newswriters, and musicians, while the same occupation for officers includes audiovisual and broadcast directors and public information officers. Then for enlisted combat specialty you'll wind up with choices like infantrymen and artillery or tank crew members, the officer counterparts being infantry, artillery, and tank officers. Each career is described. Descriptions cover such things as training provided, physical demands, work environment, and special requirements.

Links are included for the different U.S. service branches (Army, Navy, Air Force, Marine Corps, and Coast Guard). Go to a particular site in order to get information focused on whatever branch you want to know more about.

Mining

INFOMINE
HTTP://WWW.INFOMINE.COM/

When you land at InfoMine's site you'll feel like you stepped into a minefield bursting with information! This site has the latest news on the mining industry and resources for tracking down mining companies and suppliers.

Some of the resources you'll find include a mailing list for mining job opportunities, a company database so you can research prospective employers, a calendar of events, and a list of universities and colleges offering mining programs. The employers page lists companies that currently have jobs posted. You have the option of viewing all the jobs of a particular company or data on that company. From the jobs page you can view all job opportunities or designate certain criteria such as dates, category, and country. Some of the positions listed are geotechnical engineer, mine surveyor, rock engineer, and strata control officer. Most of the full descriptions (with contact details) can be viewed by members only.

You'll strike gold in the "TechnoMine" section of InfoMine. Here there are additional educational resources for mining and geology programs and resources for mining law, laboratory technology, environmental technology, geological technology, and more. Go to "EnviroMine," for example, and you'll find links to environmental policy statements, case histories of mine reclamation, mining environmental publications, and much more.

MININGUSA.COM
HTTP://WWW.MININGUSA.COM/

If you're trying to plot your future in mining, you may want to start by looking at the educational resources at this site. Universities with mining programs are listed here. The research page supplies addresses and links (where available) to mining resource sites by state, such as the Washington Division of Geology and Earth Resources and the Center for Applied Energy Research at the University of Kentucky.

The employment page lists vacancies by state and is a good spot to see the types of jobs available in this industry. Examples are openings for aggregate project engineers, asphalt project engineers, cement general managers, and underground mine project engineers. Also featured at this site are all sorts of mining-related goodies, including contact details for and/or links to pages about mining associations, companies, suppliers, and publications, as well as government agencies and mineral facts.

Museums and Cultural Centers

AMERICAN ASSOCIATION OF MUSEUMS
HTTP://WWW.AAM-US.ORG/

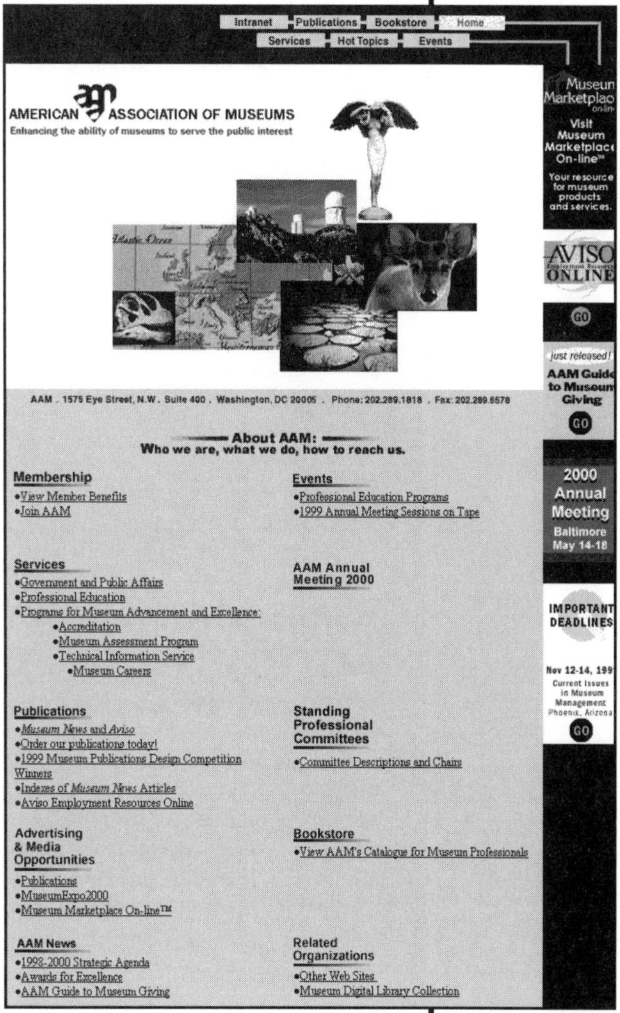

AAM offers an overview of some of the positions held and tasks performed by museum professionals. This information can be found if you go to "Services" and then to "Technical Information Service." Among the common museum positions are curator, conservator, membership coordinator, and exhibit preparator. There's also a useful discussion on how to prepare for a museum career, along with notes and links on finding a job or an internship.

"Hot Topics" presents articles addressing issues as they relate to museums, including tourism, fair use of digital images, and intellectual property. Read these to familiarize yourself with the variety of concerns held by museum workers. If you want to check out AAM job listings, you'll have to get hold of the group's newsletter Aviso, which is free to members or available by subscription.

AMERICAN INSTITUTE FOR CONSERVATION OF HISTORIC AND ARTISTIC WORKS
HTTP://PALIMPSEST.STANFORD.EDU/AIC/

If your dream is to enter a field where the goal is to preserve artifacts of artistic, historic, religious, or other importance, then don't miss this site. AIC has such a goal and affords a good opportunity for you to learn more about the activity of conservation. Under "General Information," take a look at "Definitions of Conservation Terminology" for a quick introduction to the field. "Conservation Specialties" gives much more specific and detailed information. Here you can read about caring for architecture, works of art on paper, paintings, photographs, and more. Browse the titles from the publications list if you're looking to order further reading material. If you're serious about a career in this field, you might be interested in joining one of the specialty groups, dealing, for example, with books and paper, research and technical studies, textiles, or wooden artifacts, as well as the categories mentioned earlier.

Music

AMERICAN SOCIETY OF COMPOSERS, AUTHORS AND PUBLISHERS
HTTP://WWW.ASCAP.COM/

ASCAP members are composers, songwriters and lyricists (authors), and music publishers. Some of the site's information will be applicable mainly to such professionals. An example of this is the section on licensing. "Art & Commerce Cafe" (opinion and commentary on the music business), on the other hand, should make for interesting reading to someone breaking into the business as well as to music enthusiasts.

The ASCAP Resource Guide suggests reference books, periodicals and newsletters, and professional organizations for various areas of the music business, including the recording industry, film and television, theater, jingles, and concert music. You can read ASCAP's magazine, Playback, online. Archived issues are available.

WORLDWIDE INTERNET MUSIC RESOURCES

HTTP://WWW.MUSIC.INDIANA.EDU/MUSIC_RESOURCES/

This is an extraordinary compilation of music links from the William and Gayle Cook Music Library at the Indiana University School of Music. You could spend hours browsing through them! Select a category and find out for yourself how much there is here. Say you pick "Groups and Ensembles (Except for Popular)." This will lead you to sites on chamber ensembles, dance and ballet, early music groups, and high school music departments. Or how about "Research and Study." You'll get an enormous number of subheads here, relating to ancient music, centers of musical scholarship, ethnic and national music, music education, music pedagogy, professional societies—the list goes on and on! A few of these feature more than a hundred links apiece. If you're in the process of selecting a college, "Schools and Departments of Music by Country" should be a big help.

"The Commercial World of Music" takes you to actual job listings. If you have time to look at only one link there, make sure it's IU School of Music Placement Bulletin, from the site's host. There are plenty of jobs nationwide posted in categories such as band, choral conducting, church music, musicology, strings, theory, woodwinds, and many more.

In order to use some of the sites in this directory for planning your future or advancing your career, you'll have to think creatively. Ask yourself questions such as the following: What can you learn at the site to help you decide on a career path? Can you contact somebody you find through a site concerning (unposted) educational or internship opportunities or perhaps to conduct an information interview?

Music and Recording Industry

AUDIO ENGINEERING SOCIETY
HTTP://WWW.AES.ORG/

The AES is a professional society dedicated to promoting and developing audio technology. Go to the section on education to read articles such as "Student Membership in the AES: What Is It All About?" and "Apprenticeship/Internship in Audio." Additionally, addresses and phone numbers are given for various organizations where you can get further information on careers and relevant education. Details are given on AES publications and events. Rounding out the site is an impressive collection of annotated links in such areas as audio education and research, computers and audio, professional audio companies and organizations, and radio and broadcast. Remember to think creatively when you peruse the links. Might you be able to find a mentor? an internship? or even a job?

SONGWRITERS GUILD OF AMERICA
HTTP://WWW.SONGWRITERS.ORG/

If you're curious about breaking into the songwriting business, you'll want to head straight for "New Writers." This FAQ section addresses pertinent issues like how to get started, collaboration, demo tapes, copyright, and contracts. Learn more by talking to others through the discussion forum or in the chat room. Check out the events page to find out what's going on with the SGA offices in Los Angeles, Nashville, and New York, as well as online.

Newspapers and Magazines

EDITOR & PUBLISHER
HTTP://WWW.EDITORANDPUBLISHER.COM/

Editor & Publisher magazine has covered the newspaper industry for more than a hundred years. At the site you can read industry news or check out journalism and media jobs. The listings in the classifieds section, which are updated regularly, are listed according to category, such as academic, administrative, advertising, circulation, editorial, new media, pressroom, production/tech, and public relations. Browse through a category of your choice or search by keyword. Some jobs you might find include sports copy editor, editorial artist, circulation director, online producer, and home delivery supervisor.

"Media Links" is an extensive searchable database of U.S. and international media. Use it to find details about and links to home pages of newspapers, magazines, news services, radio and television stations, and industry associations. E&P is an excellent and reliable source that you will surely want to consult frequently if you're thinking about a journalism career.

J-JOBS
HTTP://WWW.JOURNALISM.BERKELEY.EDU/JOBS/

This site has up-to-date, detailed job listings for journalism positions. The postings come from discussion lists and newsgroups and are compiled by the University of California at Berkeley Graduate School of Journalism. You can look through them by category, including freelance; internships; magazines, journals, and newsletters; new media; newspapers and wire services; photojournalism; radio; and television. Or you can browse through the entire listing the old-fashioned way. Some of the widely varied jobs you can pursue here are copywriter, weekend news associate producer, assistant metro editor, freelance reporter-photographer, investigative reporter, and Web content intern. In addition to the wealth of job listings to be discovered here, there are links to even more listings at other sites plus other related resources.

Nonprofits

ACCESS: NETWORKING IN THE PUBLIC INTEREST
HTTP://WWW.ACCESSJOBS.ORG/

This Washington, D.C.-based organization has put together a useful resource intended for nonprofit-sector job seekers and employers alike. You can browse regional nonprofit employment listings that include job descriptions presented along with the organization's mission statement, founding date, budget, and Web site address where available. Archived articles cover such topics as salaries in nonprofit jobs, nonprofit-related graduate programs, building diversity, and trends in the field. Links to other pertinent pages are provided. Career counseling is offered for a fee.

INTERNET NONPROFIT CENTER

HTTP://WWW.NONPROFITS.ORG/

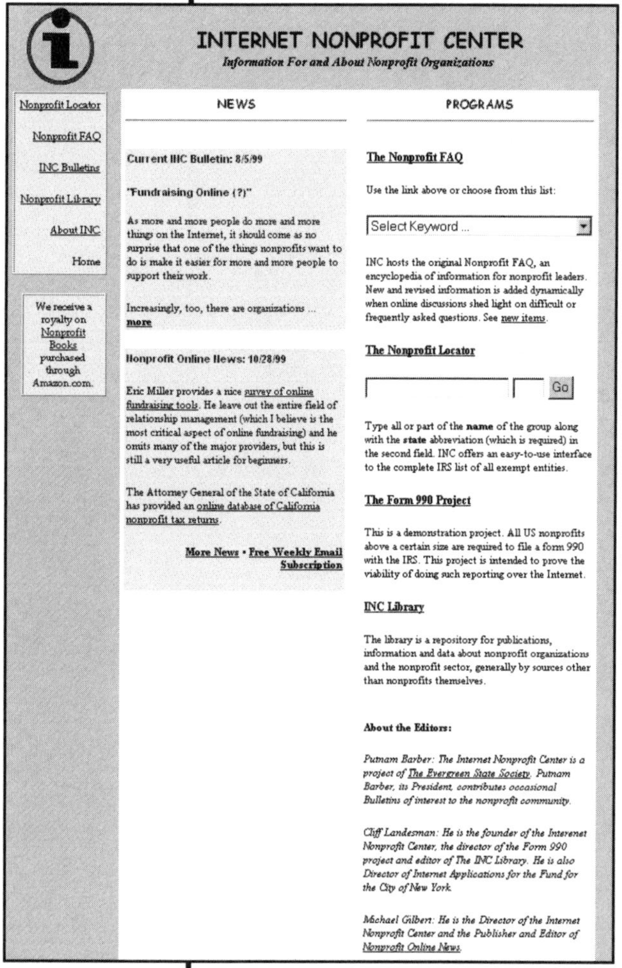

INC provides information for volunteers and donors in the nonprofit sector. There are no job listings but you'll have access to background information on hundreds of charities and nonprofit organizations (NPOs).

The "Nonprofit FAQ"—organized by several subheads (including organization, management, regulation, resources, and development), which are further divided into more specific categories—offers some great answers to common questions asked by nonprofit workers. Read about liability, automation, charitable contributions, service learning, and canvassing, just to name a few. Suggestions are given on finding volunteer opportunities.

The "Nonprofit Library" includes a handful of essays and articles and suggests publications you can turn to in order to learn about nonprofit organizations. To find addresses and phone number of NPOs, search the "Nonprofit Locator" database.

NATIONAL OPPORTUNITY NOCS
HTTP://WWW.OPPORTUNITYNOCS.ORG/

Opportunity NOCs ("Nonprofit Organization Classifieds") is a classified ads publication serving the nonprofit sector in several U.S. markets: Atlanta, Boston, Dallas, Los Angeles, Philadelphia, and San Francisco. The listings at this Web site come from nonprofit organizations nationwide and therefore will be different from what appears in the print versions. And jobs appear online about a week later than they appear in the print edition. Actually, it's up to the hiring company where the ads are posted—online and/or in print.

There are several ways to search the database. You can view all postings within a certain time period, you can call up job openings by state, or you can narrow the field by specifying certain criteria (keyword, region, state, position type). Among the many jobs posted are substance abuse counselor for an HIV program, finance manager for a conflict resolution and mediation organization, grant writer, and accountant for an environmental activist organization.

"Nonprofit Library" features links to nonprofit-related sites in the categories of books and journals, newsgroups and mailing lists, organizations and information, and technology, while "Career Resources" links direct you to other nonprofit jobs databases as well as the usual career-planning materials (for example, resumes and career development). If you have any interest in the nonprofit sector, you must not miss this site!

PHILANTHROPY NEWS NETWORK ONLINE
HTTP://WWW.PJ.ORG/

If you'd rather work for a nonprofit organization than a major public corporation, check out PNN Online. Here you'll find all sorts of information pertaining to the nonprofit sector. There are articles about foundations, volunteering, fund-raising, innovations, corporate giving, and laws and taxes. Read the brief synopsis and then follow the link if you want to read the full article content.

Go to the jobs page and decide whether you want to look at jobs by region or category (development, executive, or other). Sample positions include regional information systems manager, applications development manager, gifts officer, director of membership, and grant writer, working with schools, religious organizations, environmental groups, and the like.

Don't miss the "Meta-Index of Nonprofit Sites," a comprehensive list of links to general nonprofit organization sites, human rights sites, civil liberties sites, environmental issues and animal rights sites, and more. These aren't necessarily job-related, but if you are gearing up for a career in nonprofits, this is a great way to research different organizations and causes.

Nuclear Power

NUCLEAR ENERGY INSTITUTE

HTTP://WWW.NEI.ORG/

NEI, an organization having members worldwide, plays a major role in shaping nuclear policy. "Nuclear Energy Basics" and "The Nuclear Energy Story" serve as introductions to the world of nuclear energy and its relationship with people and the environment. News releases will keep you apprised of what's currently going on in the industry. You'll find plenty of career-related information and ideas in "Careers and Education." Details on fellowships and scholarships are given, and possible occupations, certification, and training are discussed. Looking for more? Then head for the links to related resources.

Personal and Business Services

ASSOCIATED LOCKSMITHS OF AMERICA

HTTP://WWW.ALOA.ORG/

"Getting Started in Locksmithing" (under "Industry Resources") is a great place to begin if you're considering a career as a locksmith. Job responsibilities, working conditions, qualifications, training and education, earnings and hours, and occupational outlook are all covered. Looking for a school? They're listed here too. Plus details are provided for classes regularly offered by ALOA. Other site features are legislative reports, industry news, dates of industry events, and descriptions of ALOA's publication Keynotes.

NATIONAL FUNERAL DIRECTORS ASSOCIATION
HTTP://WWW.NFDA.ORG/

NFDA provides here some excellent information on the funeral service industry and what it takes to become a funeral director. First take a look at "Careers/Education," where you can read about what skills are necessary to become an effective funeral director. There's a discussion of job duties and educational requirements as well. Licensing and educational requirements by state are provided, as are listings of schools with accredited programs in mortuary science and funeral service scholarships. Some listings are supplemented by links to home pages.

Other sections you might want to check out include "Consumer Resources," which has information on state funeral director associations, funeral service organizations, and funeral prices, and "Publications/Advertising," which features abstracts of articles from The Director, NFDA's official publication.

Petroleum

AMERICAN PETROLEUM INSTITUTE
HTTP://WWW.API.ORG/

There's plenty of materials here about the oil and gas industry: up-to-date global news, research papers on issues such as alternative fuels and clean air, and energy facts, FAQs, and statistics. API's activities and programs in the areas of environment, health, safety, information technology, and telecommunications are thoroughly covered. When viewing the extensive events calendar, you have the choice of sorting events by date, department, subject, or name. Under "Programs & Services" you can read about API's Quality Programs. These include programs having to do with oil licensing and certification, petroleum product accreditation, and inspector certification. "Educational Materials" presents facts about gasoline, natural gas, and oil, along with links to additional related resources.

OFFSHORE GUIDES

HTTP://OFFSHOREGUIDES.COM/

If you are interested in working in the offshore oil and gas or maritime industries, this site may help you decide if a life offshore is for you. The entire content of The Complete Offshore Employment Handbook is included here. This handbook is a crucial resource for anyone interested in offshore work. You'll learn about the job qualifications, typical work schedules, training programs, types of rigs, and employment outlook. It also includes job search advice and information on special service companies, such as anchor crews, fishing crews, and diving companies.

See what types of jobs are currently available in the section for job seekers. All the vacancies are listed and categorized by field, such as engineering, maritime, management, catering, offshore drilling rig personnel, and more. You can apply for openings online.

Pharmaceuticals

AMERICAN ASSOCIATION OF COLLEGES OF PHARMACY

HTTP://WWW.AACP.ORG/

Although primarily intended for AACP members, this site provides a large number of links to pharmacy colleges in the United States and abroad. There's also plenty of career publications offered here, although you will have to purchase them. The section for students presents a list of answers to frequently asked questions dealing with such issues as the North American Pharmacist Licensure Examination (NAPLEX) and the Pharmacy College Admission Test (PCAT), financial assistance, and educational and degree options. Current and archived AACP news releases are available. Additional resources and services are available to AACP members.

PHARMACY WEEK
HTTP://WWW.PHARMACYWEEK.COM/

This site is subtitled "The Health Systems Pharmacists' Employment Newsletter," so you can bet you're going to find some pertinent information here if you're considering a career in pharmacy services. Yes, there are job listings—and quite a few of them at that. Categories represented are health-systems pharmacists (for example, anticoagulation pharmacist, clinical pharmacist, nuclear pharmacist), pharmacy technicians, and retail pharmacists.

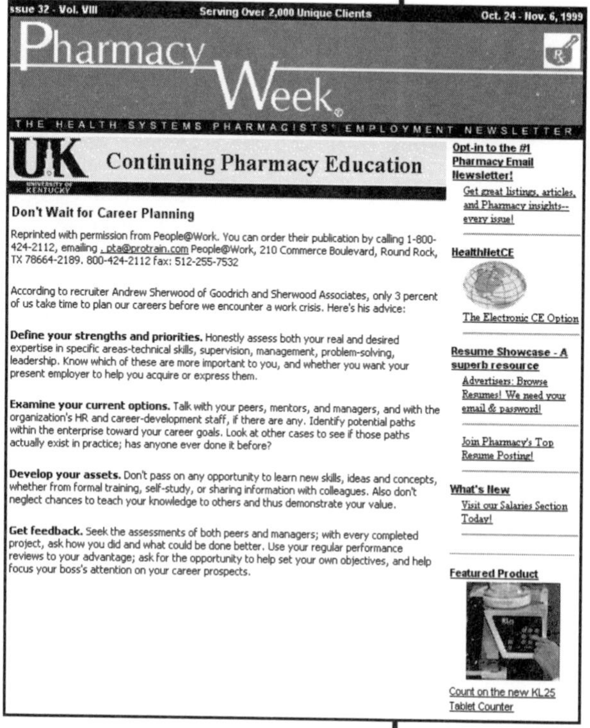

Looking to bounce some thoughts or questions off other people in the industry? Check out the site's discussion board. And don't miss the Pharmacy Week articles, which cover a broad spectrum of issues. You might find articles on pharmacy automation, salaries, interviewing and resumes, and more. The links section will point you in the direction of many other useful resources to supplement the materials presented here. Sites are listed for related organizations and associations, employment, salary and other job search topics, and of course pharmacy information.

Photography

PHOTO DISTRICT NEWS
HTTP://WWW.PDN-PIX.COM/

This is the vast online complement to the print publication Photo District News, which covers the professional photography industry, and its digital-imaging supplement, Pix. Find out about photography-related exhibits, conventions, seminars and workshops, and competitions. Among the other site features are a searchable database of past PDN articles (with ordering information), news, tools for the independent photographer (concerning contracts and agents, copyright, licensing, and insurance), "People on the Move," numerous portfolios, new product reports, and an impressive archive of related links covering such topics as copyright and legal, education, photographic organizations, photojournalism, stock photography, and technical information. And it doesn't end here!

To view the work of notable photographers, don't miss the "Legends" interactive galleries. "Photo Source" is a directory of street and Web site addresses plus phone numbers for several hundred companies in the photography industry, including dealers, retailers, equipment and service suppliers, manufacturers, distributors, and importers. At the Tech Talk bulletin board, you can discuss with others the technical aspects of the photography business. If you want to talk about photography jobs, visit the Assignment Exchange bulletin board.

Plastics

SOCIETY OF PLASTICS ENGINEERS
HTTP://WWW.4SPE.ORG/

There are a couple ways you can look here for a job in the plastics industry. First you can browse the classified listings that are also placed in Plastics Engineering magazine. Plus you can search SPE's jobs database, the Online Plastics Employment Network. Some of the jobs you might discover are materials researcher, mold engineer, production manager, and plastics engineer. Scholarship programs are described in detail, student chapters worldwide are listed, and dates are provided for conferences, seminars, and workshops. Certain members-only site features include bulletin boards and chat rooms.

Public Safety

THE CORRECTIONS CONNECTION
HTTP://WWW.CORRECTIONS.COM/

Boasting more than 10,000 links, this enormous resource has to do with the corrections industry and is actually home to a large number of corrections organizations, publications, and networks, all of which are linked from the site. Some of the other links categories cover community corrections, domestic violence, family and victims, grants and funding, juvenile issues, legislation, religious support, technology, and of course criminal justice. There are links also for criminal justice schools and programs, which you'll want to refer to if you're weighing your educational options.

The "Student Question Board" is a place where criminal justice students can pose questions to be answered by visiting criminal justice professionals. Another way to communicate with others in the field is through the numerous topic-oriented bulletin boards. Some of the topics are alternative programs, community outreach, education for inmates, gangs, health care, management and privatization, training, and juvenile, security, and correctional library issues.

Separate online networks have been established for major sectors of the corrections industry. These are in the areas of education, health care, industries, juveniles, privatization, and technology. Each network provides more focused coverage by way of news, events details, bulletin boards, job listings, reports, bibliographic citations, and more.

OFFICER.COM
HTTP://WWW.OFFICER.COM/

So you want to be a cop? This Internet directory of law enforcement sites, maintained by a couple police officers in Massachusetts, will make your head spin with all the information available. For starters, there are links to hundreds upon hundreds of police agency Web sites worldwide. There are also links to police association and organization sites, categorized as activist, labor union, Fraternal Order of Police lodges, gay and lesbian, professional, or social.

The employment page has links to law enforcement job listing sites by state. These would be police department and sheriff's office recruiting pages, university campus police employment listings, and more. There's also a link to the New Blue Line (http://www.pilotonline.com/special/blueline/), a site that provides an inside look at becoming a police officer. Check it out if you're curious to learn more about a law enforcement career.

What else is offered at Officer.Com? "Criminal Justice" has links to federal and state sites; "Special Operations" has links to SWAT, gang unit, and bomb squad pages; and "Corrections" has links to corrections departments and associations. Then there are even more links covering training and other events, community watch programs, terrorist and hate group information, and news. Interactive features include a discussion forum and a chat room.

Railroads

ASSOCIATION OF AMERICAN RAILROADS

HTTP://WWW.AAR.ORG/

While not a career resource per se, AAR offers materials that are sure to be of interest to anybody wanting to pursue a career in the railroad industry. In particular, the site features a large array of current and archived railroad news. AAR members include several main North American freight railroads (Burlington Northern Santa Fe, Canadian National, Conrail, CSX, Illinois Central, Kansas City Southern, Norfolk Southern, and Union Pacific) and Amtrak. Links to home pages lead you to industry and employment information. Back at the AAR site, you can keep up with industry issues by reading press releases, position papers, statistics and facts, and the newsletter Train-It!

Real Estate

NATIONAL ASSOCIATION OF REALTORS
HTTP://NAR.REALTOR.COM/

Dating back to 1908, NAR has a membership totaling more than 700,000. The organization's Web site is the place to go in order to find out what's happening in the industry. Here you'll have access to news releases and position papers; information dealing with community involvement issues (for example, fair and affordable housing), government affairs, and convention and trade shows; and data on home sales and mortgage rates.

NAR's affiliate site CommercialSource.com (a "global commercial real estate source") features additional resources, including a large collection of links to sites of real estate-related organizations, online property listings for the United States and abroad, and real estate news sources.

PIKENET
HTTP://WWW.PIKENET.COM/

PikeNet is a directory of commercial real estate sites. To view the complete outline arranged by topic, you'll want to select "Search on Category." This pulls up a screen alphabetically listing all the categories covered in the directory. If you're trying to figure out where you can study real estate, check here for links to the sections on education as well as on seminars and training. Get an idea of the range and availability of jobs in the field by looking at the jobs pages, which list recruiting firms and jobs databases. Some of the other categories represented are appraisers, associations (professional and realtor), brokers, consultants, listing services, and research and analysis.

Religious Ministries

AWESOME CHRISTIAN SITES
HTTP://AWESOME.CROSSDAILY.COM/

Aimed at a Christian audience, this immense directory includes annotated links to a wide range of Web sites in just about any category imaginable. There are sites having to do with arts and entertainment, the Bible, churches, history, music, news, publishing, recreation, shopping, theology, and more. Among those sections that will be of most use in your career management are education (where you can explore your educational options), ministries and organizations (where you might discover groups offering resources and support in your particular area of interest), and business (where you'll find job sites).

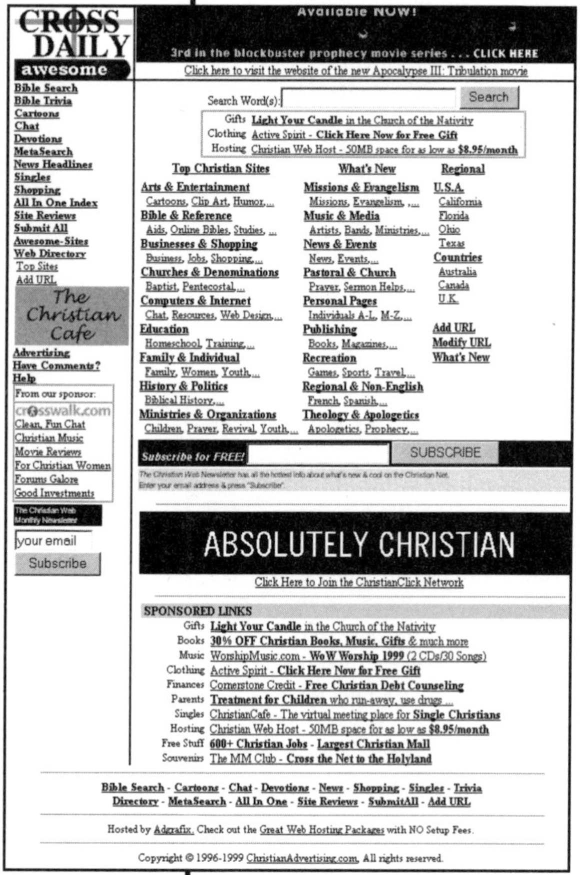

MINISTRYCONNECT
HTTP://WWW.MINISTRYCONNECT.ORG/

This is a basic job site for ministers and others looking for "meaningful work in the service of others." In addition to parish, pastoral, and spiritual ministry listings, there are listings in the areas of administration, education, health care, support services, music and youth ministry, and volunteerism, among others. Brief descriptions and contact details are offered. Educational and spiritual listings are provided as well.

Restaurants and Food Service

ESCOFFIER ON LINE
HTTP://WWW.ESCOFFIER.COM/

If spatulas and whisks are your tools of choice, stop by Escoffier On Line. This site offers a wealth of resources for anyone interested in the food industry. Perhaps the most valuable section will be that on educational resources. Here you can find links to food-related programs in the categories of culinary arts or hospitality management, scholarship information, and Web resources for education, including school listings.

Ready to find a job? Check out the employment section, where job seekers and employers can post needs and wants. You'll find openings for pastry chefs, sous chefs, and line cooks, to name a few.

Some of the many varied categories you'll find represented in the links section are associations, beverages, culinary terms, recipes, restaurant supplies, software, and vegetarian. Make sure you eat before you start looking around!

THE GUIDE TO COOKING SCHOOLS-CAREER
HTTP://WWW.SHAWGUIDES.COM/COOKINGCAREER/

ShawGuides offers searchable directories of workshops, schools, vacations, camps, and conferences in various fields of interest, including arts and crafts, photography, language, tennis, golf, writing, education, and water sports. This particular guide happens to pertain to cooking as a career. (For those of you who simply enjoy cooking, there's another ShawGuide concerning cooking as a hobby.) There are several ways to access the database of some 500 professional cooking programs. Some of your options include looking for a program by date, state, country, region, focus, or tuition range. For focus you can designate from among baking/pastry, confectionery, healthful/vegetarian, French, Italian, Eastern Asia, and other. Sponsors are highlighted on the front page.

Rubber

RUBBER WORLD
HTTP://WWW.RUBBERWORLD.COM/

Dedicated to the rubber industry, this resource offers pertinent news briefs, summaries of articles from Rubber World magazine, a forum where you can either ask or answer questions concerning rubber, an events calendar, classifieds, and links. The classifieds are for jobs or equipment. Jobs are broken down as being for chemists, for engineers, in sales or marketing, or for miscellaneous categories. Dozens of companies are listed and described in the links section. More complete details are given for companies as they're listed (by topic) in the supplier index.

Sales

NATIONAL RETAIL FEDERATION
HTTP://WWW.NRF.COM/

The retail industry is made up of buyers, sales representatives, stock clerks, merchandise displayers, retail managers, and the like. If any of these positions holds any appeal to you, you'll want to read NRF's brochure Careers in Retailing, which is presented here at the site. Learn about the common types of retailers (for example, department store, discount merchandiser, specialty store, factory outlet, catalog), typical positions from entry level to managerial, suggested preparation for a retail career, and more. The site's FAQ section provides answers to questions mainly of interest to retail industry professionals, but some (including "How do I go about opening my own retail store or gift basket business?") will hold relevance for you if you're considering retail as a career. There are directories of state, national, international, and related retail associations. Links to home pages are given for some of these listings.

Shipping

MARINER'S ALL-IN-ONE PAGE
HTTP://WWW.MMA.MASS.EDU/CAMPUS/LIBRARY/MERCH1.SSI

This basic yet useful and large directory of links was compiled by the Massachusetts Maritime Academy, a school for merchant marines. All links are described. There are lots of jumping-off points here. Among them are other merchant marine schools, U.S. and international shipping companies, government resources, law firms doing business in the maritime industry, shipping suppliers, related publications, employment pages, and shipping facts, figures, and image galleries.

THE MARITIME HOME PAGE
HTTP://WWW.MARITIMEUSA.COM/

Another hefty collection of links, this site points you in the direction of maritime-related publications, employment resources, oil and gas pages, and shipping companies, ports, and organizations, to name a few. There's a massive bibliography of related titles in such areas as navigation aids, mooring, safety, transportation of goods, ports, employment, vessel inspection, ship handling, and maritime law, training, and licensing. Titles are given in-depth descriptions. Also available are details on maritime academies and training centers as well as college and other marine programs.

Social Sciences

AMERICAN ANTHROPOLOGICAL ASSOCIATION
HTTP://WWW.AAANET.ORG/

With its brochure Careers in Anthropology, the AAA is ready to help you figure out your career direction. There's a short description of the field along with discussion of anthropology as a major, potential job opportunities, and typical career paths (academic being the standard, with corporate, nonprofit, and government the runners-up). Job vacancies are listed on-site as well as off-site at a few recommended resources. Other career-related materials are linked from the site.

You say you want to know more about the association? Wouldn't you know, but you'll get that here too! There are AAA press releases, commission reports, action alerts and other government documents, information on the AAA's more than thirty specialized sections and interest groups, abstracts from the publications Anthropology News and American Anthropologist, and a membership application. All of this plus a nice collection of anthropology-related links make for a well-rounded resource.

AMERICAN SOCIOLOGICAL ASSOCIATION

HTTP://WWW.ASANET.ORG/

Ever wondered what you could do with a sociology degree? Well, ASA can present you with some options. The student section of this site offers a guide to careers in sociology. (In case you don't really know what sociology is, the public area of the site gives a brief overview, which should clarify.) If you're intrigued, you might want to become a student member of ASA. Read up on the ways in which you can become involved. To find a school, look at the sociology departments directory (available online or in hard copy). For those of you considering an advanced degree in sociology, be sure to examine ASA's fellowship and grant programs.

Ready to find a job? Look through the ASA Employment Bulletin online. Not only can you search for sociologist jobs here, but you are given links to other job search sites, some specifically in academia and others in the corporate sector.

Pertinent materials for professionals include dates for conferences and meetings, information on obtaining research support, and details about data resources. Footnotes, ASA's newsletter, can be read online.

Social Services

MENTAL HEALTH NET
HTTP://MENTALHELP.NET/

Just about anything you would ever want to know about mental health can be found at this well-organized reference site. If you're considering a career in the mental health field, this would be a good place to conduct some research to help you make an informed decision. Materials are presented under the headings of "Disorders & Treatments," "Professional Resources," and "Reading Room."

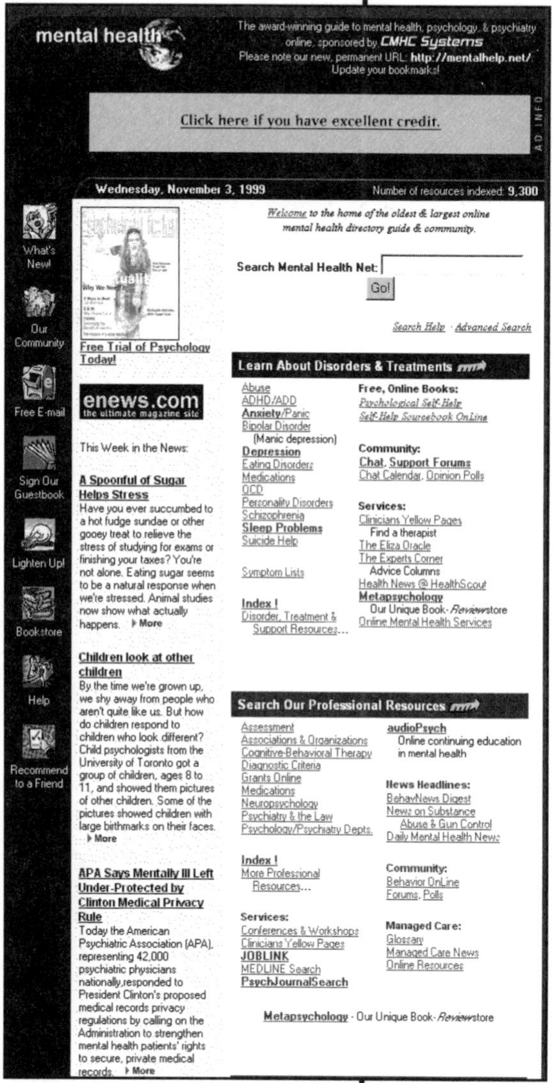

"Professional Resources" is probably the best place to begin your research. The topic section is divided into various areas; for example, assessment, behavioral and cognitive sciences, family and marriage therapy, geriatrics, health and sports psychology, and social work. Each category leads you to a list of links, each having a description along with an MHN rating. Pertinent newsgroups, mailing lists, publications, and professional organizations are included. There is a dizzying array of links!

"JobLink" announces employment opportunities (viewable by state). You'll also find a resume database and links to other employment resources on the Web. Some are related to psychology and mental health, while others are general job sites. These too are briefly described and rated.

Also featured are lists of federal and state health departments, related newsgroups and mailing lists, and U.S. and international academic departments and organizations in psychiatry, psychology, and social work; a searchable database of mental health-related events and workshops; a MEDLINE search page; and MHN news summaries and reports.

NATIONAL ASSOCIATION OF SOCIAL WORKERS

HTTP://WWW.NASWDC.ORG/

NASW is an organization of professional social workers. This site offers the usual membership details, chapter listings, news, and related links. If you want to order NASW publications, including the journals Social Work, Health & Social Work, Social Work in Education, and Social Work Research, you can do that online.

Before you make any purchases you may want to first explore your options in the field of social work. The online brochure Choices: Careers in Social Work presents detailed descriptions of several career paths a social worker can pursue, in the areas of aging, child welfare, substance abuse and addictions, corrections, developmental disabilities, mental health or clinical social work, policy and planning, and research. Related areas and typical employers are noted. For information on accreditation and licensing, follow links to the Counsel on Social Work Education and the American Association of State Social Work Boards, respectively.

If you're ready to look for employment, stop by the NASW JobLink, which enables you to search a database of social work jobs. You can select your specialty (basically the same categories that are described in the brochure mentioned above) and your U.S. geographic location. If you find a suitable opening, you can apply online or you can contact the organization directly. To get an idea of how social workers keep on top of issues, check out the up-to-date section on continuing education.

Space Exploration

AMERICAN ASTRONOMICAL SOCIETY
HTTP://WWW.AAS.ORG/

If you want to get paid for having your head in the stars, maybe you should be an astronomer! Here at the home page of the AAS, a professional organization for astronomers and other scientists, you'll find all sorts of information on the field of astronomy.

In the career resources section start out by reading the AAS pamphlet A New Universe to Explore: Careers in Astronomy. You can contact the AAS for a printed copy or read the text online. The brochure covers what to study in high school, college, and graduate school and how to prepare for an astronomy career. You can also read about the industry and where the jobs are. This is a very valuable resource for future astronomers. Other career resources include links to job listing, fellowship, and general career information sites, such as the American Institute of Physics Careers Services Division and the Network of Emerging Scientists. Select articles from The Astronomical Journal and The Astrophysical Journal are available in abstract or full-text format.

Sports

NATIONAL ATHLETIC TRAINERS' ASSOCIATION
HTTP://WWW.NATA.ORG/

How does a career in sports medicine and fitness sound to you? Check out the NATA online publication describing the certified athletic trainer and learn about the field. In addition to this, you might find the section discussing athletic injuries to be of interest. The site includes a list of contact details (names, street addresses, phone numbers, URLs) for accredited athletic training programs. You'll want to check pertinent Web sites to get hold of complete details. Tables of contents of recent issues of the official NATA publication Journal of Athletic Training can be viewed. The employment listings, however, are available to NATA members only.

ONLINE SPORTS CAREER CENTER

HTTP://WWW.ONLINESPORTS.COM/PAGES/CAREERCENTER.HTML

This site lists sports-related jobs as well as jobs in the recreation industry. Online Sports, the sponsor, produces an online catalog of sporting goods. Part of the main site is devoted to a database of products.

The "Job Bank" is where you'll find job listings. Some of the job titles you may run across include adventure travel expert, assistant varsity football coach, president of a sporting goods retail company, reporter for a sports magazine, or ticket sales account executive for a professional hockey team. Job description, requirements, and responsibilities are given, along with details on how to apply.

To add your resume to the resume database, simply send it to Online Sports in ASCII text format. You can also subscribe (for a fee) to the National Sports Employment Newsletter, which provides you with updates on new jobs in the sports industry. The e-mailed version comes out weekly, while the print edition is sent to you twice a month.

THE PHYSICIAN AND SPORTSMEDICINE

HTTP://WWW.PHYSSPORTSMED.COM/

This is the Web site for the journal Physician and Sportsmedicine. If you're interested in a career in sports medicine, be sure to page through this resource. You will have access to certain content from the current issue and from back issues. There are also many articles on personal health issues for people with an active lifestyle. Some of the areas covered include chronic disease, nutrition, rehabilitation, strengthening exercises, and weight control.

There's a section featuring resource listings, where you'll discover details on sports medicine fellowship programs and residencies, a directory of sports medicine clinics, and notes on professional organizations, with links where available for these and other sports medicine-related pages.

SPORTING GOODS MANUFACTURERS ASSOCIATION
HTTP://WWW.SPORTLINK.COM/

SGMA's site offers many features that will help keep you up-to-date with what's going on in the sporting goods industry. You can learn about the newest products, read press releases, or plan your trip to an upcoming trade show. "Hot Links" will take you to fitness-related sites, including the home pages of the U.S. Olympic Committee, Cory Everson, and the Running Network. You can also join an online discussion forum or link to nonprofit organizations such as the Women's Sports Foundation. Additional links are provided for sports products, such as apparel and footwear, equipment, and sports medicine and training supplies.

The employment section presents job listings for directors of apparel design, footwear designers, merchandisers and buyers, pro shop managers, and more. Job postings are from SGMA members. Additional job listings can be found if you follow the links to member company employment pages.

Telecommunications

TELECOMMUNICATIONS INDUSTRY ASSOCIATION
HTTP://WWW.TIAONLINE.ORG/

TIA describes itself as "the voice of manufacturers and suppliers of communications and information technology products and services." If you're thinking about entering the telecommunications industry, you'll appreciate what this site has to offer: public policy reports, press releases, standards documents, and the like, dealing with topics such as communications accessibility, broadband issues, wireless systems, building cabling standards, industry trends, and international issues. You can discuss telecommunications business through the discussion forum. Having troubles with some of the terminology? Look it up in the glossary or check the list of acronyms. Want to explore elsewhere? Peruse the extensive collection of links to related organizations, standards agencies, and more.

TOTAL TELECOM
HTTP://WWW.TOTALTELE.COM/

Here you can read current news headlines and analysis in the areas of mobile and satellite, Internet and e-commerce, business and regulatory, and network infrastructure. For access to full articles, you must first register (at no charge). The "Recruitment" section is where you'll find the jobs. Select a category and/or a region or just look at them all! Some of the vacancies are for telecommunications consultants, ISDN routers, customer technical support engineers, network controllers, analyst programmers, switching engineers, and telecommunications hardware installation supervisors. Listings are for positions situated worldwide. Events and conferences, also international, are noted in the "Diary" section, which gives you links to relevant sites where available. There's a lot of links at the site, in fact. You'll get links for manufacturers, analysts and consultants, satellite companies, operators, regulators, associations, standards bodies, and more.

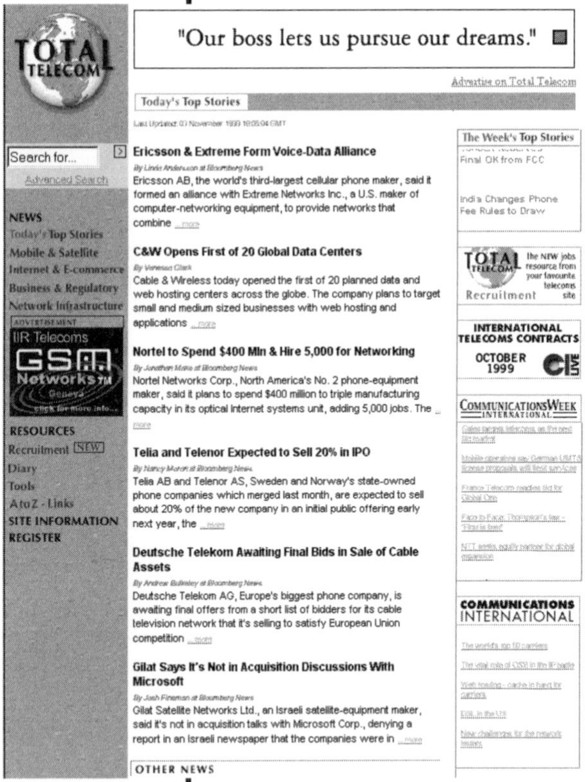

Textiles

AMERICAN TEXTILE MANUFACTURERS INSTITUTE
HTTP://WWW.ATMI.ORG/

While much of the information at this trade association site will be useful mainly to ATMI members or other textile professionals, a visit to this site will yield an overview of the industry. There is a huge products and services directory listing hundreds of companies in the areas of fabric, home furnishings, sales yarn, specialty finishing, and threads. Issues of interest within the textile industry are discussed, including labeling, flammability, health and safety, and standards. Furthermore, there are news releases, employment data, descriptions of ATMI publications that can be ordered at the site, and links to ATMI committee pages as well as to pertinent departments and agencies. Certain additional features are available to ATMI members only.

Theater

PLAYBILL
HTTP://WWW.PLAYBILL.COM/

If you've been to the theater before, you've probably seen a Playbill program. (And if you haven't yet made it to the theater, this site will quite likely motivate you to do so!) Well, this site is operated by the same company that designs them. There's so much to see here, it's hard to know where to start. So how about the news? Up-to-date and in-depth, there's news covering theater happenings around the globe: United States, Canada, international, and the Tony Awards.

Now that you're itching to get out there and join other theater professionals in their craft, let's look at resources here specifically relating to careers. Under "Industry" you can get to the school listings and jobs. You can check out college program listings according to certain criteria: college name, state, major, and/or degree. Or look at them all (it's quite a long list). Descriptions are offered for each, along with links to Web sites where available. Then for the jobs. You can browse them all or by category (performer, technical, design, administrative, academic, other). Or search on job title and state. Some of the job vacancies might be for actors and actresses, musicians and musical directors, booking associates, box office managers, stage technicians, costume designers, dancers, advertising coordinators, props masters, carpenters, and stagehands. There are many internship opportunities listed as well. To view the full details, you'll first need to register (at no charge).

Ready to catch a performance? Detailed listings are given for Broadway, Off-Broadway, regional companies, national tours, London, and summer stock. Other site features include articles and interviews, a theater industry who's who, a script database, seating charts (mainly for theaters in New York City and London), a chat room and message boards, multimedia theater art, and links. Lots of links! Most areas of the site are searchable, so if you know what you're looking for and want to get right down to it (instead of browsing endlessly, unearthing numerous other items of interest in the meantime!), then type in your keywords. If the theater is in your future, then don't miss this site!

Toys and Games

TOY MANUFACTURERS OF AMERICA
HTTP://WWW.TOY-TMA.COM/

TMA, the trade association of the U.S. toy industry, was founded in 1916. As might be expected from a site having to do with toys, this is quite a colorful, visually playful resource. Head to the "Industry" section to learn about the toy and game industry. If you've got what you think is a great idea for a new toy, you'll want to study the Toy Inventor/Designer Guide. You'll get guidance on determining what really is a good idea that might actually be worth pursuing. Legal issues are addressed. Information is also given on how to sell your invention or how you can go about manufacturing and distributing it yourself.

The Toy Industry Fact Book discusses product safety, demographic trends, retail markup, and advertising to children, with separate chapters devoted to TMA and the American Toy Institute. Another booklet available online is Fun Play, Safe Play, which focuses on the importance of play during childhood.

If you're wondering where you can get an education to prepare you for a career in this field, rest assured that you can get that information here. The Fashion Institute of Technology's Toy Design Department offers a degree program in toy design. To find out more, from the main TMA "Industry" page, go to the American Toy Institute subpage, where there will be a link for the Toy Design Department. There you can read all about the program. Also from the ATI page you can visit the "Hall of Fame," which briefly profiles major figures in the toy and game industry.

TMA doesn't stop there! "Betcha Didn't Know" presents trivia on your favorite childhood toys and toy manufacturers. Industry statements cover business practices and dangerous toys, while press releases keep you apprised of industry events and news. You can read up on association news in the newsletter TMA: FYI. Also included are lists of trade publications, online retailers, industry events, and association and government agencies (all with links where available).

Transportation

FREIGHTWORLD
HTTP://WWW.FREIGHTWORLD.NET/

This mammoth directory of resources is devoted to freight transportation and logistics around the world. What you get are links in two basic areas: modes of transportation and transportation services. Each of these is further broken down into relevant categories. Under "Modes" you'll get sites relating to airlines, logistics providers, maritime, postal services, railroads, seaports, and trucking. "Services" features sites having to do with classifieds (here you'll find sites with jobs), customs brokers, finance and leasing, law and government, organizations, software and technology, suppliers, and universities. For the most part, links are simply listed, not described. Generally you'll have the option of viewing the lists either alphabetically or geographically.

You'll have to take the initiative to fully utilize this site as a career resource. Check out organizations in an attempt to find career information or even a mentor, go to university sites to read about educational options, and visit company home pages to research potential employers and peruse job listings. The sky's the limit!

Travel and Tourism

AMERICAN SOCIETY OF TRAVEL AGENTS
HTTP://WWW.ASTANET.COM/

ASTA's site has separate sections geared toward different audiences: ASTA members, travelers, and travel industry personnel. Assuming that you're still assessing your career choices in the travel industry, you'll probably want to enter the last-named section first. Once there, check out the section on travel careers. ASTA has put together a nice introduction to becoming a travel agent. There's information about job training, necessary skills, and benefits, as well as ideas about selecting a travel school and then starting a travel agency. A few book titles are suggested for further reading. You can search for a travel school in the travel directory, which also includes listings for various other travel-related operations (for example, airlines, cruise lines, tour operators, travel agencies, travel consortiums, and so on).

There's also plenty of information on scholarships, grants, and internships. If you're already in travel school, you might want to join ASTA's Future Travel Professionals Club. Details can be found at the site. Check out the job listings if you're ready to take the plunge, or post something on the bulletin board indicating what it is you're looking for.

Some of the other things you'll find at the site are a calendar of ASTA educational programs and seminars, industry news and press releases (plus archives), legislative updates, and links to further resources.

Trucking

TRUCK NET
HTTP://WWW.TRUCK.NET/

Truck Net provides a directory of information and resources pertaining to the trucking industry. You can apply for a professional trucking job (as a driver, owner/lease operator, or diesel technician) just by filling out the online application form, which you can automatically send to Truck Net-affiliated companies that are looking to hire. Links to those companies' home pages are provided, so you can do your research before applying.

Numerous trucking and transportation associations and organizations are listed, with links where available. There are also links to sites for the Department of Transportation, trucking companies, truck magazines, new and used truck dealers, and truck stops, as well as sites offering law databases and legal services. The "Information Consortium" affords folks in the industry a place where they can discuss various trucking-related topics, covering such areas as regulations and safety, spousal issues, racing, and legal, medical, and tax matters.

Visual Arts

ARTJOB
HTTP://WWW.ARTJOB.ORG/

The Western States Arts Federation (WESTAF) publishes ArtJob, a job and news resource for people interested in the visual or performing arts. View a sample to see how you like it. You can then subscribe to the publication online (which is updated on an ongoing basis, as job openings are received) or in print (which is delivered twice a month or monthly during the summer). Employment opportunities may be listed with arts organizations, libraries, museums, or publications. Internships are featured as well. You don't have to be a subscriber to take advantage of the links to related sites, which include state arts agencies.

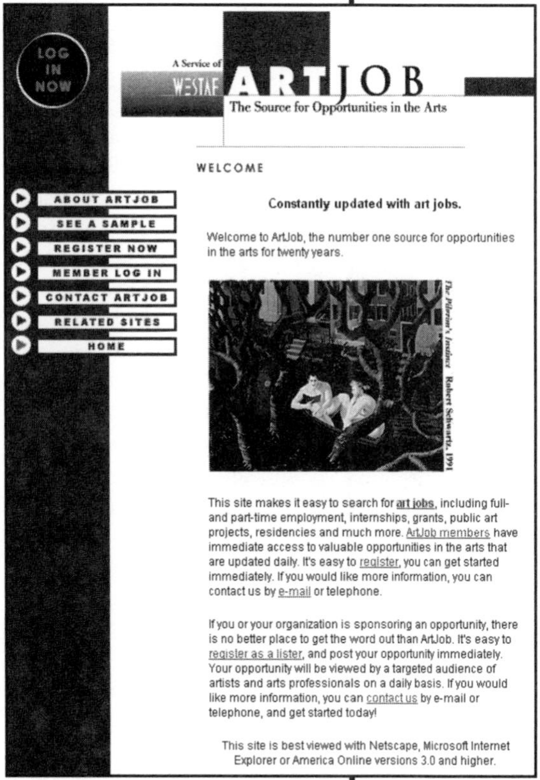

CONTEMPORARY ARTISTS' SERVICES
HTTP://WWW.ARTADVICE.COM/

This is the Web presence of Los Angeles management consultant Sylvia White's business, which is devoted to helping develop and promote the careers of visual artists. Profiles of White's artist clients are provided, as are images of their artworks.

"Art Advice" suggests ideas on how to promote yourself, how to take pictures of your artwork, how to approach an art gallery, how to handle a gallery interview, and more. In "Ask Sylvia," White addresses such questions and concerns as "Where can I go to get my art discovered?" and "I am a high school student currently wondering if I should try and get a job as an artist, but I can't seem to find anyone who will tell me anything . . ." After you read through these sections you'll come away with a clearer idea of what's involved in managing a career as an artist.

SCULPTOR.ORG
HTTP://WWW.SCULPTOR.ORG/

This is basically a directory of links to online resources aimed at professional sculptors as well as those who have a more casual interest in sculpting. Many of the links are described in some detail, while others are simply listed. There are plenty of links pertaining to sculpting in different media (for example, stone, bronze, iron and steel, wood, and computer-aided). You will also find links to sculptors' associations worldwide and also to schools offering sculpture programs. "Sculpture As a Business" is for those who want to know about commercial opportunities, partnering with others, and marketing and legal issues. Job opportunities are posted at the site. It should be noted that a good number of the site's links are appropriate to other areas of the visual arts, so even if sculpture isn't your strong suit, you will probably find something relevant to your art-related career path of choice.

Waste Management

WATER ONLINE
HTTP://WWW.WATERONLINE.COM/

Water Online is aimed at professionals in the water and wastewater industry, which goes to say that if this is where your career interests are, you should be sure to pay a visit. "News & Analysis" offers feature and regulatory articles, case studies, and more to help you keep up with what's currently happening in the industry. There's an education and training directory that lists providers of certification, management, safety, and technical training courses.

You can post your resume to the resume bank by completing the online form. Then check out the job vacancies. Search by typing in a keyword or company name or by using the drop-down list boxes where you can identify position, duties, state, and/or country. Among the positions you can select are biological scientist, civil/stormwater engineer, director of public works, field service technician, project manager, sales representative, and waste treatment specialist.

If you haven't had your fill, check out the discussion forums, product showcase, software downloads, event listings, and links to pertinent sites.

Wood

CYBER-SIERRA'S NATURAL RESOURCES JOB SEARCH
HTTP://WWW.CYBER-SIERRA.COM/NRJOBS/INDEX.HTML

This site is overflowing with links to information that can assist folks pursuing work not only in forestry but in such fields as water resources, agriculture, science and research, and others having to do with natural resources. Take the time to read the welcome and "read me" pages for insight into how to best use the site and for general advice about looking for work.

If you're only at the preliminary stage of exploring options for your future, there's plenty to glean from the materials linked from this site. Besides getting an idea of the range of career possibilities, you can link to many organizations, online courses, and reference tools.

For students deciding on colleges or just on what to do this summer, two areas could be of immediate value. The section called "Forestry and Natural Resources Schools" includes details about plus links to many of the universities and colleges where you can earn a degree in forestry, agriculture, or natural resources. Tree identification sites are listed as well. Another section, "Summer Jobs," contains links to numerous seasonal job (and internship) sites.

USDA FOREST SERVICE
HTTP://WWW.FS.FED.US/

Scratch beneath the surface of this mostly text-based government site and you'll find a useful resource for information about the Forest Service. "Human Resources" contains links (internal and external) to relevant materials on career possibilities. There's an overview of the kinds of Forest Service jobs there are with a discussion on how to get one, as well as a section on volunteer opportunities with the Forest Service. You can also access a guide to grants, fellowships, and scholarships that provides detailed descriptions of funding available to university students or professionals. If you're thinking of applying for a college scholarship, it would be worthwhile to visit this section to learn about eligibility requirements, deadlines, and contacts.

Section VII: Finding a Job

RESUMES

CHAPTER 14

Writing a resume is one of the most difficult aspects of the job search for many people. Either they do not think they will do it right or they are not confident they can represent their skills on paper (or electronically, as the case may be). Career counseling experts say that the best resume is one that gets an interview. Employers will want to interview the applicants they think have the skills to do their jobs. Smart job seekers tailor their resumes to highlight their skills that match those the employer is seeking for the position. The best resume you can compile is one that conveys your skills to an employer and reflects your experiences to document how those skills were acquired and have been used.

There is no one "right" way to write a resume. Different references, including those Web sites described in this chapter, will provide different slants on what should appear on a resume and how that information should be presented. It is important to know the practice of a given occupation—that is, what the resumes of other people applying for the same sort of jobs look like. You want your resume to stand out for the reason that your skills make you appear to be the most highly qualified, the most competitive, not because your resume looks different from others.

You are the person who is best able to create your own resume because no one knows your abilities and your work experiences better than you do. While hiring a resume-writing service may seem appealing, remember that they can only work with the information you provide. Many people find it difficult to translate what they have done in a job into the language of the resume. It is helpful to approach this task one step at a time.

• Allow yourself time to write a resume. This is not a project that can be completed in a couple of hours. It usually takes several drafts before a usable resume is produced and several more attempts before it is fine-tuned to the point of being as representative of your work history as possible. So plan to work on it across a period of time, usually several weeks to a month—and then continue to update it as your skills, experience, and objectives change.

• To help you keep track of such changes, you'd be wise to start keeping a resume-writing file. The process of redrafting your resume is made easier by keeping a file of references to remind you of academic courses taken, job descriptions, and projects you completed in both work and volunteer experiences.

• On an ongoing basis, write descriptions of specific skills you have gained in educational, work, or volunteer experiences. You will need to both summarize skills and generate broad skills categories.

• Decide on the best resume format, the content areas you want to use, and a design layout.

• Let other people critique your resume for you. They can double-check for grammatical and spelling errors. Furthermore, they might even have suggestions for a more attractive or efficient layout or ideas on how you can better emphasize your skills.

• Keep re-creating your resume. Tailor it for specific job openings. Change or rearrange headings of job skills categories, or redesign the layout. Keep it up to date, reflecting current information about your career.

Want to know more? Well, you've come to the right place if you want to find out whether to use a chronological or functional resume, what to include in your resume (for example, contact information, a career objective, work experience, details on education, professional credentials), or how to submit a resume via electronic means (as an e-mail attachment or in the body of an e-mail message). The Web sites that are described here will fill you in with specifics about all of this and more. If you're planning to post your resume online, be sure to study Chapter 10 ("Job Searching on the Internet"), especially the discussions on privacy issues.

BEST COLLEGE RÉSUMÉS
HTTP://WWW.COLLEGEGRAD.COM/BOOK/3-0.SHTML

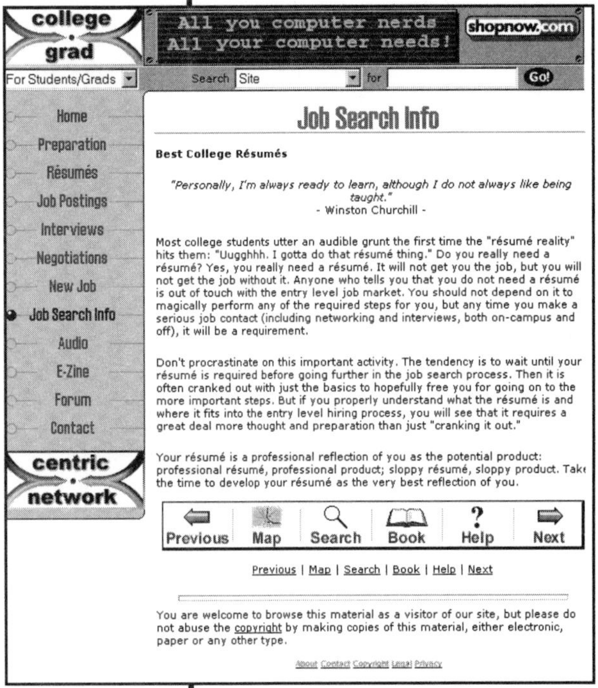

This step-by-step resume guide is a chapter from Brian Krueger's book College Grad Job Hunter. Preliminary discussion covers the importance of creating a resume—and how essential it is to keep it current. How do you go about composing an opening objective statement? And what about a summary section? What else should and shouldn't be included? How do you make your resume stand out from the crowd? Solutions to such questions are explained very matter-of-factly. You can also learn which proofreading technique to use depending on what stage your resume is at. Finally, examine the checklist to make sure you haven't forgotten to incorporate any necessary components into your resume.

ERÉSUMÉS 101
HTTP://WWW.ERESUMES.COM/TUT_ERESUME.HTML

Rebecca Smith, author of Electronic Resumes & Online Networking, explains the pros and cons of various types of electronic resumes: ASCII (plain text, rich text, or hypertext), keyword, or scannable. Especially useful is the step-by-step tutorial on creating an ASCII resume. "Web Résumé Design Guidelines" walks you through the basics of constructing a Web resume. Other tutorials deal with keyword resumes (a lengthy list of keywords is included) and "scanner-friendly vs. scanner-unfriendly" resumes. Several before and after resume samples are featured.

Smith's article "No Attachments Please!" discusses the reluctance of recipients to open attachments—mainly because of virus fears or compatibility issues. Therefore, unless it's specified otherwise, it's usually best to send your resume in the body of your e-mail message. The "Virtual Resume Gallery" consists of an assortment of links to sites where you can view or post electronic resumes.

RESUME ADVISORS
HTTP://WWW.RESUMEADVISORS.COM/

Members of this volunteer group advise students on certain aspects of resume writing. If you're looking for a way to quickly get started on your resume, a visit to this site will yield a brief, user-friendly outline covering the basics: resume content (education, work experience, awards, skills) and formatting tips. A few related links are available if you want more information.

RESUMETUTOR
HTTP://WWW1.UMN.EDU/OHR/ECEP/RESUME/

This tool helps you create a resume through an online workbook setting. You are given a choice of resume format: traditional (or reverse chronological), functional, or combination. (If you don't know what they look like, check out the examples.) For whatever the topic or question posed (regarding career objective, qualifications summary, work experience, etc.), you fill in specified fields with the relevant information, which is then gathered into a sample resume to be presented in your browser window in the format you selected. In an attempt to further clarify the process, advice is given and/or comments are made in response to the information you place in the various fields. This is a straightforward and relatively painless way to begin assembling a resume.

10MINUTE RESUME
HTTP://WWW.10MINUTERESUME.COM/

Register for free to create your resume online. You'll probably want to check out the demo before you start to get an idea of what your completed resume will look like. The interface is straightforward, so you should have no troubles figuring out what to do. Along the way, as you supply information for such resume headings as objective, major accomplishments, experience, education, and activities, you'll have access to guidance ("Expert Advice"). Suggestions are given for commonly used phrases you might want to incorporate into each section, general tips are offered to guide you in your writing, and action words are listed to give you options so you can avoid repeating the same old stagnant verbs throughout. If you like, you can work on your resume by saving a little at a time. Or come back and revamp it after you've gained new experiences. Ready for the final product? There are several available Web display options: basic, traditional, professional, or high-tech.

"WEB-ABLE" RESUMES
HTTP://TITAN.IWU.EDU/ CCENTER/RESUME/

You won't find a description of how to write your resume here. Instead you'll receive guidance on how and why to post your resume on the Web. Basic information is offered on creating ASCII (plain text), scannable, and HTML resumes. Since privacy is a major topic when it comes to conducting business online these days, you'll want to examine the section addressing concerns about issues of security. Various other tips and links to further resources are also provided.

WORKSEARCH: RESUME WRITING RESOURCES
HTTP://MEMBERS.XOOM.COM/GWWORK/ RESWRI.HTM

Author and consultant Gary Will rates and describes several resources you might want to explore when you sit down to work on your resume. A couple pertinent book titles earn his rave review (five stars), while the twenty-plus Web sites selected fall short of the highest rating, most receiving three or four stars. As you peruse the links, you'll discover step-by-step guides, assorted tips on such issues as presentation and the inclusion (or exclusion) of certain information, a discussion of "rules and regulations," and more. Resume-related articles by Will are also included.

CHAPTER 15

COVER LETTERS

Cover letters are business letters explaining to a perspective employer why you are interested in—and right for—a specific job or, more generally, career opportunities with the targeted company. No resume should be submitted for consideration for hiring without an accompanying cover letter that specifies the position for which you are applying. The cover letter affords you another opportunity to market yourself to the employer. It gives you a forum for presenting information or comments that aren't really suitable for inclusion in your resume.

Remember that most employers get many applications—sometimes hundreds—for their job openings. Usually, employers only want to interview the top three to five job applicants. In the first glance at a cover letter the decision is made to reject it or to look at the resume. The best cover letter works along with the resume to get you an interview.

It is a good idea to have some stationery printed for your job search. The same stationery (or high-quality paper) should be used for all job search correspondence: your resume, cover letters, thank you notes, and envelopes should all match. Whenever possible, it is preferable to address the cover letter to a specific individual. Sometimes it is necessary to make a phone call to find out the name of that person. Make sure you get the correct spelling of the person's name, along with his or her specific job title.

Generally, the format of cover letters must be neat, businesslike, and without errors. The content must be succinct, persuasive, and relevant to the particular employer. Your cover letter should feature the basic elements of a business letter, including (but not limited to) the following:

- return address or letterhead address,
- date of composition,
- name and address of the business or company,
- closing, and
- signature and typed name of the sender.

The language of the body of the cover letter is formal. Do not use abbreviations. Proofread the cover letter to be sure it does not contain grammar or spelling errors.

Seeing that you want to market yourself in the cover letter, what you say will vary with the position applied for and the skills you can bring to that particular job. A general rule is that the cover letter should be used to tell not what you want from the employer but what you can do for the employer. If you are responding to an advertisement, emphasize the experiences and skills you have that match the described job's qualifications. For each position you apply for, you should generate a cover letter describing your skills for that particular job. The marketing strategy you use depends on your skills, on what you know about the employer's business, and on the usual practices of the occupation in which you are applying.

As with resumes, there is no one right way to write a cover letter and you can find many sites on the Internet that offer tips on how to do so, suggesting guidelines for formatting and contents to be included. Here are some to get you started.

COVER LETTER TUTORIAL
HTTP://WWW.QUINTCAREERS.COM/COVER_LETTER_TUTORIAL_MAP.HTML

This detailed tutorial is from Quintessential Careers. You can start from the very beginning and learn about cover letter basics (why and when to use one and what kinds there are) and work your way through to the very end (writing tips and letter formatting). Or you can skip around the various topics listed in the outline.

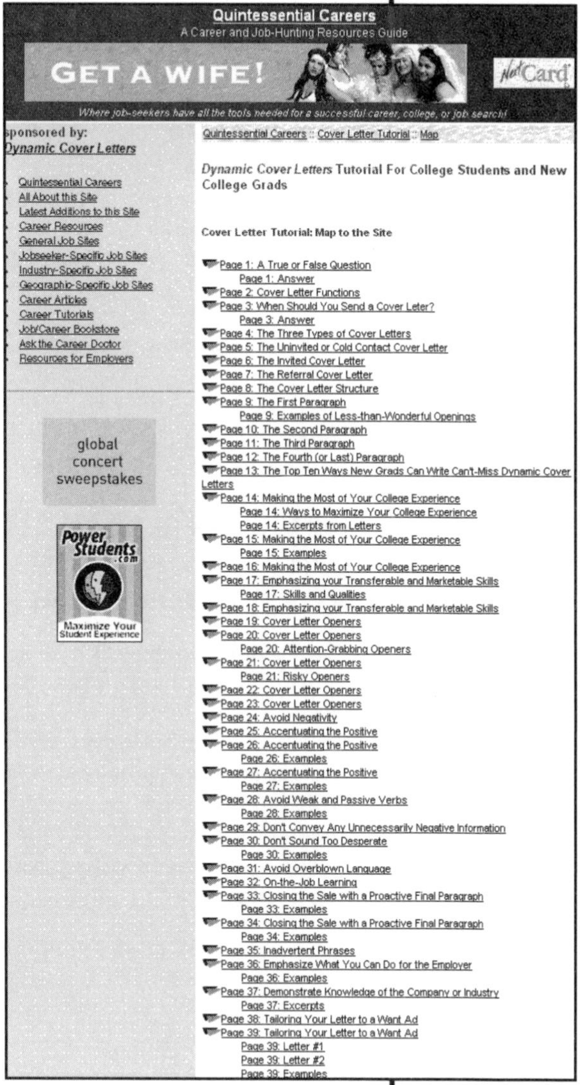

A brief step-by-step explanation is given of what to discuss in each paragraph of your letter. But what do you do if you have little actual job experience? You'll learn how to "make the most of college experience" in your cover letter. Having college students in mind, guidance is offered on how to present academic and extracurricular activities as being relevant to a work situation. This material will come in handy on down the road if you decide to switch career paths and don't feel as if you have any applicable related experience.

And there's still more. You will be presented with examples of what to avoid (negativity, rambling) or what to stress (your knowledge about the company, your skills and qualifications), as well as ideas for opening and closing paragraphs. Descriptions of commonly made mistakes and poor cover letters—along with suggested corrections—are also included.

200 LETTERS FOR JOB HUNTERS
HTTP://WWW.CAREERLAB.COM/LETTERS/

This site has more than 200 cover letters and other job-related correspondence samples for you to dig through. The letters cover a variety of categories such as letters of introduction (or sales letters), letters in response to want ads, follow-up letters, letters asking for a reference, letters seeking a salary increase, and much more.

Go to the section that piques your interest (say, for example, the one on cold calls) and you'll find plenty of advice about how to get your foot in the door—plus those cover letters! The letters in this particular section demonstrate how to sell yourself by focusing on your skills, how to approach a company you're especially interested in working for, and how to put together a blitz campaign (when you send a series of letters to a specific employer). Many letters are supplemented by suggestions for improvement or explanations of how they can be used in different industries.

In addition to the site's wide assortment of sample letters, you will also discover some useful advice about conducting a job search when you're in a hurry, organizing your ideas before you write, and how to follow up your letter, along with a list of commonly made mistakes in letter writing.

WRITING COVER LETTERS
HTTP://WWW.ANSELM.EDU/STUDENTLIFE/CAREER/COVERTUTOR1.HTML

Career and Employment Services at Saint Anselm College (New Hampshire) provides some straightforward information about cover letters. First off, you are advised on what to think about before you begin writing your cover letter, after which you are given some rules to keep in mind (for example, include a resume, proofread before sending, remember to sign). This is followed by a presentation of the components that should be included, paragraph by paragraph, along with a couple sample cover letters. Additionally, advice is offered for writing thank you notes and letters accepting or declining a job offer.

CHAPTER 16

CAREER PORTFOLIO

A career portfolio is a collection of materials documenting your skills, abilities, and achievements. Sort of like a resume in scrapbook form, it is a record of your personal career development. A portfolio can be a useful job search marketing tool because it provides examples of what you have achieved utilizing the skills you are selling.

Portfolios have a long history of use by people in creative arts, engineering, and educational occupations. Portfolios of actors and actresses include playbills from productions in which they had roles and photos of them in costume for various parts. Models use portfolios to show pictures of their employment in advertising campaigns or in fashion shows. Journalists and writers put sample articles and short stories as well as a list of their publications in their portfolios. Portfolios allow artists and photographers to display their work. Computer graphic designers sometimes present their portfolios on disk.

In today's job market, using a portfolio can give a competitive edge to job applicants in any occupational area. Many high schools and some colleges require their students to assemble portfolios as a graduation requirement. Developing a portfolio can help you by

- serving as a reminder of what you accomplished in previous jobs or in volunteer experiences. People making career transitions may know they have the ability and skills to enter a new occupation but may lack documentation. A portfolio captures what abilities were used and when skills were developed.

• providing a focus on how your skills and abilities have resulted in achievements and accomplishments.

• building your confidence as you prepare for an interview.

What you finally put in your portfolio will depend on what skills and abilities you want to emphasize. Examples of materials that should be saved for a portfolio include

• transcripts of educational course work completed,

• diplomas or proof of degrees earned,

• certificates of achievement or other awards,

• thank you letters or letters of commendation,

• job evaluations or work performance records,

• programs from conferences or conventions that you helped organize,

• newspaper articles covering your achievements,

• promotional materials of any workshop or seminar you conducted,

• work samples, such as pages showing database setup, home pages designed, desktop-published newsletters, lesson plans, and writing samples,

• professional licenses, certificates, or registrations, and

• letters of recommendation.

Remember that the portfolio is a marketing tool to get the job. It should be used to demonstrate achievements in areas relevant to the qualities the employer is seeking in a worker to fill the job. If the portfolio is not relevant to the skills and abilities needed on the job, it will not work for you.

Some experts suggest stating at the beginning of the interview that you have brought a portfolio. This approach is fine, provided you have accurately assessed what is desired for the job and designed your portfolio accordingly. If your portfolio is not on target, however, you may have hurt your chances by needlessly introducing it. Another approach is to introduce the portfolio in response to a question about the skills or abilities that you know are highlighted in the portfolio. While displaying the portfolio page, you can state how the achievement was a result of your use of the requested skills and abilities.

What are some of the advantages of using a portfolio?

• It shows that you can assimilate experiences, drawing parallels from what you have done to what will be desired on the job, and that you are aware of the skills and abilities that helped you to achieve your goals.

• It suggests credibility of your qualifications by providing documentation that backs up your resume.

• It can help you to guide the interview in such a way as to be certain your best qualifications are mentioned.

• It provides you with a tool that can help you jog your memory during the interview should anxiety impede your ability to verbalize experiences that demonstrate your skills and abilities.

Convinced yet? Or do you need more information? Either way, the following Web sites will surely give you a clearer picture of why and how to keep an ongoing career portfolio.

CAREER DEVELOPMENT PORTFOLIO
HTTP://WWW.TEMPLE.EDU/CSPD/PUBLIC_HTML/CDPCOVER.HTML

Although designed specifically for students of the School of Business and Management at Temple University (Philadelphia), this site will prove useful to other students wanting to create a career development portfolio for themselves. Such a portfolio is intended to help students understand how their academic experiences and goals as well as social interests relate to their future career path.

For each year (freshman, sophomore, junior, senior), specific guidelines are offered for what would be appropriate to cover in the portfolio. Freshmen, for example, are to describe a possible college major, while juniors are to describe current career goals. Certain categories and skills (career readiness, leadership, campus involvement, intercultural understanding) could also be documented in a career development portfolio.

EMPLOYABILITY SKILLS PORTFOLIOS
HTTP://WWW.MBNET.MB.CA/ STJAMESA/PARENTS/EMPLOYABILITY/

This resource, a project from the Winnipeg Chamber of Commerce, Manitoba Education and Training, and St. James-Assiniboia School Division, offers advice to the user, parent, and employer on how and why to use a skills portfolio. There is a section describing how students at several Canadian schools develop portfolios as part of the ongoing curriculum.

Although some of the material (such as the lesson plans) is geared more toward instructors than students, plenty of good ideas are given on how to organize a portfolio to record your accomplishments and how to use it later in your job search. For instance, the "User's Guide" outlines how to begin a portfolio, what kinds of examples to assemble, how to organize your materials, how to develop "skill statements," how to prepare a resume, and how to test out your finished portfolio on friends and family. Additionally, ideas are given for how you can clearly and creatively document certain skills (academic, personal management, and teamwork).

More great information is provided in the section called "Are You Effectively Using Your Skills Portfolio?" (Click on "Use of Portfolios.") It's important that you prepare prior to the interview and that you highlight a few skills related to the particular job you're interviewing for. And don't forget to bring along your resume, as well as your portfolio.

PORTFOLIO LIBRARY

HTTP://AMBY.COM/KIMELDORF/P_MK-TOC.HTML

Author and teacher Martin Kimeldorf offers much helpful advice to assist you in determining what you could include in a portfolio and how to compile those materials. Step-by-step instructions are given for putting together personal, professional, or high school portfolios. As you will discover, this resource will come in handy no matter what stage you're at in your career search.

There are discussions of reasons for college students to use portfolios and how the author has used portfolios through the years. The article "Using Job Search Portfolios in an Uncertain Labor Market" presents suggestions of various samples you might want to use in your career portfolio. To get a clearer picture of what a portfolio may look like, check out the portfolio samplers for examples of how to creatively document and display testimonials and achievements. References are made to a number of books where you can find additional information.

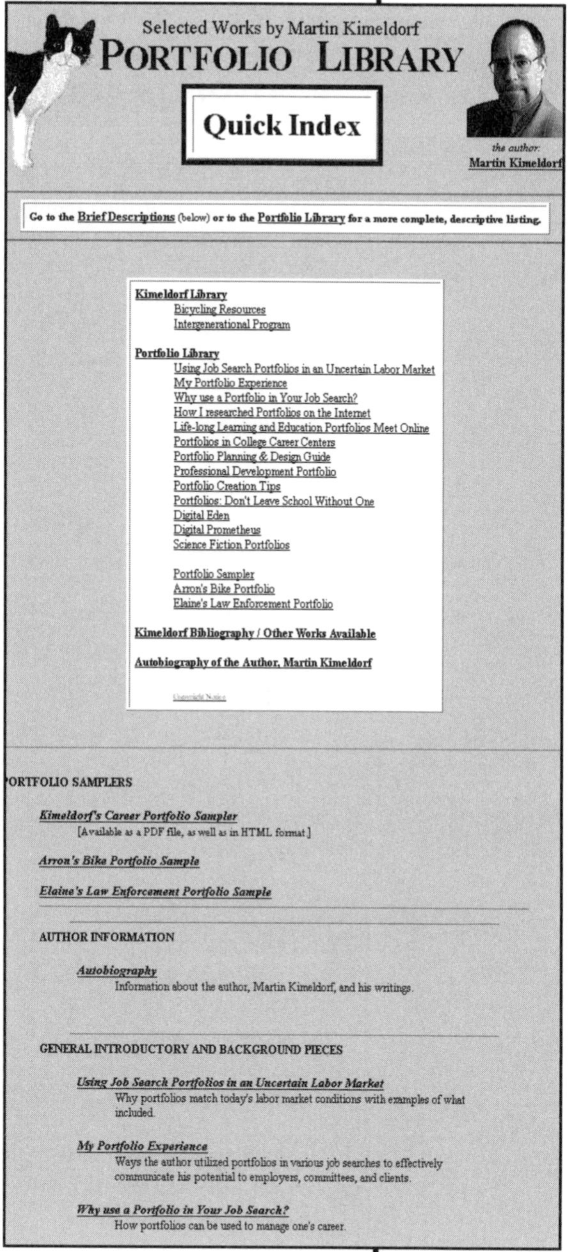

THE VERMONT STUDENT DEVELOPMENT PORTFOLIO

HTTP://WWW.STATE.VT.US/STW/PORTFOLIOMANUAL.HTML

This Vermont School-to-Work tool is appropriate for elementary or middle school through high school. But it has much to offer to anybody looking for a succinct, easy-to-understand description of what a career portfolio is and how to put one together. By keeping an ongoing portfolio, students can discover not only who they are but who they want to become by identifying their interests, skills, and achievements and learning to recognize how certain experiences may relate to particular career options. The site briefly outlines the three parts to this portfolio: "Personal & Career Exploration and Planning," "School and Community-Based Accomplishments," and "Personal Presentation and Synthesis."

CHAPTER 17

INTERVIEWING

Interviewing is when a potential employer meets with you to discuss your job qualifications. In an interview, the people interviewing you will ask questions and, usually, you will have the opportunity to ask them questions. You will be evaluated on your professional appearance and manner, as well as on your responses to questions plus any additional information you volunteer.

Interviewing is an art that must be practiced to further develop skills. Each interview should be viewed as a learning experience, even if it is unlikely you would receive or accept an offer from the employer. Never turn down an opportunity to interview. Always prepare for, and conduct yourself in, each interview as if you really wanted a job offer.

There is great variation in the way interviews are conducted by different employers in different occupational areas. Interviews may be at the employer's place of business or elsewhere, such as on-campus or during professional conventions. There may be only one interview or you may be asked to a second and even a third interview before a hiring decision is made.

Many interviews are one-on-one with an employer (often the person who will be directly supervising the employee) interviewing candidates. Candidates might be interviewed by a group of supervisors and coworkers. Large employers in some occupational fields will interview a candidate over several days.

When an employer calls to ask you to an interview, it is appropriate to ask questions about the interview format. To help you prepare for the interview, you will want to know

- where the interview will be conducted,
- when it will be conducted,
- how long it will take,
- who you will be meeting,
- what activities will be part of the process, and so on.

Other considerations you'll have in preparing for an interview are how to dress (your outfit, shoes, and accessories), what to bring (a briefcase, business cards, a pen and notepad, extra resumes, and your portfolio), and what not to bring (a friend, a pager, chewing gum, or a radio).

How can you prepare so as to present yourself as being unique among applicants for the job? Do your homework. If you haven't already done so, conduct extensive research on the employer. (Refer to Chapter 19 for in-depth coverage of this topic.) And if you already did this as part of your original application process (good for you!), then review your materials (such as the job description and annual reports) and see if you can find any current company news that you might be able to work into the interview.

Also, consider what you can say to show you have the skills and abilities to do the duties on the job description and the typical job duties in the occupation. Practice your responses to commonly asked interview questions such as

- "Tell me about yourself."
- "What are your strengths?"

- "What are your areas of weakness?"

- "What do you want to be doing in five years?"

- "What is one significant contribution you can make on this job?"

Experts suggest that the more you practice interviewing, the better you will be able to present yourself during the interview. Mock interviews with others (friends or family) is a good way to practice, particularly if they can be videotaped, allowing you to critique your own performance. Another way to prepare for interviewing is to practice relaxation techniques to reduce symptoms of anxiety, such as tense muscles, trembling hands, or a high-pitched voice.

How you follow up on an interview is an important step too. Write a thank you note to the interviewer emphasizing your desire to work for the company, incorporating information you learned in the interview to put a marketing slant on your skills and abilities. Mentally review and evaluate your own performance. What questions did you respond to well? Which ones could you have answered better? Should you have done further research? Keep records of who you interviewed with and what position you interviewed for.

However the interview turns out, use what you learn when you prepare for other job interviews in future. Even if you do not get an offer, if you made a good impression on the interviewer, this may be someone you could contact later as part of your networking process. Additional and more specific information on interviewing can be found at the following Web sites.

INTERVIEW NETWORK

HTTP://WWW.PSE-NET.COM/INTERVIEW/INTERVIEW.HTM

Public Service Employees Network's "Interview Success Plan" discusses, among other topics, inappropriate interview questions and interview preparation and behavior. The "Interview Question Bank" presents a wide assortment of sample interview questions covering such topics as leadership, prioritization, problem solving, teamwork, and telephone and pertaining specifically to such areas as accounting, customer service, purchasing, and reengineering. Think you're ready to interview for that dream job? Check out one of the mock interviews to see if you are.

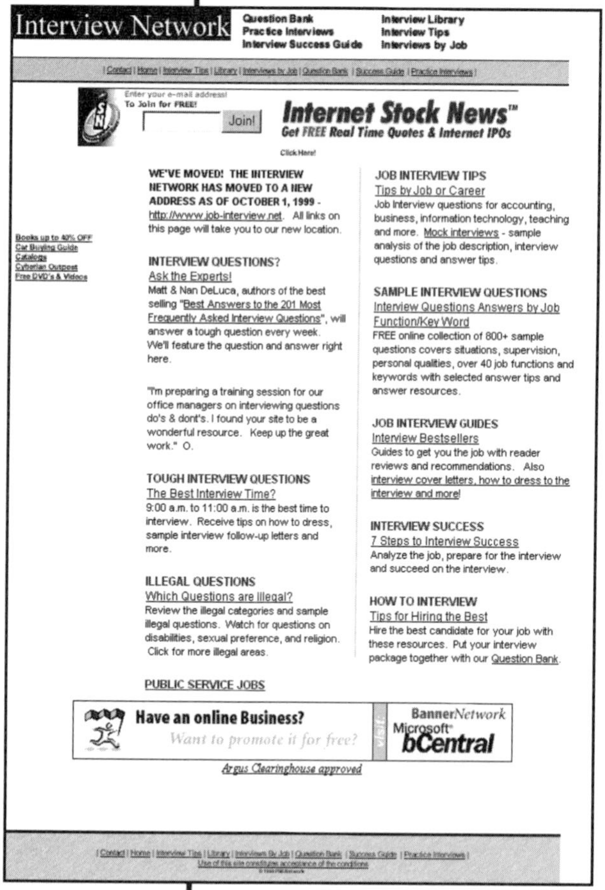

Links to other resources are abundant. You can follow these to find even more sample interview questions, interview advice and strategies, follow-up letter ideas, and information about deciding whether or not to take a job offer. If you want to read more offline, check out some of the recommended books on general career guides, cover letters, resumes, and dressing for an interview.

SUCCESSFUL INTERVIEWING

HTTP://WWW.DAC.NEU.EDU/COOP.CAREERSERVICES/INTERVIEW.HTML

If you're looking for straightforward information about job interviews, take a look at this handout from Northeastern University in Boston. It begins by listing the goals of both the candidate and the interviewer. Next is a description of how you should prepare for the interview, which is followed by an explanation of the four basic stages that make up the interview process. This leads to some notes on the different types of interviews you are apt to encounter; these include screening, one on one, and group, to name a few. Advice is offered on how to answer questions like "What are your strengths and weaknesses?" and "Why do you want to work here?" Finally, a few pointers are given for negotiating salary.

WORKSEARCH: INTERVIEWING

HTTP://MEMBERS.XOOM.COM/GWWORK/INTRES.HTM

This job search resource comes from author Gary Will and includes sample material from his book How to Prepare for an Employment Interview. One featured chapter deals with the importance of asking questions during a job interview. Another explains that when you understand how businesses operate in general, you can then determine what you have to offer the company you're interviewing with. Will also presents an assortment of interview "horror" stories and questions.

The bulk of this resource is a collection of links to other sites that deal with interviewing. As you browse through these articles, you will find extensive information on such topics as getting a job offer, behavioral interviews, how to respond to hypothetical questions, interview preparation, and more.

WORLD'S BIGGEST JOB INTERVIEW QUESTION BANK

HTTP://WWW.DUMMIES.COM/RESOURCES/JOBQUESTIONS/

This is a compilation of job interview questions that came up during research for IDG's book Job Interviews for Dummies. Some 1,000 questions are presented in various categories such as skills ("How do you go about solving a problem?"), education ("Has your education prepared you for this position?"), salary ("Why are you willing to take a cut in pay?"), and inappropriate questions ("Are you married?"). No advice or answers are provided, but this will certainly give you a lot to think about and prepare for in anticipation of your next interview.

CHAPTER 18

ON-CAMPUS SERVICES

A college campus is a good place to find an assortment of career resources. For starters, placement offices offer many different services to help people find jobs. Employers who are hiring notify placement offices of their openings. Placement offices may also help you to assess your skills and abilities and identify jobs for which you qualify. Services may be offered to help build job-seeking skills, such as dealing with job-search paperwork and correspondence, writing a resume, preparing to interview perhaps by conducting mock interviews with you, organizing a job search targeting appropriate employers, and developing personal marketing strategies. Some may even keep your resume and transcripts on file and send them out to employers when you request it. There is a wide variety in the type and quality of services provided by placement offices. Some may offer a full range of career counseling while others may do little more than list job openings.

Most educational institutions that offer training for occupations have placement services. The services offered by the institution's placement office should be a factor when considering enrollment in a training program, whether at a private career school, a community college, or a four-year college or university. An active placement office can be a critical asset in transitioning into an occupation after completing training. To use these placement offices, you must usually be enrolled as a student or be a graduate of the institution. Adults making career transitions sometimes do not realize they can often use placement offices of higher educational institutions from which they have graduated. Sometimes community college placement services are offered liberally to local people or operate in conjunction with government-sponsored programs, so it is a good idea to check them out to learn what's available.

One of the services of college and university placement offices is to arrange for employers to come to campus to recruit new graduates. On-campus recruiting efforts typically include on-campus interviewing and job fairs. Sometimes on-campus recruiting efforts are aimed at specific academic majors or colleges. For example, all recruiters interested in hiring architecture majors may be scheduled in a one- or two-week block. On-campus recruiting is very heavy in the spring, when many students are graduating. But if the labor market is tight and there is a shortage of qualified workers, recruiters will sometimes be on-campus in both fall and spring terms. Usually, only students who are nearing graduation can participate in on-campus interviewing.

On-campus recruiting offers several advantages. Employers are glad to recruit at college campuses because they will find a pool of qualified, competitive applicants. As a student, being interviewed on-campus gives you an implied referral—that is, recruiters who have had positive results hiring employees from an educational institution tend to look favorably at other applicants from that institution. Also, you save time and money by being able to interview for several jobs without having to travel to individual employers' offices.

Before the interview, placement office staff can help you learn about the businesses of employers with whom you will be interviewing. Placement offices will usually have copies of annual reports and promotional literature. Staff members will usually know about the types of job offers that the employer has made to recruits in the past, so you can go into interviews having realistic expectations regarding job titles and salaries.

On-campus recruitment may offer you the opportunity to interview with several potential employers. It is a good strategy to try to schedule interviews so those with employers who really interest you occur after you have had the chance to build interview skills by interviewing with employers of less interest to you. Remember that an on-campus recruiting interview is just like any other interview for a job. It is vital to come to the appointment on time, to be dressed professionally, to bring your resume and portfolio, and so on.

Job fairs, in bringing together a number of employers, are a good way to learn about the jobs available in occupations in various industries. Job fairs give you a chance to market yourself to employer representatives face-to-face. Schools or colleges often sponsor job fairs, as do chambers of commerce and employers themselves. Each employer has a display booth staffed by representatives who talk about job opportunities at their company. People staffing the job fair booths are often responsible for the recruitment of employees.

You should prepare yourself before going to a job fair by pulling together your job search marketing tools of business cards, resumes, and paper and pen. Business cards should indicate, at minimum, your name and contact information, such as street and e-mail addresses as well as phone number. If you have been established in the occupation in which you are seeking work, use the occupational title on the card, and indicate licenses or credentials you have. If you are not experienced, you should prepare cards for the job fair with a handwritten notation indicating the type of job you are looking for.

As a tool of networking, business cards should be handed out liberally. Whether or not their employer offers jobs in your occupational area, you should give your business card to every employer's representative you speak with. It is a good idea to bring copies of your resume to give to employers who have jobs similar to the one you are seeking. A drawback to this is that this resume can only represent your general skills and experiences rather than being tailored to a specific job description. Bring a small notepad and a pen so you can jot down the names and phone numbers of people you might want to contact later.

Marketing yourself at a job fair requires making a good first impression. In many ways, the job fair presents an opportunity that is similar to an interview. To look like someone an employer would want to hire, attend the job fair dressed neatly and professionally. How you meet the people staffing the booth will be a big part of making a good impression. You cannot afford to be shy. Notice the name of the company before you reach the booth. Smile, give an appropriate greeting, and offer to shake hands, while stating your name and saying you are interested in learning more about employment opportunities with the company—making sure to use the company's name. The representative will probably tell you the nature of the business and the occupations in which the company's employees work. If the occupation in which you are looking for work is not mentioned, ask specifically if the company has any need for workers in that field. If not, ask if the representative knows of companies who hire workers in that occupation.

It is important to listen carefully to answers to questions and to show attention. Representatives cannot allow one person to take too much of their time as they need to attend to all the people interested in their company. It is appropriate to return to booths when representatives are less busy. If there is no time for an extended conversation, and you still have questions, ask if the representative can be contacted later. If the answer is yes, get a business card with contact information or make a note of the representative's name and phone number.

Job fairs are good opportunities for making that first contact and for networking. Do not expect that you will be able to sell yourself to employers during the short time you will be able to talk at the job fair. If you leave the job fair with a better knowledge of employers who hire workers in your occupation, you have been successful. If you leave with four or five names of employers' representatives to contact later, you have begun to network and have been very successful.

As you can well imagine, the Web is home to numerous college and university placement offices, career centers, and other on-campus recruiting services. As stated earlier, this should be one of the criteria you take into account when deciding where to continue your educational pursuits. To give you an idea of what you might seek or find from on-campus resources, several offering well-rounded, comprehensive, user-friendly materials are listed here. This is only a very small sampling of what's to be found online, so you'll want to be sure and check materials available from those schools you're considering.

CATAPULT: CAREER OFFICES HOME PAGES

HTTP://WWW.JOBWEB.ORG/CATAPULT/HOMEPAGE.HTM

Part of JobWeb, a huge career resource from the National Association of Colleges and Employers, this site contains a directory of links to the placement offices and career development centers of hundreds of colleges and universities in the United States, as well as a handful in Australia, Canada, and the United Kingdom. Follow a link to discover the kinds of career and job services that are offered to students and alumni of that institution, to see a list of upcoming on-campus career-related events and job fairs, or to learn about the school's on-campus recruiting.

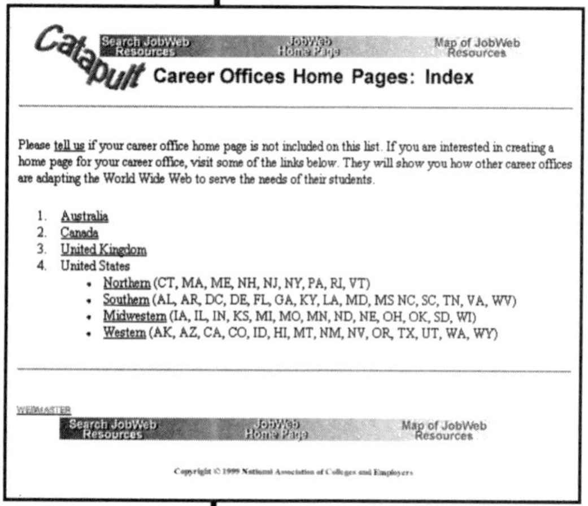

Additionally, some of these sites contain information that can be valuable to you in your job search even if you don't plan to attend the school. You'll find, for example, descriptions of conducting career research, information interviews, resumes, cover letters, and much more.

CLAREMONT COLLEGES ON-CAMPUS RECRUITING PROGRAM

HTTP://WWW.CUC.CLAREMONT.EDU/CAREERSERVICES/RECRUITING.HTML

This Web site covers the on-campus recruiting program for the five Claremont Colleges (Pomona College, Pitzer College, Scripps College, Harvey Mudd College, and Claremont McKenna College), located in Claremont, California. You can find dates and descriptions of past and upcoming career-related events when you look at the sections titled "Info Sessions & Workshops," "Open Interviews," and "Pre-Screened Interviews." Links to company Web sites are offered, as is an index of employers scheduled to visit the Claremont campuses.

You can also access resources specifically relating to each individual campus. Some of the things you might want to check out are the separate recruiting schedules and campus career centers, where you can browse through a lot more career-planning materials and read about services offered. Even though the bulk of what you'll discover in these pages is geared toward Claremont graduates, students, or prospects, you'll get a good idea of recruiting opportunities that are available at many campuses—and the kind of information you can find through a college or university placement, career, or recruiting office Web site.

INDIANA UNIVERSITY'S ASPO ON-CAMPUS RECRUITING SCHEDULE

HTTP://WWW.INDIANA.EDU/ CAREER/ASPO/ RECRUITING.HTML

The Arts & Sciences Placement Office of Indiana University in Bloomington (IUB) offers here an extensive schedule of on-campus recruiting events (past and upcoming). While this resource will be most useful to IUB students, particularly College of Arts & Sciences majors, you can learn a lot about the kinds of on-campus recruiting opportunities that are available by browsing through the site.

The schedule features the employer's name, the interview date, the position title, and required qualifications for the job. Additionally, links are provided to the employer's Web site, where you can conduct your own research about the company to learn more about its business, where it's located, and more. And while you're at the IUB site, you can check out the university's other career-planning resources.

JOB FAIR SUCCESS

HTTP://WWW.COLLEGEGRAD.COM/BOOK/ 11-0.SHTML

Before you go to your next job fair, take a look at this chapter from Brian Krueger's book College Grad Job Hunter—you'll find job fair strategies and tips to help you stand out from the crowd and make a lasting impression. What is the one mistake that most job fair attendees make? They stand in line. If you're wondering what to do instead, you'll have to go to the site to find out. Information is also offered on the various types of job fairs you might attend and what you should bring along. Have you ever considered going to another college's job fair? Consider the possibility!

JOBWEB CAREER FAIRS
HTTP://WWW.JOBWEB.ORG/SEARCH/CFAIRS/

Here is a searchable career fair database from the National Association of Colleges and Employers (NACE). You can search the database for career fairs scheduled to be held at various U.S. colleges and universities. After you select a state and a month—and perhaps even type in a keyword (e.g., business, journalism, technology)—you'll be taken to a list of career fairs. Choose one that looks interesting. Then you'll be given all the necessary details, including a brief description, dates, street and e-mail addresses, and phone number. Information (where available) is also provided for the host institutions.

MIT SLOAN CAREER CENTER
HTTP://MITSLOAN.MIT.EDU/CDO/MAIN.HTML

MIT's Sloan School of Management offers an insightful home page designed to help the MBA student with career planning. Even if you are not an MBA student—or, for that matter, an MIT Sloan student—you'll find quite a lot of universal and applicable advice. MIT really leaves no rock unturned here when it comes to career exploration.

Limited-access sections are rare. Job postings are accessible only to Sloan students with a proper password. Plus there's information on resources available at the school's Career Resource Center, which you shouldn't dismiss entirely because it may give you an idea of the types of materials you should seek out in a library or your school's placement office, such as salary information, company files, book titles, and industry files. Aside from that, most of the rest of the site will be of interest to anyone looking for career information.

"Planning and Managing Your Career" goes over the career-planning process in detail. One handy tool is the Career Management Calendar, which outlines the tasks you should undertake each month of the school year. It also breaks it down between all students, second-year students, and first-year students.

In sections devoted to networking, resumes, cover letters, interviewing, and evaluating a job offer, you'll find a lot of useful information presented in a direct and clear fashion. Different possible scenarios are depicted and various options are suggested. To provide further assistance in your career planning and job search, MIT Sloan has also included links to a manageable number of relevant Web sites, which are briefly described.

PLACEMENT AND CAREER SERVICES AT THE UNIVERSITY OF PITTSBURGH

HTTP://WWW.PLACEMENT.PITT.EDU/

This is just one of a vast number of college and university job placement or career development sites on the Web. Most of what you'll find here is targeted specifically to Pitt students or alumni; for example, the customizable searches for internships and for part-time or full-time jobs, an on-campus recruiting schedule, listings of career-related workshops, and background material on Pitt's career advisors. But as you browse through the site, you'll get a pretty good idea of the kinds of career-related resources that are being offered on the Web by educational institutions.

One section lists various college majors and for these fields describes a few relevant career opportunities, gives names of top employers for Pitt graduates, and presents data on placement rates and average starting salaries. Other site features include information on resumes, cover letters, and interviewing.

RENSSELAER POLYTECHNIC INSTITUTE CAREER DEVELOPMENT CENTER

HTTP://WWW.RPI.EDU/DEPT/CDC/

This career counseling site is dedicated to helping college students and recent graduates get a good start on their careers. While you don't have to be a student or alumnus of Rensselaer to access the data, some of the sections are only appropriate for Rensselaer students. Through the Focus Program, the Rensselaer student, after being matched with an alumnus who acts as mentor, accompanies the mentor to work. The Cooperative Education Program allows the student to get on-the-job work experience while working toward a degree. Might your college career center offer comparable programs? Something to think about.

What everyone will find useful are the sections featuring career advice ("Handouts"), salary data, and links to various job sites. The assorted handouts outline some steps to take in conducting your job search, including self-assessment, informational or on-site interviewing, resume and cover letter composition, dressing for an interview, attending a career fair, and employer research. The links offered are to a variety of career exploration sites.

THE TEN KEYS TO SUCCESS AT JOB AND CAREER FAIRS

HTTP://WWW.QUINTCAREERS.COM/JOB_CAREER_FAIRS.HTML

How should you prepare for that upcoming job or career fair you're planning to attend? This Quintessential Careers site explains what you need to know in order to make the most of your job or career fair experience. Be sure to register ahead of time, do your research, bring along plenty of resumes—well, you get the picture. Check out this site for the complete details as well as for links to other useful resources, including job fair techniques and organizations that host job and career fairs.

UC DAVIS INTERNSHIP & CAREER CENTER

HTTP://ICC.UCDAVIS.EDU/

The University of California at Davis provides its students with quite a hefty resource pertaining to career planning and placement. Among the site features available to the general public are a schedule of career-related events and workshops; a list of companies for which UCD has information files available for perusal on-campus; details about UCD job fairs, along with links to company Web sites; and notes about UCD teaching and reader assistantship openings as well as on-campus employment opportunities. Materials are offered specifically relating to internships or careers in agriculture and environmental sciences, engineering and physical sciences, health and biological sciences, or liberal arts and business. UCD Education and Graduate Placement is also linked from this site.

Certain sections require you to have a password in order to gain access. This means that you have to be a UCD student, graduate, or faculty or staff member. With the proper password you can check out such resources as a career and internship database, academic and teaching vacancy listings, and student jobs open at UCD as well as other UC campuses.

UNIVERSITY OF NEBRASKA-LINCOLN CAREER SERVICES
HTTP://WWW.UNL.EDU/CAREERS/

This career search site is by the University of Nebraska at Lincoln. Some of the information applies only to students at the university, but there's plenty to go around. Start with "Career Exploration," which provides links to Web sites that will help you assess your interests and give you some direction in figuring out what career path might be appropriate for you. If you're wondering what you might do with a degree once you get it, take a look at the pages listing what UNL graduates have done with their degrees.

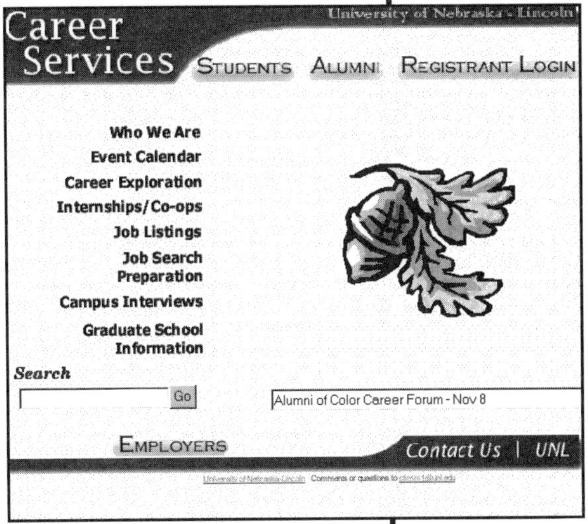

"Job Search Preparation" helps with interviews, resumes, portfolios, searching for jobs on the Internet, and researching companies. "Job Listings" has links to actual job posting sites (newspaper ads, government jobs, composite lists) and corporate sites.

Some of the UNL-specific services to be found here include events listings, details on internships and part-time or seasonal job opportunities, and notes about on-campus interviews.

YOUR CAREER PLACEMENT OFFICE
HTTP://WWW.COLLEGEGRAD.COM/BOOK/7-0.SHTML

Brian Krueger's book College Grad Job Hunter provides abundant information to help you in your job search. This particular chapter is intended to help you better utilize your college career placement office. Its main functions (career planning and career placement) are described. What job search-related materials might you find in your career placement office? There's a list of services typically offered. You're advised to develop an ongoing relationship with a placement counselor at your school. Then not only will you reap the benefits of the resources at hand, but you'll have access as well to the counselor's professional expertise and knowledge.

COMPANIES

CHAPTER 19

It has already been mentioned that you should conduct research on a company before going on an interview. And if you know something about a company when you send in your resume, you can incorporate that information into your cover letter, making its content more targeted and unique. This serves to set your cover letter apart from the more generic "one size fits all" type—and in so doing makes it more likely that an employer will take notice and be apt to contact you for an interview. But where do you go to find this background material? The Internet happens to be a good place to start.

The Internet has fast evolved into an excellent resource for information about specific companies. This is becoming more true all the time, as more and more companies go online with their home pages. Not all Web sites were created equal, of course, so you'll find that there's great variance in the amount and depth of information to be unearthed at these company home pages. But some of the things you can usually expect to discover include

- descriptions of the company's history and goals,
- an overview of the business conducted,
- specific details on products sold or services offered,
- company news and press releases, and
- employment opportunity listings.

Not only will you be able to find out what companies have to say about themselves, but you will uncover what others are reporting on certain companies. There are sites featuring commentary from actual employees as well as outside speculation and analysis. Before accepting anything as fact, however, be sure to thoroughly check your sources first, as always. Remember that anybody can put anything on the Internet, so you can't believe everything you read there.

Be creative in your research. If you don't have a specific employer in mind, or if you want to dig up data on an employer's business competitors, there are sites that present company information categorized by specific industries. These directory services enable you to find, at a single site, all sorts of information on numerous companies. This could lead you to sites of potential employers you never realized existed!

HOOVER'S ONLINE
HTTP://WWW.HOOVERS.COM/

You've probably seen Hoover's referred to pretty frequently if you've been doing much career exploration. Hoover's publishes business reference books and profiles thousands of companies, both public and private. This site, subtitled "The Business Network," is a great resource for researching companies.

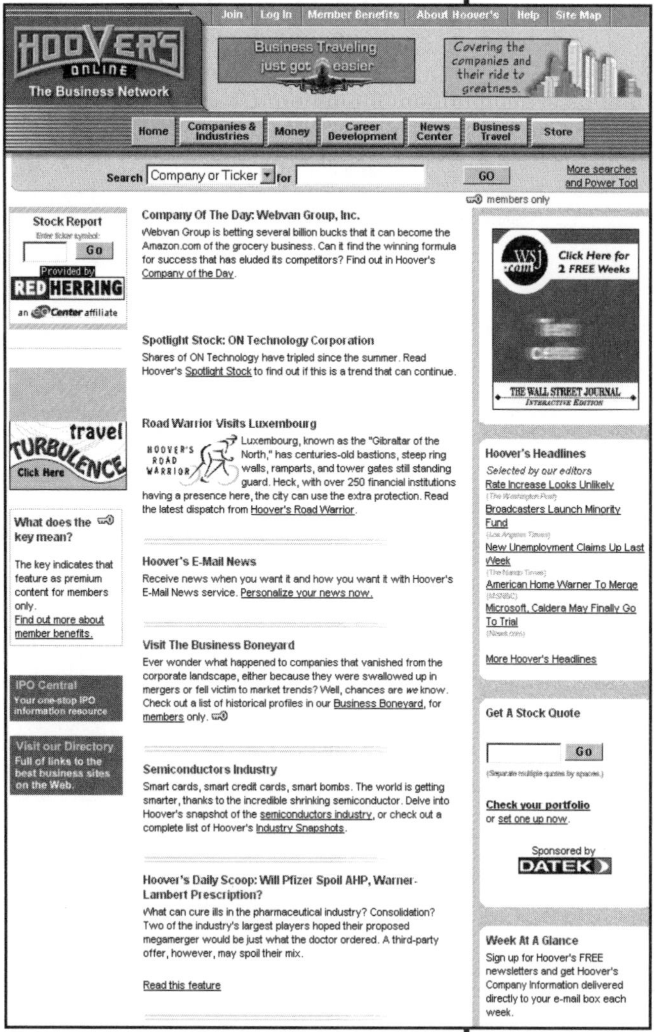

Hoover's has compiled business information on more than 50,000 companies. Thousands of these are briefly described in Company Capsules. Browse companies A to Z or search by company name, ticker symbol, keyword, or person's last name. Along with the company overview, you might also get financial data, a list of key personnel, and links to press releases, current and archived news stories, corporate history, annual reports, and employment information, as well as access to similar treatments for some of the company's competitors plus Hoover's Industry Snapshots. "Career Development" provides easy access to Company Capsules, off-site employer reports, and the company's job pages.

If you have an interest in IPOs (initial public offerings), then you'll want to drop by "IPO Central." Here you'll get some good introductory information plus news and analysis, the latest pricings, and an IPO "scorecard" presenting statistics and other data (for example, the best and worst IPO returns and the biggest first days for IPOs).

Subscribers will be able to tap into even more Hoover's features, including Company Profiles, the more in-depth reports on companies. To whet your appetite, Hoover's allows nonsubscribers to view a handful of the approximately 8,000 companies profiled.

THE INC. 500
HTTP://WWW.INC.COM/500/

Featuring Inc. magazine's annual list of America's 500 fastest-growing private companies, this site is a great tool for conducting some company and industry research. Pages for each of the top 500 include a brief company description, employee and revenue data, and, where available, access to relevant archived Inc. articles plus a link to the company home page. Lists from earlier years are also available for your perusal. If you want to learn about up-and-coming businesses, this might be the ticket.

INDUSTRYWATCH
HTTP://WWW.NEWS-REAL.COM/

Directed at business users, this tool will prove indispensable to you in your company research. Just go to the "Companies" section. Here you will type in the company's name or ticker symbol. If you get more than one result, click on the one you want. This will bring up a summary of company news.

If you want to dig deeper, take a look at the company overview. This provides basic background information, including (where available) street and Web addresses, phone number, ticker symbol, financial data, and the number of employees. Further financial details (quarterly and annual, stock quotes, and price history) might be provided as well. Also featured are lists of top executives and main competitors. Keep in mind that different companies will generate more or less information than others, but this is the gist of what you might have access to.

Industry headline news is offered in the areas of aerospace, aviation, biotechnology, computers, entertainment, insurance, pharmaceuticals, real estate, and utilities, among others. Just click on "Industries," select the industry that interests you, and read on.

JOB SAFARI
HTTP://WWW.JOBSAFARI.COM/

If you want to head straight for the company's own online information, here is a source containing links to company Web sites that include job listings. You can browse company names alphabetically or browse by location. This is a gigantic list, so it might be easier to look through the entries by location. Just go ahead and pick a state and you'll find the companies arranged by city. Links are provided for the job listings page as well as the home page for each company.

RESEARCHING COMPANIES ONLINE
HTTP://HOME.SPRINTMAIL.COM/ DEBFLANAGAN/INDEX.HTML

Part of a larger guide to conducting online research, this tutorial will provide you with the know-how to perform online company research. This guide contains basic discussion of the steps to take, supplemented by links to Web sites where you can actually conduct your research. Some of the things you'll learn how to find are company telephone numbers and addresses; a company's ticker symbol, which you will need to use at certain sites to get company profiles or, of course, financial data; company home pages; newspaper and magazine articles as well as press releases, which will enable you to stay current with the company's newsworthy activities; professional associations; and industry information.

You have the choice of following the links directly to the relevant Web sites or viewing them within frames. If you choose to view sites in frames, the left frame presents detailed instructions on finding pertinent information at the site, which then displays in the right frame.

If you require instruction on general Internet searching—for example, using search engines and subject directories—look back at the main "Web Search Strategies" tutorial. This should get you up to speed in no time.

TELL ME ABOUT THIS EMPLOYER

HTTP://WWW.DBM.COM/JOBGUIDE/EMPLOYER.HTML

The Riley Guide takes credit for this handy collection of annotated links, which will surely get you off on the right foot if you're looking for help with researching a perspective employer. The links are organized according to topic, including research guides, international business information, business rankings, financial reports, and business, nonprofit, and phone directories. These linked sites will offer you access to company home pages, stock market data, addresses and phone numbers, business news, press releases, and more.

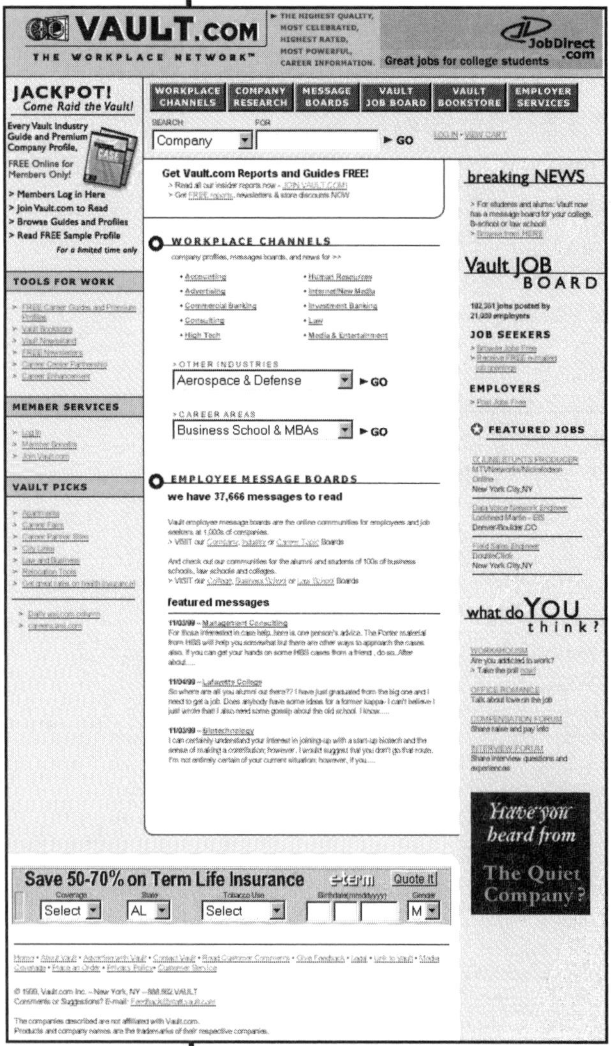

VAULTREPORTS.COM

HTTP://WWW.VAULTREPORTS.COM/

Known for its Insider Guides on companies and industries, VaultReports.com is an important resource when it comes to doing company research. Or just about any kind of career research, for that matter. Company and industry reports offer not only the facts but opinions, analysis, and speculation. A lot of the information is derived from surveys of professionals at the specific companies or working in particular industries. This should give you a different perspective from what you'll find by going directly to a company's home page.

The company database (of more than 1,000 employers) is searchable by name, keyword, or ticker symbol. If you want to just browse around, you can do that too. Company reports cover issues such as company background, the work environment, diversity, salary, dress code, benefits, and getting a job there. Industry reports feature brief industry overviews, career and personnel profiles, current job openings in the field, and links to reports on companies in the industry.

If you're ready to hit the virtual pavement, don't miss the jobs database. It consists of thousands of job openings. Specify your search criteria: location, category, experience level, job type, keyword, and date posted. There are great articles to read too. Some of the topics discussed include diversity, entrepreneurship, internships, resumes and cover letters (with lots of samples), and schmoozing. To hear what others have to say on these topics and more, head over to the message boards. You'll have a few dozen message boards to choose from, on the topics just mentioned as well as on specific companies and various industries (for example, investment banking, the Internet and new media, law, advertising, fashion, and health care). Are you in the mood to get away from your computer screen and read something in print instead? Then toss a few Vault Report Career Guides into your shopping basket.

WETFEET.COM

HTTP://WWW.WETFEET.COM/

The folks behind this site developed it with the intent to arm job seekers with pertinent company information to better prepare them for their job search. Seeing that much of the material was compiled from employee interviews, you'll get to read about companies from an insider's point of view. Search for a specific company or track one down through the alphabetical or industry listing. For most companies there will be a CompanyQuick, which is a basic overview of the company's products and services, personnel makeup, and employment opportunities. Q&As about benefits, opportunities for advancement, the workplace environment, and other topics are presented for certain companies. If you're looking for more in-depth information, check to see if there's a Company Insider available for purchase. Other site features include business news, career advice articles, and a select handful of career-related links.

CHAPTER 20

JOB LISTINGS, RESUME DATABASES, AND RECRUITING SERVICES

If you're still in the exploratory stages of your career management, you might wonder what you can do with a chapter on job listings, resume databases, and recruiting services. Well, it's never too early to begin keeping an eye on what's available in the job market, become aware of your online resume posting options, and scope out services that can help you in your job search.

The Internet is home to countless job listing sources and resume databases. Some are general, covering all industries, while others target a specific industry, region, or audience. The sites that follow fall into the "general" category. (It is important to note, however, that currently the preponderance of jobs posted online are more or less technical in nature. Given the medium [the Internet] and the audience [tech-savvy users, by and large], this shouldn't be surprising.) If instead of general resources you're looking for job listing sources or resume databases having a more specific focus, you might want to take a look at Chapters 8 ("Getting Experience"), 12 ("Resources to Meet Specific Needs"), or 13 ("Resources for Specific Industries").

As you've probably noticed already while browsing the sites discussed in this book, more and more Web sites are requiring that you register (sometimes free, other times for a fee) before you can view certain site content. As the Internet evolves, this practice is likely to continue. Therefore, registration requirements described in this chapter may have changed by the time you visit a particular site. So you'll want to carefully check the site's instructions to find out if you must register to access information. (This will be particularly common for sites containing job listings and resume databases.) Then be sure you understand the security precautions in place at the site and exercise good judgment when deciding whether or not to submit personal data online, including credit card number if you have to pay for service. Should you have concerns about your online privacy, refer back to the sites discussed in Chapter 10 for some guidance.

Recruiting is another expanding online career resource for job seekers. More often than not you'll find jobs listed at recruiter sites plus you'll also be able to post your resume. Sometimes employers pay for-profit placement services to find workers to fill specific job openings. Recruiters at these for-profit placement services are often called headhunters. They seek out highly experienced workers and woo them for hiring employers. Workers who have little experience, or who do not have advanced training, are not likely to be placed by this sort of for-profit placement service.

Many online recruiting sites charge employers to use their services. But frequently recruiters' profits are obtained from job seekers. There are several ways this can work. The for-profit placement service acts as a temporary employment agency that charges the temporarily placed workers. The fees may be a percentage of hourly earnings for as long as the worker is on the job. This can be a good way for newly trained workers to get work experience as they try to establish themselves in an occupation.

Another way that for-profit placement services make money is by contracting for a percentage of the first year's earnings of any employee who is placed. It's important to be cautious when entering into contractual agreements with for-profit placement agencies since job seekers are obliged to pay this percentage whether or not they remain with the employer for a year.

And in case this point wasn't clear enough before, always be sure to check a site carefully—read any disclaimers, privacy statements, and agreements—before submitting any personal data or signing up for anything.

ADGUIDE'S COLLEGE RECRUITER EMPLOYMENT SITE

HTTP://WWW.ADGUIDE.COM/COLLEGE/

The name says it all—this site is for college students and recent graduates looking for employment. You can search for jobs by occupation and location. There are some interesting categories listed: clergy, collections, event planning, interpreters and translators, preservation and restoration, quality control, and transcription, to name a few. Select a category and a location (or leave it blank to broaden your search). Your results page will present a listing of company names with vacancies in your chosen category. Click on the link to go to that company's Web site and check out current job openings. There are a lot of companies and jobs listed, so chances are you'll find a few things to your liking.

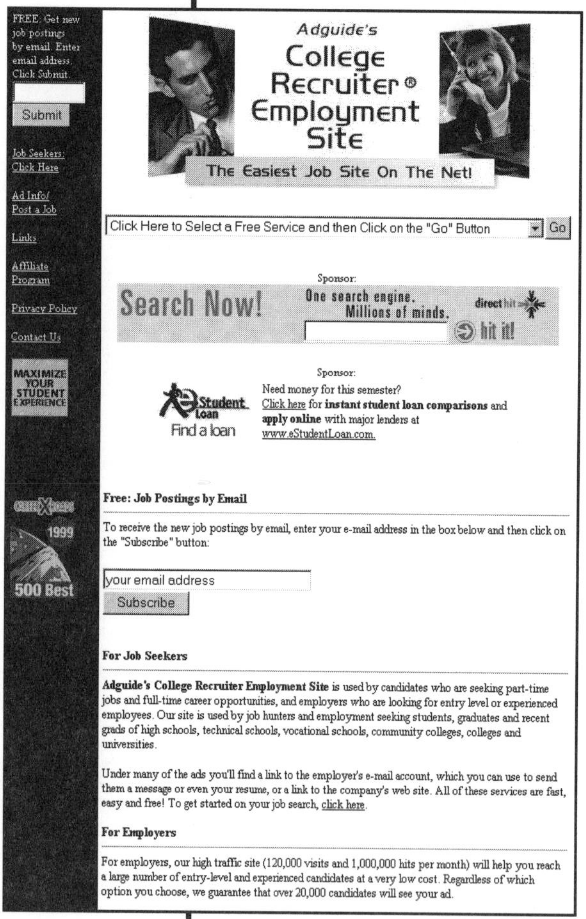

To top it off, the site offers a newsletter and links to related resources, as well as numerous career-related articles. Some of the article titles are "How to Uncover Job Leads," "The Anatomy of a Job Search," "Temping Your Way to a Career," "Evaluating a Job Offer," and "Create Your Own Resume Website?"

AMERICA'S JOB BANK

HTTP://WWW.AJB.ORG/

This extensive job search site is from the U.S. Department of Labor and the public Employment Service, a state-operated program that helps employers and job seekers. There is no fee for the employer or the job seeker. Services are funded through employer-paid unemployment insurance taxes.

In the section for job seekers you can search the job bank for a job using a menu of occupations (choices like administrative support, construction and extractive, food and lodging, protective services, and sports and recreation), each of which opens up into more specific categories. Take protective services, for example—this category breaks down into such jobs as bailiff, crossing guard, firefighter, police officer, and private detective. After you get the listings you can sort them for easier viewing. Choices include state, city, title, and salary. You can also perform your search by typing in keywords or military codes.

You can also link to affiliated sites featuring information on employers as well as on trends in wages and occupational employment (including the Occupational Outlook Handbook) in the U.S. job market. Research the fastest growing occupations, which occupations are expected to have the most openings, and more.

BEST JOBS U.S.A.
HTTP://WWW.BESTJOBSUSA.COM/

From Recourse Communications, publisher of the magazine Employment Review, this massive site is home to a huge jobs database and so much more. Browse through issues of Employment Review or look for your dream job. You can search by state, category, and/or keyword or conduct an advanced search using more specific parameters. Among the wide variety of jobs you might unearth here are tooling engineer, insurance claims analyst, Web site designer, and telecommunications construction engineer.

You'll also be able to post your resume to a resume database, read select corporate profiles (which include links to home pages for further reference), and look through listings of career fairs. Then there's a large listing of newsgroups, organized by industry or location. Click on "Career Guide" for some career resources. Here you can access "City Outlines," which gives you details on unemployment rates, employers, cost of living, and population for major cities in the United States. This site is definitely worth a visit, whether you're looking for a job or exploring your career options.

CAREER.COM
HTTP://WWW.CAREER.COM/

Sponsored by HEART (Human resources Electronic Advertising and Recruiting Tool) Advertising Network, this is a straightforward site for job seekers and employers. You can search for jobs by company, location, or discipline (category) or by selecting other unique options, such as "Hot Jobs" or entry-level positions for new graduates. The discipline option brings up many choices, including business planning, food industry, system administration, marketing, security, public relations, and technical writing. Links to international jobs databases are also offered. The resume database allows you to build a resume by filling out a questionnaire. Resumes are deleted after six months of inactivity, so keep an eye on yours.

CAREER EXPOSURE
HTTP://WWW.CAREEREXPOSURE.COM/

This site links you to thousands of corporate job postings by industry, such as financial services, high tech, manufacturing, energy, transportation, retailing, and international. Select an industry, say "transportation," and you'll find another list of categories that might include airlines, marine services, railroads, and trucking. Pick a category and you'll get a list of employers in that field. A brief description of select companies plus a direct link to the employment pages of all companies are supplied. As you can imagine, this is a great resource for checking out job opportunities with potential employers. Not only can you go straight for company job postings, but you can conduct a job search of Career Exposure's jobs database.

If you want to know the latest career news, need some job search guidance, or want to read some interviews with industry experts, you'll find it in the "Biz Center." Links to news and business resources are provided in the "Newsstand."

CAREERPATH
HTTP://WWW.CAREERPATH.COM/

Are you getting tired of looking through newspaper after newspaper to find classified ad listings that suit you? Then this might be just the solution you are looking for. CareerPath features the classified ad sections from major newspapers, including the Boston Globe, Chicago Tribune, Los Angeles

Times, New York Times, Denver Rocky Mountain News, San Jose Mercury News, and Washington Post. Newspapers from smaller markets are also available here: the Santa Rosa Press Democrat, Allentown Morning Call, Green Bay Press-Gazette, and Lexington Herald-Leader are just a few. Ads come from about ninety U.S. newspapers in all. Detailed information about each newspaper and the area it services is listed, along with direct links to home pages.

CareerPath is updated daily and offers a free, optional membership. You can search listings by newspaper, job category, keyword, and date. In addition to searching the newspaper classifieds, you can search a jobs database representing select employers. These listings are updated a couple times a week. Or check out the employer profiles to get some background information. There's a section designed to help you manage your career too. Here you'll find advice on interviewing and cover letters, as well as resume guidelines, which you can put to good use in CareerPath's resume database. You can also sign up to be notified by e-mail when the site is changed or updated.

CAREERSITE

HTTP://WWW.CAREERSITE.COM/

CareerSite is a job search site that lists a lot of vacancies. The job search is kind of tricky because you have to type in all the search parameters—your desired occupation, location, and skills—plus you can specify whether or not you wish to travel for your job. Under "Quick Job Search" you'll get the handy drop-down list boxes for occupations and locations, which should make the search process a bit easier.

Employer profiles are available for a large assortment of companies. When you select a company, you are not linked to the home page but to some background information about the company along with access to details about current job listings.

You don't have to register to use the job search tool or view the employer profiles. But if you do register (at no charge), you will be able to apply for jobs posted at the site. Additionally, you will have access to a variety of career resources. Links are offered to sites covering career exploration, resumes, interviewing, salaries, relocation, and more. Plus you can post your resume and be notified via e-mail about matching job openings.

CAREERWEB
HTTP://WWW.CWEB.COM/

Thousands of positions with more than 300 companies in any number of disciplines are waiting to be found at CareerWeb. Be sure to study the employer profiles for companies you like. There are links to home pages for some. You can go through the job listings by U.S. area, category (a drop-down list is supplied), or keyword. CareerWeb also offers a resume database and a matching service (Jobmatch).

This is more than just a jobs database. Stop by the bookstore to order books to help you with your job search. Other career resources include a career questionnaire intended to help you determine your "employment search readiness." And if your job search is ailing, you can pay a visit to the "Career Doctor." Read articles about employment and career topics such as the job interview, motivation, computer literacy, and working mothers. The doctor may provide you with just the medicine you need to get back on track!

CONTRACT EMPLOYMENT CONNECTION
HTTP://WWW.NTES.COM/

Considering work as an independent contractor? This site, hosted by National Technical Employment Services (NTES), lists contract positions and offers a resume database. Search for jobs by keywords or download all current listings. There is also a "New Jobs" section that lists only openings from the past week. You'll run across openings for systems integration engineers, technical writers, Web site developers, architectural drafters, programmers, data product managers, audio/video technicians, technical consultants, piping designers, and much more.

The list of links to the home pages of recruiters is extensive, but if you want to do some research before you contact a recruiter, don't miss the "Services Connection" section. You can subscribe to HOTFLASH, NTES's weekly jobs magazine, or order the U.S. Register of Technical Service Firms. There are links to financial services sites, training organizations, and NTES's "Contract Employment FAQ," which you can read to determine whether contract employment is for you.

CONTRACT EMPLOYMENT WEEKLY

HTTP://WWW.CEWEEKLY.COM/

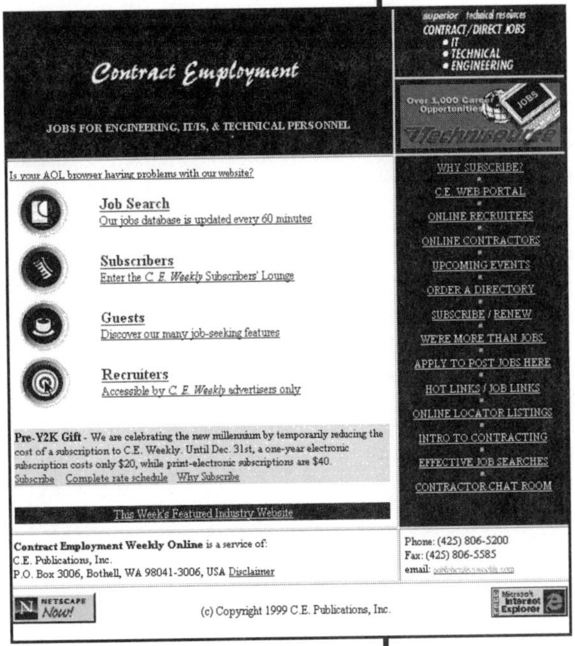

This Web site is an online version of Contract Employment Weekly, a magazine published by C.E. Publications. The magazine focuses on available temporary technical positions. While this site is a subscriber service selling print versions of or electronic supplements to the magazine, you do not have to be a subscriber to take advantage of numerous site features.

Before getting into the site too deeply, you might want to read "An Introduction to the World of Contracting" to learn about contract employment and what it entails. This should help you determine whether or not you want to pursue work of this type. If you're ready to give it a go, you'll have to get your resume in shape. Guess what? The site offers guidance on resume writing aimed specifically at contract employees!

Now it's time to head on over to the job listings, which are purportedly updated every hour. Part of the jobs database is off-limits to nonsubscribers. You can, however, run a "guest" search, which covers a healthy percentage of the jobs in the database. (Results will include data on the number of matches for guests versus subscribers, so you'll get an idea of what you're missing out on if you don't subscribe.) Your search can be quite specific—search by location, keywords, or the date the job was entered into the database.

Check out "Online Recruiters" for access to home pages of firms currently advertising jobs in Contract Employment Weekly. Plus there are annotated links to various sites dealing with relocation and housing, training and education, financial issues, and support organizations and related associations.

4WORK
HTTP://WWW.4WORK.COM/

You know you've hit upon something different when you read 4Work's motto: "Web Globally . . . Work Locally." Unlike many other sites, here you don't have to dig around for the job listings because they appear at the beginning of the main page. The job search allows you to specify whether you are looking for a job, an internship, or volunteer opportunities. You can even specify part-time or full-time, keyword, or the state in which you'd like to work. Subscribe to the free matching service Job Alert! to be notified of job matches via e-mail.

The "Human Resources Directory" includes links to sites in such categories as associations, colleges and universities, and relocation. You can read articles about different careers. If you're looking for exposure you might get it here, since 4Work features select registered job seekers on the front page and links visitors to their resumes.

HEADHUNTER.NET
HTTP://WWW.HEADHUNTER.NET/

More than 150,000 job listings and 230,000 resumes add up to one huge resource! That's what you'll get here. And everything is current. Jobs older than thirty days are purged from the system, and the resumes are no older than ninety days. The site assures you that your information is protected and registration is free. Companies wishing to have their jobs posted near the top of the list pay a premium for that service.

The job listings section allows you to conduct as specific and narrow a search as you choose. You can enter keywords, job categories, employment type (that is, employee, contract, or intern), your education, and job posting "freshness." You can also specify location and compensation. What are some of the jobs you might run across here? Electrical designer, Web developer, data entry specialist, and truck broker are but a few.

If you want to look for openings available with or through specific companies, click on "Companies." This brings up a briefly annotated list of companies (including recruiting, personnel, and temp agencies) that have used or posted on Headhunter.net. A company profile is available with access to Headhunter.net job listings, as well as a link to the company's home page.

Click on "Get Help" to receive answers to common questions, such as "I just posted my resume . . . why can't I find it?" and "I did a search, and I can't find a job." Do you want to know what other people think about this site? Then read testimonials from users—job seekers, employers, and recruiters alike—in the "Raves" section.

HOTJOBS
HTTP://WWW.HOTJOBS.COM/

HotJobs, an online recruiting company, gives users the option to either search or browse its jobs database. You can browse by state, company name, or job category. Some of the browsable categories are advertising and public relations, clerical and administrative, government and public service, hospitality and food services, new media and Internet, sales, and transportation and logistics. As you can see, quite a wide range of career fields are represented here. If you decide to browse by category, pick one and then you can see a list of job openings listed alphabetically or by industry. Or you can view them by state. If you'd rather search the database, then you'll need to enter keywords and specify job type as well as city/state. It's up to you how the results will display—sorted by date or relevance. When you find a job description that sounds right up your alley, you can apply online. You can post your resume in a separate database or copy and paste it into a form.

Are you curious to know what companies you might encounter here? Then take a look at the "Member Companies" section. There are more than 1,000 HotJobs member companies. If you click on the company name, it will bring up all the current job vacancies for that company, along with a brief company profile.

JOBBANK USA
HTTP://WWW.JOBBANKUSA.COM/

This easy-to-use site features tons of job listings plus a resume database. You can search for jobs by keyword, position, and location. Other search options include industry, newspaper, regional, or international listings. The client list is extensive and packed with well-known companies in the fields of health and medicine, computer technology, law, and more. Job descriptions are quite detailed, often indicating high and low salary as well as company Web site address.

For further and more specific information, check out the lengthy list of job-related newsgroups or the smaller list of resume newsgroups. If you're still in the early stages of career exploration, you'll probably benefit by looking at the assessment tool sites. And if you're considering an opportunity in another state, don't miss the relocation tool sites. In "This, That, & the Other," you'll find links to job sites by company, field, or location, along with links to additional career-related resources.

JOBDIRECT
HTTP://WWW.JOBDIRECT.COM/

JobDirect is a free resume database service geared toward college students and recent graduates. You must first register (free) in order to add a resume to the database. Once you've registered, you just fill in the questionnaire, which asks for your school, job experience and preferences, skills, and so on. You can also paste in a copy of your resume. After you've completed the process, your resume is made available to potential employers, who then might contact you about job opportunities. Not only does the site feature entry-level positions, but it also has listings of summer jobs and internships. And there's a searchable jobs database as well.

THE JOB RESOURCE
HTTP://WWW.THEJOBRESOURCE.COM/

Developed by students for students and continuing to feature student involvement, this resource offers job listings, a resume database, and a bit of career advice. About 700 companies recruit at this site. Search for jobs using keywords and by designating job, company type, location, and type of work (drop-down list boxes supplied). Some of the company types represented here include those in the areas of advertising, consulting, entertainment, financial, government, insurance, manufacturing, nonprofit, retail, software, and telecommunications. To find out just which companies list job openings here, check out the "Recruiter List" and select a state of your choice. You will then get a list of employers in that state. Click on a company name for a list of job openings. There's also a "Career Advice" section, which provides career-related articles for you to study.

JOBTRAK
HTTP://WWW.JOBTRAK.COM/

College students or alumni from one of more than 900 participating colleges can upload a resume to Jobtrak's database or peruse the job listings. There is no fee for the colleges or the job seekers, who in order to use these services must identify the school attended and provide that school's password. Employers pay a small fee to list their openings, and they can select the schools where they wish to advertise.

A sort of career resource center, packed full of useful information, is available to all visitors. Read through the job search tips, search for scholarships, learn about top recruiters and employers and visit their Web sites, discuss career options in the forums, or study the guide to graduate schools.

NATIONJOB NETWORK
HTTP://WWW.NATIONJOB.COM/

This site from NationJob, a private company in Iowa that has been in business since 1988, is an impressive and growing network of computerized recruitment services. The job listings are from companies that contract with NationJob, including economic development groups and chambers of commerce (every company in the community can post job openings). Most of the communities represented here are in the Midwest. This is a great way to explore the job opportunities on the local level.

You can fine-tune your job search by specifying criteria such as position, location, education, and salary, sometimes having the option to narrow down your choices through several levels. You can also search for specific companies by industry or location—or you can view the entire list of a couple thousand potential employers! Be sure to check out the "Custom Jobs Pages" section, which has mini-Web sites describing certain participating companies and offering links to their home pages. You will also want to browse through the "Specialty Pages," which lists jobs by employment category, such as aviation and aerospace, customer service, HVAC, legal, or wireless and cellular jobs. NationJob Network's matching service, P.J. Scout, will send you an e-mail when it finds a job that matches your qualifications.

PURSUITNET

HTTP://WWW.TIAC.NET/USERS/JOBS/INDEX.HTML

PursuitNet provides a free matching service to job seekers in the areas of professional, technical, sales, and management. Fill out the site's extensive resume form and you're finished! The system will then search for jobs that match your requirements and skills and notify you of those specific recruiters or potential employers. Do you need help in compiling your resume? Then take a look at "Developing a Winning Resume," which is a step-by-step guide to resume writing.

RECRUITER: FRIEND OR FOE?

HTTP://WWW.CAREERMAG.COM/NEWSARTS/SPECIAL/SERVANCE.HTML

This Career Magazine article addresses the fact that not all recruiters are alike. It could be tremendously advantageous to have certain recruiters in your corner during your job search, while others could just as well prove to have a hugely detrimental effect. How do you know which is which? There are several rules to follow that should help you figure that out, as you'll discover when you read the article. For example, you'll want to develop a good sense of rapport with the recruiter and receive notification each time your resume is distributed.

RECRUITERS ONLINE NETWORK

HTTP://WWW.RECRUITERSONLINE.COM/

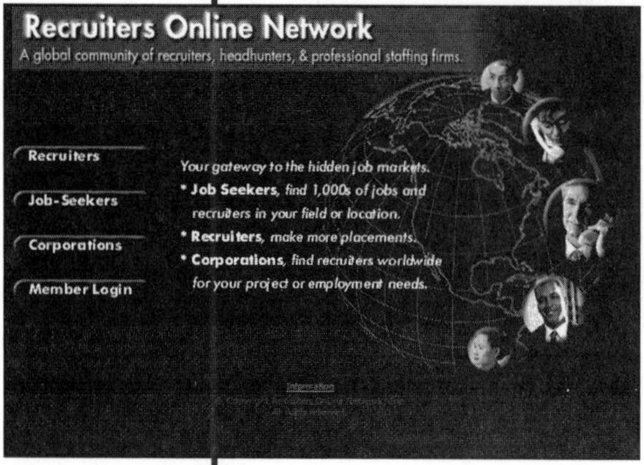

More than 8,000 recruitment and employment firms are members of Recruiters OnLine Network. That adds up to a lot of jobs!

There are many ways that you, the job seeker, can use this extensive Web site. You can search for jobs by keyword, post your resume, seek out a particular recruitment firm, and browse the member firm listing by category, of which there are more than 70, representing a wide range of fields (for example, automotive, civil engineering, computer, entertainment, marketing, and real estate). Let's say you pick civil engineering. More than 100 agency names are brought up. Most matching services look for jobs that might match your skills and needs, but Recruiters OnLine Network finds companies that may be able to help you find a job. Start tracking these companies today and improve your chances of landing a job in the future. And if you're in the market for more reading materials, visit the "Career Library" to order books about creating resumes, improving your interviewing skills, and other job search advice.

RECRUITING AGENCIES

HTTP://WWW.JOB-HUNT.ORG/RECRUIT.SHTML

NETability's Job-Hunt.Org presents a large but manageable collection of links for recruiting agencies, search firms, and employment listings. Companies are listed alphabetically, so unless you know what company you're looking for, you'll have to browse through all the names to find something suitable. Most are based in the United States, although there are some offering international placement. Fields represented are mainly in information technology, but there are links as well for organizations specializing in accounting, communications, construction, education, and engineering, to name a few others.

RECRUITING-LINKS.COM

HTTP://WWW.RECRUITING-LINKS.COM/

Sponsored by SkillSearch Corporation, a major provider of database recruiting services, this Web site features access to job listings by location, industry, or occupation. The search form initially is very general (for location, your choices are United States, Canada, or Mexico) but grows more specific as you proceed (the United States is then broken down into geographic regions). If you narrow your industry search after initially selecting "Media/Communications," you'll arrive at more specific categories, such as advertising, promotion, and public relations or new media production and services. It's a bit complicated, so you might want to read the "Help" section before you start. You can also choose to automatically send your resume via e-mail to the companies that have listings fitting your criteria. The client list includes companies representing a variety of fields, including software, telecommunications, manufacturing, and engineering.

TELECOMMUTING JOBS

HTTP://WWW.TJOBS.COM/INDEX.HTML

Don't feel like fighting commuter traffic? Then why not telecommute! This site lists job opportunities and other materials for the growing telecommuting population.

Job opportunities are listed by category and include desktop publishers, writers, photographers, engineers, programmers, and Web designers. Go to the writers area if you're interested in a telecommuting job in that area. You may find listings for Internet research librarians, Web guide writers, online content producers, editorial abstractors, or copy editors.

"Teletalk" has snippets from telecommuting articles, as well as links to pertinent telecommuting sites. Learn about books to help you start your telecommuting career in the section called "Telebooks."

TOPJOBS USA

HTTP://WWW.TOPJOBSUSA.COM/

Dynamic Information System & eXchange brings you this commercial database listing more than 55,000 jobs for professionals in a diverse range of career fields. Specify your search criteria (location, job title, date added) to pull up descriptions of job matches. The vacancies are posted by subscribing companies and other sources. There are purportedly more than 60,000 companies listed in the employer database. Look here if you wish to locate details about a specific company.

Shop the "Employment Mall" for Internet links, career advice, and comments from visitors. The links section has a huge list of links to job- and career-related sites, along with some commentary about what the sites offer. The career advice section, called "Career Central," is definitely worth checking out. Interviewing, marketing yourself, career assessment, and stress management are just a few of the topics you'll find discussed here.

TOP 100 ELECTRONIC RECRUITERS
HTTP://WWW.INTERBIZNET.COM/TOP100/

The information offered at this Web site comes from the Electronic Recruiting Index, a report published by the Internet Business Network. IBN is a consulting firm specializing in the analysis of online recruiting. This site lists what IBN considers to be the top 100 electronic recruiter sites.

Presented in lists geared toward recruiters or job seekers, results are categorized as third-party recruiters, corporate, industry niche, master sites, regional, and so on. For each, there are links (where available) that will take you directly to the site's resume database, job search agent, career tools, discussion area, or searchable jobs database.

WESTECH VIRTUAL JOB FAIR
HTTP://WWW.CAREEREXPO.COM/

This hefty site is a great spot to research those high-tech job openings. Boasting more than 1,000 employers and 30,000 jobs, it lets you search by keyword, title, technology, location, or company. U.S. as well as international job openings are to be found here. You can submit your resume online once you've registered. If that's not enough, you can always peruse the Westech Career Expo schedule, dig through articles from High Technology Careers Magazine, study the index of employers to see if you can find any suitable companies out of the 1,000 plus, or page through the links to hundreds of other related resources.

Feature magazine articles are from regular departments like "The Next Step," "Silicon Valley News," and "On-the-Job Strategies." Read about consulting, future trends in technology, electronic commerce, high-tech start-ups, and more. "Career Index" is a massive compilation of links to further resources to assist you in your job search, including newsgroups, newspapers, career articles, relocation tools, and assorted career databases, where you'll find international employment databases.

So, what if you're not interested in pursuing a high-tech career? Check out general job fair locations and dates in "JobsAmerica Career Fairs."

WORK-WEB
HTTP://WWW.WORK-WEB.COM/

Work-Web is free for both employers and job seekers. It was developed by the Private Industry Council of Columbus and Franklin County, Ohio. Some of Work-Web's partners include the National Association of Private Industry Councils and the National Alliance of Business.

The job bank is organized by state. Select the state where you would like to search for job openings and then you will be prompted to specify the service area (county or statewide). Once you have selected the general area, you can then browse by category. Some of the categories offered include financial and banking, food service and hospitality, health and medical, and skilled trades. You'll get a listing of the most current job orders then. Choose one in order to view job details such as employer name, contact information, salary, open date, number of openings, and description.

Section VIII:

Considering—and Accepting—a Job Offer

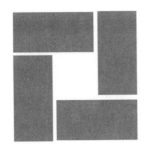

CHAPTER 21

SALARY/WAGES

Many people think that all workers receive a weekly paycheck, that the minimum wage is the least employers can pay workers, and that no employer can require a worker to be on the job for more than forty hours a week without paying overtime. These are all myths. Pay for work may be given weekly, biweekly, monthly, or when the job is completed. When and how much workers are paid depends on the practices in the occupation. For example, workers who receive tips usually take home tips received on the job at the end of each work shift. They may get a weekly paycheck but are often paid less than minimum wage. Their tips are expected to make their hourly earnings greater than the minimum wage. In some sales occupations, workers are paid, entirely or in part, by commission, which means their income depends on making sales. Workers who earn a salary—that is, a set amount per year instead of an hourly wage—may be required to work more than forty hours a week but receive no overtime pay. Before you negotiate your salary, it is useful to understand both how much workers in the occupation earn and how workers in different jobs are usually paid.

References such as the Web sites reviewed here and the Occupational Outlook Handbook (see Chapter 7) provide you with a starting place for looking at some of the issues surrounding salary. When looking at the earnings that workers make, it is important to understand the difference between entry-level, average, and median earnings. Entry-level wages, or starting salaries, is the amount of money usually paid to workers who are new to an occupation. These workers, who are often recent graduates from training programs, do not have much experience on the job. Average wages are the mean of all the earnings of all workers in the occupation from entry level to the most experienced. Because some experienced workers also have longevity on a job, they may be paid much more than workers who have some job experience but who have not worked a long time in one position. In some occupations, a very few "star players" make particularly large salaries while most of the workers in the occupation earn more moderate amounts. The way average earnings are calculated, earnings of a small number of highly paid workers will inflate the figure. This leads to the reported average earnings actually being higher than what most people make in the occupation. The median earnings is the amount that is in the middle when the earnings of all workers in the occupation are considered, the figure that best reflects what a worker with some job experience can expect to make.

The way workers receive their earnings depends on the business practices common in the occupation; for example, whether or not the employer issues paychecks from which taxes have been withheld. In the United States, all workers must pay taxes on money they earn. Taxes are paid to the federal government (for programs such as Social Security and Medicare) and to state governments. Some employers pay the taxes owed on the earnings before they pay workers. On payday, workers receive a statement of earnings for the pay period. This statement reflects the gross amount of earnings—that is, how much was earned before deductions. Deductions include money that was withheld to pay taxes and any contributions the employee makes to pay for benefits, such as health insurance. The actual amount of the check is the net earnings—that is the earnings after taxes and benefits have been paid..

In some occupations, such as outside sales, workers may be considered independent contractors. Employers do not withhold money for taxes from their earnings. Also, workers who receive tips do not have taxes withheld on this income because employers do not know the amount of tips workers receive. Remember that federal and state governments expect workers to pay taxes on income earned annually, so when an employer doesn't deduct money for your taxes, you must save money from any of your income that is not taxed throughout the year so that you will be able to pay taxes on the due dates.

Armed with this overview of salary and wages, you should be ready to explore and better understand the data and information at the following Web sites. Find out what the going rates are for workers in various occupations of interest and learn how to negotiate a pay increase.

JOBSTAR SALARY INFORMATION

HTTP://JOBSMART.ORG/TOOLS/SALARY/INDEX.HTM

JobStar (formerly JobSmart) has compiled links to many Web sites dealing with salaries and wages. You can find assorted government, magazine, and association sites offering statistics, reports, and surveys galore. In addition to resources pertaining to specific occupations, you'll be able to track down information on the minimum wage, the cost of living, benefit plans, severance pay, and salary negotiation. As JobStar is a California-based project, some of the information or links deal specifically with California.

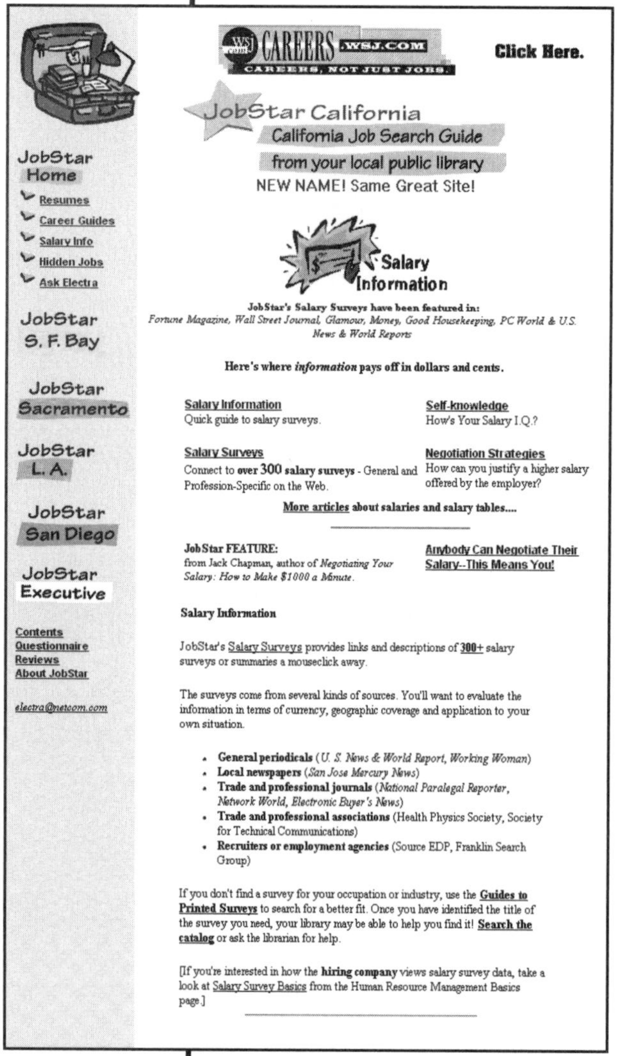

CAREERS WSJ.COM
CAREERS, NOT JUST JOBS.
Click Here.
JobStar California
California Job Search Guide
from your local public library
NEW NAME! Same Great Site!
JobStar Home
Resumes
Career Guides
Salary Info
Hidden Jobs
Ask Electra
JobStar S. F. Bay
JobStar Sacramento
JobStar L.A.
JobStar San Diego
JobStar Executive
Contents
Questionnaire
Reviews
About JobStar
electra@netcom.com
Salary Information
JobStar's Salary Surveys have been featured in:
Fortune Magazine, Wall Street Journal, Glamour, Money, Good Housekeeping, PC World & U.S. News & World Reports
Here's where information pays off in dollars and cents.
Salary Information
Quick guide to salary surveys.
Self-knowledge
How's Your Salary I.Q.?
Salary Surveys
Connect to over 300 salary surveys - General and Profession-Specific on the Web.
Negotiation Strategies
How can you justify a higher salary offered by the employer?
More articles about salaries and salary tables....
JobStar FEATURE:
from Jack Chapman, author of Negotiating Your Salary: How to Make $1000 a Minute.
Anybody Can Negotiate Their Salary--This Means You!
Salary Information
JobStar's Salary Surveys provides links and descriptions of 300+ salary surveys or summaries a mouseclick away.
The surveys come from several kinds of sources. You'll want to evaluate the information in terms of currency, geographic coverage and application to your own situation.
General periodicals (U. S. News & World Report, Working Woman)
Local newspapers (San Jose Mercury News)
Trade and professional journals (National Paralegal Reporter, Network World, Electronic Buyer's News)
Trade and professional associations (Health Physics Society, Society for Technical Communications)
Recruiters or employment agencies (Source EDP, Franklin Search Group)
If you don't find a survey for your occupation or industry, use the Guides to Printed Surveys to search for a better fit. Once you have identified the title of the survey you need, your library may be able to help you find it! Search the catalog or ask the librarian for help.
[If you're interested in how the hiring company views salary survey data, take a look at Salary Survey Basics from the Human Resource Management Basics page.]

SALARY AND JOB OFFER NEGOTIATION TUTORIAL

HTTP://WWW.QUINTCAREERS.COM/SALARY_NEGOTIATION_TUTORIAL.HTML

Quintessential Careers offers practical advice in this step-by-step tutorial on salary negotiation. Some of the issues covered are when and how to talk salary, how to determine your competitive market value, what kinds of questions you should ask and the things to consider after an offer's been made, how to respond to an unacceptable job offer, and suggestions specifically aimed at new college graduates. Much of the advice is presented in the form of sample responses of what to say when you are asked certain salary-related questions. This should give you a good head start on how to handle a variety of situations. Links to salary surveys, salary calculators, and cost-of-living resources are also featured.

SALARIES & PROFILES
HTTP://PUBLIC.WSJ.COM/CAREERS/RESOURCES/DOCUMENTS/CWC-SALARIES.HTM

This resource about salaries and more is brought to you by the Wall Street Journal and the National Business Employment Weekly. The salary tables give median salaries or salary ranges for different positions in a variety of industries. Other site features include data on future projected increases, a salary calculator, a "Relocation Toolkit," and numerous articles dealing with relocation, hiring activity in different industries, and layoffs and unemployment.

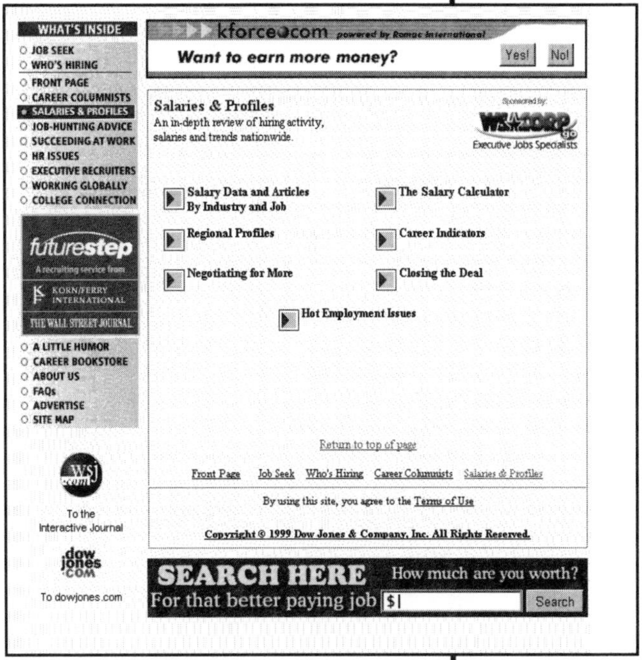

WAGEWEB
HTTP://WWW.WAGEWEB.COM/

This salary survey resource comes from Human Resources Programs Development and Improvement (New Jersey). Data, gathered from numerous organizations, is presented for more than 150 benchmark positions in such categories as administration, engineering, finance, health care, human resources, information management, manufacturing, and sales and marketing. Charts display data—number of respondents and of employees in that position in these companies; average minimum, mean, and maximum salaries; and average bonus (where applicable)—for various job titles in each category. Take manufacturing as an example. Here you will find salary information for light and heavy machine operators, machine production supervisors, assemblers, production schedulers, safety managers, and so on.

CHAPTER 22

FRINGE BENEFITS

Some employers offer no fringe benefits while others offer a wide variety of benefits. What benefits are offered usually depends on both different occupational practices and the size of the employer. Generally, larger employers are able to offer more benefits than smaller employers. Benefits packages—that is, the different types of benefits employers offer and the amount of payment they contribute toward those benefits—add compensation value comparable to actual earnings. When you are considering a job offer, it's important to not only consider the salary to be paid but the benefits package that comes with it. Benefits packages can increase the value of earnings by 33 percent. Some benefits commonly offered by employers include the following:

- paid holidays, sick leave, personal days, and vacations;
- insurance; and
- retirement plans.

Paid holidays are days off for which employees are paid. Sick leave, personal days, and paid vacation time are benefits that are often offered on an accrual system. What this means is that as employees work a certain period of time for the employer, they earn paid time off in case of sickness or personal needs. These benefits are often earned on a schedule; for example, one sick day may be earned per month. Usually, sick leave and personal days accrue if they are not used. In other words, if not used in the month earned, the time off can be saved to be used later. Sometimes there is a cutoff of how many days can be saved. Some employers pay for accrued days when workers leave their employment. Often employees must work a certain period of time, usually a year, before they begin earning paid vacation time.

Because some employers hire large numbers of workers, it is possible for employers to negotiate with insurance companies to have their employees covered at a cost lower than individual policies. This is called group insurance. Employers pay all or part of various types of group insurance policies for their workers. Health insurance is a commonly offered, and valuable, insurance benefit. Employers may pay all or part of an employee's health insurance costs and may allow employees to insure spouses and dependents at reduced cost. Other insurance packages offered include disability, which pays employees who suffer impairment and become unable to work; and life, which, in the case of an employee's death, makes payments to designated survivors. For workers in some occupations, employers pay the costs of professional insurance that protects against malpractice lawsuits.

Employers will often put money in an account, usually IRAs or 401(k) plans, that an employee may claim upon retirement. Some employers will match the amount employees choose to save toward retirement. Many times, money that employees put into a retirement account is not taxed. By contributing as much as possible to retirement accounts, employees save money by avoiding paying taxes on those earnings. In some cases, employees must work for the employer for a certain period of time before they are eligible for retirement accounts, at which time they are referred to as being vested. Some retirement accounts can be converted to cash when a worker leaves the employment. Taxes and frequently penalties must be paid on such cash payments received. People who wait until they have reached retirement age (usually 55) to cash in their retirement accounts do not pay taxes on this money.

Employers sometimes offer a variety of other benefits. What is offered often depends on the occupation. For example, food service workers are traditionally provided a meal on the job. Some jobs, such as apartment manager, provide housing for the worker. Workers required to wear uniforms may have both uniforms and laundry services provided by employers. Some employers pay fees for renewal of professional licenses or for memberships in professional organizations, or even for further job-related training and education. Some employers offer their workers shares of their business's stock, so when the company's value increases, the employee gains a profit.

When negotiating a job offer, it is important to know what benefits are usually offered by comparably sized employers in the occupation. Benefits packages are not usually negotiable—employers either offer them or they do not. But the value of a benefits package to the employee should be considered part of the total earnings gained by working for the employer. The total compensation a worker gains may be greater working at lower pay for an employer who offers a comprehensive benefits package than working at higher wages for an employer who does not offer benefits. Information to help you assess a company's benefits package can be found at this chapter's Web sites.

BENEFITSLINK

HTTP://WWW.BENEFITSLINK.COM/

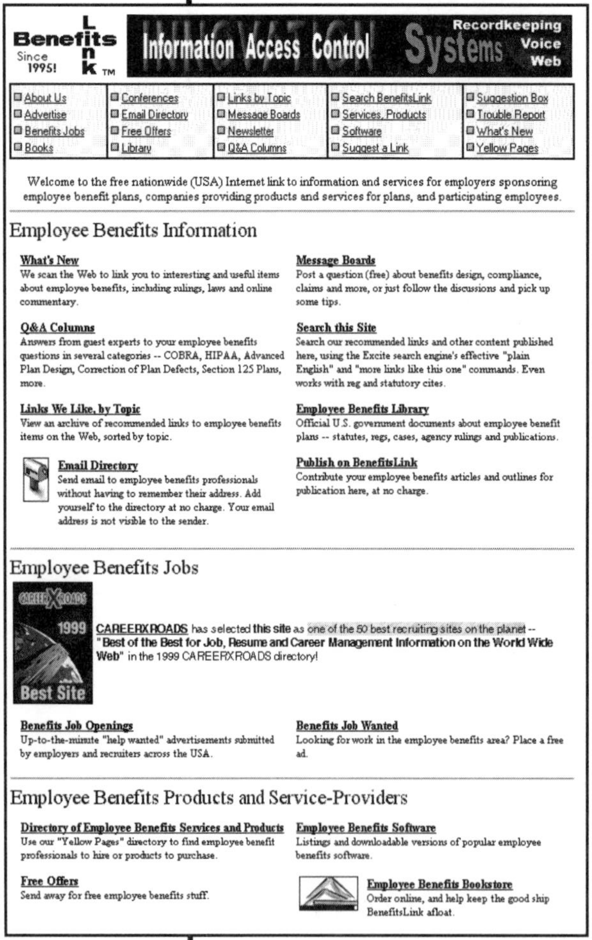

Benefits Link
Since 1995!
Information Access Control
Systems
Recordkeeping
Voice
Web
About Us
Advertise
Benefits Jobs
Books
Conferences
Email Directory
Free Offers
Library
Links by Topic
Message Boards
Newsletter
Q&A Columns
Search BenefitsLink
Services, Products
Software
Suggest a Link
Suggestion Box
Trouble Report
What's New
Yellow Pages
Welcome to the free nationwide (USA) Internet link to information and services for employers sponsoring employee benefit plans, companies providing products and services for plans, and participating employees.
Employee Benefits Information
What's New
We scan the Web to link you to interesting and useful items about employee benefits, including rulings, laws and online commentary.
Message Boards
Post a question (free) about benefits design, compliance, claims and more, or just follow the discussions and pick up some tips.
Q&A Columns
Answers from guest experts to your employee benefits questions in several categories -- COBRA, HIPAA, Advanced Plan Design, Correction of Plan Defects, Section 125 Plans, more.
Search this Site
Search our recommended links and other content published here, using the Excite search engine's effective "plain English" and "more links like this one" commands. Even works with reg and statutory cites.
Links We Like, by Topic
View an archive of recommended links to employee benefits items on the Web, sorted by topic.
Employee Benefits Library
Official U.S. government documents about employee benefit plans -- statutes, regs, cases, agency rulings and publications.
Email Directory
Send email to employee benefits professionals without having to remember their address. Add yourself to the directory at no charge. Your email address is not visible to the sender.
Publish on BenefitsLink
Contribute your employee benefits articles and outlines for publication here, at no charge.
Employee Benefits Jobs
CAREERXROADS 1999 Best Site
CAREERXROADS has selected this site as one of the 50 best recruiting sites on the planet -- "Best of the Best for Job, Resume and Career Management Information on the World Wide Web" in the 1999 CAREERXROADS directory!
Benefits Job Openings
Up-to-the-minute "help wanted" advertisements submitted by employers and recruiters across the USA.
Benefits Job Wanted
Looking for work in the employee benefits area? Place a free ad.
Employee Benefits Products and Service-Providers
Directory of Employee Benefits Services and Products
Use our "Yellow Pages" directory to find employee benefit professionals to hire or products to purchase.
Employee Benefits Software
Listings and downloadable versions of popular employee benefits software.
Free Offers
Send away for free employee benefits stuff.
Employee Benefits Bookstore
Order online, and help keep the good ship BenefitsLink afloat.

A multitude of information and links to further resources can be found here. While the site will probably be of most use to employers and plan advisors and administrators, employees and job seekers will find a wide range of interesting benefits-related subjects to explore. Site features include synopses of current news items dealing with such issues as sick pay, pensions, and health care costs, with links to full stories; several Q&A columns discussing retirement plan distributions, 401(k) plans, COBRA coverage, and more; an "Employee Benefits Library" of links to government sites offering documents concerning employee benefits plans; a wide array of BenefitsLinks articles and annotated links pertaining to disability benefits, government plans, managed care, social security, and stock options, among other topics; and job listings. There are also links sections devoted to health and retirement plan information for employees.

EMPLOYEE BENEFITS PRIMER

HTTP://WWW.EMPLOYEASE.COM/WWW/PRIMER.HTML

Employease presents a user-friendly guide to typical employee benefits. Various benefits are briefly summarized. These summaries are followed by bulleted points, which provide more detailed information on each benefit. If you want to learn about benefits relating to health and prescription drugs, short- and long-term disability, accidental death and dismemberment, pension plans, worker's compensation, and more, then you've come to the right place. A special feature is the glossary, which explains many of the terms (such as coinsurance, deductible, point of service, and portability) that you may run across as you read through your benefits materials.

EMPLOYEE BENEFITS SURVEY

HTTP://WWW.BLS.GOV/EBSHOME.HTM

This Bureau of Labor Statistics (BLS) survey provides data and information about employee benefits offered in the private and federal sectors. Some 6,000 private companies (large, medium, and small) as well as state and local government establishments are represented in the report, which documents employee participation in various employer-sponsored plans and includes tables that cover paid leave, health care and disability benefits, retirement plans, employee contributions, coinsurance rates, and more.

EVALUATING YOUR EMPLOYEE BENEFIT PACKAGE

HTTP://WWW.LAFAYETTECAREERPATH.COM/RESOURCES/STORY5.HTML

This straightforward resource, brought to you by the Lafayette (Indiana) Journal and Courier and CareerPath.com, outlines several categories to consider when you are thinking about a new benefits package or when you are rethinking your existing one. Various types of health benefits (traditional, managed care, HMOs) are explained. Also covered are retirement, life insurance, and disability benefits, as well as financial, personal, family, and travel considerations. You will additionally find suggestions of numerous questions to ask to assist in your evaluation of the overall benefits package.

SUCCESSFUL JOB OFFER NEGOTIATION

HTTP://WWW.COLLEGEGRAD.COM/BOOK/21-0.SHTML

Here is a chapter from Brian Krueger's book College Grad Job Hunter. Once you've been presented with a job offer, there are different techniques to use in determining whether or not you want to accept it. Read about these techniques here and learn some of the important questions to ask. Remember that salary is not the only thing you may want to consider when deciding whether or not to accept a job offer. Be sure to look at all the perks of the job: insurance (medical, dental, life, and disability), vacation, holidays, sick days, retirement plans, tuition reimbursement, overtime and comp time, and so on. Some benefits may be more open to negotiation than others, depending on company policy, so it's important that you find this out before getting too far along in the negotiation process. Advice is also given on how to handle counteroffers made by your current employer, how to give notice when you want to quit your job, and how to leave without burning bridges.

CHAPTER 23

PERSONNEL MANAGEMENT

Hiring workers, evaluating how well they are doing their jobs, keeping them as employees, promoting them, or firing them are all personnel management actions. Employers who have many workers usually have written personnel policies explaining

- the way workers are hired,
- what is expected for satisfactory job performance,
- how performance is evaluated,
- earnings for each position and how earnings increase,
- what promotion opportunities exist and how to be promoted, and
- what can be expected when performance is not satisfactory.

Sometimes employees in a new job will be informed that there is a probationary period during which their ability to perform satisfactorily will be evaluated. Should they fail to perform to satisfaction during the probationary period, they may well be asked to leave the company. Workers whose employers are not required to have formal personnel procedures are actually on probation no matter how long they have been working for an employer. These employers may dismiss such unprotected workers without having to follow any formal procedure.

Employers with personnel policies will have formal procedures for evaluating workers' on-the-job performance.

Adequate or satisfactory performance ratings may be necessary for retention, or being kept on as an employee. To be considered for promotion or to receive more pay, it may be necessary that an employee receive performance ratings that are better than adequate.

Usually, an immediate supervisor is responsible for rating a worker's job performance. Policies for evaluation specify that employees must be told, prior to the rating period, what duties they are expected to fulfill and the performance criteria (or standards for ratings) used in evaluating the work performed.

Keep in mind that excellent work may not be appropriately recognized unless the worker takes the initiative to document superior performance. So it would be in your best interest to keep records of achievements such as completing a project with high-quality work before a deadline, receiving high praise from customers, or troubleshooting a system flaw to save time and money. Documenting achievements is important, either to get a raise or to start looking for another job.

As they gain experience in a job, and learn to perform the duties better, most workers expect that they will earn an increased amount of money. One way employers keep good employees is by offering pay that is competitive with that offered by other employers. To keep their pay rates competitive, some employers offer cost-of-living raises. Many employers base pay rates on both length of time on the job and work performance ratings. Personnel policies provide information on pay schedules and when raises will occur. Usually, pay increases are offered for each year spent on a job. Some employers also offer merit increases to reward employees who get excellent job performance ratings.

Bonuses are a lump sum of money that is not part of earnings. Some employers offer bonuses either through tradition, like a gift Christmas bonus, or as a motivation to strive for achievement. Bonuses are frequently offered in sales occupations for exceeding a certain volume of sales.

Employers are not obliged to offer raises. In fact, many employers have no schedule for raises and no policy for increasing workers' pay. Workers must then ask for raises. Asking for a raise requires the same sort of personal marketing skills that got you the job in the first place. As noted earlier, a record of work achievements provides a convincing reason why a raise is deserved. Before you ask for a raise, you need time on the job to accomplish achievements that show you to be valuable to your employer. It is seldom wise to ask for a raise prior to having spent six months on the job.

To get promoted, it is often necessary to become better qualified through more training and by taking responsibility for more job duties. Workers who want to be promoted take advantage of every opportunity to obtain more training and to work on projects that will expand their skills.

The idea of lifelong employment with an organization that will offer excellent employees advancement opportunities is outmoded in today's job market. Career managers know that promotion usually means leaving one job to take another with a different employer. Being able to document more skills and more achievements on your resume and in your job portfolio prepares you for promotion by making you competitive for the next job.

"You're fired" are two words no employee wants to hear. Employees' tenure on their jobs is somewhat protected by personnel policies offering due process, which means that an employee cannot be immediately dismissed for unsatisfactory performance but that certain steps must be taken to try to help that employee meet job performance standards.

Most workers do not realize that employers have no obligation to provide them employment or to keep them on the job. Without due process policies in place, employment is at will, whereby employees can be immediately dismissed from a job even without cause (meaning that employment was terminated through no fault of the worker). For example, the employer lays off employees because it is no longer the "busy season" or an employer decides to downsize or restructure the organization, thereby eliminating certain positions without there being any fault on the part of the employees. With cause means the employer found some fault in the employee's performance either on or off the job. Some reasons for firing a worker with cause include

- failure to show up for work,
- failure to satisfactorily perform duties,
- sleeping on the job,
- drinking or using illegal substances on the job,
- stealing from the employer, or
- destroying the employer's property.

Employers can also terminate workers for incidents that occur off the job (for example, if an employee has been convicted of drunken driving, the use of an illegal substance, or a felony).

If you think you have been unjustifiably dismissed from a job, the courses of action available will depend on a variety of circumstances. (Do you have a contract with the employer?

Has there possibly been violation of any laws with which the employer is obliged to comply?) As most small employers are "at will" employers, the only course open may be suing in a court of law. If an employer has violated personnel policies, there is usually a grievance procedure that can be pursued. This means that there's a system in place by which employees can file formal complaints. If the worker has been employed under a union agreement, there will certainly be grievance procedures that can be followed. If the employer is bound by federal regulations, and has violated them, the worker can file a complaint with the appropriate federal agency.

New employees frequently attend an orientation session during which these policies are explained. Employees working for employers who have personnel policies are often given a handbook spelling out the policies. Personnel policies protect both employers and their workers by providing rules on how the employer will handle actions that affect their employees. Federal laws against discrimination have influenced the development of personnel policies. Unions and other bodies representing employees try to influence personnel policies to protect employees' rights.

Usually, only larger employers have formal written personnel policies. This is because the number of workers employed is a factor that determines what laws protecting workers are applicable to the employer. Employers who hire only a small number of workers do not have to meet the same legal requirements as larger employers. This means the employment rights of workers in small businesses are usually less protected than those of union workers, of government employees, or of workers in corporations doing business nationwide. Written rules or procedures help protect workers by giving grounds for an employee to file a grievance if an employer does not follow these rules.

Personnel policies usually make employment more secure for the employee by clarifying procedures for actions between employers and their employees. When considering a job offer, it is important to learn what personnel policies, if any, the employer adheres to. Following are some Web sites that will give you more specifics about personnel management issues.

ETHAN WINNING'S ARTICLES
HTTP://WWW.EWIN.COM/EWARTS.HTM

This large collection of articles dealing with personnel issues comes from California-based human resources professional Ethan Winning, author of Labor Pains: Employer and Employee Rights and Obligations. The articles cover a wide range of topics, including access to personnel records, age discrimination, corporate loyalty, downsizing, dress codes, exit interviews, the Family Medical Leave Act (FMLA), severance pay, and more. Additional articles are available if you pay for a subscription.

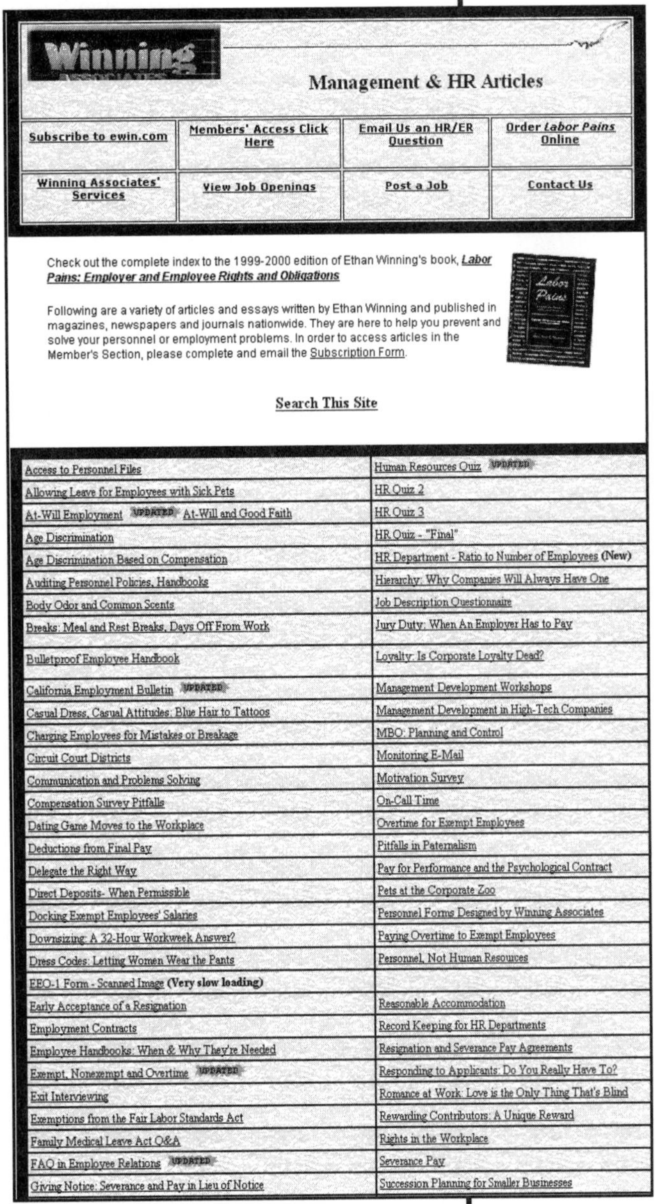

Winning
Management & HR Articles
Subscribe to ewin.com
Members' Access Click Here
Email Us an HR/ER Question
Order Labor Pains Online
Winning Associates' Services
View Job Openings
Post a Job
Contact Us
Check out the complete index to the 1999-2000 edition of Ethan Winning's book, Labor Pains: Employer and Employee Rights and Obligations
Following are a variety of articles and essays written by Ethan Winning and published in magazines, newspapers and journals nationwide. They are here to help you prevent and solve your personnel or employment problems. In order to access articles in the Member's Section, please complete and email the Subscription Form.
Search This Site
Access to Personnel Files
Human Resources Quiz
Allowing Leave for Employees with Sick Pets
HR Quiz 2
At-Will Employment At-Will and Good Faith
HR Quiz 3
Age Discrimination
HR Quiz - "Final"
Age Discrimination Based on Compensation
HR Department - Ratio to Number of Employees (New)
Auditing Personnel Policies, Handbooks
Hierarchy: Why Companies Will Always Have One
Body Odor and Common Scents
Job Description Questionnaire
Breaks: Meal and Rest Breaks, Days Off From Work
Jury Duty: When An Employer Has to Pay
Bulletproof Employee Handbook
Loyalty: Is Corporate Loyalty Dead?
California Employment Bulletin
Management Development Workshops
Casual Dress, Casual Attitudes: Blue Hair to Tattoos
Management Development in High-Tech Companies
Charging Employees for Mistakes or Breakage
MBO: Planning and Control
Circuit Court Districts
Monitoring E-Mail
Communication and Problems Solving
Motivation Survey
Compensation Survey Pitfalls
On-Call Time
Dating Game Moves to the Workplace
Overtime for Exempt Employees
Deductions from Final Pay
Pitfalls in Paternalism
Delegate the Right Way
Pay for Performance and the Psychological Contract
Direct Deposits- When Permissible
Pets at the Corporate Zoo
Docking Exempt Employees' Salaries
Personnel Forms Designed by Winning Associates
Downsizing: A 32-Hour Workweek Answer?
Paying Overtime to Exempt Employees
Dress Codes: Letting Women Wear the Pants
Personnel, Not Human Resources
EEO-1 Form - Scanned Image (Very slow loading)
Early Acceptance of a Resignation
Reasonable Accommodation
Employment Contracts
Record Keeping for HR Departments
Employee Handbooks: When & Why They're Needed
Resignation and Severance Pay Agreements
Exempt, Nonexempt and Overtime
Responding to Applicants: Do You Really Have To?
Exit Interviewing
Romance at Work: Love is the Only Thing That's Blind
Exemptions from the Fair Labor Standards Act
Rewarding Contributors: A Unique Reward
Family Medical Leave Act Q&A
Rights in the Workplace
FAQ in Employee Relations
Severance Pay
Giving Notice: Severance and Pay in Lieu of Notice
Succession Planning for Smaller Businesses

PERFORMANCE APPRAISAL
HTTP://WWW.PERFORMANCE-APPRAISAL.COM/INTRO.HTM

The Archer North System is a performance appraisal system developed by Archer North & Associates. This Web site, advocating the use of performance appraisals in the workplace, is based on it. Content is aimed toward human resources personnel, but it will serve to give you a glimpse of what all could be involved in an employer's performance appraisal process. First there's a brief introduction to the history of workplace performance appraisals. This is followed by an overview of the purposes for conducting them. Then three different types of performance appraisal are described. These are rating scales, the essay method, and the results or MBO (management by objectives) method. Pros and cons of each approach are outlined. Additionally, benefits to conducting a performance appraisal are explored, reasons are given for why to use—or not to use—a reward system based on appraisal results, and suggestions are offered on how to avoid or deal with conflict and confrontation during the review process.s.

TOWN ONLINE WORKING

HTTP://WWW.TOWNONLINE.COM/WORKING/CAREERRES/WORKPLACE.HTML

Numerous articles pertaining to assorted workplace and career issues are featured at this site, which will be of interest to job seekers, employees, and human resources professionals alike. Read about such topics as workplace diversity, telecommuting, personality tests, comp time and overtime, college tuition reimbursement, pay raises, communication, employee training, salary negotiation, networking, interviewing, and more. Much of the content is presented in a question-and-answer format.

CHAPTER 24

EMPLOYMENT LAWS

There are numerous employment laws that the U.S. government has enacted to protect the welfare and rights of workers. Among these are laws intended to

- protect workers from discrimination based on race, color, sex, national origin or citizenship, age, religion, or ability;
- ensure that, for equal work performed, women receive pay equal to that received by men; and
- provide for a safe working environment by demanding that certain safety standards are met.

The area of employment law is very complex. Some laws apply only to workers in specific occupational areas, such as agriculture or mining. Other laws are more general, but certain businesses, such as those employing few workers, may not have to comply with these laws, as was discussed in the preceding chapter. Web sites having to do with some of the major U.S. employment laws are covered in this chapter.

AGE DISCRIMINATION IN EMPLOYMENT ACT OF 1967

HTTP://WWW.EEOC.GOV/LAWS/ADEA.HTML

Text of U.S. legislation (plus ADEA amendments) prohibiting employment discrimination against workers aged forty or older, from the U.S. Equal Employment Opportunity Commission.

AMERICANS WITH DISABILITIES ACT INFORMATION ON THE WEB

HTTP://WWW.USDOJ.GOV/CRT/ADA/

This page contains a collection of links to U.S. Department of Justice (DOJ) resources pertaining to the Americans with Disabilities Act (ADA) of 1990. You can read the statute itself or find answers to select questions about the ADA (for example, "Does an employer have to give preference to a qualified applicant with a disability over other applicants?" and "Must an employer modify existing facilities to make them accessible?"). There is also a section on ADA myths and facts and one devoted to the ADA in regard to individuals with HIV/AIDS. For even more materials, check out the link to the ADA home page, which offers related publications for sale, status reports pertaining to ADA enforcement, texts of select DOJ settlement and consent agreements, and information on new or proposed legislation.

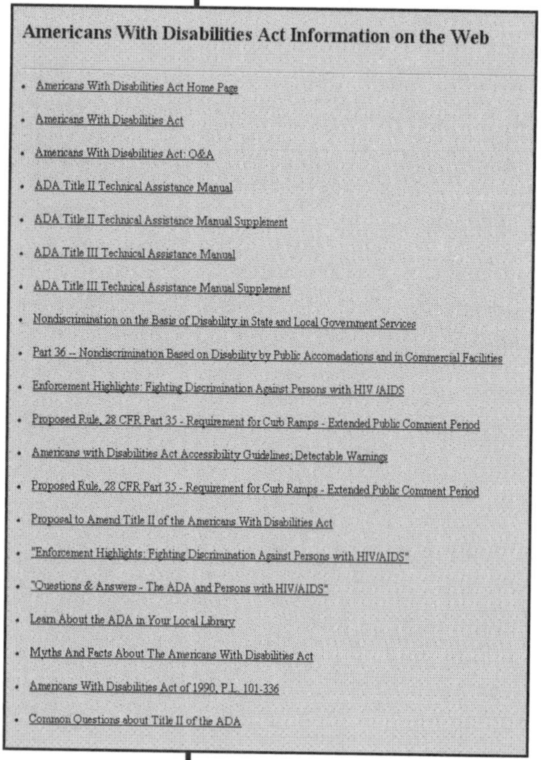
Americans With Disabilities Act Information on the Web

- Americans With Disabilities Act Home Page
- Americans With Disabilities Act
- Americans With Disabilities Act: Q&A
- ADA Title II Technical Assistance Manual
- ADA Title II Technical Assistance Manual Supplement
- ADA Title III Technical Assistance Manual
- ADA Title III Technical Assistance Manual Supplement
- Nondiscrimination on the Basis of Disability in State and Local Government Services
- Part 36 -- Nondiscrimination Based on Disability by Public Accomadations and in Commercial Facilities
- Enforcement Highlights: Fighting Discrimination Against Persons with HIV /AIDS
- Proposed Rule, 28 CFR Part 35 - Requirement for Curb Ramps - Extended Public Comment Period
- Americans with Disabilities Act Accessibility Guidelines; Detectable Warnings
- Proposed Rule, 28 CFR Part 35 - Requirement for Curb Ramps - Extended Public Comment Period
- Proposal to Amend Title II of the Americans With Disabilities Act
- "Enforcement Highlights: Fighting Discrimination Against Persons with HIV/AIDS"
- "Questions & Answers - The ADA and Persons with HIV/AIDS"
- Learn About the ADA in Your Local Library
- Myths And Facts About The Americans With Disabilities Act
- Americans With Disabilities Act of 1990, P.L. 101-336
- Common Questions about Title II of the ADA

EQUAL PAY ACT OF 1963
HTTP://WWW.EEOC.GOV/LAWS/EPA.HTML

Text of U.S. legislation forbidding gender-based wage discrimination among employees having similar positions and responsibilities who are employed at the same place of work, from the U.S. Equal Employment Opportunity Commission. EPA amendments from volume 29 of the United States Code are noted.

FAIR LABOR STANDARDS ACT
HTTP://WWW.DOL.GOV/DOL/ESA/PUBLIC/REGS/STATUTES/WHD/ALLFAIR.HTM

Text of U.S. legislation dealing with minimum wage, overtime compensation, maximum workweek hours, and child labor provisions, originally dating from 1938 and later amended, from the Wage and Hour Division of the U.S. Department of Labor's Employment Standards Administration. FLSA history and other provisions are also included. You will need Adobe Acrobat Reader to view the files.

FAMILY AND MEDICAL LEAVE ACT OF 1993
HTTP://WWW.DOL.GOV/DOL/ESA/FMLA.HTM

This U.S. Department of Labor site presents the text of the U.S. legislation whereby eligible workers are entitled to unpaid leave under certain circumstances, during which time the worker would receive health benefits and after which time the worker could return to work. Also available are an FMLA fact sheet, a compliance guide, poster images, and further explanatory materials.

THE MINIMUM WAGE
HTTP://WWW.DOL.GOV/DOL/ESA/PUBLIC/MINWAGE/MAIN.HTM

This Employment Standards Administration site offers supplementary materials to the Fair Labor Standards Act. FLSA and minimum wage history is discussed, an employer fact sheet is included, employee information is presented, and a printable poster image is available. A chart shows the changes in minimum wage through the years—it was 25 cents back in 1938 when the law was first enacted..

OCCUPATIONAL SAFETY AND HEALTH ADMINISTRATION COMPLIANCE ASSISTANCE AUTHORIZATION ACT OF 1998

HTTP://WWW.OSHA-SLC.GOV/OSHACT_TOC/OSHACT_TOC_BY_SECT.HTML

Text of U.S. legislation that requires certain standards of safety at the workplace, originally dating from 1970 and amended in 1998, enforced by OSHA. You can view the text in full or in parts. If you're looking for a particular section or topic, check out the search function.

TITLE VII OF THE CIVIL RIGHTS ACT OF 1964

HTTP://WWW.EEOC.GOV/LAWS/VII.HTML

Text of U.S. legislation prohibiting employment discrimination, as amended by the Civil Rights Act of 1991, from the U.S. Equal Employment Opportunity Commission. It addresses issues of discrimination based on race, color, religion, sex, and national origin.

CHAPTER 25

YOUR RIGHTS AS AN EMPLOYEE

There is no one blanket law or comprehensive document that defines the rights of all employees. Various federal laws cover some workers. State laws provide certain protections to other workers. Employees do not normally cede any of the usual protections of penal codes; for example, employers cannot assault workers, because such behavior is illegal. While there is no "Bill of Rights for Employees," workers should generally expect certain criteria to be met while on the job. This includes safe working conditions, pay for performance as scheduled, and a nonhostile working environment.

Workers should not be asked to perform duties or be expected to work in conditions that flagrantly endanger their physical well-being. Workers in some occupations, such as firefighters or police officers, are required to perform some duties that have a measure of jeopardy. Other occupations, such as medical personnel, require workers to be in environments, like hospitals, that may put them at risk. Nevertheless, even in occupations where some hazards can be expected, there are safety measures that must be in place. In all occupational areas, employers must provide reasonably safe working conditions. Safe working conditions also include not requiring an employee to perform duties that act against the penal code—that is, employers cannot ask employees to break the law.

Furthermore, employers must pay workers for work performed at the agreed-upon rate of compensation and at the agreed-upon time.

And finally, employers must ensure that workers are not subject to discrimination or harassment (a persistent condition of abuse: physical, verbal, or sexual) in their place of work or in their normal performance of duties. Employers must protect their employees from on-the-job harassment by either supervisors or other employees.

Now that you've landed a job, be sure you know what your rights are. These sites should give you an overview of the manner of on-the-job treatment you can expect and are entitled to. Of course, if you realize that you require legal advice or representation, ask around to find a reputable attorney to advise and assist you rather than relying exclusively on material presented online, which, though it may be helpful, doesn't address your specific circumstances.

DISCRIMINATIONATTORNEY.COM
HTTP://WWW.DISCRIMINATIONATTORNEY.COM/

This collection of articles and resources relating to employment law is from the California-based Law Offices of David H. Greenberg. You will find much of interest here even if you know little of this area of the law. There are summaries of sexual harassment, different kinds of discrimination (for example, age, disability, pregnancy, racial, and sexual orientation), wrongful termination, and breach of contract. Whistle-blowing, class action lawsuits, and damages are also briefly described. After you visit this site you will have gained a good overview of various aspects of employment law, but if you require legal assistance with an actual case, the site advises you to contact a lawyer directly. Tips are offered on doing just that.

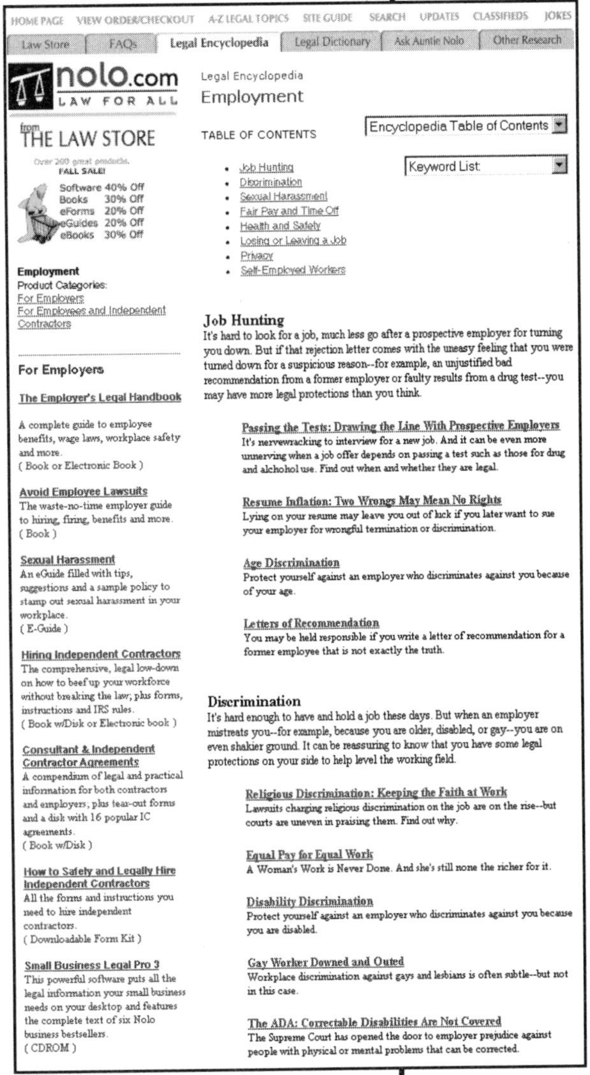

EMPLOYMENT: WORKPLACE RIGHTS AND RESPONSIBILITIES
HTTP://WWW.NOLO.COM/ENCYCLOPEDIA/EMP_ENCY.HTML

Nolo Press, staffed by a team of in-house lawyers and having close affiliations with others in the legal profession, is a publisher of self-help law books and software. This section of the Nolo Web site features essays on topics having to do with what you're entitled to and held accountable for in the workplace. Articles cover such issues as job hunting, discrimination, sexual harassment, wages, workplace safety, job termination, privacy, and self-employed workers. Contact addresses and links for organizations providing additional information are offered. If you want to purchase any Nolo Press titles, you'll find order details at the site.

EQUAL EMPLOYMENT OPPORTUNITY COMMISSION

HTTP://WWW.EEOC.GOV/

The EEOC, a U.S. government agency, is responsible for enforcing various employment-related legislation, including Title VII of the Civil Rights Act of 1964, the Age Discrimination in Employment Act of 1967, the Equal Pay Act of 1963, Titles I and V of the Americans with Disabilities Act of 1990, the Civil Rights Act of 1991, and Sections 501 and 505 of the Rehabilitation Act of 1973. This vast resource includes texts of these acts plus much more.

EEOC press releases will help you keep up-to-date on court rulings and other matters. Read fact sheets to find out more on racial, age, and religious discrimination as well as on sexual harassment. Learn about your rights as an individual with a disability. There are sections devoted to filing a discrimination charge, the EEOC mediation program for resolving workplace disputes, small business concerns, enforcement and litigation, enforcement statistics, and EEOC's Technical Assistance Program Seminars (TAPS). Additionally, the text of the Freedom of Information Act is presented, along with a reference guide and other pertinent documents.

INFORMATION ABOUT SEXUAL HARASSMENT

HTTP://WWW.DE.PSU.EDU/HARASS/INTRO.HTM

This guide from Penn State should leave you with a better understanding of what constitutes sexual harassment, how to recognize it, what to do when faced with it, and how to avoid behaving in a way that could be interpreted as such. The term is defined and examples of the behavior are spelled out. Two specific types of sexual harassment are described: quid pro quo sexual harassment and hostile environment sexual harassment.

To demonstrate the types of situations involving sexual harassment (alleged or actual) that might arise in a university setting, a few hypothetical cases are presented. After reading accounts of events as told by each participant, you are to determine whether or not the accusation of sexual harassment is accurate. The "Theory and Analysis" section discusses sexual harassment history, its existence in schools and the workplace, the affect it has on the victims, and men who harass. Links to other sources are included, as is access to pages pertaining to Penn State's policy and procedures. While much of the material relates to sexual harassment in a university setting, the information featured will be of use to anyone wanting to know more about the issue.

LAW ABOUT EMPLOYMENT

HTTP://WWW.LAW.CORNELL.EDU/TOPICS/EMPLOYMENT.HTML

Cornell Law School's Legal Information Institute has compiled a useful collection of employment-related law materials. Topics covered are collective bargaining, employment discrimination, unemployment compensation, pensions, workplace safety and health, and worker's compensation. A brief overview is provided for each, supplemented by such sources as texts of state and federal statutes, judicial decisions, and agency regulations, along with links to relevant Web sites.

NATIONAL LABOR RELATIONS BOARD

HTTP://WWW.NLRB.GOV/

NLRB, an independent U.S. federal agency, is responsible for enforcing the National Labor Relations Act, which deals with the relationship between labor unions and private-sector employers. Through this act employees are given the right to organize and conduct collective bargaining negotiations with their employers—as well as the right not to do so. In addition to the text of the act, the site features NLRB facts, summaries of current cases, case decisions, press releases, rules and regulations, and manuals and other publications. There is a section devoted to the NLRB and the Freedom of Information Act. To read some of the materials, you'll need to use Adobe Acrobat Reader. Certain selections are also available in Spanish.

OCCUPATIONAL SAFETY AND HEALTH ADMINISTRATION
HTTP://WWW.OSHA.GOV/

OSHA, an agency of the U.S. Department of Labor, is responsible for enforcing worker safety guidelines according to the Occupational Safety and Health Administration Compliance Assistance Authorization Act of 1998. This site contains the text of that act and assorted other materials pertaining to the agency, its history, and its functions.

Among the many resources offered at the site are compliance guides; information on OSHA training and state programs; fact sheets, press releases, and other publications concerning ergonomics and other workplace safety issues; guidelines discussing health hazards of numerous chemicals, protective equipment to be used, what to do in the event of spills or leaks, and so on; and answers to frequently asked questions.

SITE INDEX

A

Academic Employment Network 234
Academy of Television Arts & Sciences: Education Programs 87
ACCESS: Networking in the Public Interest 275
Accountemps Campus 205
Accounting & Finance Jobs 205
ACM SIGGRAPH 225
ACT 21
Adguide's College Recruiter Employment Site 352
Advancing Women 164
Adventures in Education 33
Advertising Age 206
Advice for Volunteers 87
Ag-Biz.com 209
Age Discrimination in Employment Act of 1967 390
Agriculture Online 209
Airwaves MediaWeb 219
AJR NewsLink: Newspapers 172
Alaska Jobs Center 186
Alaska State Parks 88
All about College 62
AltaVista 128
America's Career InfoNet 49
America's Charities 89
America's HealthCareSource 250
America's Job Bank 352
America's One-Stop Career Center System 78
American Anthropological Association 289
American Association for Adult and Continuing Education 78
American Association of Colleges of Nursing 248
American Association of Colleges of Pharmacy 280
American Association of Cosmetology Schools 231
American Association of Museums 271
American Astronomical Society 293
American Bankers Association 214
American Dental Association 232
American Holistic Health Association 211
American Hotel & Motel Association 253
American Indian Science & Engineering Society 157
American Institute for Conservation of Historic and Artistic Works 272
American Institute of Chemical Engineers 224
American Institute of Aeronautics and Astronautics 208
American Institute of Architects 228
American Institute of Biological Sciences 216
American Institute of Physics 266
American Library Association 257
American Mathematical Society 267
American Medical Association 249
American Petroleum Institute 279
American Planning Association 246
American Red Cross 88
American Society for Engineering Education 239
American Society for Information Science 257
American Society of Travel Agents 300
American Society of Agronomy 209
American Society of Composers, Authors and Publishers 272
American Sociological Association 290
American Textile Manufacturers Institute 296
American Veterinary Medical Association 212
American Zoo and Aquarium Association 213
Americans with Disabilities Act Information on the Web 390
AmeriCorps 89
Archaeological Fieldwork Opportunities 90
Argus Clearinghouse 136
Arkansas Employment Register 179
ArtJob 301
ASAE Gateway to Associations Online 203
Asia-Net 193
Ask Jeeves 128
Associated Locksmiths of America 278
Association of American Railroads 284
Association of Internet Professionals 259
Association of Schools of Public Health 250
ASVAB Career Exploration Program 22
Audio Engineering Society 274
AutoCareerNet 214
Awesome Christian Sites 286

B

Bay Area Jobs 186
BBBOnLine 124
BenefitsLink 378
Best College Résumés 310
Best Jobs U.S.A. 353
The Black Collegian 157
Black Voices Career Center 158
Bona Fide Classified 172
Boston.com Careers 174
Botanical Society of America 216
Broadcast Education Association 219
Broadcasters Training Network 219
Building Brand You 7
Bureau of Apprenticeship and Training 79
Bureau of Labor Statistics 49
Business Job Finder 215

C

CampusTours 62
Career and Educational Guides 33
Career Decision Making 19
Career Development Manual 7
Career Development Portfolio 320
Career Doctor 33
Career Exploration Links 34
Career Exploration on the Internet 124
Career Exposure 354
Career Guides 8
The Career Interests Game 19
The Career Key 20
Career Magazine 138
Career PlanIt 8
A Career Planning Center for Beginning Scientists and Engineers 239
Career Planning Process 9
Career.com 354
CareerBabe 136
CareerBuilder 137
CareerCity 137
CareerLink 138
CareerMart 139
CareerMosaic 139
CareerMosaic Canada 191
CareerPath 354
CareerPost 175
Careers & Jobs 140
Careers in Dentistry 233
Careers OnLine 194
Careers.wsj.com 140
CareersColorado 184
CareerSite 355
CareerWeb 356
Carolina's Preferred Jobs 179
The Carter Center 90
Catapult: Career Offices Home Pages 334
CDT's Guide to Online Privacy 125
Central Indiana.com Classified Ads 181
Chemistry & Industry 225
Chicago Tribune CareerPath 181
The Chronicle of Higher Education 235
Claremont Colleges On-Campus Recruiting Program 334
CNET Web Building Jobs 260
College Compass: College Selection 62
College Grad Job Hunter 141
College Is Possible 63
College of William & Mary Office of Career Services 142
College Pro Painters (U.S.) Ltd. 105
CollegeNET 64
CollegeView Career Center for Career Planning 143
Communication Arts 207
Community College Web 64
Conducting Research on the Internet 125
Contemporary Artists' Services 302
Contract Employment Connection 356
Contract Employment Weekly 357
Cool Works 106
Corporation for Public Broadcasting 220
The Corrections Connection 283
Council for Higher Education Accreditation 65
Council on International Educational Exchange 91
Cover Letter Tutorial 315
CyberAir Airpark 210
Cyber-Sierra's Natural Resources Job Search 303

D

Dance Magazine 232
DanceArt.com 231
Dave's ESL Cafe 235
Deja.com 129
Department of Hospitality Management at the University of New Hampshire 253
dice.com 226
DiscriminationAttorney.Com 395
The Distance Education and Training Council 81
The Distance Learning "Getting Started" Booklist 81
Division of Indian & Native American Programs 159

E

Earthwatch Institute 92
Editor & Publisher 274
.edu 65
EE-Link 241
EFLWEB 236
Electronic Field Trip to Kentucky Educational Television 220
Employability Skills Portfolios 320
Employee Benefits Primer 378
Employee Benefits Survey 379
Employment Information 194
Employment: Workplace Rights and Responsibilities 395
Energy Information Administration 238
ENR 229
EnviroLink 92
Environmental Careers Organization 93
Environmental Sites on the Internet 241
Equal Employment Opportunity Commission 396
Equal Opportunity Publications 171
Equal Pay Act of 1963 391

eRésumés 101 310
Escape Artist 195
Escoffier On Line 287
Ethan Winning's Articles 387
Evaluating Your Employee Benefit Package 379
Excite 130
Exercise Science, Fitness/Wellness, and Health Promotion Internship Information 93
Experimental Medicine Job Listing 217
Exploring Occupations 35

F

Fair Labor Standards Act 391
FairTest 22
Family and Medical Leave Act of 1993 391
FASTaiD.com 113
fastWEB 113
Federal Jobs Digest 167
Feminist Majority Foundation Online 164
The Film, TV, & Commercial Employment Network 242
FinAid 114
FinanceNet 168
Financial Aid 101 115
FindLaw 261
1st Steps in the Hunt 143
Flight Attendant Corporation of America 211
Food Processing Machinery & Supplies Association 245
Foundation for Interior Design Education Research 252
4Work 358
Freightworld 299
FutureScan 35

G

Gary Johnson's BraveNewWorkWorld and NewWork News 50
Gaywork.com 159
Geological Society of America 233
GEOSCI-JOBS 234
Getting Real! 9
Global Volunteers 94
GO Network 130
Goalmap 10
GoldSea Career Success Center 160
Graduate School Guide 66
GRE 23
The Great American Web Site 168
Great Summer Jobs 106
Greenpeace International 94
The Guide to Cooking Schools-Career 287
Guide to Job-Hunting on the Internet 126

H

Habitat for Humanity International 95
Hampton Roads CareerConnection 180
Headhunter.net 358
Health Care Job Store 250
HealthWeb 251
HeraldLink Employment Classifieds 180
Hoover's Online 343
Hospitality Jobs Online 254
Hospitality Net 255
HotBot 130
HotJobs 359
How to Decide What to Do with Your Life 11
How to Respond to Help Wanted Ads 173

I

ICYouSee: T Is for Thinking 126
Idealist 95
IEEE-USA 237
The Inc. 500 344
Independent Insurance Agents of America 258
Independent Means 165
Indiana University's ASPO On-Campus Recruiting Schedule 335
Industrial Designers Society of America 264
IndustryWatch 344
InfoMine 270
Information about Sexual Harassment 396
Information by National Occupational Classification Code 39
Information on Majors 36
The Information Professional's Career Page 227
Informational Interviewing Tutorial 44
Inkspot 262
Institute of Industrial Engineers 265
Institute of Food Technologists 245
Institute of Physics 268
InterAction 96
International Association of Administrative Professionals 223
International Hotel & Restaurant Association 255
International Webmasters Association 260
Internet Career Connection 169
The Internet Fashion Exchange 242
Internet Job Source 169
Internet Nonprofit Center 276
The Internet Pilot to Physics 268
Internship Resources On the Web 97
InternshipPrograms.com 97
Interview Network 326
Iowa: The SmartCareer Move 182
IPL Associations on the Net 203
Iron & Steel Society 269
iVillage Career 165

J

J-JOBS 275
Job Accommodation Network 155
Job Bank of Canada 192
Job Fair Success 335
Job Hunting in Planning, Architecture, and Landscape Architecture 230
The Job Resource 360
Job Resources by U.S. Region 173
Job Safari 345
Job Search 188
Job Search Networking: Worth the Effort! 44
JobAccess 155
JobBank USA 359
JobDirect 360
jobEngine 227
Jobfind 175
Job-Hunt.Org 144
JobHunter 187
JobHuntersBible.com 143
jobNET 144
JobOptions 145
JobProfiles.com 36
Jobs in Government 247
JobServe 195
JobsHawaii 188
Jobsite 196
JobsOK 184
JobStar 189
JobStar Salary Information 372
Jobtrak 361
JobWeb 145
JobWeb Career Fairs 336

K

Kaplan 23
Keirsey Temperament and Character 25
Kids' Camps 106
Krislyn's Strictly Business Sites 145

L

Law about Employment 397
Law News Network 262
Liberal Arts Job Search 37
Librarians' Index to the Internet 130
Library Job Postings on the Internet 258
Local U.S. Work Opportunities 173
Los Angeles Times 189

M

Management and Teams 11
Mariner's All-in-One Page 289
The Maritime Home Page 289
MarketingJobs.com 207
Mental Health Net 291
MetaCrawler 131
Michigan Works! 182
Military Career Guide Online 269
Mind Tools 11
The Minimum Wage 391
MiningUSA.com 270
MinistryConnect 286
MinnesotaJobs.com 183
Minorities' Job Bank 160
MIT Sloan Career Center 336
Monster.com 146
Montana Job Service 184
My Future 79

N

National Association of Broadcasters 221
National Association of Manufacturers 265
National Association of Social Workers 292
National Association of Asian American Professionals 161
National Association of Professional Insurance Agents 259
National Association of Realtors 285
National Athletic Trainers' Association 293
National Black MBA Association 161
National Business Employment Weekly 147
National Current Employment Statistics 51
National Fire Protection Association 244
National Funeral Directors Association 279
National Grocers Association 248
National Labor Relations Board 397
National Opportunity NOCS 277
National Retail Federation 288
National School-to-Work Learning & Information Center 107
National Society of Black Engineers 161
National Society of Accountants 206
National Society of Professional Engineers 240
National Writers Union Job Hotline 263
NationJob Network 361
NCS Career Assessments 20
Networking 45
Networking and Informational Interviewing Tips 45
Networking Skills 46
New England Opportunity NOCs 175
New Mobility 156
Newsgroups GetAJob 174
Nonprofit Career Network 98
Nuclear Energy Institute 278

O

O*NET 40

Occupational Outlook Handbook 51
Occupational Safety and Health Administration 398
Occupational Safety and Health Administration Compliance Assistance Authorization Act of 1998 392
Officer.Com 283
Offshore Guides 280
Ohio Careers Resource Center 183
One-Stop Career Field Search 37
The Online MBA 224
Online Sports Career Center 294
Online Women's Business Center 166
Overseas Jobs Express 196

P

Part-time Jobs for Teenagers 108
Peace Corps 98
PennsylvaniaJobs.Com 176
People for the Ethical Treatment of Animals 99
Performance Appraisal 387
Peterson's 66
Peterson's LifeLongLearning 81
Peterson's: The Summer Opportunities Channel 108
Pharmacy Week 281
Philanthropy News Network Online 277
Photo District News 281
The Physician and Sportsmedicine 294
PikeNet 285
Placement and Career Services at the University of Pittsburgh 337
Planning Your Future . . . A Federal Employee's Survival Guide 170
Playbill 297
Poets & Writers 264
Policy.com 247
Portfolio Library 321
PowerStudents.com 67
President's Committee on Employment of People with Disabilities 156
President's Student Service Challenge 99
Princeton Review Online: Career 147
Privacy in Cyberspace 126
Project America 100
Prospects Web 196
PSAT/NMSQT 23
Publishers Weekly 218
PursuitNet 362

Q

Quintessential Careers 148

R

Rainforest Action Network 101
Recruit Media 197
Recruiter: Friend or Foe? 362
Recruiters OnLine Network 362
Recruiting Agencies 363
Recruiting-Links.com 363
REEI Employment Opportunities 197
Rensselaer Polytechnic Institute Career Development Center 337
Researching Companies Online 345
Resources for Women, Minorities, and Other Affinity Groups and Audiences 171
Resume Advisors 311
ResumeTutor 311
Right of Way 230
The Riley Guide 149
Rubber World 288
RWM Vocational School Database 80

S

Salaries & Profiles 373
Salary and Job Offer Negotiation Tutorial 372
Saludos Hispanos 162
SAT 24
Scholarly Societies Project 204
Science Professional Network 217
Screenwriters & Playwrights Home Page 243
Sculptor.Org 302
Search Tools 128
SearchIQ 132
SeasonalEmployment.com 109
Second Harvest 101
Self-Directed Search 21
Semiconductor.Net 228
The Seven Challenges: Cooperative Communication Skills Workbook & Reader 12
SF Gate: Who's Hiring? 190
Showbizjobs.com 244
Silicon Alley Jobs 176
SmartDog 177
Soba.net 190
Society for Human Resource Management 256
Society of Plastics Engineers 282
Songwriters Guild of America 274
Sporting Goods Manufacturers Association 295
Standard Occupational Classification 40
Stanford 9 24
STC Regional and Chapter Information 228
Student Conservation Association 102
Student Financial Assistance Programs 116
Study Abroad Directory 67
Successful Interviewing 327
Successful Job Offer Negotiation 379

Summer Jobs 109

T

Teach For America 102
Teaching Jobs Overseas 198
Team Technology 25
Telecommunications Industry Association 295
Telecommuting Jobs 364
Television and Radio News Research 222
Tell Me about This Employer 346
The Ten Keys to Success at Job and Career Fairs 338
10Minute Resume 311
Texas-Jobs.net 185
Therapeutic Recreation Directory 252
Think College 68
Title VII of the Civil Rights Act of 1964 392
Today's Careers 191
TodoLatino Career Center 163
Top 100 Electronic Recruiters 365
TOPjobs USA 364
Total Telecom 296
Town Online Working 177
Town Online Working 388
Toy Manufacturers of America 298
Transition Assistance Online 12
Traveling in Cyberspace? Be Savvy! 127
Tribal Employment Newsletter 163
Tri-State Jobs 178
Truck Net 300
TV Jobs 222
200 Letters for Job Hunters 316

U

U.S. Department of Labor 51
U.S. State Department Internships Index 103
UC Davis Internship & Career Center 338
University of Nebraska-Lincoln Career Services 339
University/Education Disability Resources 157
USA Jobs 170
USA Jobs: Summer 110
USDA Forest Service 304
Using the Internet in Your Job Search 127
Utah's Career Center 185
The Utility Connection 238

V

VaultReports. com 346
The Vermont Student Development Portfolio 322
Virginia Tech Career Services 149
Virtual Volunteering Project 103
Volunteer Organizations on the Web 104
VolunteerMatch 104
VTJOBS 178

W

Wageweb 373
Water Online 303
Web Exchange: Liberal Arts Career Network 38
"Web-able" Resumes 312
Webgrrls International 166
Westech Virtual Job Fair 365
Western Governors University 82
WetFeet.com 347
What Can I Do with a Major In 38
Wisconsin Jobs On-line 183
Women's Careers and Professional Organizations 167
WorkAvenue.com: Phoenix 185
WorkinfoNET 192
WorkSearch: Interviewing 327
WorkSearch: Resume Writing Resources 312
Work-Web 366
World's Biggest Job Interview Question Bank 328
Worldwide Internet Music Resources 273
Writing Cover Letters 316
WWW Virtual Library: Environment 242

Y

Yahoo! 132
Your Career Placement Office 339
Youth@Work 191